ITALIAN FOOD

ITALIAN FOOD

ELIZABETH DAVID

BARRIE & JENKINS
LONDON

First published by Macdonald in 1954
This edition first published in Great Britain in 1987 by
Barrie & Jenkins Ltd
289 Westbourne Grove
London W11 2QA

British Library Cataloguing in Publication Data
David, Elizabeth, *1913*-
    Italian Food. —— 3rd ed.
    1. Cookery, Italian
    I. Title
    641.5945   TX723

    ISBN 0-7126-2000-1

Typeset by SX Composing Ltd, Rayleigh, Essex
Printed in Italy by A. Mondadori Editore, Verona

CONTENTS

INTRODUCTION 7
   Introduction to the First Edition 8
   Introduction to the Penguin Edition 12
ACKNOWLEDGEMENTS 17
ITALIAN DISHES IN FOREIGN KITCHENS 19
THE ITALIAN STORE CUPBOARD 23
KITCHEN EQUIPMENT 37
   Quantities, Timing, Temperatures, Measuring and Weighing
HORS D'ŒUVRE AND SALADS 43
SOUPS 53
PASTA ASCIUTTA 61
RAVIOLI, GNOCCHI ETC. 73
RICE 81
HARICOT BEANS, CHICK PEAS, POLENTA ETC. . . 89
EGGS, CHEESE DISHES, PIZZE ETC. 93
FISH SOUPS 101

FISH 109
MEAT 129
POULTRY AND GAME 151
VEGETABLES 161
SWEETS 173
   Fruit 179
   Ices 181
SAUCES 189
PRESERVES 197
CHEESES 205
NOTES AND BOOKS ON ITALIAN WINES 209
SOME ITALIAN COOKERY BOOKS 213
GUIDES TO FOOD AND WINE IN ITALY 217
VISITORS' BOOKS 219
INDEX 225
NOTES ON THE ILLUSTRATIONS 240

KITCHEN SCENES
from *Opera* by Bartolomeo Scappi, 1570
Left *The cool kitchen, with a water tank, is used for pastry work and the filtering of sauces and jellied stocks.* Right *In the well-equipped main kitchen, a bundle of straw for knives and other implements keeps rust at bay.*

ᴵNTRODUCTION

 HIS 1987 EDITION OF *Italian Food* DIFFERS FROM several of its predecessors chiefly in that revisions made over many years in the form of footnotes to recipes have now been incorporated into the main body of the text. References to numerous shops, at one time sources of supply of imported Italian foodstuffs, but now vanished, have been eliminated. When it came to my original chapter on the wines of Italy I found that almost everything I wrote in 1954 had receded into history. In fact already by the 1970s it wasn't only the variety and diversity of Italian wines available to us in England which had changed beyond recognition, it was the entire Italian wine industry which had undergone a revolution.

In 1954, and I suppose until 1960 or thereabouts, we bought unidentified – and perhaps unidentifiable – Chiantis, flabby Soaves and rough Valpolicellas, plus the odd bottle of Marsala kept handy for concocting a little sauce for a veal piccata or to add the necessary alcoholic kick to a zabaglione. Then one day, when writing this book, I came across a reference by André Simon, at the time the most revered of wine gurus, to white Orvieto, a wine of which I had affectionate memories. But all that André could find to say about it was that it made a good accompaniment to pineapple. That struck me, and strikes me still, as uncommonly unhelpful, not to say insulting to a wine which at its best has much character and which even at its worst would hardly be improved by marriage with so sharp and acid a fruit as pineapple. I realised that the attitude of French experts such as André to Italian wine and, although to a slightly lesser degree, to Italian food, was incurably patronising. Only the French – oh well perhaps at a pinch the Germans too – knew how to make wine, only the French could compose and cook a decent meal. The realisation of what that attitude implied wasn't encouraging to someone already fully committed to the writing of a full-length book on the cooking of Italy. Well, it was no time to turn back. At last, in November 1954 the book crept into print, predictably too late for reviews in the Christmas numbers of the monthlies. One piece of news, a Recommendation by the Book Society – unheard of at that time for a cookery book – was cheering, and eventually there were enthusiastic reviews, two of them by writers of the stature of Freya Stark and Margaret Lane. I am still grateful to those two much respected authors for their support, all the more so because although I had never met them I was aware that in both cases their knowledge of the subject would have justified sharp criticism had either of them felt inclined to make it.

The mid-1950s, it must be said, were not the most propitious times for the sales of cookery books. Food rationing, first imposed in 1939, came to an end only in the summer of 1954, and many ingredients vital to Italian cookery returned very gradually. Maybe you could at last buy veal, but if your butcher knew how to cut escalopes you were lucky. The purchase of a supply of olive oil, and for that matter even a small amount of Parmesan in the piece, entailed a bus trip to the Italian provision shops of Soho and heavily laden shopping bags to tote home. Still, the efforts involved did make cooking and entertaining in those days very rewarding and enjoyable. Then came the early sixties, the heyday of Italian fashion, Italian knitwear, Italian furniture, Enzo Apicella's Italian trattorias, in short of anything Italian from Parma ham to Ferragamo shoes. It was in 1963, at the height of Italy-fever, that Penguin books acquired *Italian Food* for paperback publication, but it was not until 1971 that the same firm judged that popular interest in Italian wine was growing sufficiently to justify a paperback edition of Cyril Ray's *Wines of Italy*. To the best of my knowledge this was the first English book, and Cyril Ray the first English author, to treat the subject in depth. Italian wines were at last to be taken seriously by English wine experts and English wine merchants.

Apart from a brief new chapter on Italian wines written for this 1987 edition, together with a list of English-language books on the same subject, for those interested there are much expanded lists of Italian cookery books, of guides to food and wine in Italy, and of relevant reference books. A list entirely new to this edition is one which I have called Visitors' Books, in other words a selection from the accounts written by scores of English and French visitors to Italy from the end of the fifteenth century down to the 1980s. This list gives hardly more than a hint of the vast range of relevant books – shamefully, for example, I now see that I have omitted any mention of Stendhal, most celebrated of French observers of the Italian scene. My only excuse for that and any other omissions of similar enormity is that my lists were compiled while I was in hospital and without benefit of reference to my own books or of a check in libraries.

To my original Introduction I have made only one significant revision, and that concerns the paragraph dealing with the influence on French cookery traditionally exercised by Catherine de Medici and the Florentine cooks she is said to have brought with her to France. Those cooks, I now find, are part of a myth originating in mid-nineteenth-century France, perhaps in the imagination of one of the popular historical novelists who flourished at that period, and certainly without existence in historical fact. As briefly as possible, what *is* historical fact is that when Catherine arrived in France in 1533 to marry Henri Duke of Orleans, younger brother of the Dauphin, she was fourteen years old, had barely emerged from the Florentine convent in which she had been brought up, and had already been granted French nationality. All her attendants were French.

Whatever the Italian influence exercised on French cultural life in general and on culinary developments in particular by Catherine's marriage to the boy who was later to become Henri II of France, that transalpine influence had already been active at least since the end of the previous century. It was Charles VIII, King of France from 1483 to 1498, and indirect predecessor of Catherine's father-in-law, François 1er, who had imported Italian gardeners to recreate in the Loire valley gardens such as he had seen in Italy, and to cultivate in France the attractive green vegetables, the garden peas, the cauliflowers, the spinach, some say even the artichokes, which had so impressed him in Italy when in 1495 he had attempted, unsuccessfully, to seize the Kingdom of Naples. One of those imported gardeners, Paolo di Mercogliero, had even planted orange trees in the grounds of the royal Château Gaillard, not in an orangery, but over-optimistically in the open air. Unsurprisingly, the trees never bore fruit.

Catherine's own reign as Queen Consort, and for thirty more years as Queen Dowager – many of them as officially recognised Regent – from 1559 until her death in 1589 did inevitably coincide with a great deal of artistic and cultural activity on the part of Italians working in France. Jewellers, glove-makers, sugar-workers, pastrycooks, confectioners, were brought from Italy by Catherine during the years of her widowhood. One of her pastrycooks is credited with the invention or at any rate with the introduction of flaky pastry, but then so are other personages, among them the much later painter Claude Lorrain, who is said to have learned how to make it in Rome. Many food historians would say that some form of fine-leaved pastry had been known at least since the days of the Romans, and I think they would be right, but equally I have doubts about the claim that Catherine's pastrycooks made their *feuilleté* with butter rather than with oil or lard. One does not hear much about the use of butter in France at this period. But then almost as many legends are attached to Catherine's name as later became encrusted around that of Napoleon. In Catherine's case, many of the stories, whether apocryphal or factual, do point to the advanced state of civilised life in Italy as compared with that of France in the first half of the sixteenth century, and to the improvements achieved by the French during the second half. That some of those improvements were directly due to Catherine and her Italian craftsmen and architects, cooks and confectioners is undeniable. To credit her with all of them would be a distortion of history.

E.D. – 1987

INTRODUCTION TO THE FIRST EDITION
The origins of Italian cooking are Greek, Roman, and to a lesser extent, Byzantine and oriental.

The Romans, having evolved their cookery from the sane traditions of Greece, proceeded in the course of time to indulge in those excesses of gluttony which are too well known to bear repetition here; but what must in fact have been a considerable understanding of the intricacies of cookery has been overlooked in the astonishment of less robust ages at their gigantic appetites and at the apparently grotesque dishes they consumed. Owing to the necessities of preservation, a good deal of the food of those days must have been intolerably salt; to counteract this, and also presumably to disguise a flavour which must often have been none too fresh, the Romans added honey, sweet wine, dried fruit, and vinegar to meat, game, and fish, which were, besides, heavily spiced and perfumed with musk, amber, pepper, coriander, rue.

Similar methods of cookery prevailed in all the more primitive parts of Europe until the nineteenth century, when the development of rapid transport began to make the large-scale salting and pickling of food unnecessary. In Italy Roman tastes are still echoed in the *agrodolce* or sweet-sour sauces, which the Italians like with wild boar, hare and venison. The Roman taste for little song-birds – larks, thrushes and nightingales – also persists in Italy to this day; so does the cooking with wine, oil, and cheese, and the Roman fondness for pork, veal, and all kinds of sausages.

COOKING VESSELS AND UTENSILS
from *Opera* by Bartolomeo Scappi, 1570
including left *deep and shallow tart pans and covers, boiling and stewing pots and an*
egg poaching pan; middle *a hair sieve, dripping pans and strainers; and* right *a fried egg pan*

When all the arts of a civilized world were swept away by the waves of barbarism which engulfed Europe after the final extinction of the Roman Empire, the art of cooking also vanished, surviving only in the books preserved in the monasteries. With the fifteenth-century renaissance of art and letters, fostered by the great families of Venice, Milan, Florence, Rome, Genoa, and Naples, came the renewal of interest in the food and cooking of classical times. The first printed culinary work, written by Bartolomeo Sacchi, librarian at the Vatican, appeared about 1474; it is a sign of the great interest displayed in the subject that the book, called *Platina de honesta voluptate et valitudine vulgare*, usually known as Platina's book, was printed in six different editions within the next thirty years.

Some twenty years after the first printing of Sacchi's book the so-called book of Apicius was printed in Milan (1498; there had been an earlier printed edition of this work undated, in Venice). This was the cookery book purporting to contain fragments of the culinary writings of Marcus Apicius, noble and erudite Roman gourmet of the time of Tiberius. Apicius is said to have derived his gastronomic learning from Greek cookery books and to have founded a school devoted to the culinary arts. His own manuscript was in fact lost, and the work which was printed under his name was derived from notes supposed to have been written by one of his pupils; these notes were copied, apparently, two hundred years after the death of Apicius. (Having spent a vast fortune in the course of a dissolute life, he committed suicide at the age of fifty-five, about A.D. 30, rather than be forced to modify his way of living.) Throughout the Middle Ages various copies of the manuscript were made.

These enthusiastic studies of Greek and Roman methods of cooking found expression in the vast banquets and displays of gorgeous splendour with which the Doges of Venice, the Medici, the Este, the Borgia, the Visconti, the Sforza, the Doria, and the rest of the powerful Italian rulers impressed each other, the populace, and foreign potentates.

The spice trade, which had originated with the Phoenicians and never entirely died out, had a lasting influence on Italian cookery. Spices from the East Indies, Southern India, and Ceylon were shipped from Calicut, on the south-west coast of India, via the Red Sea port of Jidda to Suez; from Suez they were transported across the desert to Cairo, thence down the Nile to Rosetta; from Rosetta the cargoes were shipped to Alexandria, from Alexandria to Venice and to Genoa. At each stage of the journey there were import dues, landing charges, and transport costs to be paid. In their turn the Genoese and the Venetians exacted heavy toll and grew rich on the profits. It was, in fact, not only

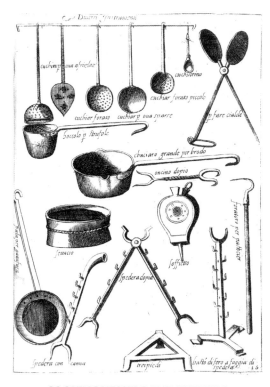
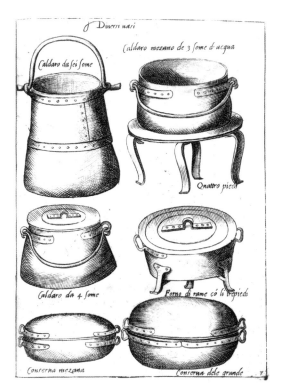

COOKING VESSELS AND UTENSILS
from *Opera* by Bartolomeo Scappi, 1570
including left *a fish pan, copper and bronze sieve, large leather bags for flour and small
ones for spices;* middle *wafer irons;* and right *large capacity cauldrons and preserving pans*

the fall of Constantinople in 1453 and the consequent threat to the spice route, but the ever more exorbitant profits demanded by these traders, and the promise of vast financial reward which spurred on the search for a sea route to India and the spice islands. Although that route was discovered by Vasco da Gama in 1498, the Venetians continued to handle the bulk of the spice and sugar trade via the overland route to Europe for the next fifty years. In those days the galleys of the Venetian merchants must have been a familiar sight in English seaports.

At about the same time as the sound teachings of the Medical School of Salerno with regard to diet and health were penetrating for the first time to England, Catherine de Medici became the bride of the Duke of Orleans who in 1547 succeeded as Henri II of France. The marriage was solemnised in Marseille in 1533, when bride and bridegroom were both fourteen years old, and while it is no doubt true that at the time the French were a long way behind the Florentines and the Venetians in knowledge of the culinary arts, it was much later, during the reign of Catherine's third son, Henri III (he succeeded his elder brother Charles IX in 1575) that the Italian influence in the skills of elegant cookery became effective.

By 1600, when a second Medici bride, Maria, arrived in France as the new Queen of Henri IV, the French had seemingly absorbed Italian cookery to a point where among others the Venetian chronicler Gerolamo Zanetti was complaining that imported French cooks were ruining Venetian stomachs 'with so much *porcherie* (filth), sauces, broths, extracts . . . garlic and onion in every dish . . . meat and fish so transformed that they are scarcely recognisable by the time they get to table. . . . Everything masked and mixed, with a hundred herbs, spices, sauces. . . .'

Complex cookery of the kind castigated by Zanetti would have been confined to the tables of the rich, and even then probably only to banquets and ceremonial occasions. The everyday food of the Italian people can have been little affected by the import of French cooks, and remained, as it does to this day, very much their own, based on local ingredients and traditional methods.

Whereas only the very credulous would suppose that today that diet consists entirely of *pasta asciutta* and veal escalopes, the enormous variety of local dishes to be found in Italy remains little appreciated by the general public and is grasped only by those who have actually set out in search of it, or have studied cookery books dealing with the subject.

The term 'Italian' used in relation to food would in fact mean very little to most Italians. To them there is Florentine cooking, Venetian cooking, there are the dishes of Genoa, Piedmont, Romagna; of Rome, Naples, and the Abruzzi; of Sardinia and Sicily; of Lombardy, Umbria, and the Adriatic coast. United Italy was created only in 1861, and not only have the provinces retained their own traditions of cookery, but many of their products remain localized.

In London or Paris can be found (or *could* be, before the system of export and import became so fanciful) the best of everything which England or France produces. In Italy the best fish is actually to be eaten on the coast, the finest Parmesan cheese in and around Parma, the tenderest beef in Tuscany, where the cattle are raised. So the tourist, having arrived in Italy via Naples and there mistakenly ordered a beef steak which turns out to be a rather shrivelled slice of veal, will thereafter avoid *bistecca*, so that when he visits Florence he will miss that remarkable *bistecca alla Fiorentina*, a vast steak, grilled over a wood fire, which, tender and aromatic, is a dish worth going some way to eat. How many transatlantic travellers landing in Genoa have dined in some Grand Hotel or other and gone on their way without ever suspecting that Genoa possesses a cookery of a most highly individual nature, unique in Europe? Everyone has heard of the *mortadella* sausage of Bologna, but how many hurrying motorists drive past the rose and ochre coloured arcades of Bologna quite unaware that behind modest doorways are some of the best restaurants in Italy? Alas for them, they will remain ignorant of those remarkable dishes consisting of a breast of chicken or turkey cooked in butter, smothered with fine slices of those white truffles which are one of the glories of Italian cooking. Every Italian restaurant abroad serves a dish of so called *tagliatelle Bolognese*; it is worth visiting Bologna to find out what this dish really tastes like, and to accompany it with a bottle of that odd but delicious Lambrusco wine which combines so well with the rich Bolognese cooking. In Venice, nursing aggrieved memories of woolly Mediterranean fish, the traveller will refuse sole on the grounds that it can be eaten only in London or Paris. He will miss a treat, for the soles of the Adriatic have a particularly fine flavour. In Parma he will scarcely fail to eat Parma ham; but if he is not sufficiently inquisitive he will not taste another first-class local speciality, the Felino *salame*, which is one of the most excellent sausages produced in Italy. Now, the blame for this state of affairs lies to a certain extent with the waiters and restaurant keepers. So convinced are these gentlemen that foreigners will accept only spaghetti in tomato sauce, to be followed by a veal cutlet, that the traveller, unless of an unusually determined nature, gives in over and over again, and finally returns home with the conviction that there is nothing else to be had in the whole country.

In Italy, therefore, it is always worth finding out what is to be had in the locality in the way of wines, cheeses, hams, sausages, fruit, and vegetables. They should be asked for, if possible, beforehand; but at the same time it must be borne in mind that as in any country which relies largely on its own agricultural produce, the seasonal character of the food remains intact. Although in Italy, as in France, frozen food has made deep inroads it is still happily quite useless to ask for, say, figs in January or white truffles in July. There are still dishes which are made in certain seasons or for certain festivals and at no other time of the year. Heavy winter dishes such as the *polenta pasticciata* of Lombardy, the *lasagne verdi al forno* of Bologna and the brown bean soup of the Veneto give way after Easter to lighter dishes of *pasta in brodo*, or *antipasti* (hors d'œuvre) of raw vegetables, or little *crostini*, fried bread with cheese and anchovies. One of the summer dishes common to all Italy is *vitello tonnato*, cold veal with a tunny fish flavoured sauce (this sounds outlandish, but is, in fact, a most excellent combination).

The names of Italian dishes are, to say the least, confusing, and vary immensely from region to region. Ravioli as we think of it in England is called ravioli only in Piedmont and Genoa, but it is never stuffed with the coarse mixture met with outside Italy and never smothered with an oily tomato sauce. In other districts there are endless varieties of ravioli called *tortellini, anolini, tortelli, cappelletti, malfatti, agnolotti*. The *pasta* which we should call noodles, is known variously as *fettuccine, tagliatelle, tagliarini, pappardelle*; there are thin, match-like strips of the same paste called *tagliolini* in Florence, *trenette* in Genoa, *tonnarelli* in Rome. *Pasticciata* is a meat stew in Verona, a *polenta au gratin* in Milan. The names of fish are particularly hard to disentangle. The squid and cuttle-fish family are known as *seppie, totani, calamari, calamaretti, moscardini, fragole di mare, sepolini*, and several other names according to the local dialect. Mussels are *cozze* in Naples, *peoci* in Venice, *telline* in Florence: they are also known as *muscoli* and *mitili*, and *telline* are also clams, which are *vongole* in Rome and Naples, *capperozzoli* in Venice, *arselle* in Genoa and Sardinia.

Saltimbocca, bocconcini, quagliette di vitello, braciolette, uccelletti scappati, gropetti, involtini, are all variations of the same little slices of veal with a piece of ham or some kind of stuffing inside; they may be rolled up or they may be flattened out, they may be fried or baked or grilled. *Frittelle* may indicate anything from a very small rissole of meat and herbs (also called *polpette*) to a huge rustic potato cake made with yeast. Its unpredictable nature adds the charm of surprise to the discovery of Italian cooking, a charm which will perhaps replace that operetta conception of romantic Italy in which the tourist lolled in eternal sunshine on a vine-hung terrace, drinking wine for a song, while the villagers in peasant costume danced and sang in the piazza below. The present-day traveller in Italy will be quick to perceive that those cherished fantasies bear about as much relation to the Italy of today as does modern Britain to Merrie England.

The sober facts are that in a town of any size at all the nerve-racking, ceaseless roar and screech of traffic make eating in the open air an endurance test. As for the singing, there is no lack of it. In Rome, Naples, Capri, Genoa, Venice, those romantic musicians with their guitars, their violin bows which may well get entangled with your spaghetti, and their operatic voices vibrating in too confined a space, soon become exasperating. . . . Summer visitors to the Bay of Naples and the Sorrento peninsula should not expect too much; it is not in overgrown seaside villages or tourist-infested islands in the heat of a Mediterranean summer that gastronomic treats will be found. On the other hand, there is no need to depart from the well worn pilgrim roads of Italy in the search for good food. It can be successfully sought in the small and famous towns of Tuscany and Umbria, in Siena and Perugia, at Aquila in the Abruzzi, at Ancona and the port of Ravenna on the Adriatic coast, at Ascoli and Rimini and in the Veneto, in Turin and Modena and Mantua, in Parma, Bologna, Verona and Vicenza. In Italy, the traveller who arrives at any hour within the bounds of reason need rarely make do with a sandwich at his hotel; it is, in fact, a mistake to eat at grand hotels (there are exceptions, naturally), and in any case the display of food in the restaurants is always worth seeing. Pink hams, golden coils of *pasta*, pale green fennel and dark green artichokes, rose-coloured *scampi* and mullet, in the autumn the orange and scarlet and brown of funghi, the whites and creams of cheeses spread out on a table so that the customers can choose, are an important part of the enjoyment of eating in an Italian restaurant. As for the splendid food markets of Florence, Bologna, Turin, Genoa, and Venice, especially Venice, few sightseers bother to go and look at them. A pity, for they are fascinating and beautiful, and an integral part of the life of any great city.

E.D.—1954

INTRODUCTION TO THE PENGUIN EDITION

It is now well over ten years since I returned to England after nearly a year spent in Italy for the express purpose of collecting material for the book which eventually became *Italian Food*.

When about to embark on my travels, English friends who knew Italy far better than I did at the time had been ready with unencouraging predictions. 'All that *pasta*,' they said. 'We've got enough stodge here already; you won't find much else in Italy. You'll have to invent.'

How we cling to our myths, we English. The French, we believe, have been forced to perfect the art of cooking owing to what we like to think is a necessity to disguise poor materials. We ourselves have, we comfortably imagine, no need for either art or artifice in the kitchen. Our basic ingredients are too superb to need the application of intelligence or training to their preparation. As for the Italians, they live, according to our mythology, on veal and tomatoes, spaghetti, cheese, and olive oil.

In the original edition of *Household Management*, published in 1861, the very year of the unification of Italy under the rule of the House of Savoy, young Mrs Beeton asserted that 'modern Romans are merged in the general name of Italians, who, with the exception of macaroni, have no specially characteristic article of food'. She was expressing, no doubt, the general belief of her day – and, I fancy, very largely of our own, one hundred years on.

It is now 1963. During the last decade provision shops and supermarkets selling a high proportion of Italian and other imported produce have multiplied. In our big towns new Italian restaurants open almost monthly. The Espresso Coffee Bar, phenomenon of the early fifties, has developed into the Roman or Neapolitan-type *trattoria*, and spreads far beyond the confines of Soho into the outer suburbs of London and our great industrial cities and seaports. Scarcely a week passes but somebody writes an article in a national newspaper or magazine extolling the glories and subtleties of Italian cooking. Every year appear new cookery books giving more or less accurate versions of the best Italian recipes. And still the general public finds it difficult to equate these happenings with anything having any bearing upon Italy itself as a nation or a geographical entity.

Italy is a place to which you go for a summer holiday. (That is very much what it would have been to me, had I not had the opportunity of writing this book.) You go to Positano, to Capri, to Amalfi, to the Italian Riviera, to the Adriatic coast. You go to soak up sun and to soak in Mediterranean waters. Fair enough. And fair enough, too, is the food you get in Italian seaside resorts. It is representative of holiday food everywhere in Southern Europe. The hotels and restaurants are crowded. The staffs are overworked. The cooking may have an Italian accent, but the majority of foreign visitors (of whom vast numbers are German and Scandinavian as well as British) would be too suspicious of the unknown to accept genuine regional specialities were they offered. Besides, there is the language difficulty and there is the question of what is suitable or in season during the hot summer months, and for people uprooted from familiar routine and surroundings and therefore peculiarly sensitive to changes of diet. So the cooking is reduced to a general level of international mediocrity. Indifferent beefsteaks, chips, the ubiquitous veal, spaghetti and tomato sauce, the evening broth thickened with *pasta*, the eternal *Bel Paese* cheese; and, in the land of fresh figs and peaches, apricots, grapes, and pears, there will be imported bananas for dessert.

Oh yes, I know those meals; too well I know them. And their French equivalents too. And every time I am faced with one and feel angry and frustrated, I remember also the kind of meals served in our own seaside hotels and in the English counterparts of an Italian *pensione*; then I think, well, after all, would I in such establishments expect fine smoked Scotch salmon and roast English lamb? Bradenham ham, home-made Cumberland sauce, and matured Lancashire cheese? Breakfast mushrooms picked in the meadows and bacon sweet-cured according to a traditional Suffolk farmhouse recipe?

On the whole I think it is easier to find the best Italian cooking in Italy than to come by its English equivalent in our own country.

In England – apart from a few obvious delicacies such as the aforementioned smoked salmon, and luxuries like oysters and grouse, which may be found and enjoyed by anyone who can, in the appropriate seasons, afford the most expensive restaurants and hotels – good native English cooking is confined mainly to private houses. For the casual tourist it would be difficult to locate.

In Italy, matters are markedly different. In the south, it is true, careful cooking is not common, although I am told that the opening up of Calabria to tourists has improved the standards of cooking and accommodation almost beyond recognition since the days when Norman Douglas wrote such thundering denunciations of both. In central Italy, however, and in the north, in the provinces of Lombardy, Piedmont, the Veneto, Tuscany, Umbria, Emilia, Parma, and Lazio restaurants

KITCHEN SCENES
from *Opera* by Bartolomeo Scappi, 1570
Left *As the cauldron boils, a joint and fish roast on spits turning in front of the fire.
Smoke is carried upwards by the conductors rotating on either side of the fire.* Right
*Dairy work: the central figure beats egg whites to snow; the one on the right makes
whipped cream in a churn.*

serving the local regional specialities abound. To get such dishes one does, to be sure, need to know a little kitchen and menu Italian. It is a help, and one out of all proportion to the small amount of preparatory study involved, to have some idea of what the regional traditions of cooking are and of what the particular geographical, climatic, and agricultural conditions of the country have produced.

I tried, when I wrote this book, to indicate some of these circumstances and to explain a little how to get the best of Italian food in whichever province one happens to find oneself. A few people have been kind enough to say that in this respect it has helped them to enjoy their visits to Italy, and has been a stepping-stone to further discoveries of their own. That is reward enough for the work I put into the book.

I know that finding the kind of food one is looking for in Italy can be hard work. My own voyage of discovery in that country was far from easy. My command of the Italian language is decidedly the wrong side of adequate. The amount of money I had to spend was not boundless. Neither is my eating capacity. Italians are on the whole abstemious drinkers but big eaters. Sometimes I was asked to plough through a five-course meal and then start all over again with some dish for which I had particularly asked. My kind hosts would be astonished, and cease to believe that I was at all a serious person, when I could do no more than taste a spoonful. There were times when I was very close to despair at the proverbial Italian disregard for their own and other people's time. When it came to getting details of a recipe there were days when I scarcely knew how to find the patience to wait. There was the occasion when I hung about in Anacapri for some three weeks inquiring daily of Mafalda at the Caffè whether today she considered the red peppers just sufficiently and precisely ripe enough to make her bottled *peperoni*.

Another time, after I had already spent far too long dawdling about Sardinia, someone said: 'Ah, Signora, wait a few more days. There will be a *festa*. A wild boar will be roasted in such and such a village.' Such opportunities are not after all to be resisted, at least not by anyone with the curiosity which in the first place makes me undertake these journeys and which sometimes I find myself regretting. Anxiety to return home and get down to practical work on my notes nearly – thank heavens, not quite – prevented me from breaking my homeward journey at Turin in order to eat those magical white truffles brought straight in from Alba at the peak of their season, towards the end of November.

I had been naggingly aware, even during long and contented days spent in other people's kitchens, that a tremendous task still awaited me when I should return to England. For one thing, scales appear to be almost unknown in many Italian kitchens, and neither do Italian cooks use the American cup-and-spoon method of measuring ingredients. They use their memories, their instincts, and, literally, their hands.

'Signora,' I would say, 'what weight, do you think, is a handful of cheese?' 'Ah, now, let us see, perhaps one *etto*.' (One *etto* is 100 grammes or just over 3 oz.; I subsequently discovered that this standard reply was very far indeed from reliable.)

'Then how much is a handful of spinach?' 'One bunch.'

For liquid measurements there were bowls, glasses, cups: each cook using vessels of different sizes and capacity. Some of my recipes I had in fact worked out on the spot, but all, in any case, had to be cooked with ingredients as far as possible available in England.

And rationing was still with us.

Eggs, butter and cream were scarce. (At one time I was buying turkey eggs at 1s. 3d. apiece for my experiments.*) With meat, it was not only a question of the restricted quantity: cuts were often unidentifiable – they were hunks of meat designated as suitable for roasting, frying, grilling, or stewing. To ask you butcher for special cuts (and foreign ones at that) was to ask also for a sardonic laugh or a counter-request to remove your registration elsewhere.

In Soho, but almost nowhere else, such things as Italian *pasta* and parmesan cheese, olive oil, *salame*, and occasionally Parma ham were to be had. There too Italian rice, Tuscan haricot beans, chick peas, and brown lentils were beginning to come back. In the rest of the country such commodities were all but unobtainable. With southern vegetables such as aubergines, red and green peppers, fennel, the tiny marrows called by the French *courgettes* and in Italy *zucchine*, much the same situation prevailed. The only cream cheeses at all possible for cooking, unless you made your own – and milk was still rationed – were the French Gervais and a Scandinavian boxed product. Meat stock, fresh herbs such as basil and tarragon, and for that matter even dried ones, and minor ingredients such as pine nuts and various spices were stumbling blocks. Flour was of very poor quality, bad for sauces, inadequate for *pasta*, and worse for pastry.

Writing of the feelings of authors towards their own work, Mr Raymond Mortimer once observed that they usually prefer, perhaps wrongly, the book which has given them the most trouble.

That this book was uncommonly troublesome cannot be denied. But I do not think that was the only reason that I felt, and feel, less detached from it than from any other work I have done before or since.

Italy was a country to which I had come long after Provence and Greece had put me under lasting spells. Towards Italy I felt more critical, my emotions were less engaged. It was possibly for this reason that the sense of discovery which in the end Italian cooking brought me was so potent. As recipe after recipe came out and I realized how much I was learning, and how enormously these dishes were enlarging my own scope and enjoyment, the fever to communicate them grew every day more urgent.

How wrong they had been, all those pessimists, from Mrs Beeton down to my own contemporaries. Where had they been looking? Had they been looking at all? Invent indeed. I had so much material that a vast deal had to be rejected. (Anyone who truly knows Italy and Italian food will know also that this is nothing but the truth.) What I kept were mainly those recipes which would, I believed, be of use in our own kitchens when normal conditions returned. Those I thought entirely unpractical or hopeless to attempt in England I confined to references or descriptions. Even so, when finally I delivered my typescript to my publishers they looked at it coldly. I had been a long time

---

*The equivalent in the late 1980s would be about 75p.

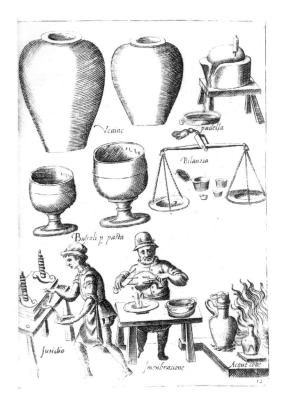

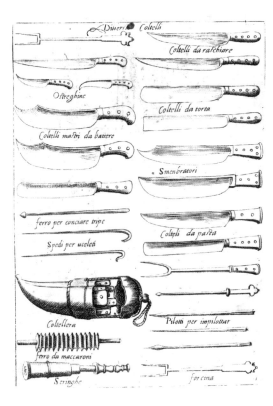

KITCHEN SCENES AND COOKING UTENSILS
from *Opera* by Bartolomeo Scappi, 1570
including left *storage jars, scales, using a gravy press and carving;* middle *washing up*
and knife sharpening; and right *a sheath for knives, a macaroni iron or roller and a syringe for fritters*

about it – it was twice as long as they had been led to expect . . . paper shortage . . . printing costs . . . they hoped the expenditure would be justified.

I hoped so too. And went home to a house empty, divested of the evidence of two years' work.

The whole Italian project was relegated to the back of my mind. During the long months while the typescript was going through the first stages of production and printing, I occupied myself with work on another and less taxing book.

It was not until Renato Guttuso's illustrations, long awaited, started arriving one or two at a time from Rome, that I began again to feel that the Italian venture had after all been worth while.

To have for my book those magnificent drawings and the dazzling jacket picture by one of Italy's most remarkable living artists, I would have gone through the whole agony of writing it all over again.

Here were no sentimental decorations (nor, from Guttuso, had I exactly expected any), no vine-hung terraces or strings of onions in the conventional-romantic cookery book tradition. Here was a well-worn cheap aluminium *tegamino*, the double-handled egg dish so beloved of Italian cooks, every dent and defect implied. Here was a ravenous

Italian workman, every nerve concentrated on the shovelling of *pasta* into his mouth; here a chunk of coarsely cut *salame*, its squares of fat glistening; slices of Parma ham laid like pieces of silk over the edge of a dish; leaf-artichokes on the stalk, tied in a bunch exactly as they are offered for sale in Roman markets, but by Guttuso invested with a quite dangerously blazing vitality; for this artist even the straw round the neck of a wine flask is unravelling itself in a manner positively threatening in its purpose and intensity.

Long before the pictures were out of my hands and delivered into those of the publishers, they had become for me an integral part of my book. Once again the whole idea made sense.*

As I have already mentioned on page 7, reviewers were unimaginably kind and welcoming. (So far as I remember only one expressed the view that Italian food should be left to the Italians and we to our puddings and cabbage.)

When Mr Evelyn Waugh, a writer whose books have given me more

---

*Unhappily, at some stage the Guttuso illustrations and cover picture fell off the back of my then publishers' lorry, and cannot be reproduced for the present edition. For that loss we have compensated with four reproductions of the same artist's arresting still-lifes.

pleasure that I have powers to acknowledge, actually named this book in the *Sunday Times* as one of the two which in the year 1954 had given *him* the most pleasure I was, and still am, stunned by the compliment and by Mr Waugh's tolerance of my amateur's efforts at writing.

Do not think I wish to imply that criticisms, queries, and corrections from readers did not come in. They did and do. I do not think there is one which has not been enlightening, constructive, and encouraging. It is in view of such criticisms and requests for more detailed explanations, and in the light of ten years' further cooking experience, as well as in consideration of conditions much changed during these ten years, that I have made some highly necessary revisions to my recipes and instructions.

Because so many of the recipes have become trusted familiars in my own kitchen, some have evolved over the years, as recipes do, into something rather different from the originals, most of my revisions have been made in the form of footnotes.*

This is, I think, a book for those readers and cooks who prefer to know what the original dishes are supposed to be like, and to be given the option of making their own adaptations and alterations according to their taste and their circumstances. There is, I know, a school of writers who seem to believe that English housewives are weak in the head and must not be exposed to the truth about the cooking of other countries; must not be shocked by the idea of making a yeast dough, cleaning an ink-fish, adding nutritive value to a soup with olive oil, cutting the breast off a raw chicken in order to fry it in butter rather than buying a packet of something called 'chicken parts' from the deep-freeze and cooking them in a cheap fat or tasteless oil substitute.

If I believed that English women really needed this kind of protection – censorship it almost amounts to – I would have packed in cookery writing long ago.

What I in fact believe is that the English are now more creative and inquiring about cooking than they have ever been before. I am sure that they are – and rightly so – annoyed and exasperated when recipes for celebrated foreign specialities dished out to them in books, magazines, and newspapers prove to be false. As I write this, I have just come across, in a respected monthly magazine, a recipe for a risotto made with twice-cooked Patna rice and a tin of tomato soup. What way is that of enlarging our knowledge and arousing our interest? *Minestrone*, that

hefty, rough-and-ready, but nutritionally sound traditional midday soup of Northern Italian agricultural and manual workers, features frequently in such publications. Often the readers are told that it can be made with some such ingredients as a bouillon cube, a tin of chicken noodle soup, and a few frozen french beans. A crumpet or a made-up scone-mix spread with tomato purée and a slice of processed cheese turns up regularly as a Neapolitan *pizza*.

I can't help wondering how we should feel if Italian cookery writers were to retaliate by asserting that a Welsh Rabbit is made with polenta cakes and Gorgonzola, or steak and kidney pudding with veal and tomatoes and a covering of macaroni. The point is, how far can you go in attaching the names of internationally known specialities to concoctions which have only the flimsiest relation to the originals? To what extent can you rely on the ignorance of your readers to get away with the practice? Should that ignorance be exploited in the cause of selling some nationally advertised ingredient? Should it be exploited at all?

Adaptations do of course have to be made, alternatives to the original ingredients sometimes used. Knowledge, they say, is power. Knowledge, as Norman Douglas observed, is also fun. Knowledge in the case in point helps one to discriminate in the matter of deciding what is or is not an acceptable substitute or alternative in a recipe.

In London and in other big cities, or in any town or village where there are enterprising delicatessen stores and enlightened greengrocers, such manipulation of recipes may these days indeed be unnecessary. I have also taken into consideration that there are still many towns and country areas where no such shops exist, where imported vegetables are still rare, fresh herbs other than parsley unknown, and even such commodities as Italian *pasta* and rice hard to come by. For these reasons I have left as I wrote them ten years ago the suggestions I then made as to ways of getting round the difficulties. (Some cannot be got round. In those cases best leave the recipes alone; there are still very many for which quite everyday ingredients only are required.) Here and there I have appended a footnote to the effect that I no longer entirely agree with what I thought in 1953, or in some cases that there are now better alternatives than those of that far-off period.

For the rest, I do ask, although diffidently, that readers unfamiliar with Italian ingredients, or in doubt as to what to buy, should summon up the courage and the patience to have a look at the chapter in this book which is entitled *The Italian Store Cupboard*, as well as at the introductory pages to each section of recipes.

---

* Most of them have now (1987) been incorporated into the main text.

E.D. – 1963

Acknowledgements

Y TRAVELS IN ITALY IN SEARCH OF REGIONAL FOOD and traditional recipes were to a great extent made possible by the generosity of the On. Dr Pietro Romani, High Commissioner for Italian Tourism, and by the Conte Sigmund Fago Golfarelli of the Ente Nazionale Industrie Turistiche in Rome. I am deeply grateful to them, and to the officials of the Ente del Turismo all over Italy who were so hospitable, and so understanding of my rather special problems of research. Particularly in Siena, Perugia, Florence, Bologna, Parma, Verona, Ravenna, Venice, Como, Stresa, Milan, Turin, Genoa, Sanremo, and in the island of Sardinia, the kindness, enthusiasm, and often the erudition of members of the Ente del Turismo led me to discoveries about Italian food and wine which would otherwise have been most difficult, if not impossible, to make.

Restaurant proprietors and their chefs, and cooks in the houses of friends, were equally generous in the matter of disclosing recipes, cooking special dishes, and demonstrating the individual characteristics of the Italian kitchen.

I am particularly indebted to Signora Ramusani of the Aurora restaurant in Parma, Signor Zoppi of the Taverna Fenice in Venice, Signor Oswaldo* of Il Buco in Rome, Signora Mafalda of the Caffè Caprile in Anacapri, and Signor Bolognini of Bolognini's in Bologna, in whose kitchens I have spent most delightful and instructive days. I also gratefully record my thanks to the proprietors and chefs of the Pappagallo, the Sampiero, and the Trattoria Nerina, all in Bologna, of the Molinara in Verona, the Hotel Diana in Milan, the Locanda on the island of Comacino, the Ristorante al Sole at Ravenna Marina, the Tre Galline in Turin, the Panteon in Rome, Delfino's in Portofino, Sabatini's in Florence, the Antico Martini and the Peoceto in Venice, the Tre Re at Chieri, Giacometti's in Positano, the Trasimeno in Perugia, and Caruso's at Ravello. All of them have given me valuable information and recipes. I wish also to acknowledge my debt to several most admirable and fascinating Italian cookery books. Without a thorough study of these books, as well as first-hand knowledge of eating and cooking in Italy, it would have been impossible for me to write about Italian food. For those who read Italian I have given a brief list of Italian cookery books on page 213.

A good many of the recipes in this book were originally published by Harpers Bazaar, and three of four by Messrs Saccone and Speed, to whom my thanks are due for permission to reprint them here.

Several extracts from G. Orioli's book *Moving Along* are reprinted with the permission of Messrs Chatto and Windus, and a passage from *Siren Land* by Norman Douglas with the permission of his executors and of Messrs Secker and Warburg. The Maison Stock & Cie of Paris have courteously allowed me to quote a paragraph from Guillaume Apollinaire's *L'Hérésiarque & Cie*, and Messrs Seeley Service Ltd and Mr Robin Fedden a recipe from Romilly Fedden's *Food and other Frailties*.

To Mr John Lehmann, who originally fostered the idea of this book, and to all those friends in Italy and in England who have helped me in my researches, extended the hospitality of their houses and their kitchens, and tolerantly offered most helpful criticisms while I have been working on my book, I here express, although in inadequate terms, my very great gratitude.   E.D. – 1954

* Later of La Fontanella, Largo Fontanella Borghese 86, Rome.

GIOVANNI BATTISTA RECCO (c. 1615-60)
KITCHEN STILL LIFE
Naples, Museo Nazionale e Gallerie di Capodimonte

ITALIAN DISHES IN FOREIGN KITCHENS

HE DIFFICULTIES OF REPRODUCING ITALIAN COOKING abroad are much the same as the difficulties attendant upon any good cooking outside its country of origin, and usually they can be overcome.

Italians, unlike the thrifty French, are very extravagant with raw materials. Butter, cheese, oil, the best cuts of meat, chicken and turkey breasts, eggs, chicken and meat broth, raw and cooked ham are used not so much with reckless abandon as with a precise awareness of what good quality does for the cooking.

In most Italian households the marketing is done twice a day. Everything is freshly cooked for every meal. What the Italian kitchen misses in the form of concentrated meat glazes, *fumets* of fish and game, the *fonds de cuisine* of the French, it makes up for in the extreme freshness and lavishness of its raw materials. It is worth bearing in mind that when an Italian has not the wherewithal to cook one of the traditional extravagant dishes she doesn't attempt to produce an imitation. No amount of propaganda could persuade her to see the point of making, let us say, a steak and kidney pudding with tinned beef and no kidneys, neither would she bother to make a ravioli stuffing with leftovers, because the results would not at all resemble the dish as it should be, and would therefore be valueless. So her method would be to produce some attractive and nourishing little dish out of two ounces of cheese and a slice of ham, or a pound of spinach and a couple of eggs. A hefty *pizza* made of bread dough and baked in the oven with tomatoes, cheese and herbs costs very little and is comforting, savoury food.

Gnocchi made of potatoes, or of semolina flour, or of spinach and *ricotta* (fresh white sheep's milk cheese*), are cheap and easy to make, so are little envelopes of paste containing slices of cheese and *mortadella* sausage, and *mozzarella in carrozza*, a fried cheese sandwich. Because Parmesan cheese is expensive, many people eat their spaghetti in the rough-and-ready but extremely good Neapolitan way, with olive oil and garlic. From such methods I believe we could learn much of value from the Italians. Not that Italian cooking is without its faults. The excessive use of cheese, the too frequent appearance of tomato sauce, the overworking of the frying pan (expert as Italian cooks are with it), too heavy a hand with powerful herbs, are some of the points at which fault could be found with the Italian kitchen.

There is no reason, however, why we should not combine the best which it has to offer (and the best in Italy is extremely good) with materials at our disposal in this country. The number of different ways of making use, for example, of a small quantity of veal is astounding. (I have given a dozen such recipes in this book, and there are plenty more.) We could benefit from Italian methods of frying and grilling fish; and as we have not one single fish soup in common use in this country, could we not invent one? Again, once the delicate flavour of genuine Bolognese or Parma stuffings for *anolini* or *cappelletti* have been compared with the coarse mixtures contained in bought ravioli, the idea of making these things at home cannot fail to appeal.

The delicacy and intrinsic goodness of the simplest white risotto

---

*Also now made with cow's milk.

GIOVANNI PAOLO SPADINO (active 1687-1703)
STILL LIFE
Rome, Pinacoteca Capitolina

SCHOOL OF CARAVAGGIO (c. 1600)
STILL LIFE WITH FLOWERS AND FRUIT (detail)
Rome, Galleria Borghese

eaten only with Parmesan cheese and good fresh butter will also quickly be appreciated. Tied as we are by tradition in the matter of the roast turkey, we complain that it is a dull and dry bird, but continue to eat it cooked in the same way; the Italian fashion of cooking the breast with butter, ham and cheese will be a revelation. Home-made cream cheese can be turned to good account in twenty different dishes in the Italian manner. To make *pasta* at home may sound a formidable undertaking, but if any Italian peasant girl can make it without effort we should presumably be able, after two or three attempts, to master the technique. And now of course pasta machines, whether hand-operated or electrically powered, are easily obtainable.

Some interesting sidelights emerge from a study of Italian cooking. The beautiful colours of their food is one most characteristic point. The vivid scarlet dishes of the south, the tomato sauce and the pimentos, the oranges and pinks of fish soups, the red and white of a Neapolitan

pizza, contrast strikingly with the unique green food of central and northern Italy; the spinach *gnocchi* of Tuscany, the *lasagne verdi* of Bologna, the green *pesto* sauce of Genoa, the green peas and rice of the Veneto, green artichokes in pies, in omelettes, in salads; the green and yellow marbled stuffings of rolled beef and veal dishes – such food can scarcely fail to charm. Then there is the point of the endless hours Italian cooks are willing to spend over the pounding of intricate stuffings and sauces, and the startling rapidity with which the actual cooking is carried out (five minutes in boiling water for the ravioli, into the frying pan and out with the *polpette*, the *crocchette* and the *fritelle* which have been most patiently chopped, sieved, and rolled out on the pastry board).

The seemingly deliberate misunderstanding by French cooks of Italian food is another curious point. 'Two tablespoons of rice for a risotto for four'; 'the Milanese like their rice half-cooked' – one reads

FOLLOWER OF PIETRO LONGHI (18th century)
A COUNTRY PICNIC (detail)
Venice, Museo Correr

with astonishment such instructions from otherwise irreproachable French cookery books. Ali-Bab, in his monumental work *Gastronomie Pratique*, falls into the common trap of asserting that 'poultry and butcher's meats are (in Italy) frankly mediocre', and 'the most common vegetables are broccoli and fennel'. It is scarcely to be wondered at that in their turn a good many Italians jeer at French cooking (French dishes are rarely well cooked in Italy), although they make a mistake in deriding the slowly simmered, patiently amalgamated dishes of wine, meat, and vegetables which play such an important part in the marvellous regional food of France. There *are* long-cooked meat dishes in the Italian kitchen, and soups containing haricot beans or chick peas which must be cooked for several hours; but on the whole Italian cooks neither like nor understand these methods. As I have already sufficiently explained, quality and freshness of flavour are the all-important elements in Italian cooking; and in describing the dishes in this book I have deviated as little as possible from the correct ingredients and quantities, so that the food may retain its authentic flavour.

VINCENZO CAMPI (1536-91)
THE FRUIT SELLER
Milan, Pinacoteca di Brera

THE ITALIAN STORE CUPBOARD

LE ERBE ODOROSE
(HERBS)

SWEET BASIL (Lat. *ocymum basilium*. It. *basilico*). Why is this lovely aromatic herb now so rare in England? It is true that it needs sunshine and a certain amount of care in cultivation, but I have myself grown it with success even in boxes on a London roof. It was introduced into England in the sixteenth century and evidently flourished, for English herbalists, among them Tusser (*Five Hundred Points of Good Husbandry*, 1577), Parkinson (*The Earthly Paradise*, 1629), and Culpeper (*The English Physitian*, 1652), appear to take its presence in the herb garden for granted, although it was employed for perfumes and as a strewing herb rather than in the kitchen. Its only traditional use in English cooking is as an ingredient of turtle soup, so presumably it must have been common during the nineteenth century.

Basil has a deliciously spicy and aromatic scent, and is worth growing for that reason alone. In Italy basil leaves are used a great deal to flavour tomato sauce, salads, and soups, especially in the south, and are essential to the marvellous Genoese *pesto*, perhaps the best sauce yet invented for all kinds of *pasta*.

Nothing can replace the lovely flavour of this herb. If I had to choose just one plant from the whole herb garden I should be content with basil. Norman Douglas, who had a great fondness for this herb, would never allow his cook to chop the leaves or even to cut them with scissors; they must be gently torn up, he said, or the flavour would be spoilt. I never agreed with him on this point, for the pounding of basil seems, on the contrary, to bring out its flavour. Possibly he had been influenced by the legend, which I discovered only after it was too late to ask him, that 'the properties of that hearbe was that being gently handled it gave a pleasant smell but being hardly wrung and bruised would breed scorpions ... it is also observed that scorpions doe much rest and abide under those pots and vessels wherein Basill is planted' (Parkinson's *Earthly Paradise*, 1629).

Dried basil is an improvement on no basil at all, but it cannot be used in the making of *pesto* or in salads. Buy it in small quantities. Dried herbs bought in enormous jars go stale.

Besides the ordinary sweet basil the Italians grow a giant variety called *basilico a foglie di lattughe*, lettuce-leaved basil.

WILD MARJORAM (Lat. *origanum vulgare*, It. *origano*). Although this herb grows wild on the South Downs, it is seldom used for cooking in England. In Italy, where its scent is stronger than the English variety, it is a characteristic flavouring of many dishes, particularly of the *pizza Napoletana*; it grows, says Professor Ghinelli (*Le Conserve di Carne*, Parma, 1950), in uncultivated areas and in poor and arid soil. Freshly picked from the scrubby hillsides of the south, it scents the kitchens where it is hung up to dry, and has an unmistakable flavour, quite distinct from that of sweet marjoram. Dried, it is sold in little sausage-like cellophane bags all over Italy and is a passable substitute for the home-dried herb. The *rigani* which is used in Greece to flavour mutton *kebabs* is still another variety, *origanum dubium*, of which the dried flowers have a far more powerful scent than the leaves of the Italian plant.

SAGE
from *Tacuinum Sanitatis* (c. 1390-1400)
Paris, Bibliothèque Nationale, MS Nouv. Acq. 1673

MARJORAM
from *Tacuinum of Sex Rebus* (15th century)
Rouen, Bibliothèque Municipale

BASIL
from *Tacuinum Sanitatis*
Paris, Bibliothèque Nationale, MS Nouv. Acq. 1673

SWEET MARJORAM (Lat. *origanum marjorana*, It. *maggiorana*) can be used instead of *origano*, and in Italy goes into soups, stews, and fish dishes.

SAGE (Lat. *salvia officinalus*, It. *salvia*) is used a good deal in Italian cookery, particularly with veal and calf's liver. I find its musty dried-blood smell overpowering, and prefer to use in its place mint or basil. Most English people are accustomed to it, however, from having so frequently eaten pork, or duck, or goose as a background to sage and onion stuffing.

THYME (Lat. *thymus vulgaris*, It. *timo*) is used less in Italy than in France, but in English kitchens it often has to serve as a substitute for marjoram or *origano*. Wild thyme from the downs has the most lovely scent and flavour. Lemon thyme is worth cultivating in gardens.

MINT (Lat. *mentha viridis*, It. *menta*) and PEPPERMINT (Lat. *mentha peperita*, It. *mentuccia, menta Romana*) are used a good deal in Roman cooking, with vegetables, fish, in salads and soups. Anyone who has walked among the ghostly ruins of Ostia Antica will remember the haunting scent of the wild mint which rises from the ground, for one cannot help treading it underfoot. In Florence there is a slightly different variety called locally *nepitella*. (The mint tribe is notoriously difficult to classify.) Since all mints retain their flavour well when dried, they should be used more liberally in the kitchen, with all manner of dishes. Try mint, for example, with stewed mushrooms.

ROSEMARY (Lat. *rosmarinus officinalis*, It. *rosmarino*). Italians are inordinately fond of rosemary. It is an essential flavouring of *abbacchio*, the roast baby lamb of which the Romans are so fond, and of *porchetta*, roast sucking pig. In the market of Florence rolled fillets of pork are most exquisitely tied up ready for roasting, adorned, almost embroidered, with rosemary. They overdo it, to my way of thinking. Rosemary has great charm as a plant but in cookery is a treacherous herb. The oil which comes from the leaves is very powerful and can kill the taste of

FENNEL
from *Tacuinum Sanitatis*
Paris, Bibliothèque Nationale, MS Nouv. Acq. 1673

PARSLEY
from *Tacuinum Sanitatis*
Paris, Bibliothèque Nationale, MS Nouv. Acq. 1673

GARLIC
from *Tacuinum Sanitatis*
Paris, Bibliothèque Nationale, MS Nouv. Acq. 1673

any meat. Finding those spiky little leaves in one's mouth is not very agreeable, either. Dried, it loses some of its strength, but should still be treated with caution.

FENNEL (Lat. *foeniculum dulce*, It. *finocchio*). The bulbous root stem of the Florentine fennel has an aniseed flavour and is eaten both raw and cooked. In Italy it is often served raw at the end of a meal instead of fruit, as well as at the beginning, seasoned with oil and salt. The leaves, which are used so much in the South of France for flavouring fish and fish soups, are not commonly employed in Italy, but both the stalks and leaves of wild fennel (*foeniculum vulgare*) are chopped up with garlic and used as a stuffing for roast sucking pig as cooked in Umbria, with excellent results. An improvement on the rosemary of Rome.

FENNEL SEEDS (It. *semi di finocchio*) go into a number of sausages, particularly *finocchiona*, the Florentine *salame*, which to my taste is one of the two best in Italy (the other one being Felino, from the province of

Parma). Fennel seeds are also used to flavour the delicious dried figs of Bari.

CELERY (Lat. *apium graveolens*, It. *sedano*). The leaves as well as the stalks of celery, with carrot and onion, form the basic soup vegetables of most Italian cooking. It is rarely served raw, possibly because it appears to be mostly of a rather stringy and thin growth.

Turner, in his *Herbal* of 1538, says of celery: 'The first I ever saw was in the Venetian Ambassador's garden in the spittle yard, near Bishop's Gate Streete.'

PARSLEY (Lat. *petroselinum sativum*, It. *prezzemolo*) is said to have been originally a native of Sardinia. A great deal of parsley goes into Italian soups and salads. With garlic and anchovies it is chopped for the stuffing of aubergines, pimentos, small marrows, onions.

The flat-leaved parsley commonly used in Italy is more aromatic than our English curled parsley, and in England is often to be found in the shops of greengrocers specialising in Cypriot, Greek and Indian products.

TARRAGON (Lat. *artemisia dracunculus*, It. *dragoncello, serpentaria*). The only region of Italy where I have found tarragon in common use is Siena. In that town it is used to flavour stewed and stuffed artichokes, and if asked for will be put into salads or cooked with sole in the Sienese restaurants.

It is always a battle to get plants of the true French tarragon out of nurserymen, but it can be achieved, and if planted in light soil with room to root deeply it seems to grow quite well.

BAY LEAVES (Lat. *Laurus nobilis*, It. *alloro, lauro*). Everyone who has a garden, however small, can find room for a little bay tree, if only in a wooden tub. Bay trees must be well watered and carefully cherished. An ailing bay tree is a woebegone sight, and according to Italian tradition the withering of a bay tree is a bad omen. Certainly in 1629, as reported by John Evelyn, all the bay trees in the garden of the University of Padua died, and soon afterwards the town was struck with a fearful pestilence; but the tradition must have been well established long before that, for Shakespeare refers to it in that foreboding line spoken by the Welsh captain in *Richard II*: 'The bay trees in our country are all withered.' This same event was recorded by Holinshed in 1399 (the year of Richard's downfall): 'Throughout all the realme of England, old baie trees withered, and afterwards, contrarie to all men's thinking, grew greene againe; a strange sight, and supposed to import some unknown event.'

In Italian cooking bay leaves are used in the same way as in France and England – in soups, stews, and in the brine for salted food.

A freshly picked bay leaf gives out a strange scent, bitter and aromatic, with something of both vanilla and nutmeg, and can be boiled in the milk for a béchamel sauce or a sweet cream with good results. To extract a stronger flavour from dry bay leaves, mince them up very fine before putting them in a soup.

MYRTLE (It. *mirto*). Myrtle grows all over the stony hillsides of Sardinia, right down to the sandy beaches, and Sardinians are fond of flavouring their food with it. Sprigs of myrtle are wreathed round the roast baby pig (*porceddù*), which is so good in the *rosticcerie* of Cagliari and Sassari, and the old peasant women who bring herbs to the market offer bunches of myrtle for sale, as well as fennel, marjoram, parsley, bay leaves, wild mint, and basil. A Sardinian delicacy called *tàccula* consists of roasted thrushes or blackbirds stuffed while they are still hot into little bags lined with myrtle leaves and left until they have absorbed the scent of the myrtle. In some parts of the island the country people even make oil from the ripe berries of the myrtle (this is forbidden, but Sardinians are not notably law-abiding), and they claim that this myrtle oil is far superior to olive oil for frying fish.

BORAGE (Lat. *borago officinalis*, It. *boraggine*). Borage has always been said to have exhilarating properties, and to give courage, which no doubt accounts for its traditional use in wine cups. In and around Genoa, but so far as I know nowhere else in Italy, borage is used in a stuffing for ravioli, and the leaves are also made into fritters. Borage grows wild on the chalk soil of the Sussex downs, and occasionally one comes across little bunches of it for sale in London greengrocers' shops. It withers very rapidly. Lady Rosalind Northcote (*The Book of Herbs*, 1912) says that 'bees love borage and it yields excellent honey'. It has a pronounced flavour of cucumber, and is delicious when finely chopped and mixed into freshly made cream cheese.

JUNIPER (It. *ginepro*). The Italians often put juniper berries into stuffings for game; they have an aromatic-bitter scent, which greatly enhances the flavour of any bird which in the process of transport or cold storage may have become dry or a little flavourless. Juniper berries are also excellent with pork and mutton. They can be bought at Harrods, Selfridges, in Soho shops, and in the many establishments now specializing in Indian and Chinese provisions and spices.

SPEZIE
(*SPICES*)

The great galleys of Venice and Florence
Be well laden with things of complacence;
All spicerye and of grocers ware
With sweet wines, all manner of fare....
Adam de Molyneux, Bishop of Chichester (d. 1450)

The use of spices in Italian cooking dates back to the Romans. The prosperity of the Venetian and Genoese republics, and to a certain extent that of Florence, was founded on the handling of the spices which reached Italian ports by the overland route from the East. From Italy they were distributed throughout Europe (England and Flanders being supplied by the Venetian merchant fleet). Tomasso Garzoni, listing the herbs and spices in use in sixteenth-century Venice, mentions cloves, pepper, saffron, cinnamon, nutmeg, coriander, mustard, fennel, basil, parsley, sage, rosemary, bay leaves; almonds, pine nuts, sultanas, figs, and pistachios were also commonly cooked with meat and fish dishes.

With the development of the sea route from the Indies in the sixteenth century, the Italian spice trade declined; but the taste for spiced food remained.

NUTMEG (It. *noce moscata*). The customary one nutmeg found in a dusty corner of English kitchen cupboards would not go far in Italy. It is a spice which goes into dozens of dishes, particularly in the region of Bologna, where it is an essential ingredient of the stuffing for *anolini*,

MYRTLE
from *Tacuinum Sanitatis*
Paris, Bibliothèque Nationale, MS Nouv. Acq. 1673

CINNAMON SELLER
from *Tractatus de Herbis* (15th century)
Modena, Biblioteca Estense, MS Latino 993, ∝ L 9.28

NUTMEG
from *Tacuinum Sanitatis*
Paris, Bibliothèque Nationale, MS Nouv. Acq. 1673

tortellini, tortelli di erbette (a kind of chard or spinach ravioli which is a speciality of Parma). In fact, nutmeg goes into all dishes which contain spinach, and all dishes whether sweet or savoury made from *ricotta* (see page 19).

CLOVES (It. *chiodi di garofano*). Besides being used to flavour spiced cakes such as the famous *panforte* of Siena, cloves are still occasionally put into meat dishes, such as *stracotto*, a beef stew, and those game dishes which are served with a sour-sweet sauce.

CINNAMON (It. *cannella*) is occasionally used in meat and game dishes, as well as in cakes and puddings.

VANILLA (It. *vaniglia*). Keep a special jar of caster sugar with a stick of vanilla in it, and use the sugar when making sweet pastry or creams. In Italy they sell little packets of vanilla sugar especially for this purpose.

CORIANDER SEEDS (It. *coriandro*). A neglected but useful spice in the kitchen. A few crushed coriander seeds make an excellent flavouring for roast lamb or pork, and its orange-peel scent goes well, too, with fish.

SAFFRON (Lat. *crocus sativus*, It. *zafferano*). The use of saffron as a spice is of ancient origin. The Phoenicians were apparently inordinately addicted to it, and its use in southern France in *bouillabaisse* and other fish dishes, and even in the saffron buns of Cornwall, has been attributed to Phoenician influence. In Italy the saffron crocus is cultivated in the Abruzzi and in Sardinia, and as everyone knows it is saffron which gives *risotto Milanese* its beautiful pale butter colour and its characteristic flavour. There are one or two districts where saffron is used to spice the *zuppa di pesce*, but a great many Italian cooks turn up their noses at saffron ('too strong, it kills the flavour of the fish'), in which I don't altogether agree with them.

Saffron comes from the pistils of the autumn-flowering crocus, and since there are three only to each flower it is easy to understand in what large quantities the flower must be cultivated and why genuine saffron is so expensive.

Jeanne Savarin, editress of *La Cuisine des Familles*, wrote in October 1905: 'About half a million crocus pistils are needed to make one kilo of authentic saffron powder, and a druggist cannot buy a pound of saffron powder for less than sixty francs.' Sixty francs would have been about three pounds at that time, and it is not surprising that the adulteration and falsification of saffron was common.

To avoid being fobbed off with imitation saffron, it is best to buy the kind which is sold not in powder but in the actual pistils of the flower, frail little threads which on being steeped in water give out their beautiful saffron colour and rather bitter flavour. It is used in very small quantities. It is the most expensive of all spices, and in Italian cooking there is no substitute.

SALT (It. *sale*). Out past Poetto, the long white beach of Cagliari in Sardinia, can be seen a curious and fascinating sight, the salt lagoons which provide all Italy with marine salt. In rectangular, loaf-like shapes which echo the long ridges of the Sardinian hills, the newly extracted salt from the lakes is heaped, hard and crusty, blinding white in the sunlight, with blue and rose and lilac shadows, a moon landscape. Sea salt (In French *gros sel, sel gris*) can now be bought in many delicatessen shops as well as in wholefood and health food stores, and at one or two kitchen utensils shops. Our own Maldon salt, in crunchy flakes, can be found at Fortnum's, Harrod's, Selfridge's, and the Army & Navy Stores, or ordered direct from the Maldon Crystal Salt Company, Maldon, Essex.

Food cooked with sea salt tastes so much better than that cooked with powdered salt that people who are accustomed to it notice a startling difference when deprived of it. For Maldon salt, mills are pointless. Use your fingers, or if you prefer pound it in a wooden mortar.

PEPPER (It. *pepe*) is one of the oldest, most valuable, and most widely known of all spices. Use black pepper, freshly ground from a pepper mill, whenever possible.

AGLIO
(GARLIC)

It is a mistake to suppose that all Italian food is heavily garlic-flavoured.

In the south, particularly in Naples, a good deal of garlic goes into the tomato sauce and the fish soups. Spaghetti with oil and garlic is much beloved of the Neapolitans (and how I agree with them). In Rome the only common restaurant dish which contains a quantity of garlic is *spaghetti alle vongole* (described on p. 67).

Piedmont has its garlic dish, the *bagna cauda* sauce, and Genoa its delicious garlic-flavoured *pesto*, but on the whole Italian cooking contains far less garlic than that of Provence or south-west France. Even the *salame* and the sausages are only very mildly garlic flavoured, and some not at all.

A clove or two of garlic should go into most soups and stews, into the stuffings for pimentos, aubergines, and small marrows, and into mixed salads. Beetroot salad is infinitely the better for a little chopped garlic, and so are stewed mushrooms and spinach soup.

ALICI, ACCIUGHE
(ANCHOVIES)

Anchovies in oil or brine are used a great deal in southern Italy and in Piedmont and Liguria as an ingredient of sauces, salads, and stuffings, sometimes in unexpected ways. *Crostini di provatura*, a dish nearly always to be found in the more humble Roman *trattorie*, are croûtons of bread and melted cheese with a sauce of anchovies cooked in butter, a particularly successful combination. As a garnish for pimentos in oil a few fillets of anchovies are excellent.

Anchovies and garlic are the basis of *la bagna cauda*, the traditional sauce of Piedmont. At one time they were used a good deal in England to lard meat, but the only survival of this taste seems to be that rather unpleasant anchovy sauce. . . . Anchovy toasts made with genuine anchovy paste used to be so good. . . . Anchovies in oil of good quality can be found quite easily in England. Some are inclined to be over-salted, and should be washed in warm water or vinegar before they are added to a sauce. As an occasional change there is nothing wrong with pounded anchovies in the salad dressing, but the taste is apt to pall.

TONNO SOTT'OLIO
(TUNNY FISH IN OIL)

This appears in a dozen unfamiliar ways: mixed with potatoes or french beans for a salad; with pimentos; made into a kind of sausage for an *antipasto*; in a sauce for cold veal; as an important part of the delicious Tuscan dish of white beans *fagioli col tonno*. The choice part of the tunny fish is the stomach (*ventresca*), which is very tender and of an appetising creamy-pink colour. In Italy tunny fish in oil is most commonly sold by the kilo, out of barrels or very large tins. For a salad one must always ask for *ventresca*. If the tunny is to be pounded into a sauce or made into *polpettone*, the cheaper quality will do.

The netting, canning, and export of tunny is one of the important industries of the island of Sardinia; there I have eaten fresh tunny of a tenderness and flavour quite unequalled elsewhere in the Mediterranean, but so far as I am aware we do not import Sardinian tinned tunny to this country. There is, however, a certain amount of Spanish, Portuguese, and French tinned tunny fish obtainable.

FUNGHI SECCHI
(DRIED MUSHROOMS)
These are usually boletus, the kind called *cèpes* in France and *porcini* in Italy.

Used in small quantities, they are a good addition to soups and sauces, but contrary to general supposition they do not need long cooking. They should be soaked in warm water for a few minutes, and can then be added to the dish. In 15-20 minutes they will be perfectly tender. If cooked too long, they lose all flavour. Be careful to buy the dried mushrooms which look cream coloured and brown and have been recently imported. When they are black and gnarled they have a disagreeably strong flavour.

PIGNOLI, PINOLI
(PINE NUTS OR PINE KERNELS)
The nuts which come from the cones of the stone pine. They are about ¼ in. long, cream coloured, slightly oil-flavoured little nuts, which in Italy are used in meat and game dishes, more specifically in those which are cooked with an *agrodolce* or sour-sweet sauce. They also appear sugared in small cakes, biscuits, and macaroons.

Nothing quite replaces *pinoli*, for they have a consistency and flavour entirely their own. (Incidentally they are good prepared in the same way as salted almonds, or fried in butter, to serve with drinks.)

In England *pinoli* can usually be bought from those shops which specialize in nuts and vitamin and vegetarian foods. They are best stored in a covered jar in the refrigerator.

PROSCIUTTO CRUDO,* PROSCIUTTO COTTO
(RAW HAM AND COOKED HAM)
Raw ham and cooked ham are used a great deal, usually in small quantities, in stuffings for *anolini*, *tortellini*, *agnolotti*, and all the ravioli tribe, also in sauces, in *risotto*, with vegetables, in soups, and in a number of pastry fritters, in *pizze*, and with cooked cheese; and also in conjunction with veal escalopes.

Raw ham other than imported Italian is not usually available in this country except in the

VINCENZO CAMPI (c. 1536-1591)
THE RICOTTA EATERS
Lyons, Musée des Beaux Arts

whole piece, which means that often one must make do with gammon, which has rather too powerful a flavour for delicate stuffings. The *spalla* or cured shoulder of pork which is sold in Soho under the name of *coppa* is very good, but expensive. *Mortadella* sausage is a useful standby for cooking and can sometimes take the place of ham.

---

*See also pages 144 and 50.

FORMAGGIO
(CHEESE)
The three cheeses essential to Italian cooking are: *grana*, known all over the world as Parmesan; *mozzarella*, that elastic white buffalo-milk cheese of the south; and *ricotta*,* a soft sheep's milk cheese, unsalted, which is at its best in the spring, in Rome and round about.

Parmesan we can get, although expensive (it is far from cheap in its native country) and often of rather dubious quality. *Mozzarella* is rarely imported, probably for the very good reason that it is only fit to eat if absolutely dripping fresh. No doubt the dozens of dishes in which it appears have been invented partly to utilize the quantity of insufficiently fresh *mozzarella* which cannot be eaten as a straight cheese. I have used *Bel Paese* as a substitute for *mozzarella* in a great many dishes, with perfect success. Sometimes it is in fact an improvement. *Mozzarella* at its best has great charm, but badly cooked it is disastrous.

Ricotta is another cheese which must be eaten very fresh. With a little salt and ground black pepper it has a lovely countrified flavour. It is pounded up and mixed with spinach to make the most delicious *gnocchi* and *ravioli*, and is turned into a number of good sweet dishes, as is its counterpart in Greece and as some fresh cream cheeses are in France.

Other cheeses used in Italian cooking are *fontina*, a very creamy kind of gruyère, *groviera* (gruyère) *provolone, pecorino*, a hard sheep's milk cheese for grating, and *caciotta*, a semi-hard Tuscan sheep's milk cheese.

---

*I.e., re-cooked; from the whey left from the draining of semi-hard cheeses such as caciotta. See also page 19.

TARTUFI BIANCHI
(*WHITE TRUFFLES*)

To me these white truffles are one of the most delicious of all foods anywhere. They are called white presumably to distinguish them from the black ones, for they are in reality a dirty brownish colour on the outside, beige inside. They grow in Tuscany, in Romagna, and in Piedmont, where the best and largest are found (in the country round Alba, not far from Turin); they are hunted out by specially trained dogs. In the height of the season, which lasts from October to March, white truffles as large as tennis balls are to be seen in the shops in Turin, which at the same season are wonderfully decorative with orange and brown and yellow *funghi*, every kind of feathered game, lovely cream cheeses, and rich looking sausages.

White truffles have an immensely powerful flavour and penetrating scent, quite unlike that of black truffles. They are almost always eaten raw, sliced very finely on a special instrument over a plain *risotto*, on top of the cheese *fonduta* of Piedmont, or on to very fine home-made *tagliolini*, or in a green salad. In Bologna white truffles are served with turkey or chicken breasts cooked in butter and cheese, and on top of thin veal escalopes. They can be cooked 2 or 3 minutes in butter and smothered with Parmesan cheese (their

TARTUF ALBA
TRUFFLES
20th-century postcard from the author's collection

affinity with cheese is remarkable), a wonderfully rich dish; and to the galantines of turkey and chicken, which are two of the specialities of the Pappagallo restaurant in Bologna, they give the most remarkable flavour.

In Piedmont white truffles are preserved for 2 or 3 weeks in a jar of rice. Zia Nerina, proprietress of the charming restaurant in Bologna now, alas, vanished which bore her name, preserved them buried in sawdust. In this way they kept for a month. Zia Nerina also tinned her truffles in such a way that they preserved nearly all their aroma in the most astonishing way.

At the Café Procacci in Florence the proprietor makes a purée of white truffles which, made into little sandwiches, goes down particularly well at eleven o'clock in the morning with a glass of good white Tuscan wine.

Rossini, who was almost as famous a gourmet as he was a composer, lived in Bologna, and it was no doubt a love for the local white truffles which originally caused his name to be tagged on to any dish containing truffles or *foie gras truffé* on pompous menus all over the world.

CECI
(*CHICK PEAS*)

These are the *garbanzos* so beloved of the Spaniards, the *pois chiches* of France. In shape and size not unlike nasturtium seeds, they are corn yellow in colour and very hard when dried, so that they need prolonged soaking in water before cooking, and lengthy simmering, with a pinch of bicarbonate of soda in the water in which they are cooked.

In Italy they are cooked and then mixed with *pasta* to form a heavy and filling *minestra*. They are often sold already soaked by the grocers in Italy. Boiled, and seasoned with plentiful oil, salt, and pepper, they make an excellent salad, and their nutty consistency makes them a good accompaniment to drinks instead of salted almonds; I have always found them very popular whenever I have cooked them for English people. (See also p. 89.)

In Sardinia, Piedmont, in Genoa and Liguria, there is a kind of thick pancake or galette called *faina* or *farinata*, made from chick-pea flour mixed to a batter with water and olive oil and baked in very shallow round earthenware or iron pans. *Faina* is market or street food, sold hot from portable ovens or from perambulating barrows as soon as winter sets in. There is an equivalent in the Niçois region called *socca*.

PANE GRATTUGIATO
(*BREADCRUMBS*)

One of the important elements of Italian cooking for stuffings and sauces, as well as for coating veal *escalopes* and other food to be fried. Crisp breadcrumbs, the kind generally used for the latter purpose, can be made at home by baking slices of stale bread in a slow oven; they are then pounded or grated. Or they can be bought by the pound at bakeries which make their own bread.

Crumb of bread (*mollica* or *midolla di pane*) is used a good deal in Italian cooking to give consistency to stuffings and sauces, sometimes to thicken soups. The crust is cut off a thick slice of white bread, which is then softened in milk, stock, or water and pressed dry.

POMIDORO E CONCENTRATO DI POMIDORO
(TOMATOES AND CONCENTRATED TOMATO SAUCE)

The large ripe soft tomatoes of the south cook much faster and produce better tomato sauce than any we can buy in England. (Our home-grown variety are at their best uncooked.*) Often the quantity of fresh tomatoes used in an Italian recipe has to be nearly doubled when English tomatoes are used. (This has been taken into account for the directions in this book.)

When fresh tomatoes are scarce or expensive, use the Italian tinned peeled tomatoes (Cirio brand is one of the best known), which are excellent and cheap. They are very extensively used in Italy in the winter in restaurants and in households which have no facility for preserving their own tomatoes.

Before the days of tinned food and preserves, concentrated tomato paste was made by drying the cooked tomato sauce in the sun. It was sold in 'loaves the colour of dark mahogany, of the consistency of stucco, cylindrical in form, well oiled and wrapped in oiled paper. In the winter it was also eaten by children, spread on bread.' (*Gastronomia Parmense*, Ferrutius, Parma, 1952.)

The commercial production of concentrated tomato paste on a large scale was started in the province of Parma over fifty years ago. There are varying grades of *concentrato*. To make *doppio* (double) *concentrato* the tomatoes are reduced to less than a seventh of their original volume; thus 250,000 tons of tomatoes are needed to produce 35,000 tons of *concentrato*: the same amount reduced to *triplo* (triple) *concentrato* produces 32,000 tons – figures which give some idea of the scale on which tomatoes are cultivated in the area. The province of Naples also produces large quantities of *concentrato* made from the little oval tomatoes known as *pomidori da sugo* (sauce tomatoes).

OLIVE OIL LABEL
from *Poggio Lamentano*

This concentrated purée is extremely cheap, which is, however, no reason for using it in unlimited quantities. It has an all-pervading flavour and must be used sparingly. A teaspoonful in a sauce, a tablespoonful in a stew or soup is usually sufficient to give flavour or consistency. A little *concentrato* mixed with fresh tomatoes for a sauce is a good combination. An opened tin of purée can be kept for some time, if the purée is covered with olive oil. To my mind the kind which comes from Parma is the best. Nowadays it is also sold in tubes, like tooth-paste.

*Commercially-grown varieties are now mostly all-purpose tomatoes; which is beginning to mean no-purpose.

PANNA
(CREAM)

Fresh cream, *panna fresca*, is rarely used in Italy for the cooking of meat, fish, or sauces as it is in France. Only in Bologna, where the cooking is very luxurious, do they occasionally add cream to the *ragù Bolognese*, and they have a way of heating up *tortellini* in cream, which is good but so rich that it is unwise to eat more than a minute quantity.

For sweet dishes whipped cream (*panna montata*) is piled in vast quantities upon elaborate cakes and confections of all kinds, usually sweetened to a very nearly uneatable degree. *Mascherpone*, or *mascarpone*, a kind of double cream cheese resembling the French *cœur à la crème*, of the consistency of soft butter, is whipped up with brandy or a liqueur and is extremely good.

LATTE
(MILK)

In central and northern Italy there is a highly commendable way of stewing meat or poultry in milk. These dishes are well worth a trial. The milk finally emerges as a creamy sauce. The stages of its transformation are fascinating to watch.

OLIO DI OLIVA
(OLIVE OIL)

On the Ligurian coast, in Genoa, in Tuscany, in Piedmont, in Naples and southern Italy, olive oil is the basis of cooking. In Roman cooking it is used about equally with *strutto* (lard or pork fat). Half oil and half butter is an excellent combination for slow frying; the oil prevents the butter from burning.

Throughout Italy olive oil is used for deep frying. The Italian genius for fried vegetables of every kind, for fritters, for the famous *fritto misto*, for fried cheese, for croquettes of rice, potatoes, brains, spinach, for fish, especially *scampi*, prawns, small red mullet, and squid, is well known. In some miraculous way the smell of frying seldom penetrates into the dining-room of a restaurant or a home. This method of cooking will, however, appeal less to English women who are their own cooks, for the smell penetrates clothes, hair, and kitchen; and, moreover, it is food which must be cooked at the last moment and eaten sizzling and crackling from the frying pan.

In any case, whatever kind of cooking one intends to do, a supply of good olive oil is essential, even if it is only for salads. Italy produces such an immense quantity of good oil that it is difficult to decide which is the best. It depends upon whether one prefers a light golden limpid oil, or a heavy greenish fruity one; but remember that the earthy flavour of a rich oil which may be good on salads will taste too strong when used for cooking or for making a mayonnaise, which has the curious quality of accentuating the flavour of whatever oil is used. On the other hand, some of the Italian oil sold in this country is refined out of all recognition and is quite tasteless. Some people prefer this, and it is perfectly good for frying. My own preference is for the oil of Liguria, or for the extra virgin cold-pressed oil of Tuscany. The miles of olive trees which make the country round Sassari in Sardinia so beautiful yield wonderful oil; some Italian connoisseurs rate it higher than that of Lucca.

The olive crop has its good and bad years, and the oil we buy in this country is usually a blend, so that a uniform standard may be maintained. It is well worth paying the little extra for good quality oil (anything marked simply 'Salad Oil' is best left alone).

Make generous use of olive oil for salads, and as a seasoning for spaghetti or Tuscan beans, and for frying; be circumspect with it when making the initial preparations for stews and soups.

In April 1911 that perspicacious English gourmet Colonel Newnham Davis wrote that 'an Italian gentlemen never eats salad when travelling in foreign countries, for his palate, used to the finest oil, revolts against the liquid fit only for the lubrication of machinery he so often is offered in Germany, England, and France' (*The Gourmet's Guide to Europe*, Grant Richards, London). The circumstances have not greatly changed.

TELEMACO SIGNORINI (1835-1901)
THE OLIVE HARVEST, 1863
Bari, Pinacoteca Civica

BRODO DI CARNE, BRODO DI POLLO
(MEAT AND CHICKEN STOCK)

A great many Italian soups, *minestre*, and *risotti* are based on good chicken or meat broth.

In a large household it is possible to have a pint or two of good broth always to hand, and the advent of the deep freeze has made it easy to store chicken and meat stocks. In 1953, when I was writing this book, meat was still rationed, and sometimes I had no alternative but to use the then recently introduced Swiss bouillon cubes. In those days they seemed quite acceptable. Now (1987) I don't find them so. They appear to taste predominantly of salt and monosodium glutamate.

LIEVITO
(YEAST)

Indispensable in Italian cooking for making *pizza* dough. In England yeast must be bought from a bakery which makes its own bread on the premises. Buy not more than 1 or 2 oz. at a time, according to needs, as it does not keep any length of time, although it can be stored in a refrigerator for 2 or 3 days, so long as it does not get wet.

Nowadays (1987) I use the fast-acting dried yeast called Harvest Gold, which is added direct to the flour, and needs no preliminary preparation with water or other liquid. I find that about half the quantities specified on the packet are quite enough.

WINE IN ITALIAN COOKING

The use of wine in Italian cooking dates from Roman days. In a certain number of Italian dishes it is indispensable, and there is a definite technique for its treatment. In a *stufato* or *stufatino*, which are stews or ragoûts, a small quantity of wine is poured over the meat, after it has been browned in oil or butter, and is then reduced by fast cooking to almost nothing. The meat is then barely covered with stock, and simmered slowly until it is tender, so that it is the concentrated aroma of the cooked wine which permeates the meat rather than a wine sauce which finally emerges. Some risottos, notably the Milanese and the Genoese versions, are cooked with the addition of wine; the principle employed is the same as for the meat stews.

For certain fried dishes, such as the little slices of veal called *scaloppine* or *piccate*, Marsala is always used. As soon as the meat is cooked it is moistened with a tablespoon or two of Marsala, which is allowed to cook only a minute. The wine amalgamates with the butter in which the meat has cooked and the juices which have come out of it, and makes a syrupy and extremely delicious little sauce. Marsala is employed considerably in Italian cooking, for meat and fish dishes as well as for sweets. It can be used in discreet quantities to temper the dryness of a red wine for a beef or veal stew. In a tomato sauce Marsala or one of the many other sweet Italian wines works wonders. In the making of *minestrone* (robust vegetable soups thickened with rice or pasta, of which there are innumerable versions) wine is not generally employed, although it would often be an improvement.

Fish soups are usually made with white wine, but for a most excellent stew of *calamari* (inkfish) with tomatoes and onions, red wine is used.

THE MARINADING OF MEAT

It is not, I believe, fully understood that the purpose of putting meat into a marinade is to break down the fibres and to impart the aromas of wine, spices, and herbs to a piece of meat which would otherwise be tough, dry, and lacking in flavour. The time required, therefore, for the marinading must depend upon the quality of the meat. Too long a bath in the wine mixture may spoil the meat, destroying what flavour it has

GUGLIELMO CIARDI (1842-1917)
THE GOLDEN HARVEST (detail)
Rome, Galleria d'Arte Moderna

EARLY COOKING SCENES
from *Theatrum Sanitatis* by Ububchasym de Baldach (14th century)
Rome, Biblioteca Casanatense

EARLY COOKING SCENES
from *Theatrum Sanitatis*
Rome, Biblioteca Casanatense

and making it sodden. Venison and boar (not that they lack flavour, but they can be very dry) can advantageously be left 2 or 3 days in the marinade. Six to twelve hours is sufficient for a hare, and in any case only old and dried-up animals should be so treated. Stewing beef, and the ewe mutton* which proves such a problem in England, can be much improved by a 6-8 hour bath in wine.

When the meat, whatever it is, which has been marinaded is to be roasted, it must be very carefully dried when taken out of the marinade, or the liquid dripping from it in the roasting-pan will prevent it from browning, so that it will be braised rather than roasted. If the meat is to be stewed this is not so important, but in any case the vegetables and herbs of the marinade will be sodden, and should be thrown away, fresh ones being put into the pan with the meat. For a stew, the wine of the marinade is strained and poured over the meat in the pan, stock or water being added later. When the marinaded meat is roasted, the

*Past history now. Should such meat chance to come one's way, it is useful to know how to deal with it.

marinade is usually reduced until it is thick, and with the addition of sugar or red-currant jelly, pine nuts, and a little stock, is served as a separate sauce.

Marinades can be cooked, in which case the vegetables are usually first lightly browned in a little olive oil, the wine added, cooked for about 15 minutes, and poured over the meat when it has cooled; or the wine can simply be poured over the meat, and the herbs and vegetables steeped in it. The system of first cooking the marinade has the advantage of bringing out the flavour of the various vegetables, spices, and herbs and of rendering the wine itself more aromatic and concentrated. The second method is more economical with the wine, as there is no loss from reduction.

IMPORTERS OF ITALIAN PRODUCTS
Many grocery, provision, and delicatessen merchants are disposed to be helpful to their customers in the matter of stocking imported products for which they are asked. When they seem less than receptive

to new ideas, it is only fair to consider that they have many difficulties. Small shopkeepers are understandably wary of ordering wholesale supplies of a perishable commodity like fresh cream cheese simply for the benefit of one or two customers. Others are cramped for space, and cannot stock a large variety of brands of a bulky product such as olive oil or imported packet *pasta*. Dried pulses and vegetables such as haricot beans, chick peas, and lentils do not remain in good condition for ever. Most Italian cured-pork products owe much of their finesse to the fact that they are lightly cured and must be fairly quickly consumed. Many of these are to be found only in certain Soho shops, because they are imported direct from Italy by the shopkeepers who retail them, rather than bought through a London wholesaler or agent.

Where less fragile products are concerned it can be of some help to the customer to know the name of importing and wholesaling firms and distributing agents, who can be contacted for information as to local stockists of their goods. If they are lively and enterprising, these wholesale firms will also make a note that there is a possible demand for their products in a district or small town where their representatives have not hitherto been calling. Our traders are by no means as stick-in-the-mud as would sometimes appear; but those dealing in quality products imported for and sold to a minority market, without benefit of national newspaper or television advertising, have to contend with formidable competition; and they cannot offer their retailers the inducements in the way of quick profits, free display material, lightning turnover, and daily deliveries which are the merchandising assets of the mass-market firms.

Under the circumstances it is astonishing that the country's provision and delicatessen shops offer as much choice and variety as they now do. We still need more, much more; and better quality.

NOTE ON IMPORTS OF ITALIAN PORK PRODUCTS

From 1966 to 1970, the import into this country of Italian cured but uncooked pork products such as Parma ham, salame sausages and *coppa*, was banned owing to repeated outbreaks of African swine fever in Italy.

In April 1970 the ban was at last lifted, and, at the time of going to press with this edition, genuine Parma ham and Italian salame are once more to be found in English shops and restaurants.

Because, however, the import of any kind of ham on the bone is still banned, all the prosciutto of Parma and other districts destined for export to England is boned, most of it prior to the curing process. Boned hams are very much easier and more economical to slice, and are very commonly sold in Italy. Unfortunately these products very often lack the subtlety and the savour of ham cured on the bone. The imitations and substitutes which crept in during the years when Italian pork products were unobtainable are also still currently on the English market. Many people, including some who should know better, are unable to distinguish between a Parma ham and any other raw ham of whatever provenance. In a newly established and very expensive little French provision shop in Knightsbridge I was told, quite recently, that 'Bayonne ham and Parma ham are the same'. Since, for a start, Bayonne ham (a French product of ancient origin) is smoked and Parma ham is not, and since the curing methods are very different, the main resemblance between the two products is that they both come from the pig.

It is as well also to note here that no uncooked ham, bacon, sausage or other pork product is allowed into this country without an import licence.

EARLY COOKING SCENES
from *Theatrum Sanitatis*
Rome, Biblioteca Casanatense

JOACHIM BEUCKELAER (*c.* 1530/5-1573/4)
KITCHEN INTERIOR
Paris, Musée du Louvre

KITCHEN EQUIPMENT

PART FROM THE NORMAL EQUIPMENT OF A GOOD kitchen, Italian cooking demands few special pans or out of the ordinary devices.

Sharp, pliable cook's knives are needed for any good cooking. Without them it is impossible to achieve any kind of swift, efficient, or satisfactory work in the kitchen. Not enough people seem to grasp this rudimentary fact. There are now various stainless steel kitchen and carving knives on the market; these are better than they used to be, but they are still not so good as the thin rapier-pointed carbon steel knives which age so wonderfully, wearing thinner and more springy until they are almost worn through. . . . One of the endearing features of Italian restaurant life is the little sharp knife always provided when steak is ordered. This is not to be taken as a sign that the steak will be tough, but if it *is* tough at least it cannot be blamed on the knife.

Anyone who wishes to cook pasta or boil rice successfully must be provided with at least one very large pan of about eight quarts capacity when full, which will also be of the greatest service for many other purposes. Nothing is more maddening than trying to cram a large bird or piece of meat into too skimpy a pan.

Electric blenders and modern food processors apart, the most useful single labour-saving device is, to me, the *mouli légumes*, a metal food mill or purée maker. For soups, purées, mashed potatoes, and so on, it is invaluable, saving literally hours of boring work. Get the medium or large size; this is important, as the smallest size is only adequate for very small quantities. The price of the medium-sized *mouli* is still very reasonable for the service it gives.

A good cheese-grater is a necessity in any household where pasta or rice is eaten. A traditional Italian one is in the shape of a round box, with the grater forming the lid, so that the cheese falls inside as it is grated. Swedish stainless steel graters, in a conical shape and with several different grating surfaces, make an adequate alternative. For Parmesan, the essential is a very sharp grating surface.

For making pasta at home a large pastry board and a long rolling pin are absolutely essential. The board should be at least 16 × 22 in. When wooden boards have been scrubbed, do not put them near the fire or on top of the boiler; a warped board is useless, and so is one with a join down the middle, which will eventually wear apart and harbour particles of meat and vegetables, like a decayed tooth.

Rather large round or square cake tins, both deep and shallow, are used in Italian cooking for baked dishes of meat, vegetables, and rice as well as for pies and cakes.

A crescent-shaped two-handled chopper called a *mezzaluna* or *lunetta* (surely some English manufacturer could produce these?)* is found in every Italian kitchen. Square and round cutters with scalloped edges for ravioli, frying pans both for deep and shallow frying, skewers for grilling meat, a perforated spoon for lifting *gnocchi* and ravioli out of the pan, palette knives, large dishes which can be put in the oven to keep the pasta hot, two-handled metal or china egg dishes (*tegamini*), a heavy cutlet bat (the sound of the ceaseless bashing of the veal cutlets is

---

*Either English-made or imported stainless steel choppers are now to be found in almost all self-respecting kitchen supply stores in this country.

familiar to anyone who has frequented Italian taverns and restaurants), a nutmeg grater, a small thick pan for sauces, a pestle and mortar, a pepper grinder, a mincer, are all utensils frequently in use in an Italian kitchen. A pair of scissors for cutting parsley and other fresh herbs is a great asset and saves endless time.

It is interesting to note that in the plates of Bartolomeo Scappi's famous cookery book *Dell'Arte del Cuoco*, first published in 1570, a great many of the knives, choppers, spoons, vegetable cutters, saucepans, and casseroles which were presumably those of the Vatican kitchen of the period* are identical in form with those we associate with a well-stocked French kitchen of today. The basic equipment shown for making pasta is also very little changed, except that nowadays there are machines for turning out spaghetti and macaroni and other more complicated shapes, made in sizes suitable for a moderate household as well as for restaurants and large establishments.

Where the cooking stove is concerned it should be remembered that an enormous number of Italian households, particularly in country districts, still use a charcoal stove and grill, and a *forno di campagna*, a country oven, which is placed on the top of the charcoal, or over the burner if they have Calor gas (*pibigas* or *liquigas* in Italy). Italian cooks achieve very good results with these rather capricious ovens. As for the charcoal or wood fire, nothing can equal it for the savour of grilled meat or fish, but since these methods are scarcely practical for English town-dwellers I merely suggest that anyone who is fond of grilled food should furnish their kitchen with an extra electric or gas grill to supplement that provided on the normal cooker, which is never large enough. Personally, I would always choose a cooker, whether gas or electric, designed with a capacious eye-level grill, and if I had to cook on a solid-fuel stove like an Aga or a Rayburn I would supplement it with a separate electric grill. (A solid-fuel stove does after all presuppose a kitchen of a certain size, so the extra space for a supplementary grill should not present a problem.)

QUANTITIES, TIMING, ETC.

As far as quantities, times of cooking and oven temperatures are concerned I find it misleading to give exact details. So much depends upon appetite, mood and habit, that what may, for example, be an ample dish of rice for four people in one household may only feed two in another. Much depends also upon what other dishes are to be served. Approximate quantities of the recipes in this book, unless otherwise stated, are for four to six people. Times of cooking vary according to the quality of meat, *pasta* or vegetables, on the kind of cooking stove used, and upon the pans.

Gas and electric cooking stoves are so diverse that I have found it only makes for confusion to give Regulo oven or Fahrenheit temperatures. Very slow, medium, moderate, fairly hot, hot, very hot, should be sufficient indication to anyone who has even a little experience. As a guide, I append the tables which follow. But do remember, when roasting or grilling, to heat the oven or the grill beforehand so that as

*Scappi was private cook to Pope Pius V, who was elected in 1566 and died in 1572.

GIOVANNI BATTISTA CRESPI (c. 1575-1632)
THE COOK
Florence, Meridiana Collection Contini Bonacossi

soon as the food is put on to cook the juices will be sealed, and concentrated *inside* the meat or fish, instead of seeping out into the pan, which is what happens when food is cooked very slowly. The same principle applies to deep frying. If the oil or dripping is not hot enough it soaks into the food, making it sodden; whereas when it is really hot it instantly causes the formation of a crisp coating on the outside, preserving the inside from contact with the oil.

TABLE OF EQUIVALENT OVEN TEMPERATURES

	Solid Fuel	Electricity	Gas
Slow		240-310°F.	¼-2
Moderate		320-370°F.	3-4
Fairly hot		380-400°F.	5
Hot		410-440°F.	6-7
Very hot		450-480°F.	8-9

EQUIVALENT FAHRENHEIT AND CENTIGRADE TEMPERATURES

Degrees Fahrenheit	Degrees Centigrade
240-310	115-155
320-370	160-190
380-400	195-205
410-440	210-230
450-480	235-250

MEASURING AND WEIGHING

How much cheese is a handful? How much more or less is a cupful? What is the capacity of a glass, a tumbler, a soup ladle? How much is a pinch? How much greater is a good pinch?

In the Introduction to this editon I have referred to the rather rough-and-ready methods by which Italian cooks tend to measure their ingredients. To a certain extent all household cooks everywhere use such methods. (In the Middle East, I remember, an English round fifty cigarette tin was a common kitchen measuring unit; simply as 'a tin' of this or that ingredient I have come across this unit in published recipes, to me obviously authentic, but baffling to anyone not familiar with kitchen procedure in the countries concerned.*)

In Italy there is an explanation over and above the question of a tradition which grew up in the days when so many cooks could neither read nor write and measured by instinct and memory. It is to be found in the method by which household shopping is (or was) conducted – which I have also described in the chapter on Italian Dishes in Foreign Kitchens, pages 19-21 – which means that over and over again, perhaps even twice a day for years, the cook has bought the same weight of cheese, so many bunches of spinach, so many grammes of tunny fish or anchovies from the huge open tin on the grocer's counter. She has just the amount she wants, and so has no need for scales to weigh these commodities at home. When it comes to store-cupboard ingredients such as flour or rice, she uses her hands, a glass, a cup. And there's the rub. Her cup and her glass are not necessarily the same capacity as yours or mine. Such things as standard measuring cups, spoons, and glasses may exist in Italy. If so, I certainly never saw any; and so far as I know not even the Americans, with their passion for measuring every-thing down to a sixteenth of a teaspoon of pepper and the ultimate three drops of lemon juice, have laid down a standard handful of rice, grated cheese, or parsley.

While I was writing this book and still much under the influence of

GIUSEPPE RECCO (1634-95)
THE KITCHEN (detail)
Vienna, Akademie der Bildenen Kunste

Italian cooking as practised in Italy, some of these vague terms did, I am afraid, creep into my recipes. Nowadays I would probably write them quite differently. They would be more precise, they would fill a volume twice the size of this one; in the transition, I think, they would also lose something of their authenticity and spontaneity. So I have left them substantially as I first wrote them, appending here and there a footnote when it seemed necessary for the sake of clarity. Below, also, are tables

*The capacity of these tins was in fact 8 oz., just that of an American cup.

ANON (18th century)
THE BAKERY (detail)
Rome, Museo da Roma

instructions with mention of varying grades of olive oil, thick or thin, refined or unrefined, and take into consideration the differences between solid fuel, gas burners, and electric hot plates.

If recipes were all written on these lines there would be no end to them. Nobody would use cookery books. They would be too dull, too forbidding, and too bulky to handle. To specify therefore, 'enough oil to cover the bottom of your saucepan' or 'about a teacup of olive oil' is a short cut. It is also an indication that a precise quantity is not of great moment. Except for sauces, one does not often measure oil by tablespoons. One pours it out of a bottle into the pan. One uses one's eyes and one's loaf. The same may be said when one is adding a glass of wine, a handful of parsley. A little more, a little less – it is up to you. Of course there are the exceptions which prove the rule. Ingredients for sauces, pastries, and ice-cream recipes, for example, should be carefully weighed and measured. I would never advocate that a kitchen should be without scales. (I find the kind with weights more satisfactory than the spring-balance type.) And one of the most frequently used utensils in my own kitchen is a measuring jug marked with both English ounces and pints and metric grammes. For those who use French, Italian, and other European-language cookery books as well as English ones, or who employ continental cooks, such a measuring utensil is invaluable, and when we convert to the metric system will become essential. Such jugs can now be found in any well-stocked hardware or kitchen shop.

of comparative measurements which I hope will provide further guidance to readers who feel in need of it.

While I think that the degree of precision required is largely a question of the individual temperament of each cook (some are positively irritated by the appearance of a lengthy list of ounces and tablespoons, half-teaspoons, grains, and quarter-cups on a page), I would also remind readers that reliance on precise recipes alone can be a trap. 'The dangerous person in the kitchen,' wrote Marcel Boulestin, 'is the one who goes rigidly by weights, measurements, thermometers, and scales.'

That was well put. It is like this. Suppose that I tell you to put two tablespoons of olive oil into a pan before starting off say a vegetable stew or a pot-roast. Then what pan are you using? How wide is it? How thick is it? With what kind of fuel are you cooking? What, in fact, you need is enough oil to cover the bottom surface of your pan; enough for your onions and other vegetables to be evenly spread out in it, neither swimming in oil because there is too much nor rapidly drying out, catching, and burning because there is not enough. So if I am going to tell you precisely how much oil you must use, then I must also tell you precisely the dimensions and weight of the pan you require, qualify the

MEASUREMENT TABLES
Measurements as used in this book

(1) SOLID INGREDIENTS

1 level tablespoon of flour	= ½ oz.
rice	= ½ oz.
sugar	= 1 oz.
grated Parmesan	= ¼ oz.
1 teacup of rice (Italian)	= 6 oz.
grated Parmesan	= 2½ oz.

(2) LIQUID INGREDIENTS

1 tablespoon	= ½ fl. oz.
1 coffee cup (after-dinner size)	= 2½ fl. oz.
1 soup ladle	= 4 fl. oz.
1 teacup	= 6–7 fl. oz.
1 liqueur glass	= approx. ½ fl. oz.
1 sherry glass	= approx. 2½ fl. oz.

EQUIVALENT METRIC AND ENGLISH MEASUREMENTS
As used in cooking

(1) SOLID MEASUREMENTS

Metric	English
1 kilogramme	= approx. 2 lb. 2 oz.
500 grammes	= approx. 1 lb. 1 oz.
250 grammes	= approx. 8½ oz.
125 grammes	= approx. 4¼ oz.
100 grammes (1 *etto*)	= approx. 3⅓ oz.

(2) LIQUID MEASUREMENTS

1 litre	= approx. 35 fl. oz.	= approx. 1¾ British pints (the American pint is 16 oz. to the British 20 oz.)
½ litre	= approx. 17½ fl. oz.	= approx. ¾ pint plus 5 tablespoons
¼ litre	= approx. 8¾ fl. oz.	= approx. ½ pint less 2½ tablespoons
1 decilitre (100 grammes)	= approx. 3 fl. oz.	= 6 tablespoons
1 centiletre (10 grammes)	= approx. ⅓ fl. oz.	= 1 dessertspoon

EQUIVALENT ENGLISH AND AMERICAN MEASUREMENTS

(1) SOLID MEASUREMENTS

English	American
1 lb. butter or fat	= approx. 2 cups solidly packed
½ lb. butter or fat	= approx. 1 cup solidly packed
¼ lb. butter or fat	= approx. ½ cup solidly packed
2 oz. butter or fat	= approx. ¼ cup = 4 tablespoons
1 oz. butter or fat	= approx. 2 tablespoons
1 lb. caster sugar	= approx. 2⅓ cups powdered sugar
½ lb. caster sugar	= approx. 1 cup plus 3 tablespoons
¼ lb. caster sugar	= approx. 8 tablespoons
2 oz. caster sugar	= approx. 4 tablespoons
1 lb. plain flour sieved	= approx. 4½ cups sieved cake flour
¼ lb. plain flour sieved	= approx. 1 cup plus 4 tablespoons
2 oz. plain flour sieved	= approx. 8 tablespoons
1 oz. plain flour sieved	= approx. 4 tablespoons
¼ oz. plain flour sieved	= approx. 1 tablespoon
¼ lb. dry grated cheese	= approx. 1 cup
½ lb. rice, raw	= approx. 1 cup

GIOVANNI DOMENICO FERRETTI (1692-1766)
HARLEQUIN AS COOK (detail)
Florence, Collection Cassa di Risparmio

(2) LIQUID MEASUREMENTS

English	American
1 gallon = 4 quarts = 8 pints	= 10 pints = 1¼ gallons
1 quart = 2 pints = 40 oz.	= 2½ pints = 5 cups
1 pint = 20 oz.	= 1¼ pints = 2½ cups
½ pint = 10 oz.	= 1¼ cups
¼ pint = 5 oz. = 1 gill	= ½ cup plus 2 tablespoons
2 oz. = 4 tablespoons	= ¼ cup
1 tablespoon = ½ oz.	= ½ oz.
1 teaspoon = ¼ tablespoon	= 1 teaspoon = ⅓ tablespoon

CHRISTIAN BERENTS (1658-1722)
THE ELEGANT SNACK
Rome, Galleria Nazionale

Hors d'Oeuvre and Salads

MONG ITALIAN *ANTIPASTI* (HORS D'ŒUVRE) ARE TO be found some of the most successful culinary achievements in European cooking. Most midday meals in Italy start with some small dish of *antipasti*, particularly if the meal is to be without *pasta*. The most common *antipasti* are some kind of *salame* sausage, olives, anchovies, ham, small artichokes in oil, funghi in vinegar (rather tasteless and unsatisfactory, these last), pimentos in oil, raw fennel, raw broad beans.

Of varieties of *salame* sausage there is seemingly no end. Some are garlicky, some not; some are eaten very fresh; others are considered best when they have matured.

Apart from sausages, there are a number of interesting pork products which are eaten as *antipasti*. *Lonza*, which is fillet of pork cured in much the same way as ham and served raw in very thin slices, can, if not oversalted, be quite delicious, with its background scent of spices, wine, and garlic. *Coppa* is another name for the same sort of product, but this word can be misleading, for in Rome it signifies pig's head brawn, in the Veneto a remarkable kind of loaf comprising whole slices of cooked ham, tongue, and *mortadella* sausage. This *mortadella*, most famous although to my mind least alluring of all Italian sausages, is found at its best in Bologna, its own home. As an ingredient of various stuffings and little pastries it is useful, but as an hors d'œuvre frankly dull.

Prosciutto di Parma and *prosciutto di San Daniele* are at their best perhaps the most delicious hams in the world and the most perfect hors

d'œuvre.* Whose was the brilliant idea of combining fine slices of these hams with fresh figs? Or melons? (Although melons are very much a second best.)

Antipasti of fish, all kinds of small fry served in oil and vinegar sauces, as well as anchovies and the inevitable tunny fish, are at their best in Italy. Prawns, *scampi*, shrimps, *seppie, calamaretti, totani, moscardini* (the last four are of the squid family), mussels, clams, sea dates, sea truffles, oysters, crabs, cold sturgeon in oil, all appear on the hors d'œuvre tray.

Vegetables are presented in a number of ways, and there are plenty of ideas from which we could borrow. It is the unexpected which makes the charm of many of these little dishes: papery slices of raw artichokes; anchovies garnishing a salad of raw mushrooms; slices of gruyère cheese with crisp fennel or rounds of uncooked pimento; salty sheep's milk cheese with raw broad beans; tunny fish with cooked french beans; an unorthodox mixture of cooked mushrooms and prawns in a tomato-flavoured mayonnaise; cooked artichoke hearts mixed into a salad of green peas, broad beans, and potatoes; tunny fish encased in rolled-up red peppers. To the enterprising there is no limit to the number of dishes with which, without overdoing the mixtures, a promising start to a meal may be contrived.

Another welcome and unusual feature of Italian cooking is the hot *antipasto*. Usually this consists of *crostini*, rounds of fried or baked bread underneath a slice of melting cheese, garnished, in some form or another, with anchovies. Occasionally the *crostini* are served with a

---

*The methods of curing some of these pork products are described on p. 144.

chicken-liver sauce instead of cheese, or with cooked shellfish; then there are miniature *pizze*, one for each person, or *frittelle* (fritters) containing ham and cheese, in fact the sort of things which in England were once served as savouries. These little dishes are comforting in the cold weather, are good at lunch or supper, and facilitate life for the cook. But they should, I think, remain simple and small. Enlarged to the size of hefty Welsh rabbits or club sandwiches, they lose their point and their charm. Recipes for the *crostini* and the *frittelle* will be found in the chapter dealing with cheese cookery.

The importance of good olive oil in the making of *antipasti*, so many of which take the form of salad, cannot be overstressed. The excellence of the oil can turn the most primitive of dishes, such as a plateful of haricot beans flavoured only with oil, into a meal which any person with a taste for natural food will appreciate. People unaccustomed to the natural taste of olive oil may perhaps prefer the refined and almost tasteless variety. The flavour which it lacks must then be replaced with extra seasoning of some kind – not vinegar (though many Italian cooks are too free with the vinegar, and it is a sound policy in Italian restaurants to ask for the oil and vinegar to be brought to the table and to watch the mixing of the dressing). Lemon juice is usually preferable to vinegar, although of course if you do have good wine vinegar by all means use it, but very sparingly.

Salads are included with the *antipasti* recipes. Apart from the ordinary green salads, many of these dishes can be served either as an hors d'œuvre, as a salad, or even as a main dish. It is a question of adjusting the quantities.

ANTIPASTO ALLA GENOVESE
(GENOESE HORS D'ŒUVRE)
One of the best and simplest hors d'œuvre is the one beloved by the Genoese. A big dish of young broad beans, still in their pods so that you may peel them yourself and so eat them as fresh as possible, is served with a plate of the local rather strong *salame*, and a large hunk of *Sardo*, a white pungent sheep's milk cheese made in Sardinia. When fresh, *Sardo* has a sharp salty tang, and together with the beans, the *salame*, some crusty fresh bread, and a glass or two of the good white Coronata wine of the district, provides a perfect beginning to a country meal. We have no cheese comparable to *Sardo* in England, but there is no reason why the same sort of combination should not be tried with a fresh, slightly salted cream cheese, any good *salame*, and, when the fleeting season of broad beans is over, celery, or raw fennel, or a dish of those little wrinkled-up sharp black olives which bring with them such a strong flavour of the south.

INSALATA DI FRUTTI DI MARE
(SHELLFISH SALAD)
This consists of mussels, prawns, and *fragoline di mare*, a very small, incredibly tender variety of inkfish. The cooked and shelled mussels and prawns are mixed with twice their quantity of a minuscule white boneless fish called *gianchetti*, which, plainly boiled, forms a basis on which to make the rest of the salad. Flaked

crab does very well instead. Season the mussels, prawns, and crab with oil and lemon, salt, pepper, and parsley; garnish the dish with squares of either lobster or scallops (cooked 5 minutes in a *court-bouillon*), which effectively replace the *fragoline di mare*.

PAOLO PORPORA (1617-73)
MUSHROOMS, BUTTERFLIES AND QUAILS (detail)
Strasbourg, Musée des Beaux Arts

INSALATA DI FUNGHI E FRUTTI DI MARE
(SALAD OF RAW MUSHROOMS* AND SHELLFISH)
Prepare ½ lb. of raw mushrooms as described for the salad on p. 45. Have them ready an hour or two before they are to be served, and season them with plenty of good olive oil, a little lemon, garlic, salt, and pepper.

The shellfish used in Italy are either *scampi* or *gamberoni*, the large prawns of the Genoese coast, and the tiny tender squid called sea-strawberries (*fragoline di mare*). In England use scallops and prawns. Clean 4 medium sized scallops and stew them for about 5 minutes in a little salted water, with a piece of lemon peel and a slice of onion. Add the red part of the scallops for the last 2 minutes only. Drain them, mix them with about 2 oz. of cooked prawns, and while they are still warm season them with oil and lemon. A few minutes before serving mix the mushrooms and the shellfish together and garnish them with a little cut parsley.

Enough for two or three.

---

*When I first wrote about these raw mushroom salads they appeared to strike readers as a startling novelty. Such dishes are now firmly entrenched in English kitchens. They provide an excellent way of using cultivated mushrooms.

INSALATA DI FUNGHI E SCAMPI
(SALAD OF MUSHROOMS AND SCAMPI)
A variation of the preceding recipe, the mushrooms being cooked and mixed with *scampi*, and the sauce being a tomato-flavoured mayonnaise instead of oil and lemon.

A good dish, but rather rich.

INSALATA DI RISO E SCAMPI
(SALAD OF RICE AND SCAMPI)

Cold rice makes an excellent first course. There should not be too much rice in proportion to other ingredients, it must on no account be overcooked, and it is best to season it while still hot.

Boil 1 cupful of rice in salted water. Drain it, season it with pepper, salt, nutmeg, plenty of olive oil, and a little vinegar or lemon juice. Stir in a few shreds of raw onion. When it is cold add a dozen cooked *scampi* or Dublin Bay prawns,* a cupful of green peas cooked with shredded ham (as for *piselli alla romana*), and a handful of chopped parsley.

A rice salad can be made with any number of different ingredients: raw or cooked mushrooms, cold chicken, any shellfish, pine kernels, almonds, cooked or raw pimentos, celery, fennel, ham, olives. There should always be one crisp element to counteract the softness of the rice.

---

*When I wrote this book it was quite common to find fresh Dublin Bay prawns. Now they are rare. Use frozen ones if you must.

INSALATA DI FUNGHI
(SALAD OF RAW MUSHROOMS)

Wash and drain ½ lb. of firm white mushrooms. Slice them fairly thinly and put them in a bowl with olive oil, pepper, a little lemon juice, and, if you like a scrap of garlic. Add salt only just before serving. Mushrooms are scarcely ever eaten raw in this country, yet they are excellent; and cultivated mushrooms, often lacking in flavour when cooked, are at their best presented in this way. The Genoese like their *insalata di funghi* garnished with a few anchovy fillets – an unexpected and successful addition.

CROSTINI DI MARE
(SHELLFISH ON FRIED BREAD)

Cut the crust off slices of a French loaf, fry them in oil or butter, and serve them spread with a few mussels, cooked as for *cozze al vino bianco* (p. 111) or *vongole alla marinara* (p. 112) and shelled.

GIOVAN BATTISTA RUOPPOLO (1629-93)
STILL LIFE WITH CRAB AND FISH (detail)
Naples, private collection

GRANCEVOLE
(CRAB)

Grancevole, or *granceole*, are the spider-crabs of the Adriatic – large, bright scarlet, spiky beasts with a most spectacular appearance but a rather less sensational flavour.

They are boiled, cleaned, the insides scooped out, and the edible portions put back into the shell, dressed with oil and lemon or with mayonnaise.

In Venetian restaurants the *grancevole* are served resting in a special metal stand, and form a splendid part of the gorgeous colours of Venetian food.

INSALATA DI PEPERONI GIALLI
(SALAD OF YELLOW PEPPERS)

Cut 3 or 4 large raw yellow peppers into strips and mix them with a bunch of radishes cut into thin rounds, a very little celery cut into small pieces, and 2 or 3 sliced tomatoes, liberally seasoned with oil.

PEPERONI SOTT'OLIO
(PIMENTOS IN OIL)
Preserved pimentos* (the method is described on p. 198) are very good. They are served as an hors d'œuvre, cut into strips and dressed with a little fresh oil and chopped garlic.

---

*Beware commercially bottled pimentos in vinegar strong enough to blow off your head.

INSALATA DI CARCIOFI
(SALAD OF RAW ARTICHOKES)
As a component of an hors d'œuvre for four people you need 2 medium sized artichokes; if the dish is to be served as a salad, have twice as many. The other essential elements are a sharp knife, a lemon, and olive oil. Draw your knife through the lemon and at the same time squeeze lemon juice all over the artichoke in order that it may not turn black. Cut off the stalk close to the head, remove all the tough outer leaves, then cut off the top half of the artichoke, which is discarded. Now cut the half which is left in half again, lengthways, exposing the choke, or 'hay' as the French call it. This is now easily removed with the knife. Squeeze more lemon over the artichoke, and cut each half, downwards, into the thinnest possible slices, so that they emerge fan-like and delicate. When all the artichokes are sliced, season them with oil, salt and possibly a little more lemon. Treated in this way, artichokes have an unexpected, slightly nutty flavour. The combination of this salad of raw artichokes with a few fine slices of wind-dried beef or raw ham is a very good one.

CARCIOFI ALLA MAIONESE
(ARTICHOKE HEARTS WITH MAYONNAISE)
Prepare the artichoke hearts as directed on p. 164. Cook them for 25 minutes in boiling salted water. When they are cold put a spoonful of mayonnaise into each.

FAGIOLI TOSCANI COL TONNO
(TUSCAN BEANS WITH TUNNY FISH)
The white beans, fat and tender, so beloved of all Tuscans, are not usually obtainable in this

PIETRO LONGHI (1702-85)
LUNCH ON THE ESTUARY (detail)
Venice, Ca' Rezzonico

country, but good quality white haricot beans *can* be found.

Beans and tunny fish are one of the best known of Florentine dishes, and should be served in large helpings as a robust *antipasto* (no dainty little dishes with a spoonful of beans and a crumb or two of tunny).

Boil the beans (soaked overnight if they are dried), with plenty of water to cover them. They will take roughly 3 hours to cook.* Add salt at the end. Strain them, add a few strips of raw onion, plentiful oil, and when they are cold put on the top a generous amount (i.e. the contents of a 6 to 8 oz. tin) of the best-quality tinned tunny fish in oil, in large squares.

The Tuscans are, or were, much addicted to these beans, and even had a special flask-shaped earthenware pot, called a *fagiolara*, in which they were cooked over the open fire. The *fagiolara* was a beautiful and sturdy pot, but it is now (1987) many years since I have seen one for sale.

---

*If they are the new season's beans, which come into the shops here around early November, 1½ hours is often enough; 6 to 8 oz. should be sufficient for 4 people for an hors d'œuvre. Ask for cannellini or borlotti beans. The latter are fat, round, pinkish-brown in colour.

FAGIOLINI COL TONNO
(FRENCH BEANS WITH TUNNY FISH)
For 4 people boil 1 lb. french beans, and while they are still hot pour olive oil over them, a little lemon juice, salt, and pepper. Serve with squares of tunny fish in oil on the top.

TARTINE AL TONNO
(BREAD SPREAD WITH TUNNY FISH)

Cut squares of bread from a small sandwich loaf and remove the crusts. Mash the contents of a small tin of tunny in oil with 1 oz. of butter and a few capers. Spread the mixture on the prepared bread and decorate with slices of hard boiled eggs.

UOVA TONNATE
(EGGS WITH TUNNY FISH SAUCE)

Hard-boiled eggs cut in half lengthways and covered with a tunny fish mayonnaise (p. 195).

UOVA SODE AGLI SPINACI
(HARD-BOILED EGGS STUFFED WITH SPINACH)

½ lb. of spinach, 1 oz. of Parmesan cheese, 3 oz. of white cream cheese, 12 eggs.

Cook the spinach, drain it absolutely dry, and chop it. Mash it to a purée with the cream cheese, the Parmesan, the yolks of 6 of the hard-boiled eggs, salt, black pepper, and nutmeg.

The eggs should be cut lengthways. Stuff them with the mixture piled up conically, but do not spread it all over the surface of the eggs, as half the point of the dish is the fresh-looking green-and-white appearance of the eggs.

POMIDORO COL TONNO
(TOMATOES STUFFED WITH TUNNY FISH)

Raw tomatoes cut in half, the insides scooped out, and stuffed with a tunny-fish mayonnaise, made as explained on p. 195.

INSALATA DI PATATE COL TONNO
(POTATO AND TUNNY FISH SALAD)

4 medium sized potatoes, an onion, a small tin of tunny fish in oil, capers, salt, pepper, oil and vinegar, parsley.

Boil the potatoes in their skins, peel and slice them while still warm, season them with salt and pepper; slice the onion (which should be a large one) very thinly and mix it with the potatoes. Pour over them a liberal amount of good olive oil and a very little wine vinegar.

About an hour before serving, mix in the tunny fish, divided into squares, and garnish the dish with capers.

POLPETTONE DI TONNO
(POLPETTONE OF TUNNY FISH)

2 small tins of tunny fish of 150 grammes (approx. 5 oz.) each, 2 eggs, a tablespoonful of capers, pepper.

Put the contents of the tins of tunny fish through the food mill with the oil from the tin, or mash the fish if it is easier. Beat in the 2 eggs, season with pepper (and salt if necessary, but it probably won't be), and stir in the capers so that they are evenly distributed. On a floured board form the mixture into a fat sausage. Flour a cloth or a piece of butter muslin (doubled), roll the sausage up in it, and tie it with string, as *salame* sausages are tied, but not too tightly. Lower the parcel into a pan of boiling water. The pan must be large enough to accommodate the sausage lengthwise, or the size of the sausage must be adjusted to the size of the pan. Simmer gently for an hour or a little more. Unwrap the *polpettone* only when it is cold. Serve on a long dish, cut into thin slices. A potato salad makes quite a good accompaniment.

INSALATA DI TONNO E CIPOLLE
(TUNNY FISH AND ONION SALAD)

Tunny fish, raw onion rings, and red radishes dressed either with a thin mayonnaise or with oil and lemon.

RUTILIO MANETTI (1571-1639)
BEATO DOMENICO DEL POZZO (detail)
Florence, Certosa del Galluzza

PEPERONI COL TONNO
(*PIMENTOS WITH TUNNY FISH*)

6 large pimentos, red and yellow mixed, if possible; a small tin of tunny fish, oil, parsley.

Put the peppers under the grill, as explained for the preserved pimentos on p. 198. Peel off the burnt skin, and put them to marinate for 15 minutes in olive oil and a very little lemon juice. Divide each pimento into wide length-wise strips, 3 to each pepper if they are large. Place a spoonful of tunny on each strip and roll it up, so that it looks like a small sausage.

GIOVANNI ANTONIO BAZZI, 'IL SODOMA' (1477-1549)
THE STORY OF ST. BENEDICT (detail)
Siena, Abbazia di Monte Oliveto

Arrange them on a flat serving dish, pour over the oil in which they have soaked, and garnish them with parsley.

Not a well-known dish, but a delicious one, with a beautiful appearance. It can be managed also with tinned roasted peppers.

PEPERONI CON ALICI E CAPPERI
(*PIMENTOS WITH ANCHOVIES AND CAPERS*)

Made in the same way as the foregoing, but instead of tunny fish put a chopped anchovy fillet and a few capers into each slice of pimento, and garnish them when they are arranged in the dish with a few extra pieces of chopped anchovy and a caper or two.

PEPERONI ALLA PIEMONTESE
(*PIEDMONTESE PIMENTOS*)

Cut some red, yellow or green pimentos, or some of each if they are obtainable, in half lengthways. Take out all the seeds and wash the pimentos. If they are large, cut each half in half again. Into each piece put 2 or 3 slices of garlic, 2 small sections of raw tomato, about half a fillet of anchovy cut into pieces, a small nut of butter, a dessertspoonful of oil, a very little salt. Arrange these pimentos on a flat baking dish and cook them in a moderate oven for about 30 minutes. They are not to be completely cooked; the pimentos should in fact be *al dente*, the stuffing inside deliciously oily and garlicky.

Serve them cold, each garnished with a little parsley.

AGONI
(*LAKE SARDINES* [ALOSA LACUSTRIS])

A small flat freshwater fish, held in high esteem by the inhabitants of the shores of Lake Como.

For an hors d'œuvre it is cooked in oil, then marinaded in vinegar which has been boiled with a quantity of wild thyme, and served cold.

It has a pleasant smoky flavour. Anyone who likes vinegary food could cook smoked cod fillets in this way, or for that matter any firm white fish.

Agoni are also salted, dried in the sun, and packed in tins or barrels for export to other parts of the country. In this guise they are called *misoltini*, and they are served grilled, with vinegar or *salsa verde*.

INSALATA DI PATATE
(*POTATO SALAD*)

To make a good potato salad it is essential to have yellow, waxy potatoes. They must be cooked in their skins, and care must be taken that they are firm and not overcooked. Peel them while they are still warm, cut them into dice, and season them straight away with salt, pepper, a good deal of the best olive oil, and a little lemon juice. Garlic and raw onion can then be added, and whatever herbs may be available. The Italians often add capers and

anchovies, which make a welcome change, but the mixture becomes monotonous if used too often.

INSALATA DI POMIDORO
(*TOMATO SALAD*)

Slice ripe tomatoes and season them with oil, salt, and pepper (no vinegar or lemon), and garnish them liberally with green onion tops and parsley, or, when in season, basil. Arrange them in a large flat dish so that they are not piled up on each other and so do not become clammy.

An excellent accompaniment to almost any dish of meat.

ANTIPASTO MISTO
(*MIXED ANTIPASTO*)

A nice summer hors d'œuvre.

On a long dish arrange at one end a salad of raw pimentos cut into fine rings. Next to this put a salad of cucumbers or potatoes cut into squares, then a salad of very ripe small red tomatoes (in the south they use the plum-shaped *sugo* tomatoes) mixed with raw onion. Cover the whole dish with slices of hard-boiled eggs cut lengthways.

INSALATA DI FINOCCHI E CETRIOLI
(*SALAD OF FENNEL AND CUCUMBER*)

Cut half an unpeeled cucumber into slices ¼ in. thick, then cut each slice into 4 small squares. Slice a bulb of fennel into thin strips, cut 3 or 4 radishes into slices, and mix with the cucumber. Add a little chopped mint and season with salt, pepper, garlic, olive oil, and lemon juice. Before serving add 2 quartered hard-boiled eggs.

The addition of an orange cut into segments makes this an excellent salad to serve with duck or game.

INSALATA DI FINOCCHI E RADICCHIE
(*FENNEL AND RADISH SALAD*)

Sliced raw fennel and rounds of red radishes, seasoned with oil and lemon.

CARLO CANE (1618-88)
THE HUNTING PICNIC
Milan, Museo Castello Sforzesco

CAPONATA ALLA MARINARA

A primitive fisherman's and sailor's dish, found in slightly varying forms all round the Italian coasts.

Ship's biscuits are soaked about 10 minutes in water, broken into pieces the size of a slice of cake and generously moistened with olive oil. Garlic, stoned black olives, anchovies, and origano or basil are added. The *caponata* should be prepared some little time before it is

LEMON TREE
from *Tacuinum Sanitatis* (c. 1390-1400)
Paris, Bibliothèque Nationale, MS Nouv. Acq. 1673

to be eaten, to give the oil and the garlic time to penetrate. It is no bad dish, rough though it is, to accompany coarse red wine. It can be made with stale bread instead of ship's biscuits, and pimentos in oil, pickled aubergines, capers, and onions can be added.

BUTTÀRIGA

Compressed and dried eggs of the grey mullet (*muggine*), a Sardinian delicacy similar to the *botargue* of Provence and the eastern Mediterranean.

It is eaten in thin slices, plentifully seasoned with olive oil and lemon.

UOVA DI TONNO

Dried and salted tunny-fish eggs, another Sardinian speciality. In the market place of Cagliari the *buttàriga* and the *uova di tonno*, in mysterious dark-red and rusty-brown sausage-like shapes, hang up on the stalls where cheese, oil, ready made *pasta*, and *salame* are sold. These dried fish-eggs are primitive tasting foods but remarkably expensive. Our own smoked cod's roe, infinitely cheaper, is really better but absurdly neglected. One of these days smoked cod's roe will be discovered by the expensive restaurants* and offered with the same conjurer-like triumph at present reserved by waiters for the announcement that the management is in a position to provide that most uninteresting of dishes, potted shrimps.

---

*It has happened. A smoked cod's roe paste made in the Greek manner is now a quite common hors-d'œuvre in London restaurants *E.D. 1963.*

PROSCIUTTO DI PARMA
(PARMA HAM)

A properly matured Parma ham should be of a good pale-red colour, mild, sweet-flavoured and tender, and at its best is perhaps the most delicious food in all Italy.

To serve Parma ham, have it cut in the thinnest possible slices. Serve fresh figs or slices of melon with it. When neither of these is in season, the very best butter should be eaten with Parma ham – not with bread, but simply a little piece of butter with every mouthful of ham. It is debatable whether butter is not an even finer accompaniment to Parma ham than fresh figs.

San Daniele ham, from north of Udine, is every bit as good as Parma ham, but it is made

in very small quantities and is therefore infrequently obtainable.

It should be remembered that the centre part of a Parma or San Daniele ham is the best; the first few slices cut from a ham are often too salty or tough; in Italy the end pieces are sold cheaply for cooking. *Prosciutto di montagna*, country ham which may come from almost any part of Italy, is often passed off in restaurants as Parma ham. *Prosciutto di montagna* can be very good, with plenty of character, but it is usually a much coarser product than Parma or San Daniele ham.

The method of curing Parma hams is described on p. 144. Allow a minimum of 2 oz. per person; and buy it only on the day you intend to eat it.

CULATELLO DI ZIBELLO

Rump of pork cured in the same way as ham, a speciality of the province of Parma.

In winter the *Culatello* is wrapped in a cloth, steeped in white wine for two or three days before being cut, and served in thin slices with butter. In summer the steeping is not considered necessary, as the meat does not need extra moisture. One of the very best Italian pork products, and the most expensive.

SALAME

Salame are served as *antipasti*, cut into thin slices, skinned or not, according to how refined you wish to be, and accompanied by plenty of butter (as for the Parma ham). Allow 1½ to 2 oz. per person.

In Italy it is always safe to order a plate of *salame* to start a meal, for there is scarcely any variety that is not good. Danish *salame* simply does not compare; and as for Irish *salame*, the less said the better.

PROSCIUTTO COTTO
(COOKED HAM)

Slices of cooked ham are served as a first course in Italy, often together with raw ham. Curiously enough, Italian cooked ham cannot compare in flavour with the raw variety.

LINGUA CON SALSA VERDE
(TONGUE WITH GREEN SAUCE)
Finely sliced tongue served with a sauce composed of oil, lemon juice, capers, parsley, and chopped anchovies.

INSALATA DI LINGUA DI BUE
(TONGUE SALAD)
2 aubergines, a pimento, a thick slice of cooked tongue, parsley, oil, garlic.

Cut the unpeeled aubergines (egg plant) into small squares, sauté them gently in oil, and when they are cooked stir in a chopped clove of garlic and a handful of chopped parsley. While they are still warm, mix them with a red pimento in oil cut in strips and the tongue cut into dice. Season with salt if necessary, more oil, and a little lemon juice.

BRESAOLA
(DRIED BEEF)
A Lombard speciality, which has probably crossed the border from Switzerland into the Valtellina. It varies a good deal, but when not too dry makes a very good hors d'œuvre. It is served cut in thin slices, with oil, lemon juice, and chopped parsley.

OLIVE
(OLIVES)
Italian olives present a fine variety of colours, shapes, sizes, and textures. There are dark, luminous black olives from Gaeta; little coal black olives of Rome, smoky and wrinkled; sloe-like black olives of Castellamare, like bright black eyes; olives brown and purple and yellow from Sardinia; Sicilian black olives in oil; olives of a dozen different greens; the bright, smooth, newly-gathered olives before they have been salted; the slightly yellower tinge they acquire after a week or two in the brine (how delicious they are before the salt has really penetrated); the giant green olives called *cerignola*, from Puglie; the bitter green

THE OLIVE HARVEST
from *Theatrum Sanitatis* by Ububschasym de Baldach
Rome, Biblioteca Casanatense

olives with a very large stone known in Italy as *Olive Spagnuole* (Spanish Olives); olives of all the greens of the evening sea.

As part of a simplified hors d'œuvre, consisting of *salame*, tomatoes, and a country cheese, black olives* are by far the best. If they seem too salt when bought, put them in a jar and cover them with olive oil. This is, in any case, the best way to store them at home. Generally speaking, for green olives, the small oval ones are the best. They can be kept in the same way as the black; and, if you like, add a little cut garlic to the oil and a piece of chilli or dried red pepper.

---

*Buy small ones. With the exception of a certain Greek variety, the large ones tend to be acrid and over-salt.

OLIVE RIPIENE
(STUFFED OLIVES)
A dish of which I long doubted the existence, but arriving very late for luncheon in the town of Ascoli, of which these stuffed olives are a speciality, I was lucky enough to find a wedding feast still in progress in the very excellent little restaurant, and these stuffed olives had been made for the occasion.

The stuffing consists of a fine forcemeat, similar to the filling for *agnolotti* or *anolini*. When stuffed the olives are coated with egg and breadcrumbs and fried. Very large stoned green olives are used. The taste is good, but not so extraordinary as to justify the labour involved, unless the stuffing were already being prepared for other dishes at the same time.

JOACHIM BEUCKELAER (*c.* 1530/5-1573/4)
A COUNTRY MARKET
Naples, Museo di Capodimonte

Soups

NON TEME ZVPPE

ASCIVTTO

TALIAN SOUPS TAKE ROUGHLY THREE FORMS: PLAIN broth or consommé, made from meat, chicken, or vegetables; thick soups containing a variety of vegetables both fresh and dried and further thickened either with rice or some form of *pasta* (this is, broadly speaking, the composition of a *minestrone*); and the *minestre in brodo,* which consist of *pasta,* or sometimes of rice, cooked and served in broth. There are, besides, various vegetable purées and cream soups; and although these are mostly of the sophisticated kind and derived from French cooking, the Italians add their own characteristic touches, often with good results.

A notable variation on the traditional croûtons served with such soups is the Italian *crostini,* a round of bread spread with cheese, which is heated in the oven until the bread is crisp and the cheese melted. What gives all Italian soups, whether thick or thin, rustic or elegant, their unmistakable character is the lavish use of grated Parmesan or Pecorino cheese, both stirred into the soup to thicken it and served separately at the table. In Tuscany good fresh olive oil will sometimes take the place of cheese; in Liguria no cook can resist the addition to a vegetable soup of *pesto,* that admirable Genoese compound of basil, garlic, oil, and *Sardo* cheese. The Abruzzesi are fond of an excessive quantity of fiery red pepper in their soups and *minestre.* Characteristic of Rome is a flavouring of wild mint (good, and unexpected, in a soup of lentils and tomatoes). In the south the haunting perfume of *origano* is as familiar in the kitchens as it is upon the hillsides. Most amateur cooks have found out in recent years that a good soup does not necessarily demand an impossible quantity of meat stock; that the flavouring need not be confined to white pepper and cooking sherry; and that there are other ways of thickening a soup than by means of flour-and-water paste. Italian cookery should provide plenty of ideas in this respect, and slavish adherence to the book is not necessary for the recipes which follow.* The dishes which make up the rest of the meal must determine to a certain extent the composition of a soup. Equally important are the personal taste, imagination, and fantasy of the cook. Incidentally, soup, unless it be a plain clear consommé, is invariably served instead of, never at the same meal with, a dish of rice or *pasta asciutta,* and these soups must be served in large deep soup plates; dainty little pottery bowls in which the cheese cannot be stirred into the soup for fear of it spilling will not do.

Apart from the soups mentioned in these notes, there is of course a considerable variety of *zuppe di pesce* (fish soups); but since these are in fact not really soups but fish stews constituting almost a meal in themselves, they are included in the chapter on fish.

---

*Amounts of seasonings, herbs, cheese, and so on are in any case left to the discretion of the cook.

BRODO DI MANZO
(*BEEF CONSOMMÉ*)

2 lb. of lean beef, a carrot, an onion, a small piece of celery, 3 pints of water, salt.

Put the meat in one piece, the carrot, onion, and celery into a large saucepan, season very lightly with salt, cover with the cold water, and heat very gently. As the water is just coming to the boil, remove the scum very carefully with a spoon dipped in a bowl of cold water. Cover the pan and cook as gently as possible, so that the broth is barely moving, for 5-6 hours. Strain it, leave it to cool, and remove the fat from the top. The broth should be perfectly clear.

This is a simple form of meat consommé in which various kinds of *pasta* are cooked, or which is used as a stock for sauces and for *risotto*.

BRODO RISTRETTO
(*CONCENTRATED CONSOMMÉ*)

2 lb. of lean beef, a boiling chicken, a carrot, an onion, a piece of celery, 4 pints of water.

Cook exactly as for the beef consommé, but when the chicken is cooked remove it from the broth so that it can be served as a separate dish. Continue to cook the consommé with the meat for another hour or two. Next day, when the fat has been taken off, put the broth into a pan and boil it until it is reduced to half the original quantity of water. Add salt and other seasonings only when the second boiling is nearly finished.

A stewing pigeon can be included with the hen and the beef, and helps to give a good flavour, a useful function for this rather dull little bird.

BARTOLOMEO BIMBI (1648-1730)
CAULIFLOWER
Florence, Istituto Botanico

ZUPPA PAVESE

Zuppa pavese appears regularly upon the menu of practically every restaurant in Italy. Rightly, for it is a capital invention, admirable when one is tired, and also for solitary meals, for it is not only quickly prepared but one dish provides the elements of a nourishing meal – broth, eggs, bread, cheese. You need chicken or meat or vegetable consommé. Naturally upon the flavour of the consommé depends the excellence of the result. You also need an egg per person, small slices of bread, and grated cheese.

While the consommé is heating up fry your slices of bread (3 for each plate of soup) in butter. Poach the eggs in the hot consommé, lift them out into the heated plates, pour the consommé over them (through a fine strainer if there are any pieces of white of egg floating about). Spread a little grated cheese over each slice of fried bread, and arrange 3 round each egg. Serve more grated cheese separately.

Some Italian cooks break the eggs into the plates and simply pour the boiling consommé over them, but this method does not, to my mind, cook the eggs sufficiently.

STRACCIATELLA

A Roman soup, but common all over Italy, and extremely good. A safe dish to order in any restaurant.

The basis is a good broth, preferably chicken. For four people beat 2 eggs in a basin, and with them incorporate 2 tablespoonfuls of grated Parmesan and a tablespoonful of fine semolina. To this add a cupful of the broth, and stir it to a smooth cream. Heat the broth, and when it is nearly boiling pour in the mixture and beat it vigorously with a fork for 3 or 4 minutes, then leave the soup to come barely to the boil. The egg mixture should not be absolutely smooth, but just breaking up into little flakes or threads. Serve it quickly.

PASSATELLI

This is a *minestra*, a kind of *pasta in brodo*, a speciality originally of the neighbourhood of Modena and Bologna. To make it as it should be you need a special kind of sieve, rather like a potato ricer, with holes about the size of large spaghetti. An ordinary metal sieve with large holes, a colander, or even a perforated draining spoon, will do. The ingredients for four large helpings are 4 eggs, 4 good tablespoonfuls of grated Parmesan, 4 of fine breadcrumbs, 2 oz. of butter, salt, pepper, and a scrap of grated nutmeg. Mix all the ingredients thoroughly together until they form a paste; heat it in a saucepan for barely a minute; holding the sieve over the saucepan containing bubbling meat or chicken broth – allow 2 pints for four people – push the paste through so that it falls into the consommé in the form of short pieces of spaghetti. (Or the prepared paste can be rolled out on a board into thin sausages, cut into inch lengths, and dropped straight into the broth.) They need only cook a minute or two. Serve the soup with grated cheese.

At one time the Bolognesi seldom served *tagliatelle* or *lasagne* in the summer, and after Easter replaced the heavier *pasta* with *passatelli*. Traditional Italian cooking abounds in such small refinements, unsuspected outside the country itself.

BARTOLOMEO BIMBI (1648-1730)
GIANT MARROWS
Florence, Istituto Botanico

BUDINO DI POLLO IN BRODO
(*CHICKEN MOUSSE IN BROTH*)
6 oz. of uncooked white chicken meat, 4 eggs, 2 oz. of grated Parmesan, salt, pepper, nutmeg, 3 pints of very good clear chicken broth.

Mince the chicken meat (the Bolognese use the breast of the chicken, making the broth out of the rest of the bird). Pound the minced chicken meat in a mortar, adding from time to time a little of the broth (about 3 fluid oz. in all); it must now be put through a sieve,* so that a fine cream is obtained. Beat the eggs, pour them through a strainer into the chicken mixture, and mix them thoroughly. Add the grated cheese, and season with salt, pepper, and nutmeg. Put the chicken cream, which should be very smooth, into 6 small buttered moulds or china ramekins, of the kind in which eggs are baked. Put the ramekins in a pan containing water, about halfway up the little pots; cover, and cook gently for 15 minutes, until the chicken mixture is firm. Turn each one out on to a soup plate and pour over them the hot chicken broth. Enough for six.

This is a very delicate and delicious soup, worth taking the trouble over for an occasional treat. It makes a light and excellent beginning to any meal. I am indebted for the recipe to the Pappagallo restaurant in Bologna, for good reason one of the most famous in all Italy at the time I was working on this book.

---

*Or puréed in the electric blender.

PASTA IN BRODO CON FEGATINI E PISELLI
(*PASTA IN BROTH WITH CHICKEN LIVERS AND PEAS*)
I first came across this *minestra* in Verona; it is one of the nicest *pasta in brodo* mixtures, mild, soothing, and freshly flavoured.

The quantities for two people are a pint of chicken broth, 4 or 5 chicken livers, 6-8 oz. of shelled green peas, about 1½ oz. of fine *pasta*

(it should be home-made, in short strips about the thickness of a match, but ready-made *pasta* will do), Parmesan cheese, a little butter.

If using ready-made *pasta*, first cook it for 5 minutes, with the green peas, in plenty of boiling salted water. Drain it, and then heat the broth to boiling point and put in the *pasta* and the peas, which should be young and very fresh, so that they will be cooked at the same time as the *pasta*. Clean and chop the chicken livers, not too small. Heat them through in the butter, and add them to the *pasta* and broth, with their butter. Add some grated Parmesan when the broth is ready to serve.

PASTA IN BRODO AL PESTO
(*PASTA IN CONSOMMÉ WITH PESTO*)
Cook a handful of fine *pasta*, broken into small lengths, in good chicken or meat broth. Before serving stir in a tablespoonful or two of prepared *pesto* (p. 193).

MINESTRA DI FUNGHI
(MUSHROOM SOUP)

¾ lb. of mushrooms, 1½ pints of béchamel sauce, a breakfastcupful (7 to 8 oz.) of stock, a large bunch of parsley, pepper, salt, garlic, nutmeg, a sherry glassful of Marsala, butter.

Prepare the béchamel with 1 oz. of butter, 2 tablespoonfuls of flour, and 1½ pints of hot milk. Season it with salt, pepper, and nutmeg, and let it cook for at least 15 minutes.

Wash the mushrooms, chop them up very small, and cook them gently in 1½ oz. butter for about 10 minutes. Then add a little finely-chopped garlic, the parsley (also chopped), salt, pepper, and the Marsala. After 2 or 3 minutes pour in the béchamel, then the stock. Let it heat thoroughly, and if the soup is too thick add a little more stock or milk. Enough for four people.

The Marsala and the large quantity of parsley give the soup a flavour rather different from that of the usual mushroom soup.

PAPAROT

A spinach soup, from the Istria district.

1 lb. of spinach, 2 oz. of butter, a clove of garlic, nutmeg, 2 tablespoonfuls of fine *polenta* flour, a tablespoonful of ordinary flour, salt and pepper.

Cook the cleaned spinach in the usual way, and put it through the food mill. Stir the flour into the melted butter. Add the prepared spinach, the chopped garlic, the salt, pepper, and nutmeg. Add 2½-3 pints of water. Let the soup cook for a few minutes after it has come to the boil and add the *polenta*. Cook for another 30 minutes, stirring frequently. Instead of putting the spinach through the sieve to start with, the whole soup can be sieved after the *polenta* has cooked, which is perhaps more satisfactory.

ZUPPA DI FAGIOLI ALLA TOSCANA
(TUSCAN BEAN SOUP)

½ lb. of white beans, parsley, garlic, salt and pepper, olive oil.

Put the previously soaked beans to cook, covered with 3 pints of water. When they are tender (about 3 hours)* put half the beans through a sieve and return the resulting purée

to the rest of the beans in the pan. Season with salt and pepper. In a little olive oil heat the chopped garlic (the quantity depends entirely upon individual taste) and add a good handful of chopped parsley. Stir this mixture into the soup, and before serving add a little fresh olive oil.

---

*See footnote, p. 46.

PIER FRANCESCO CITTADINI (1613/16-1681)
STILL LIFE WITH CAT (detail)
Modena, Galleria Estense

MINESTRA DI LENTICCHIE E PASTA
(LENTIL SOUP WITH PASTA)

6 oz. of brown lentils, 3 or 4 large tomatoes, 1 oz. of ham or bacon, a stick of celery, a medium-sized onion, several cloves of garlic, a bunch of parsley, salt, pepper, basil or mint, bacon fat, 2 oz. of *pastine* (*pasta* made in the shape of long grains of rice) or broken-up spaghetti, 3½ pints of water.

Soak the lentils in cold water for 2 hours. Fry the thinly-sliced onion in olive oil, then add the bacon cut into squares, the peeled and quartered tomatoes, the garlic, and the celery cut into short lengths. After 5 minutes put in the strained lentils and stir them so that they absorb the oil. Season them, and add the basil or mint (the latter is preferable for lentils).

Pour over 3½ pints of hot water, and let the soup cook fairly fast for about an hour, when the lentils should be done. Throw in the *pasta* and cook for 10 minutes more. Enough for six people. A warming winter soup.

ZUPPA DI PATATE
(POTATO SOUP)

For four people prepare 10 oz. of potatoes, a medium-sized onion, and 8 small slices of bread. You also need about 2 pints of broth, 3 tablespoonfuls of olive oil, thyme, salt, pepper, grated cheese, nutmeg, 2 oz. of butter.

Cut the potatoes in thin strips, as if you were going to make very small chips. Heat the olive oil in the saucepan, brown the onion, then add the potatoes and season them with salt, pepper, nutmeg, and thyme. Pour over the boiling broth. In 15 minutes the soup will be cooked.

To go with it, prepare the following *crostini*: saturate the slices of bread with melted butter; spread them thickly with grated Parmesan and cook them in a moderate oven for 10 minutes.

This soup, which is good and so easy to cook, can be made with water instead of stock, provided a little bacon or ham (about 2 oz.) is cooked with the onion to give flavour.

ZUPPA DI CASTAGNE
(CHESTNUT SOUP)

½ lb. of chestnuts, 2 onions, a carrot, a small piece of celery, 1½ oz. of butter or bacon fat, salt, pepper, 2½ pints of stock or water.

Score the chestnuts across on the rounded side and bake them in a slow oven for 15 minutes. Both shell and skin should come off easily if they are peeled while still warm.

Brown the chopped onion, carrot, and celery in the butter or bacon-fat; add the chestnuts, the seasoning, and the stock. Cook for about 40 minutes, until the chestnuts are completely tender and have started to break up. Put the soup through a sieve, heat up, and serve with slices of fried bread.

MINESTRONE (1)

4 pints of stock, ½ lb. of fresh kidney beans, a small head of celery, a small marrow, ¼ lb. of

spinach, a small onion, 10 oz. of fresh peas, ¼ lb. of gammon, 2 carrots, a small cabbage, ½ lb. of tomatoes, 2 leeks, 2 sprigs of parsley, a few sage leaves, a clove of garlic, a few tablespoonfuls of grated Parmesan cheese, salt and pepper.

'Chop the gammon and the celery and put them in a saucepan and cover with the boiling stock. Bring to the boil and add the peas, then simmer for 30 minutes. Then add the other chopped vegetables, stir, and season with salt and pepper. Continue to simmer for about 40 minutes till all the vegetables are quite soft. Just before serving add the Parmesan cheese. This is a thick and very substantial soup, enough for six persons. Hot toast cut in small squares can be served with it.' (Romilly Fedden, *Food and other Frailties*, Seeley Service & Co. 1948.)

MINESTRONE (2)

¼ lb. of dried haricot beans, 2 carrots, 2 small potatoes, a small turnip, 2 onions, a piece of celery, 4 tomatoes, half a small cabbage, 2 rashers of bacon, garlic, herbs, and seasoning, olive oil, a small glassful of red wine, 2 oz. of broken-up macaroni or spaghetti, or *pastine*, or any of the *pasta* made in small shapes, such as little stars, little shells, etc.

Put the haricot beans to soak overnight. Next day prepare all the vegetables, and melt the sliced onions in the oil, adding 2 cloves of garlic, the bacon cut into pieces, and plenty of herbs, marjoram, thyme, basil, or whatever may be available; add the chopped tomatoes, or a tablespoonful of concentrated tomato purée; pour in the red wine, let it bubble a minute or two, then add the drained haricot beans; cover them with 3 pints of hot water and let them boil steadily for 2 hours. Now put in the carrots and about 15 minutes later the turnip and potatoes. Ten minutes before serving, add the celery, the cabbage cut into strips, and the pasta. See that the soup is properly seasoned, stir in 2 tablespoonfuls of grated Parmesan, and serve more Parmesan separately.

According to the season almost any vegetable can be added to a *minestrone*: peas, beans, spinach, leeks, small marrows; rice can be substituted for the pasta.

MINESTRONE (3)

'Chop 6 or 8 oz. of bacon, put it into a stewpan with a piece of raw ham, a savoy cabbage shredded large, and 2 or 3 handfuls of fresh haricot beans, either white or green; moisten all these vegetables with 3 quarts of broth, and place the stewpan on a brisk fire. After it has boiled for 10 minutes, add to the liquid 4 tablespoonfuls of tender celery roots cut into small dice, the same of cabbage, and again the same of haricot beans cut in pieces. Eight or 10 minutes after, add 2 handfuls of fresh broad beans, the same of green peas and asparagus heads, a chopped tomato, 12 or 14 oz. of Piedmont rice (not washed) as well as 2 or 3 smoked Milan sausages. Continue boiling until the rice is done – 12 or 14 minutes will be enough. At the last moment add to the soup a handful of grated Parmesan; then take out the ham and sausages; pour the broth and vegetables into the soup tureen, cut the sausages and put them into the soup, which serve.

'The Milanese, be it remarked, are undoubtedly the best cooks in Italy.' (G. A. Sala, *The Thorough Good Cook*, 1895.)

MINESTRONE GENOVESE
(*GENOESE MINESTRONE*)

¼ lb. of white haricot beans, 2 large aubergines, a cabbage, 1 lb. of tomatoes, 2 or 3 small marrows or a piece of pumpkin, 3 oz. of fresh mushrooms or a few dried mushrooms, 3 tablespoonfuls of oil, 3 oz. of *pastine* or vermicelli, 2 tablespoonfuls of *pesto* (p. 193), grated Parmesan.

Boil the previously soaked haricot beans until they are three-quarters cooked. Strain them and put them into 3 pints of fresh water. Add the peeled aubergines cut into squares,

GIUSEPPE BISI (1787-1869)
PANORAMA OF GENOA
Milan, Museo Nazionale d'Arte Moderna

GIOVANNA GARZONI (1600-70)
A DISH OF BEANS
Florence, Palazzo Pitti, Galleria Palatina

tomatoes are cooked to the consistency of a sauce. Now add the french beans, cut into lengths of about ½ in., and the potato, cut into small dice. Cook for a few more minutes and then pour in 3 pints of hot water. Cook over a fairly fast flame for 10 minutes, then add a handful of noodles broken up small and the haricot beans with their liquor but minus the pork rind. The soup should be ready in 10 minutes. Before serving stir in another handful of parsley and fresh herbs. Serve Parmesan cheese separately.

ZUPPA DI VERCOLORE
(GREEN SOUP)
An onion, ¼ lb. of french beans, half a cucumber or 2 or 3 small marrows, half a carrot, a small potato, 4 tomatoes, a little watercress, mint, a bunch of parsley, a clove of garlic, olive oil.

Brown the sliced onion in olive oil, add the chopped carrot and potato, the skinned tomatoes also chopped, the diced cucumber or marrows, the watercress and mint. Season with salt and pepper and let them all simmer for a few minutes. Put in the french beans cut in small lengths, cover with 2 pints of water and simmer until all the vegetables are cooked.

In the meantime pound the garlic and the parsley together with a little salt until they are a pulp. Stir this mixture into the soup a minute or two before serving.

Grated cheese to be served separately. Enough for four or five.

ZUPPA CREMA DI PISELLI
(FRESH GREEN PEA SOUP)
A small onion, a slice of ham, a stick of celery with the leaves, 12 oz. of green peas (weighed when shelled; about 2 lb. in the pod), butter, a pint of water, about ½ cupful of milk.

Melt the chopped onion in the butter, then add the chopped ham and the celery. After 5 minutes put in the shelled peas, and let them get thoroughly impregnated with the butter before adding the water. Simmer gently until the peas are thoroughly cooked. Put the whole contents of the pan through the food mill.

Add the milk when the soup is heated up. Enough for three.

the peeled and chopped tomatoes, all the other vegetables also cut into small pieces, and the olive oil. When the beans and the vegetables are all but cooked put in the *pasta*, and when it is tender stir in the *pesto*. See that there is sufficient seasoning, and serve with grated cheese.

The vegetables for this *minestrone* can naturally be varied according to the season; carrots, cauliflower, french beans, celery, and potatoes can be added. The *pesto* makes Genoese *minestrone* one of the best of all.

MINESTRONE VERDE
(GREEN MINESTRONE)
2 oz. of dried haricot beans, ½ lb. of french beans, 2 leeks, 2 large tomatoes, parsley, garlic, basil, chives, or any fresh green herbs, olive oil, a medium sized potato, Parmesan cheese, a handful of noodles, a strip of salted pork rind.

First soak the haricot beans overnight, and next day put them on to boil, with water to cover them by 2 or 3 in., a piece of garlic and the pork rind. Boil them steadily for about 2½ hours. Salt them only when they are nearly cooked. (This is a precaution which it is always wise to take with haricot beans, in case the water boils away too fast, leaving the beans oversalt.)

When the time comes to make the soup heat the oil in a large pan, and put in the leeks, cut into thin rounds, the tomatoes chopped into small pieces, a crushed clove of garlic, a tablespoonful of parsley and the other herbs chopped, but not too finely. Season with salt and pepper. Stew this mixture gently until the

GIOVANNA GARZONI (1600-70)
A DISH OF PEAS
Florence, Palazzo Pitti, Galleria Palatina

pepper, sugar, basil or marjoram, 2 pints of meat broth.

Chop the skinned tomatoes and put them in a saucepan with salt, pepper, sugar, a little basil or marjoram. Let them melt and reduce a little, and then pour the meat broth over them.

In a bowl mix 2 tablespoonfuls of ground rice with a little of the soup. Add the mixture to the soup, and stir for 2 or 3 minutes. Let it cook for another 15 minutes.

The soup can be put through a sieve to make it quite smooth or left as it is. The egg yolks should be added to the soup before serving, after which it must not boil again.

Serve with *crostini* (as for potato soup, p. 56).

MINESTRA DI POMIDORO
(*TOMATO SOUP*)

Melt 1½ lb. of chopped and skinned tomatoes in olive oil; add a clove of garlic and some fresh parsley or basil or marjoram. Cook for 5 minutes, then add a pint of meat or chicken stock, salt and pepper, and a pinch of sugar. Cook for 5 minutes more only.

By this method the flavour of the tomatoes is retained, and the soup tastes very fresh.

Enough for four.

In the summer this soup can be eaten iced, accompanied by hot *crostini* (as for potato soup, p. 56).

ZUPPA CREMA DI POLLO
(*CREAM OF CHICKEN SOUP*)

For four people, allow 3 pints of chicken broth, 4 dessertspoonsful of ground rice, 2 eggs, lemon, nutmeg, a few strips of cooked chicken, a teacupful of milk.

Make a paste with the ground rice and the milk, adding also a little of the cold broth. Heat the broth, add the ground rice mixture to it, and simmer for 20-30 minutes. Season with a little lemon juice, nutmeg, and ground black pepper. Pour the soup through a very fine strainer. Return it to the pan to re-heat, and

beat 2 eggs in a basin; add to them some of the hot soup, and then pour this mixture back into the pan. Once the eggs have been added to the soup it must not boil.

A good soup for people who like creamy food.

ZUPPA CREMA DI POMIDORO
(*CREAM OF TOMATO SOUP*)

A quickly and easily made soup.

Ingredients are 1½ lb. very ripe tomatoes, 2 tablespoonsful of ground rice, 2 egg yolks, salt,

MINESTRE FREDDE
(*COLD SOUPS*)

Italians rarely eat iced soups, but in the summer a *minestra* of vegetables and *pasta* is sometimes served cold, or *tiepida*, and is, perhaps contrary to expectations, rather good. The green soup described on p. 58 is a good one to serve cold, so is the *minestrone Genovese*. Rather thinner versions of the tomato, the green pea, and the chicken cream soups on pp. 58-9 make excellent iced soups. The quickest and simplest to make is the tomato soup above, which is excellent iced.

ANON
THE PASTA EATER
Oneglia, Museo della Pasta Agnesi

PASTA ASCIUTTA

N THE 15TH OF NOVEMBER 1930, AT A BANQUET AT the restaurant Penna d'Oca in Milan, the famous Italian futurist poet Marinetti launched his much publicized campaign against all established forms of cooking and, in particular, against *pastasciutta*. 'Futurist cooking', said Marinetti, 'will be liberated from the ancient obsession of weight and volume, and one of its principal aims will be the abolition of *pastasciutta*. *Pastasciutta*, however grateful to the palate, is an obsolete food; it is heavy, brutalizing, and gross; its nutritive qualities are deceptive; it induces scepticism, sloth, and pessimism.'

The day after this diatribe was delivered the Italian press broke into an uproar; all classes participated in the dispute which ensued. Every time *pastasciutta* was served either in a restaurant or a private house interminable arguments arose. One of Marinetti's supporters declared that 'our *pastasciutta*, like our rhetoric, suffices merely to fill the mouth'. Doctors, asked their opinions, were characteristically cautious: 'Habitual and exaggerated consumption of *pastasciutta* is definitely fattening.' 'Heavy consumers of *pastasciutta* have slow and placid characters; meat eaters are quick and aggressive.' 'A question of taste and of the cost of living. In any case, diet should be varied, and should never consist exclusively of one single element.' The Duke of Bovino, Mayor of Naples, plunged into the fight with happy abandon. 'The angels in Paradise', he affirmed to a reporter, 'eat nothing but *vermicelli al pomodoro*.' To which Marinetti replied that this confirmed his suspicions with regard to the monotony of Paradise and of the life led by the angels.

Marinetti and his friends proceeded to divert themselves and outrage the public with the invention and publication of preposterous new dishes. Most of these were founded on the shock principle of combining unsuitable and exotic ingredients (*mortadella* with nougat, pineapple with sardines, cooked *salame* immersed in a bath of hot black coffee flavoured with eau de-Cologne, an aphrodisiac drink composed of pineapple juice, eggs, cocoa, caviar, almond paste, red pepper, nutmeg, cloves, and Strega). Meals were to be eaten to the accompaniment of perfumes (warmed, so that the bald-headed should not suffer from the cold), to be sprayed over the diners, who, fork in the right hand, would stroke meanwhile with the left some suitable substance – velvet, silk, or emery paper.

Marinetti's bombshell contained a good deal of common sense; diet and methods of cookery must necessarily evolve at the same time as other habits and customs. But behind this amiable fooling lurked a sinister note: the fascist obsession with nationalism and patriotism, the war to come. 'Spaghetti is no food for fighters.' In the 'conflict to come the victory will be to the swift', '*Pastasciutta* is anti-virile. . . . A weighty and encumbered stomach cannot be favourable to physical enthusiasm towards women.' The costly import of foreign flour for *pastasciutta* should be stopped, to boost the national cultivation of rice. The snobbery of the Italian aristocracy and haute bourgeoisie, who had lost their heads over American customs, cocktail parties, foreign films, German music, and French food, was damned by Marinetti as *esterofil* (pro-foreign) and anti-Italian. In future a bar should be known as a *quisibeve* (here-one-drinks), a sandwich as a *traidue* (between-two), a cocktail as a *polibibita* (multi-drink), the maître-d'hôtel would be addressed as *guidopalato* (palate-guide), an aphrodisiac drink was to be called a *guerra in letto* (war-in-the-bed), a sleeping draught a *pace in letto* (peace-in-the-bed). Marinetti's tongue was by no means wholly in his cheek. A message from Mussolini, to be published in *La Cucina Futurista* (F. Marinetti, 1932), was dedicated 'to my dear old friend of the first fascist battles, to the intrepid soldier whose indomitable passion for his country has been consecrated in blood'.

The origin of *pasta* is lost in the mists of antiquity. There is a popular legend, entirely without foundation, to the effect that it was introduced into Italy by Marco Polo on his return from China. The Futurists knew better. *La Cronaca degli memorabilia*, by Dacovio Saraceno, they claimed, 'is fortunately here to bear witness' that it is a barbarous legacy from the Ostrogoths who 'frequently and gladly solaced themselves with this food. The said *macarono* was made from *spelta* (small brown wheat) and first made its appearance in the reign of the magnanimous Prince Teodoric in Ravenna, the said Prince having revealed the secret to Rotufo, his cook. A kitchen woman, in love with one of the palace guards, revealed to him the existence of the said *macarono*. From this beginning the taste for *macarono* spread to the people. They boiled it with onions, garlic and turnips, and licked their fingers and their faces'.

By the end of the Renaissance, according to Marinetti, the wretched macaroni was all but buried in oblivion (although it is on record that Boccaccio liked his macaroni in a sauce of milk and bitter almonds), 'when that noisy rascal of an Aretino once more raised it to the skies; guests who had feasted at his table, to ingratiate themselves into his favour, composed sonnets and eulogies in praise of the macaroni served at his banquets'.

For the rest, Marinetti's effort was not the first that had been made to reform the Italian diet. In the sixteenth century a Genoese doctor had denounced the abuse of *pasta*. Towards the end of the eighteenth century a campaign was instituted against the consumption of excessive quantities of macaroni. Innumerable volumes from the hands of eminent scientists and men of letters proved unavailing. Not only was the passion for *pastasciutta* too deeply rooted in the tastes of the people, but there was also a widely diffused superstition that macaroni was the antidote to all ills, the universal panacea.

Another effort was made in the first half of the nineteenth century by the scientist Michele Scropetta; he, again, achieved nothing concrete. Had it not been for the war Marinetti's campaign might have achieved a certain success; but however aware enlightened Italians may be of the unsuitability of *pasta* as a daily food, the fact remains that the majority of southern Italians (in the north it is replaced by rice or *polenta*) continue to eat *pastasciutta* at midday and probably some kind of *pasta in brodo* at night. Considering the cost of living, this is not surprising; freshly made *pasta* such as *tagliatelle* and *fettuccine* is cheap and versatile. According to circumstances it may be eaten economically with tomato sauce and cheese, with fresh tomatoes when they are cheap, with butter and cheese, with oil and garlic without cheese. The whole dish will cost rather less than two eggs, is immediately satisfying, and possesses the further advantage that every Italian could prepare a dish of spaghetti blindfold, standing on his head in his sleep.

Figure-conscious Italians claim that no fattening effect is produced

ANON
PULCINELLA DISTRIBUTES FOOD
Source unknown

by *pasta* provided no meat course is served afterwards; vegetables or a salad, cheese and fruit, are quite sufficient. People mindful of their digestions will also tell you that the wise drink water with their spaghetti and wait until it is finished before starting on the wine.

As to the different varieties of *pasta*, they are countless. The catalogue of one big firm alone gives fifty-two different varieties; and to add to the confusion each province has different names for almost identical kinds of *pasta*. In the following chapter I have endeavoured to describe the main varieties.

There are two main distinctions to be made with regard to genuine Italian *pasta*. There is *pasta fatta in casa* (home made *pasta*), and the kind which is mass-produced and dried in the factory, sold in packets or by the pound, and which will keep almost indefinitely; this is the

ANON
THE PASTA EATER
Oneglia, Museo della Pasta Agnesi

pasta to a fine art, and the difference between home-made and dried *pasta* is chiefly one of texture. Dried or factory *pasta* must, of course, be cooked for about 15 minutes, whereas freshly made *pasta* takes only about 5 minutes.

In all large Italian towns freshly made *tagliatelle, fettuccine, vermicelli,* and some stuffed pastes such as *tortellini* and *ravioli,* can be bought in the shops, to be cooked at home the same day. In the restaurants of Rome home-made *fettuccine* are a speciality, but as a matter of fact a great many of these restaurants buy their *fettuccine,* or *tagliatelle,* from the shop round the corner, and so do the cooks in private houses, although every Italian cook can, and does, make her own *pasta* if called upon to do so. I have explained the process to the best of my ability in the chapter which follows. Anyone who has a good hand for pastry – and so many English people have – should be able to master the idea after one or two tries. Spaghetti and macaroni require a special machine, and although as a general rule it is less trouble to use bought *pasta,* it is useful to know how to make it, and there are some varieties which cannot easily be bought ready made. There are any number of different sauces to be served with *pasta,* and there are still possibilities to be explored.

Do not, I implore, be influenced against *pasta* by the repugnant concoctions served in restaurants under the name of *spaghetti Napolitaine, Bolognese* and the like; a good dish of *pasta* is admirable food for one or two days a week, but it must be cooked with as much care as any other dish. Giuseppe Marotta, the Neapolitan writer, has made the point about spaghetti: 'The important thing is to adapt your dish of spaghetti to circumstances and your state of mind.'

THE COOKING AND SERVING OF PASTA
In Italy the amount of *pasta* allowed for each person is 3-4 oz., whether home made or dried. The latter is usually cooked in a large quantity of boiling salted water, say 6 quarts to 12 oz. of *pasta.* It should be cooked *al dente,* that is, very slightly resistant, and it should be strained without delay. A warmed serving dish should be ready, and the *pasta* should be eaten as soon as it has been prepared.

An alternative, but little known, way of cooking manufactured pasta is to calculate one litre or 1¾ pints of water to every 125 gr. or ¼ lb. of dried *pasta.* Bring the water to the boil; add a tablespoon of salt for every 2 litres or half gallon of water. After it comes back to the boil let it continue boiling for 3 minutes. Turn off the heat, cover the saucepan with a towel and the lid, leave it for 5 to 8 minutes according to the thickness of the *pasta,* e.g. 5 minutes for *spaghettini,* 8 for *maccheroni rigati* which are short tubes, ridged and thick. At the end of this time the *pasta* should be just *al dente.*

I learned this excellent method from the directions given on a packet of Agnesi *pasta* bought in the early 1970s. I find it infinitely preferable to the old-fashioned way.

The addition of a generous lump of butter left to melt on the top of the *pasta* as it is served, or of a little olive oil put into the heated dish before the cooked *pasta* is turned into it, are both valuable improvements. Whether the sauce is served separately or stirred into the *pasta* is a matter of taste.

pasta most familiar to us in England, the best-known brands being imported from Naples, where the quality of the water is said to account for its superiority over *pasta* produced in all other parts of Italy.

When you see the words *pasta di pura semola di grano duro* printed on the label of a packet of spaghetti or other *pasta,* it means that the product is made from fine flour obtained from the cleaned endosperm or heart of the durum (hard) wheat grain; the cream of the wheat, in fact. What we know as semolina is produced in a similar way, but is more coarsely milled.

Some kinds of factory-produced *pasta* are made with eggs (the best with 5 eggs to a kilo), some without. *Pasta* coloured green with spinach is also sold in packets. The Italians have brought the manufacture of

TAGLIATELLE

Tagliatelle are the most common form of home-made *pasta*. In Rome they are usually called *fettuccine*. To make *pasta* at home it is essential to have either a very large pastry board (see the chapter on kitchen utensils) or marble-topped table, and a long rolling pin. To make *tagliatelle* for six people the ingredients are: 1 lb. of flour (preferably strong unbleached bread flour which has a high gluten content), 2 or 3 eggs, salt, a little water. Pour the flour in a mound on the board, make a well in the middle, and break in the 2 eggs. Add a good teaspoonful of salt and 4 tablespoonsful of water.

Fold the flour over the eggs and proceed to knead with your hands until the eggs and flour are amalgamated and the paste can be formed into a ball. Having obtained a fairly solid consistency, you continue to knead the paste on the board, holding it with one hand while you roll it from you with the other, with the heel of the palm.

During the process, flour your hands and the board from time to time. After about 10 minutes the dough should have the right somewhat elastic consistency. Divide it into two halves. Now roll out the first half, wrapping it round the rolling-pin, stretching it each time a little more. After each turn round the rolling-pin sprinkle flour over the paste; if it is not quite dry it will stick to the board and the rolling-pin and get torn. After the operation has been repeated nine or ten times the paste is very thin and greatly enlarged, but when you think it is thin enough you will still have to roll it out two or three times more until it is transparent enough for the graining of the wooden board to be visible through it. It will be like a piece of material, and can be picked up exactly as if it were a cloth, laid on a table or over the back of a chair (on a clean cloth) while the other half of the dough is being rolled out. Having finished the second half of the dough, both sheets can be left for 30 minutes. Each one is then rolled up lightly, like a newspaper, and cut, with a sharp knife, across into strips rather less than ¼ in. wide. Spread them all out on a cloth or a flat basket and leave them until it is time to cook them. All that has to be done is to drop them into a large deep pan full of boiling salted water. As soon as they rise to the top, in about 5-7 minutes, they are ready. Drain them, put them into a heated dish with a generous lump of butter, and serve them as hot as possible, either with more butter and plenty of Parmesan cheese or with any of the sauces for *pasta* which are described elsewhere in this book.

As will be fairly clear from this description, although the making of *pasta* is neither an intricate nor highly skilled process, it does require patience and time, and a certain knack which can be acquired.

People who have a gift for making pastry will probably be able to make *pasta* easily; those who are cramped for space or who find the processes of kneading and rolling the dough too irksome will be better advised to buy Italian imported *pasta*, or one of the freshly-made types now available in many delicatessen shops and some supermarkets.

TAGLIATELLE ALLA BOLOGNESE

The cooked *tagliatelle*, or whatever *pasta* is chosen, is mixed with the famous *ragù Bolognese*, described in the chapter on sauces. Fresh butter must be served as well, and plenty of grated Parmesan. This dish of *pasta*, known by name all over the world, is served in such a vast number of astounding ways, all of them incorrect (which would not matter if those ways happened to be successful), that it is a revelation to eat it cooked in the true Bolognese fashion.

FETTUCCINE AL BURRO
(FETTUCCINE WITH BUTTER)

Fettuccine is the Roman name of home-made egg *tagliatelle*, or noodles. When cooked, very generous helpings of butter and grated cheese are stirred into the *pasta* and left a minute or two to melt.

More butter, more cheese, on the table. With good unsalted country butter this is a dish worth eating.

TAGLIATELLE COL PROSCIUTTO
(TAGLIATELLE WITH HAM)

Cook the *tagliatelle* in boiling salted water, drain them, and put them into a hot dish, while in a small pan you sauté in butter a fair quantity, say 2 oz. per person, of good ham cut into strips. It need only cook for 2 or 3 minutes. Pour it over the *pasta*, with the butter in which it has cooked, add some grated Parmesan, and serve it quickly, with more cheese separately. A Bolognese dish.

LASAGNE VERDI AL FORNO
(BAKED GREEN LASAGNE)

Lasagne verdi are large strips of *pasta* coloured green with spinach. The Bolognese way of cooking them makes a rich and sustaining dish; a salad and fruit is about all one can eat after a good helping of *lasagne*. The proportions for *lasagne verdi* for six are: 1 lb. of flour, 3 eggs, 3 oz. (weighed when cooked) of purée of spinach, and 2 teaspoonfuls of salt. It is most important that the spinach should be very thoroughly drained before being mixed with the flour and eggs. Heap the flour up on the pastry board, make a well in the centre, break in the 3 eggs, add the salt. With the hands, fold the flour over the eggs and mix them thoroughly, then add the spinach. This paste must be thoroughly kneaded and worked, pushing it away from you on the board with the palms of the hands. It will be at least 10 minutes before the paste has attained the required elasticity. Now divide the paste into two pieces. Flour the board and the rolling pin, and roll out the dough again and again, stretching it as you do so round the rolling pin, pulling it out thinner all the time, and lightly flouring the flattened paste between each rolling to keep it from sticking. By the time it has been rolled and pulled about twelve times it should be like a piece of cloth which you can fold or roll up in any way you please without its breaking. Put this prepared paste over a clean cloth on a table while you work the second half of the paste. When both are ready, cut them into pieces about half the size of an ordinary postcard.

Having ready a large pan of boiling water, throw in the *lasagne* and let them cook for 5 minutes. Drain them, and put them into a bowl of cold salted water. You should have ready a *ragù Bolognese* as described on p. 190, and an equal quantity of very creamy béchamel sauce flavoured with nutmeg (nutmeg plays an important part in Bolognese cooking). You also need a wide and fairly deep fireproof dish of earthenware, porcelain, or copper, or a large cake tin. Butter it well, and on the bottom put a first coating of ragù, then one of béchamel, then one of *lasagne*. Start again with the ragù and béchamel, and continue until the dish is filled, finishing with a layer of ragù with the béchamel on the top, and a final generous coating of grated Parmesan cheese.

Put the dish into a previously heated but moderate oven for about 30 minutes. Keep an eye on it to see that the *lasagne* are not drying up, although it is inevitable that they will get slightly crisp around the edges of the dish.

A very adequate dish can be made from bought green *lasagne* or noodles as long as they are of good quality. But beware those English-made green noodles which are artificially coloured. The colour comes out in the water when you cook them. Check the list of ingredients before you buy a packet. The preliminary cooking will take 10-15 minutes instead of 5 minutes; otherwise proceed in the same manner.

SPAGHETTI ALL'AGLIO E OLIO
(*SPAGHETTI WITH OIL AND GARLIC*)

Since the cost of living in Italy is very high, many people cannot now afford meat sauces, butter, or even Parmesan with their daily *pasta*; it is often eaten with no embellishment but oil and garlic. Those who are particularly addicted to spaghetti and to garlic will find this dish excellent, others will probably abominate it. It is essential that the oil be olive oil and of good quality. When your spaghetti is cooked, barely warm a cupful of oil in a small pan, and into it stir whatever quantity of finely chopped garlic you fancy. Let it soak in the oil a bare minute, without frying, then stir the whole mixture into the spaghetti. You can add chopped parsley or any other herb, and of course grated cheese if you wish, although the Neapolitans do not serve cheese with spaghetti cooked in this way. If you like the taste of garlic without wishing actually to eat the bulb itself, pour the oil on to the spaghetti through a strainer, leaving the chopped garlic behind.

ANON (19th century)
THE PASTA SELLER
Oneglia, Museo della Pasta Agnesi

FETTUCCINE ALLA MARINARA
(FETTUCCINE WITH FRESH TOMATO SAUCE)
Fettuccine are home-made ribbon noodles. The ready-made kind will, however, do just as well for this dish, which is Neapolitan. Cook them as usual; 5 minutes before they are ready make the sauce. Into a frying pan put a good covering of olive oil; into this when it is hot but not smoking throw at least 3 cloves of sliced garlic; let them cook half a minute. Add 6 or 7 ripe tomatoes, each cut in about 6 pieces; they are to cook for about 3 minutes only, the point of the sauce being that the tomatoes retain their natural flavour and are scarcely cooked, while the juice that comes out of them (they must, of course, be ripe tomatoes) amalgamates with the oil and will moisten the *pasta*. At the last moment stir in several leaves of fresh basil, simply torn into 2 or 3 pieces each, and season the sauce with salt and pepper. Pour the sauce on top of the *fettuccine* in the serving dish, and serve the grated cheese separately.

This sauce is also thoroughly to be recommended for all kinds of *pasta*, rice, and dried vegetables such as haricot beans and chick peas.

MACCHERONI ALLA CARBONARA
(MACARONI WITH HAM AND EGGS)
A Roman dish, and a welcome change from the customary *pasta* with tomato sauce. It can be made with any shaped *maccheroni*, spaghetti, or noodles. Cook the *pasta* in the usual way, in plenty of boiling salted water. Strain it and put it into a heated dish. Have ready 4 oz. (for four people) of ham, or *coppa* (Italian cured pork shoulder) cut into short matchstick lengths, and fried gently in butter. When the *maccheroni* is ready in its dish add to the ham or *coppa* 2 beaten eggs and stir as you would for scrambled eggs, pouring the whole mixture on to the *maccheroni* at the precise moment when the eggs are beginning to thicken, so that they present a slightly granulated appearance without being as thick as scrambled eggs. Give the whole a good stir with a wooden spoon so that the egg and ham mixture is evenly distributed, add some grated Parmesan, and serve more Parmesan separately.

Sometimes *rigatoni* (short, thick, ribbed macaroni) are used for this dish; and streaky salt pork rather than ham or bacon.

SPAGHETTI ALLA MATRICIANA
(SPAGHETTI WITH SALT PORK AND TOMATO)
A Roman dish, often served in the *trattorie* of Trastevere.

For the sauce melt a tablespoonful of pork fat

1930S *ADVERTISING*
PASTE ALIMENTARI
for *Pastificio Triestino*

in a saucepan and in this fry a chopped onion; add about 3 oz. of pickled pork cut into short strips. When it has cooked a few minutes, add 1 lb. of skinned and chopped tomatoes. Cook over a fast flame for about 5 minutes only so that the tomatoes retain their fresh taste. Cook about ¾ lb. of spaghetti (for four or five), and as soon as it is strained and in a hot dish, pour the well-seasoned sauce over it.

Instead of Parmesan, grated *pecorino Romano* cheese is eaten with *spaghetti alla matriciana* (and with many *pasta* dishes). *Pecorino* is a hard and pungent sheep's milk cheese, with a similar texture to Parmesan; in Italy it is a good deal cheaper than the best-quality Parmesan. On the rare occasions when I have come across *pecorino* in London it has cost as much as, or more than, Parmesan.

PAPPARDELLE CON LA LEPRE
(PAPPARDELLE OR TAGLIATELLE WITH HARE SAUCE)
When you have a hare, of which the saddle is to be roasted separately, the legs can be stewed to make this admirable sauce for *pasta*. Cut all the meat of the hare off the bones, and divide it into small strips. In a thick pan melt some pork fat and 3 or 4 oz. of Italian *pancetta* (cured belly of pork obtainable in Italian delicatessens). Add a sliced onion, a piece of celery cut into strips, and a clove of garlic. When these have browned a little put in the pieces of hare, half a dozen dried mushrooms, previously soaked in water for ten minutes, a generous amount of fresh or dried thyme or marjoram, salt and pepper. Let the pieces of hare simmer for a few minutes, then add a good tablespoonful of flour. When this has thickened add half a tumbler of red wine or about half that quantity of Marsala. Let this reduce a little, and pour in ½-¾ pint of hot stock or water. Cover the pan, and cook on a moderate fire for a good hour; the mixture should be of the consistency of a good thick sauce by the time it has finished cooking. Before serving, stir in a few drops of lemon juice and a teaspoonful of grated lemon peel.

Cook the *pappardelle* (wide ribbon noodles), which can be either home-made or bought in Italian groceries, in plenty of boiling salted water for 10-15 minutes according to the quality (freshly made noodles or *tagliatelle* need only a few minutes' cooking), put them into the heated serving dish, stir in grated Parmesan and the hare sauce, and serve more cheese separately. The sauce can also be served separately in a bowl, which is perhaps the better method. A Tuscan dish.

TRENETTE COL PESTO
(TRENETTE WITH PESTO)
Trenette are the Genoese version of fine *pasta*, about the thickness of a match, and the same shape, but in long pieces. *Pesto* is the marvellous Genoese basil sauce described on pp. 193-4. The *pasta* is cooked as usual, and when it is ready in the serving dish, about 2 tablespoonfuls of *pesto* (which is neither cooked nor heated) are heaped up on the top, and on top of the *pesto* a large piece of butter. The butter and the sauce are mixed into the *pasta* at the table. Grated Parmesan or *pecorino* are served separately. This is perhaps the best *pasta* dish in the whole of Italy. Spaghetti, *lasagne, tagliatelle*, in fact any *pasta* you fancy, can be served with *pesto*.

SPAGHETTI ALLE VONGOLE
(SPAGHETTI WITH CLAMS AND TOMATO SAUCE)
One of the regular dishes of Roman restaurants as well as of Naples and the southern coast.

Vongole are small clams, unobtainable in England except in tins. Try using mussels or cockles, but fresh ones, not the lethally vinegared kind in jars.

For four people, buy 4 pints of cockles if they are in their shells, ½ lb. if they are already cooked and shelled. If using mussels, allow 5 pints for four people.

Clean the shellfish carefully, scrubbing them first and leaving them under running water until all the grit and sand have disappeared. Put them into a pan over a fairly fast flame and let the shells open. Strain them. Remove the shells. In a little warmed olive oil, sauté a chopped onion and 2 or 3 cloves of garlic (more if you like). Add 1½ lb. of chopped and skinned ripe tomatoes (or the contents of a 1 lb. tin of Italian peeled tomatoes), and when this has been reduced somewhat, add the clams, cockles, or mussels and a handful of chopped parsley. As soon as the shellfish are hot the sauce is ready. Pour it over the cooked spaghetti in the dish.

Cheese is never served with *spaghetti alle vongole*.

If ready-cooked cockles are bought from a fishmonger, keep them in a colander under running water for as long as possible, for they are sure to be gritty and probably salty.

PASTA CON LE SARDE
(PASTA WITH SALTED SARDINES)
One of the famous dishes of Sicily.

The *pasta* is mixed with a tomato sauce, salted sardines or anchovies, onions, pine nuts, sultanas, saffron, and fennel.

I have never experienced this dish in its native country. Paolo Monelli (*Il Ghiottone Errante*, 1935) describes it as discordant but exhilarating.

1930S *ADVERTISING*
PASTA ALL'UOVO
for *Pastificio Triestino*

SPAGHETTI ALL'OLIO, AGLIO E SAETINI
(SPAGHETTI WITH OIL, GARLIC AND RED PEPPER)
Cook the spaghetti in the usual way, put it into a hot dish, and pour over it a generous amount of very hot olive oil in which have been fried several coarsely-chopped cloves of garlic and some ground red pepper. (Dried red peppers to be ground up for this dish can be bought in Italian delicatessens.)

PASTA ALLA CHITARRA
Alla chitarra is the Abruzzesi fashion of making *pasta*. The *chitarra* is a wooden board with wire strings (hence the name – guitar) on which the prepared *pasta* dough is cut, forming long thin strips. The sauce may be simply olive oil and strips of hot red pepper, of which the Abruzzesi are extremely fond, or *paesana* (p. 70) or Genovese (p. 190).

The Abruzzi region produces good cooks; their food has a particularly savoury countrified quality, not refined, but with much character, deriving from local hams, cheese, and rustic garlic sausages.

PASTA ASCIUTTA ALLA MARCHIGIANA
(A DISH OF PASTA FROM THE MARCHE)
Bread dough instead of the ordinary *pasta* dough is used for this dish. When you are making bread, or a *pizza*, keep aside some of the dough, roll it out thin, cut into strips as for *tagliatelle*, and leave to rise. Cook as for *pasta*, and serve with a meat sauce or any other sauce suitable to *pasta*.

This recipe, and the one which follows it, were given to me by the late Lord Westbury, author of an interesting cookery book, *With Gusto and Relish* (Deutsch, 1957), which contains some good Italian recipes.

PASTICCIO DI MACCHERONI ALL'ANZIANA
(ANZIO MACARONI PIE)
Line a soufflé dish with sweetened short dough (see the recipe for *pasticcio di anolini*). Fill with cooked spaghetti (rather underdone) and a layer of minced beef or veal, mixed with a little grated orange peel; moisten with a very little good stock; season highly with salt, pepper, and cinnamon. Cover with more dough and bake in a slow to moderate oven. Turn out of the dish and serve very hot. A meat sauce can be served with it.

TONNELLINI CON FUNGHI E PISELLI
(TONNELLINI WITH MUSHROOMS AND GREEN PEAS)
Tonnellini are very fine, match like noodles, home-made with fresh egg *pasta* dough. This dish can also be made with spaghetti.

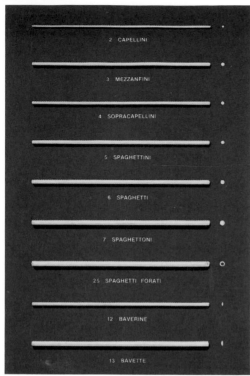

2 CAPELLINI

3 MEZZANFINI

4 SOPRACAPELLINI

5 SPAGHETTINI

6 SPAGHETTI

7 SPAGHETTONI

25 SPAGHETTI FORATI

12 BAVERINE

13 BAVETTE

168 RADICCHIO

165 BARBINA

167 RADICCHINO

170 NASTRINI

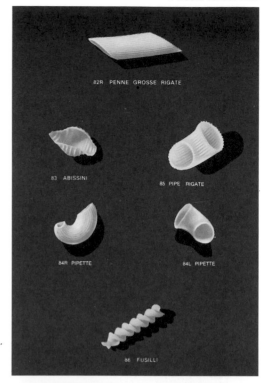

82R PENNE GROSSE RIGATE

83 ABISSINI

85 PIPE RIGATE

84R PIPETTE

84L PIPETTE

86 FUSILLI

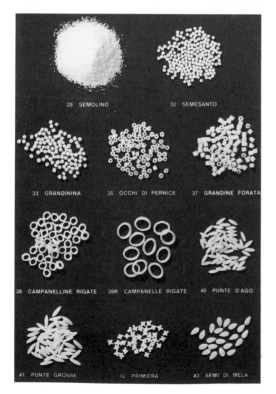

29 SEMOLINO

32 SEMESANTO

33 GRANDININA

35 OCCHI DI PERNICE

37 GRANDINE FORATA

38 CAMPANELLINE RIGATE

39R CAMPANELLE RIGATE

40 PUNTE D'AGO

41 PUNTE GROSSE

42 PRIMIERA

43 SEMI DI MELA

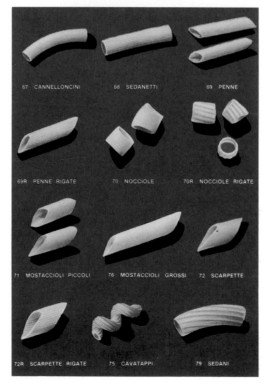

67 CANNELLONCINI

68 SEDANETTI

69 PENNE

69R PENNE RIGATE

70 NOCCIOLE

70R NOCCIOLE RIGATE

71 MOSTACCIOLI PICCOLI

76 MOSTACCIOLI GROSSI

72 SCARPETTE

72R SCARPETTE RIGATE

75 CAVATAPPI

79 SEDANI

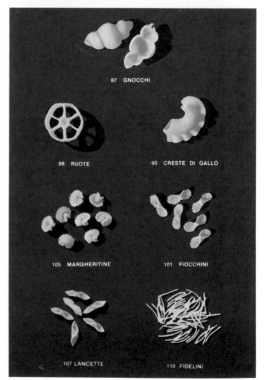

87 GNOCCHI

88 RUOTE

90 CRESTE DI GALLO

105 MARGHERITINE

101 FIOCCHINI

107 LANCETTE

110 FIDELINI

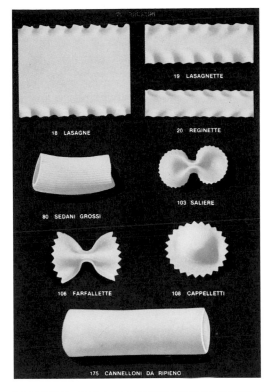

18 LASAGNE
19 LASAGNETTE
20 REGINETTE
80 SEDANI GROSSI
103 SALIERE
106 FARFALLETTE
108 CAPPELLETTI
175 CANNELLONI DA RIPIENO

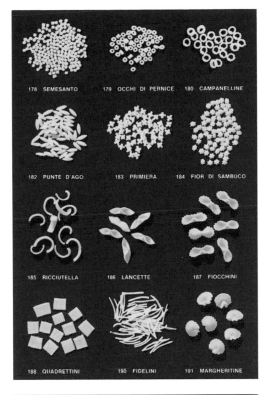

178 SEMESANTO
179 OCCHI DI PERNICE
180 CAMPANELLINE
182 PUNTE D'AGO
183 PRIMIERA
184 FIOR DI SAMBUCO
185 RICCIUTELLA
186 LANCETTE
187 FIOCCHINI
188 QUADRETTINI
190 FIDELINI
191 MARGHERITINE

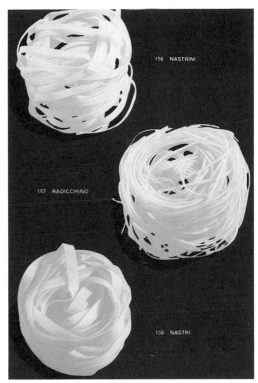

156 NASTRINI
157 RADICCHINO
158 NASTRI

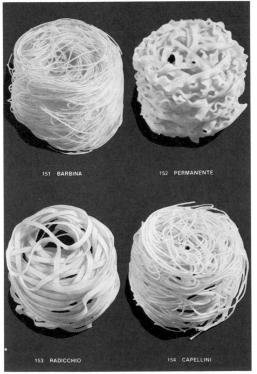

151 BARBINA
152 PERMANENTE
153 RADICCHIO
154 CAPELLINI

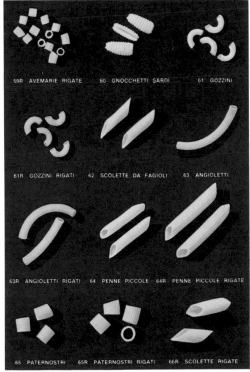

59R AVEMARIE RIGATE
60 GNOCCHETTI SARDI
61 GOZZINI
61R GOZZINI RIGATI
62 SCOLETTE DA FAGIOLI
63 ANGIOLETTI
63R ANGIOLETTI RIGATI
64 PENNE PICCOLE
64R PENNE PICCOLE RIGATE
65 PATERNOSTRI
65R PATERNOSTRI RIGATI
66R SCOLETTE RIGATE

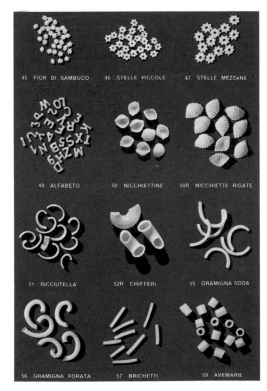

45 FIOR DI SAMBUCO
46 STELLE PICCOLE
47 STELLE MEZZANE
49 ALFABETO
50 NICCHIETTINE
50R NICCHIETTE RIGATE
51 RICCIUTELLA
52R CHIFFERI
55 GRAMIGNA SODA
56 GRAMIGNA FORATA
57 BRICHETTI
59 AVEMARIE

ANON (19th century)
THE MACARONI SELLER
Oneglia, Museo della Pasta Agnesi

The sauce consists of ½ lb. of mushrooms cut into thin slices, 2 oz. of bacon in small squares, and 1 lb. of green peas. Cook the green peas in butter with the bacon and an onion, adding a very little water. After 10 minutes add the mushrooms.

When the peas and mushrooms are cooked, pour them over the prepared *pasta*, and serve cheese separately.

TONNARELLE ALLA PAESANA
(*TONNARELLE WITH CURED PORK AND MUSHROOMS*)
Yet another variety of thinly-cut *pasta*, very little different from *tonnellini* and *tagliolini*. *Alla paesana* they are served with a thick ragù made with ½ lb. of finely sliced mushrooms and ¼ lb. of diced cured pork stewed together in butter. When the mushrooms are cooked stir a handful of grated cheese into the sauce so that it amalgamates with the butter. Pour it over the *pasta* and add fresh butter. More cheese separately.

TAGLIATELLE ALLA PAESANA
(*TAGLIATELLE WITH TOMATOES, PROSCIUTTO AND PORK*)
½ lb. of mushrooms, ¼ lb. of fresh tomatoes, 2 oz. of *prosciutto*, 2 oz. of cold roast pork, garlic, parsley, basil, salt and pepper, oil, cheese.

Wash the mushrooms and cut them into fine slices; cook them gently, in a frying-pan or small saucepan, in a little oil. Add the *prosciutto*, cut into small pieces, a chopped clove of garlic, then the peeled tomatoes, cut in small pieces. When they have cooked for 5 minutes add the cooked pork, also cut in thin pieces, and the herbs and seasoning. Mix this sauce into the cooked and drained *pasta* (12 to 16 oz.) in a deep, heated dish. Stir in 2 table-spoonfuls of grated Parmesan, and serve more cheese separately.

To make a richer dish, add 2 or 3 eggs to the sauce and cook them until they are almost scrambled, as for *carbonara* (p. 66).

For four to six people, according to their capacity.

SPAGHETTI COL TONNO
(*SPAGHETTI AND TUNNY FISH SAUCE*)
Spaghetti cooked in the usual way, served with butter and the *salsa di tonno* described on p. 193.

PASTA CON LA RICOTTA
(*PASTA WITH RICOTTA*)
For 10 oz. of *pasta* allow 6 oz. of *ricotta* or home-made cream cheese, 2 oz. of Parmesan, ½ oz. of butter, nutmeg, salt, black pepper.

Pound the cream cheese until it is smooth; add the grated Parmesan, and season with a little salt, nutmeg, and black pepper.

When the *pasta* is cooked, put it in a hot dish and stir the cheese mixture into it. Add the butter and put the dish into a warm oven for 2 minutes, so that the cheese melts a little.

CHIOCCIOLE AL MASCHERPONE E NOCE
(*PASTA SHELLS WITH CREAM CHEESE AND WALNUTS*)
Mascherpone is a pure, double cream cheese made in Northern Italy, sometimes eaten with sugar and strawberries in the same way as the French Crémets and Cœur à la Crème. We have several varieties of double cream cheese here. None has the finesse of mascherpone but there are one or two which make a most excellent sauce for *pasta*.

Boil 6 to 8 oz. of *pasta* shells. Some are very hard, and take as long as 20 minutes; and although they are small they need just as large a

proportion of water for the cooking as other factory-made *paste*.

The sauce is prepared as follows: in a fire-proof serving dish melt a lump of butter, and for 3 people 4 to 6 oz. of double-cream cheese. It must just gently heat, not boil. Into this mixture put your cooked and drained *pasta*. Turn it round and round, adding two or three spoonfuls of grated Parmesan. Add 2 oz. or so (shelled weight) of roughly chopped walnuts. Serve more grated cheese separately.

This is an exquisite dish when well prepared, but it is filling and rich, so a little goes a long way.

SPAGHETTI CON SALSA DI ZUCCHINE
(*SPAGHETTI WITH BABY MARROWS*)

Cut a good quantity (about 1½ lb.) of small unpeeled marrows into thin rounds. Sprinkle them with salt and put them in a colander so that the water drains away.

Fry them gently in oil or butter, or a mixture of the two, and when they are soft pour them over a dish of spaghetti or any other *pasta*.

A way of serving spaghetti which I believe is known only in the south, more particularly in Positano.

G. DUROI (19th century)
EATING MACARONI
Paris, Bibliothèque des Arts Decoratifs

SPINELLI (19th century)
GOLDEN RAIN
Florence, Hotel Monna Lisa

RAVIOLI, GNOCCHI ETC.

 NYONE WHO HAS THE TIME AND THE INITIATIVE will find it worth making an effort to master the confection of the paste and the stuffings for *anolini, cappelletti, tortelli di erbette*, or any of the ravioli family described in the pages which follow. They are among the best and most original of all Italian dishes. At what stage of Italian cooking these dishes originated I do not know, but they have certainly been evolving for over 300 years, for Garzoni, writing in the sixteenth century, mentions *gnocchi, tortelli, tortelletti, ritortelli, truffoli, ravioli*. . . . I cannot believe that anyone who has once tasted them in their genuine form would ever again care to eat the absurd travesties sold as ravioli in this country, or served in the restaurants under a blanket of tomato sauce, and with what should be their delicate texture killed by a hard brown crust. In Italy the whole object of these little cases of paste is the delicacy and variety of the stuffings which they contain, and there is great rivalry between the different provinces of central and northern Italy as to the merits of their respective traditional stuffings for *tortellini, agnolotti, anolini, ravioli*, and the rest. It follows that, having gone to the trouble of evolving these very elegant dishes, nobody wants to eat them drowned with an overpowering sauce. They are served either in a clear consommé, as a *minestra in brodo*, or with butter and cheese, as *minestra asciutta*, both forms in which the subtlety of the stuffing and the excellence of the home-made paste can be fully appreciated.

As far as the making of this paste is concerned the best ravioli is made with egg paste, in the way described for *tagliatelle* (p. 64), but to those unfamiliar with the process I would suggest first experimenting with the paste given for the *ravioli caprese* (p. 74), which is very much simpler and, although unorthodox, gives excellent results for any of the dishes here described.

Those, however, who have neither time nor inclination to experiment with new techniques should at least try some of the stuffings, for instance the highly original spinach and cream-cheese mixture of the *tortelli di erbette* or the really remarkable pork and veal stuffing of *cappelletti*, and use them for some more familiar dish, perhaps stuffed pancakes, or patties, or little *vol-au-vents*.

As for the *gnocchi* family, their merits as inexpensive, attractive, and original little dishes will be quickly perceived; they are easier to make than ravioli, as no rolling out of paste is involved. The spinach and cream cheese *gnocchi* described on pp. 78-9 are particularly to be recommended. They are simple enough to make.

RAVIOLI CAPRESE
(CAPRI RAVIOLI)

This recipe was the one used by Antonio, who cooked for Norman Douglas. Edwin Cerio, the Caprese writer, told me that the only herb in the filling should be marjoram, and that to put basil as well was a 'foreign habit'. Slightly differing versions of the cheese stuffing are made in other parts of Italy.

For the paste, mix 2 oz. of butter with ½ lb. of flour. Add salt and enough *boiling* water (approximately a cupful) to make a stiff dough. Knead it a little, divide it into two parts, and roll each one out on a floured board. This is a very easy paste to work, and takes less time than the paste made with eggs. It is quickly rolled out very thin and need not be stretched round the rolling-pin like egg paste.

If you have not a sufficiently large board, divide the dough into four parts, as it is impossible to get the sheets of paste thin enough if space on the board is inadequate.

When making this or any other paste, remember to have a clean cloth or towel ready on a table or dresser on which to lay the ready-prepared sheets of paste; and while the rest are being rolled out cover them with another cloth or they will, even in a short time, become crusty, which will cause the paste to break when the filling and cutting out of the ravioli is to be done. Remember also to have a bowl of flour ready to hand; the surface of the paste must be repeatedly sprinkled with flour while it is being rolled out to prevent it from sticking; turn it over fairly often so that both sides are well floured.

Paste for ravioli should be as thin as is consistent with it remaining intact and not tearing during the filling and cutting-out process. Having made the paste once or twice, knowledge of the right manageable thickness comes automatically.

Lastly, do not forget the salt.

For the filling mix together 4 oz. of grated Parmesan and 6 oz. of *caciotta* (a sheep's milk cheese made both in Tuscany and in the south; there is a local one made in Capri from goat's milk – in England use *provolone* or gruyère). Add a cupful of milk, 3 eggs, pepper, nutmeg, and either basil or marjoram or both.

When the two sheets of paste are ready, put little mounds (about a teaspoonful) of the cheese mixture at regular intervals, about 1½ in. apart, on one of them. Cover with the second sheet of paste, letting it lie loosely, not stretched over the stuffing. With a round cutter, about 1½ in. in diameter, separate each of the ravioli. See that the edges are well closed, but it should not be necessary with this paste to brush them with egg. Put the prepared ravioli on to a floured board or dish, in one layer only. Cover them with a floured cloth until it is time to cook them. They will keep a day or so, if necessary. Slide them into gently boiling salted water, and cook them for about 4 minutes, until they rise to the top. Lift them carefully out with a perforated spoon, put them in a heated dish, and pour some melted butter and grated cheese over them. Serve more cheese separately.

A few of these cheese ravioli cooked and served in a chicken or meat broth make a delicious soup.

Ravioli made with this paste also make excellent little hot pasties. Instead of cooking them in water fry them in very hot dripping or oil for about half a minute only on each side, lift them from the pan with a perforated spoon, and serve them at once as the cheese filling is just about to melt. Good to serve with drinks.

CAPPELLETTI IN BRODO
(CAPPELLETTI IN BROTH)

Cappelletti (little hats) are a form of ravioli which appear with varying stuffings in Tuscany, Umbria, Emilia, Romagna, Rome, and northern Italy. This particular recipe is the one from Perugia, where *cappelletti in brodo* is the traditional Christmas Eve dish.

6 oz. of lean pork, 6 oz. of lean veal, 2 oz. of ham, 2 oz. of veal brains, a carrot, a small piece of celery, a glassful (2 oz.) of Marsala, an egg, 2 oz. of grated Parmesan, nutmeg, 1 oz. of butter.

AUGUST, THE HARVEST (15th century fresco)
Trento, Castello del Buonconsiglio

Put the chopped meat and ham, the cleaned brains, and the chopped carrot and celery in a pan with the butter, and let them cook gently for 5 minutes. Add the Marsala. Cook for another 20 minutes. Put the whole mixture through a fine mincing machine. Add the egg, the grated cheese, and the seasoning of salt, pepper and nutmeg. Leave the mixture to cool. Make a paste in the way described for the *tortelli di erbette* (below) or the easier one as for the Capri ravioli (p. 74).

Put teaspoonfuls of the prepared stuffing at about 1½-in. intervals on the paste, cover with a second sheet of paste, and cut into small rounds about 1½ in. in diameter. Have ready a saucepan containing bubbling chicken or veal broth (approximately ½ pint per person) and drop the *cappelletti* carefully into it. They will rise to the top in about 4 minutes. Serve in soup plates with the broth and grated cheese.

The quantities given for the stuffing make approximately 7 dozen *cappelletti*; the right quantity of paste will be produced with ½ lb. of flour, 2 oz. of butter, and a cupful of water; or if egg paste is used ½ lb. of flour and 3 or 4 eggs.

If necessary, *cappelletti* can be prepared the day before they are to be used. Put them on to a large floured dish or board, in one layer only, so that they do not stick to each other. Cover them with a floured cloth, and keep them in a cool place (but not in a refrigerator).

The stuffing may be made successfully with all pork instead of a mixture of pork and veal.

CAPPELLETTI

To make *cappelletti* see *cappelletti in brodo* in the foregoing recipe.

To serve them *asciutti* (dry) poach them in gently simmering salted water for about 4 minutes. Lift them out with a perforated draining spoon, put them into a shallow serving dish and spread them liberally with grated Parmesan and butter. Allow 15-16 per helping.

TORTELLI DI ERBETTE

These *tortelli*, a kind of ravioli, are one of the summer specialities of the province of Parma, where a number of original dishes are to be

SILVESTO LEGA (1825-95)
THE HARVESTERS
Milan, Museo Nazionale d'Arte Moderna

found. The filling is made with the green leaves of young beets, spinach, spinach beet, or chard (the French *blettes*).

For the paste, for six people, pour ½ lb. of flour in a mound on to a pastry board. Make a hole in the centre and into it break 3 or 4 eggs and a teaspoonful of salt. Fold the flour over the eggs (without the addition of water) and knead until you have a soft dough. Divide this into 2 or 4 pieces. Roll each piece out, stretching it round the rolling pin in the way described for making *tagliatelle* (p. 64) until it is very thin and you can pick it up like a piece of fine material. It need not be quite so thin as for *tagliatelle*, but the process requires patience, until one gets used to it.

For the filling put 6 oz. of cooked spinach, thoroughly drained, through the food mill, and mix it with the same quantity of cream cheese (*ricotta* is used in Parma), 1 oz. of grated Parmesan, salt, pepper, a liberal grating of nutmeg, and 2 eggs.

Cut the prepared paste into pieces about 2 by 2½ in., if possible with a cutter which has scalloped edges. On to half the squares put small spoonfuls of the spinach mixture. Cover them with the other squares and press down the edges, moistening them a little so that they are well closed. Cook them in plenty of boiling salted water for 4 or 5 minutes, until they rise to the top. Serve them in a heated dish with melted butter and plenty of grated Parmesan poured over.

ANOLINI

The stuffing for *anolini* is made with *stracotto*, the beef stew described on pp. 140-41.

Having prepared the *stracotto* with the quantities given, the other ingredients for the stuffing are 3 oz. of breadcrumbs, 2 oz. of grated Parmesan, 2 eggs, nutmeg.

Soak the breadcrumbs in the sauce from the *stracotto* and put the meat itself through the mincing machine. Stir in the breadcrumbs, the cheese, and the eggs, and flavour with a little nutmeg.

Prepare a paste with 9 oz. of flour, 3 eggs and a little water. Roll it out as usual. (See the recipe for *tagliatelle*, p. 64.)

Make the *anolini* in the same way as for

cappelletti in brodo (pp. 74-5) and cook them either in meat or chicken broth, or dry, served with a quantity of butter and grated Parmesan.

The amounts given will produce about 100 *anolini*, so half quantities can be made.

PASTICCIO DI ANOLINI
(*ANOLINI PIE*)

A curious dish, for the pie is made with sweet pastry, and the combination of two kinds of paste, that of the *anolini* themselves with the pastry, would at first seem an unsuitable one; but the flavours and textures produced, though odd, are good and unlike anything one has tasted before. This *pasticcio* was at one time the great Sunday midday dish in the province of Parma.

Having prepared the *anolini* as in the previous recipe, make a *pasta frolla* (short pastry) with 10 oz. of flour, 5 oz. of butter, 3 oz. of sugar, a whole egg and a yolk.

Knead the pastry as little as possible and roll it out quickly. (This dish is not usually made in the summer, owing to the difficulty of making a good short pastry in the hot weather – it breaks to pieces.)

Line a deep pie dish with the pastry; put in about 4 dozen *anolini*. Cover with pastry. Make small holes all over it with a fork, and brush it with yolk of egg. Cook in a slow oven for as long as 2 hours.

GIAMBATTISTA TIEPOLO (1696-1770)
THE PEASANT FAMILY AT TABLE (detail)
Vicenza, Villa Valmarana

TORTELLINI BOLOGNESE

Tortellini, one of the famous dishes of Bologna, are little coils of paste filled with a rich stuffing, served either in broth, or dry, with cheese and butter, and sometimes with the addition of sliced white truffles. Although *tortellini* are always to be had in the restaurants of Bologna, in private houses they are still the great dish for Christmas Eve.

There are several different versions of this stuffing; a typical one is made with 3 oz. of lean pork, 2 oz. of lean veal, 2 oz. of breast of turkey or capon, 2 oz. of ham, 1 oz. of *mortadella*, 2 oz. of veal brains, 3 oz. of grated Parmesan, 2 eggs, salt, pepper, plenty of nutmeg, 1 oz. of butter.

Clean the brains and soak them for an hour in salted water. Chop the rest of the ingredients. Melt the butter, and very gently brown the pork, veal, and the turkey or chicken meat. Add the ham, the *mortadella*, the brains, and the seasoning. Cover the pan and simmer very gently for 15 minutes. Put the whole mixture through a fine mincer. Add the eggs and the grated cheese. The resulting purée should be very fine and smooth.

Make an egg paste with 1 lb. of flour and 3 eggs. Roll out as described for *tagliatelle* (p. 64), but not quite so thin. Cut out rounds of the prepared paste about 1½ in. in diameter. On each put half a teaspoonful of the stuffing.

Now fold each disc in half so that you have a half-circle, but the top edge should come just short of the under edge. Bring the two points of the half-circle together, curling the *tortellini* round the finger so that you have a little ring. Arrange all the prepared *tortellini* in a floured dish, cover them with a cloth, and leave them until the next day.

Cook them as for *cappelletti* or *anolini*, and serve them with butter and grated cheese.

Since the confection of *tortellini* is rather a tricky job, requiring some practice, this stuffing, which is one of the best of all, can be used to make *anolini*, *cappelletti*, or *ravioli*.

TORTELLINI ALLA PANNA
(*TORTELLINI WITH CREAM*)

Having prepared the *tortellini* as described above, cooked them in broth, and drained them, heat some cream in a frying-pan and put

M. DE VITO (19th century)
MACARONI SELLER AND EATERS
Naples, Museo Nazionale di San Martino

in the *tortellini*. Let them thoroughly imbibe the cream, and serve them on a heated dish. One of the very rare traditional Italian meat dishes in which cream appears. Rich and very filling.

RAVIOLI GENOVESE
(*GENOESE RAVIOLI*)

In its traditional form the stuffing for Genoese ravioli would be very difficult to make in England; but for the sake of interest and to show how greatly the stuffings for ravioli vary according to district, I give here the recipe from *La Vera Cuciniera Genovese* (compiled by Emanuele Rossi, Casa Editrice Bietti, Milano).

'Four *scarole* (small Batavian endives), a bunch of borage, 1 lb. of lean veal, ½ lb. of calf's udder, half a calf's brain or 2 lamb's brains, a sweetbread, butter, 4 whole eggs and 2 yolks, a handful each of breadcrumbs and grated Parmesan, seasoning.

'Wash the *scarole* and remove the outside leaves. Cook them for 5 minutes in boiling water with the borage. Drain them well, pressing out every drop of water.

'Cook the veal in butter, taking care it does not brown too much on the outside.

'Boil the udder for 10 minutes.

'Blanch the brains and the sweetbread.

'Chop all the ingredients finely and pound them to a paste in a mortar. Add the eggs, the breadcrumbs softened in broth or in the gravy from the veal, and the cheese.

'Make the paste, allowing half the weight of the stuffing in flour. The quantities given produce about 3 lb. of stuffing, so take 1½ lb. of flour, pour it in a mound on the board, make a well in the middle, and break in 2 eggs, adding 2 tablespoonfuls of tepid water, but no salt. With a spoon amalgamate the flour little by little with the eggs, and when the dough becomes too thick to be stirred with a spoon start to knead it with the hands, adding a little water if the dough is too thick, or a little more flour if it is too soft. This paste should have the consistency of bread dough.

'Cut off a piece sufficient to make a sheet of *pasta*. Cover the rest with a bowl, so that the air is kept out and it will not dry up to form a crust.

'Roll out the first sheet, sprinkling from time to time with flour so that it sticks neither to the board nor the rolling pin.

'As soon as it is rolled out, take the prepared stuffing and with the handle of a spoon arrange small portions in line, about the thickness of two fingers distant from each other. Cover this first line with a strip of paste, and press it down, with the fingers forming so many little cushions. Divide them with a roller-cutter. When the first sheet of paste is used up, roll out the second and continue in the same way until all the paste and the stuffing are used up.

'Prepare some excellent broth (1 litre, nearly 2 pints, for every 4 dozen ravioli). Let it boil on a fast flame, and throw in the ravioli a few at a time; the broth must continue to boil. In 15-20 minutes the ravioli will be cooked. Pour them with the broth into a soup tureen and serve them with good grated Parmesan cheese.'

CANNELLONI

Cannelloni are squares of *pasta*, cooked in boiling water, stuffed, rolled up, and browned in the oven, preferably with butter and cheese. The stuffed pancakes so often called *cannelloni* on the menus of Italian restaurants abroad are a very coarse version of the genuine *cannelloni*. Any old scraps of meat, corned beef, or cold roast mutton, gingered up with fried onions and tomato sauce, will not make good *can-*

nelloni; the stuffing should be fresh and delicate.

It is also important that the filling be put on with a light hand, or it makes too compact a mass, cloying and heavy.

The paste for *cannelloni* may be made in any of the ways described for *tagliatelle, ravioli* (p. 64), or *anolini* (p. 76). When rolled out, cut it into pieces about 4 by 3 in. Put these into boiling salted water for 5 minutes. Take them out carefully so that they do not break, and when they have cooled spread on each square

some stuffing made as for *cappelletti, anolini, ravioli Genovese*, or *tortelli di erbette*. Roll up the *cannelloni* and arrange them side by side in a generously buttered fireproof dish. Put more butter on the top, then a layer of grated Parmesan, and a ladleful of chicken or meat broth. Cook them in a moderate oven for 10-15 minutes, until they are well heated through and the butter, cheese, and broth amalgamated into a little sauce.

RAVIOLI O GNOCCHI VERDI
(*GREEN RAVIOLI OR GNOCCHI*)

Although this dish is now usually known as *gnocchi* (and the most delicious of all the tribe), they were originally, and in some parts of Tuscany still are, called *ravioli*, while what we know as *ravioli* have, as I have explained elsewhere in this book, a host of other names.

The ingredients are 12 oz. of cooked and chopped spinach (i.e. 1 lb. to start with), 8 oz. of *ricotta*, 1½ oz. of grated Parmesan, 2 eggs, 3 tablespoonfuls of flour, a little butter, salt, pepper, nutmeg, and for the sauce plenty of melted butter and grated Parmesan.

Cook the cleaned spinach with a little salt but no water. Drain it, press it absolutely dry, then chop it finely. Put it into a pan with salt, pepper, nutmeg, a nut of butter, and the mashed *ricotta*. Stir all the ingredients together over a low flame for 5 minutes. Remove the pan from the fire and beat in the eggs, the grated Parmesan, and the flour. Leave the mixture in the refrigerator for several hours, or, better, overnight.

Spread a pastry board with flour, form little croquettes about the size of a cork with the spinach mixture, roll them in the flour, and when they are all ready drop them carefully into a large pan of barely simmering, slightly salted water.

(Do not be alarmed if the mixture seems rather soft; the eggs and the flour hold the *gnocchi* together as soon as they are put into the boiling water.)

Either the *gnocchi* must be cooked in a very large saucepan or else the operation must be carried out in two or three relays, as there must be plenty of room for them in the pan. When they rise to the top, which will be in 5 to 8 minutes, they are ready. They will disintegrate if left too long. Take them out with a perforated draining spoon, drain them carefully in a colander or sieve, and when the first batch is ready slide them into a shallow fireproof dish already prepared with an ounce of melted butter and a thin layer of grated Parmesan cheese. Put the dish in the oven to keep hot while the rest of the *gnocchi* are cooked. When all are done, put another ounce of butter and a generous amount of cheese over them and leave the dish in the oven for 5 minutes.

This quantity is sufficient for four people for a first course. If they are to be the mainstay of a meal make the quantities half as much again; but as the cooking of these *gnocchi* is an unfamiliar process to most people, it is advisable to try out the dish with not more than the quantities given.

I am indebted for this recipe to Mr Derek Hill's Florentine cook Giulia. I wonder how many people who saw Mr Hill's portrait of Giulia in his Whitechapel exhibition in 1961 would have realized that this arresting-looking woman was a cook. She looked more like a Roman matron.

GNOCCHI DI RICOTTA
(CREAM CHEESE GNOCCHI)

½ lb. of *ricotta* or double-cream cheese, 2 oz. of butter, 4 tablespoonfuls of grated Parmesan, 2 eggs, 3 tablespoonfuls of flour, salt, pepper, and nutmeg.

Sieve the cream cheese, stir in the softened butter, Parmesan, eggs, and flour. Season with salt, pepper, and nutmeg. Form into *gnocchi* about the size of a cork, roll them in flour. Poach them in gently boiling water for 8-10 minutes. Lift them out and drain them when they rise to the top of the pan. Serve them with butter and grated cheese. Easier to make if the mixture is left to set for several hours, or overnight, in the refrigerator.

GNOCCHI DI PATATE
(POTATO GNOCCHI)

2 lb. of potatoes, ½ lb. of flour, 2 eggs, 1 oz. of butter.

Make a purée of the cooked potatoes, as dry as possible. Mix in the flour, the butter, and the eggs. Season with salt and pepper and knead to a dough.

Roll it out into long sausage-like rolls of the thickness of a finger. Cut into pieces about ¾ in. long, and in each of these little cylinders make a dent with the finger, lengthways, so that they become almost crescent shaped, like a curl of butter. Drop them one by one into a large pan of gently boiling salted water and cook them for about 3 minutes. When they float to the top they are done. Take them out of

1980s *PASTA PACKAGING*

the pan with a perforated spoon and put them into a heated fireproof dish with butter and grated cheese. Leave them a minute or two in a warm oven, and serve them either plain or with a chicken liver sauce (p. 190), or in the Genoese way with *pesto*, or with a meat *sugo*.

GNOCCHI DI SEMOLINO
(SEMOLINA GNOCCHI)

A pint of milk, 4 to 6 oz. of semolina, 3 oz. of grated Parmesan, 2 eggs, salt, pepper, nutmeg.

Bring the milk to the boil, season it with salt, pepper, and nutmeg, pour in the semolina, and stir until you have a thick mixture in which the spoon will stand up. (This operation is best carried out in a double boiler, which takes longer but ensures a smooth mixture.) Stir in the cheese and the beaten eggs (away from the fire) and pour the semolina on to a flat buttered dish or tin in one layer about ¼ in. deep.

When it is cold cut into rounds with a cutter about 1½ in. in diameter and arrange these in circles, overlapping each other, in a fireproof dish. Put a generous amount of butter on the top and brown under the grill or in the oven. A few minutes before serving add a handful of grated cheese; when this has melted the *gnocchi* are ready.

A variation of this dish is the addition of 3 oz. of chopped ham to the original mixture at the same time as the eggs and cheese are added. The exact proportions of semolina to milk depend upon the quality of semolina used; the finer the semolina, the more is needed.

Like all gnocchi mixtures this one is easier to work if left to set overnight. It is also easier and quicker to cut the semolina mixture into squares or lozenges with a knife than to stamp it into rounds, although the knife system does not give quite such an elegant appearance.

Semolina should be bought in small quantities, kept in a dry place, and used up quickly. If damp or stale, it tends to turn lumpy.

ANGELO MORBELLI (1853-1919)
FOR EIGHTY CENTS, 1895 (detail)
Vercelli, Civico Museo Antonio Borgogna

RICE

ICE IS TO THE NORTHERN PROVINCES OF ITALY (Lombardy, Piedmont, and the Veneto) what *pasta* is to the south. I wish I knew who was the genius who first grasped the fact that Piedmontese rice was ideally suited to slow cooking and that its particular qualities would be best appreciated in what has become the famous Milanese *risotto*. The fact that this rice can be cooked contrary to all rules, slowly, in a small amount of liquid, and emerge in a perfect state of creaminess with a very slightly resistant core in each grain gives the *risotto* its particular character.

The Chinese, the Arabs, the Greeks, the Indians, the Spaniards, the Turks, the Persians, have their marvellous national rice dishes: spicy pilaffs, golden fried rice, lovely deep pots full of rice shining with oil, mountains of dry white flaky rice. . . .

The Italian *risotto* is a dish of a totally different nature, and unique. One comes across some odd directions in French and English cookery books as to the making of *risotto*. The rice is to be first boiled and then stewed in tomato sauce, one learns; or baked in the oven, or steamed, or even cooked with the addition of flour. (The French, curiously enough, have never really taken to rice cookery.)

In Italy rice is never served *with* chicken, meat, or fish. These ingredients, if they are to be used, are always integrated *into* the dish. The one important exception to the rule is the *risotto milanese* always served with *ossi buchi*.

I have explained the making of a *risotto milanese* in detail in the following recipe. The elementary rules once grasped, it remains only to be borne in mind that the simpler the *risotto* the better. On p. 87 I have elaborated on the importance of using good quality Italian rice which is now widely distributed throughout the country.

RISOTTO ALLA MILANESE

There are various versions of *risotto alla Milanese*. The classic one is made simply with chicken broth and flavoured with saffron; butter and grated Parmesan cheese are stirred in at the end of the cooking, and more cheese and butter served with it. The second version is made with beef marrow and white wine; a third with Marsala. In each case saffron is used as a flavouring.

Risotto is such a simple and satisfactory dish, so universally appreciated, that it is well worth mastering the principles of cooking the rice, after which any amount of different dishes can be improvised. It can be served absolutely plain with butter and cheese, or it can be elaborated with the addition of chicken, duck, game, lobster, mussels, oysters, prawns, mushrooms, truffles, goose or chicken livers, artichoke hearts, peas, aubergines, almost anything you like. But not more than one or two of such ingredients in one risotto.

For *risotto alla Milanese* with white wine,

proceed as follows: into a heavy pan put a good ounce of butter (in northern Italy butter is always used for *risotto*, in the south it is very often made with oil). In the butter fry a small onion cut very fine; let it turn pale gold but not brown; then add 1 oz. of beef marrow extracted from marrow bones; this gives a richer quality to the *risotto*, but can perfectly well be left out. Now add the rice, allowing about 3 oz. per person (in Italy they would allow a good deal more; the amount rather depends upon whether the *risotto* is to constitute a first course only or a main dish). Stir the rice until it is well impregnated with the butter. It must remain white. Now pour in two thirds of a tumbler of dry white wine and let it cook on a moderate flame until the wine has almost evaporated. At this moment start adding the stock, which should be a light chicken consommé and which is kept barely simmering in another pan; add about a breakfast cupful (in American terms, a regular measuring cup) at a time, and keep your eye on the *risotto*, although at this stage it is not essential to stir continuously. As the stock becomes absorbed add more; in all you will need about 2 pints for 10-12 oz. of rice, and if this is not quite enough, dilute it with hot water. Towards the end of the cooking, which will take 20-30 minutes, stir continuously using a wooden fork rather than a spoon, which tends to crush the grains. When you see that the rice is tender, the mixture creamy but not sticky, add the saffron.

The proper way to do this is to pound the filaments to a powder (three or four will be enough for 12 oz. of rice), steep the powder in a coffee cupful of the broth for 5 minutes, and strain the liquid obtained into the rice. Having stirred in the saffron, add 1 oz. each of butter and grated Parmesan, and serve the *risotto* as soon as the cheese has melted.* More butter and grated cheese must be served separately.

To make *risotto* with Marsala, proceed in exactly the same way, omitting the beef marrow, which would make too rich a combination, and using only half a glass of Marsala.

---

*Should it be necessary to slow down the cooking of a risotto or to keep it waiting, put your pan not over a mat but on a toasting rack or trivet placed over the burner; turn the heat as low as possible, and keep the pan uncovered.

LUCA SIGNORELLI (*c.* 1441/50-1523)
STORY OF ST. BENEDICT, MONKS AT TABLE
(detail)
Siena, Abbazia di Monte Oliveto Maggiore

RISOTTO BIANCO
(*WHITE RISOTTO*)

A plain *risotto* cooked in the same way as *risotto Milanese*, omitting the beef marrow and the saffron, and using water instead of stock. White wine can be added, as for *risotto Milanese*, or not, as you please. For a fish *risotto* it is best to add it.

RISOTTO IN CAPRO ROMAN

In spite of its name, a Venetian *risotto*, one of the few Italian rice dishes made with mutton.

An onion, 6-8 oz. of lean mutton cut into small squares, ¼ lb. of tomatoes, a small glassful of white wine, butter, meat broth, rice.

Melt the chopped onion in butter, then brown the meat; add the chopped and skinned tomatoes, the white wine, salt and pepper, and a little of the stock. Cover the pan and simmer until the meat is nearly cooked. Stir in the rice. Let it soak up a good deal of the liquid from the meat before adding the meat stock, a little at a time, and finish cooking as for any other *risotto*, adding grated cheese when the rice is almost ready.

RISOTTO DI SECOLE

A Venetian dish. *Secole* are the scraps left on beef or veal bones when a joint for roasting has been boned. In Venice they are bought from the butchers especially for making this *risotto*.

In a frying pan melt some butter. In it soften a little celery and a sliced carrot. Add 6-8 oz. of raw beef or veal cut into thin strips. Season with salt, pepper, and nutmeg. When the meat has browned, pour over it a small glassful of white wine. Cover the pan, and let it simmer gently while you prepare a plain *risotto*. When it is all but cooked, add the *secole*, stir for another minute or two, and serve with a knob of butter on the top and grated cheese separately.

RISOTTO CON QUAGLIE
(*RISOTTO WITH QUAILS*)

4 quails, an onion, 1 oz. of butter, a glassful (4 oz.) of white wine, bay leaves, salt and pepper.

Melt the sliced onion in the heated butter. Brown the quails on both sides, pour the wine over them, season with salt and pepper, and place a bay leaf in each little bird. Cover the pan and cook gently for 30 minutes. While the quails are cooking prepare a white *risotto*, or a *risotto Milanese*. Five minutes before it is ready stir in the sauce from the quails, and, having added the usual butter and cheese, put the quails on the top of the *risotto* in the serving dish.

In England farmed quails are the only ones available. I'm not sure that they are worth their high price. Perhaps the recipe should be regarded as more for the history books than for today's kitchens.

RISO ALLA GENOVESE
(GENOESE RICE)

This is a rice dish cooked by a different method from that used for the classic *risotto*.

First of all prepare the following sauce: 8 oz. of raw minced beef or veal, 3 or 4 carrots, a half head of celery, a large onion, seasonings, herbs, and ¼ pint of white wine. Sauté the chopped vegetables in hot butter or oil or a mixture of the two; let them turn golden but not brown; add the meat and stir it until it has browned a little, then pour in the wine; let this reduce by half and then cover the pan; leave it to simmer for an hour, until the sauce is syrupy.

In the meantime boil 12-16 oz. of rice in a very large pan of boiling salted water; let it be very slightly underdone (about 12 minutes, but the exact time must depend upon the quality of the rice). Drain it very thoroughly, put it into a clean pan, and shake it over a low flame so that it dries. At this stage pour in half the sauce and a small lump of butter; stir it for 5 mintues over a low fire, turn it out on to a dish, and pour the rest of the sauce over it. Grated cheese is served separately.

RISOTTO ALLA SBIRRAGLIA
(CHICKEN RISOTTO)

Half a boiling chicken, a small onion, 3 or 4 tomatoes, a piece of celery, a clove of garlic, a green or red pimento, a few dried mushrooms, a glassful of white wine, seasonings and herbs, a slice of ham or Bologna sausage, rice, butter, Parmesan cheese.

For four people use half a boiling chicken weighing about 3½ lb. (the other half can be used for another meal). Remove the skin, take all the flesh off the bones, and cut into fairly large, long slices. In a thick pan sauté the sliced onion in butter or oil, and when it is golden add the pieces of chicken, the ham, and the other vegetables. Let them fry for a few minutes, then pour in the wine, leaving it to bubble for 3 or 4 minutes. Add seasoning and fresh herbs (marjoram, thyme, or basil). Add hot water barely to cover the contents of the

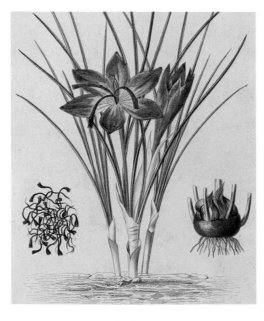

ANON (19th century)
THE SAFFRON CROCUS (*Crocus Sativus*)
Paris, Bibliothèque des Arts Décoratifs

pan, put on the lid, and cook very slowly for about 2 hours, preferably in the oven. (This preparation can be made beforehand and heated when the time comes to make the *risotto*.)

For the *risotto* allow 2 good teacupsful of rice for four people. In a large, shallow, and heavy pan heat 1 oz. of butter or olive oil, and in it melt a small very finely sliced onion; add the rice and stir, allowing it to soak up the butter. Now add boiling water to cover the rice, stir again, and when the water is absorbed add

more, cooking all the time over a moderate flame, and stirring frequently so that the rice does not stick. Season with a little salt. When you see that the rice is all but cooked pour in the chicken mixture, sauce and all, and continue stirring until the liquid is absorbed and the rice tender. At this moment stir in 2 tablespoonsful of grated Parmesan and 1 oz. of butter. The *risotto* can be served in the pan in which it has cooked, or it can be turned out on to a hot dish.

Most recipes for chicken *risotto* require a chicken stock made from the bones of the bird, but in this case the liquid from the previously stewed pieces of chicken supplies sufficient richness, so that it is really preferable to use water and reserve the carcass and bones of the chicken for a soup.

RISOTTO ALLA VERONESE
(VERONESE RISOTTO)

Make a plain white *risotto* (p. 82), and before stirring in the final butter and cheese add about 2 oz. of cooked ham cut into dice.

Serve separately the Veronese mushroom sauce described on p. 193.

RISOTTO DI FRUTTI DI MARE
(SHELLFISH RISOTTO)

To make a shellfish *risotto*, follow the method for *risotto Milanese*, leaving out, of course, the beef marrow and using either a light fish broth instead of the chicken stock or else a concentrated *fumet* of fish made from the heads and shells of lobster, crawfish, or prawns, an onion, herbs, celery, garlic, a glassful of white wine and one of water. The *risotto* can be cooked mainly with water (kept boiling on the stove) and the strained *fumet* of fish added towards the end of the cooking. The shellfish, cut into decent-sized pieces, is best heated in butter, left to cook a minute or so, and added to the *risotto* immediately before the final butter and cheese is stirred in.

RISOTTO DI SCAMPI
(RISOTTO WITH SCAMPI)

Allow half a dozen *scampi* for each person. Make a white *risotto* (p. 82). In the meantime heat the cooked *scampi* in butter with a scrap of garlic, and season them well with salt and pepper. Add them to the *risotto*, with their butter, just before the final cheese and butter is stirred in. A typically Venetian risotto.

Lobster, or prawns, or a mixture of the two, can be used instead of *scampi*, and make a lovely *risotto*. For a special dish, pour a small glassful of warmed brandy over the heated shellfish, set light to it, and continue cooking for a minute after the flames have burnt out.

RISOTTO DI PEOCI
(*RISOTTO WITH MUSSELS*)

Allow a pint of mussels per person. When they are scrubbed and cleaned heat a little olive oil in a large pan, and add to it 1 oz. of butter, a chopped clove of garlic, and a little chopped parsley. Put in the mussels and cook them until they open. Remove them at once from the pan, and when they have cooled shell them.

In the meantime have ready a white *risotto*. When it is nearly cooked add the liquid from the mussels, 1 oz. each of butter and grated cheese, and the shelled mussels. (A few of the mussels can be left unshelled, to decorate the dish.) Another Venetian risotto.

Risotto with clams or cockles is cooked in the same way.

RISOTTO IN SALTO

An excellent dish, although a tricky one, for using left-over *risotto*. Form the rice into a thick omelette shape and coat it with fine breadcrumbs. Heat some butter in a heavy frying pan, put in the rice, let it brown on one side, and turn it carefully over, so that it does not break. It should have a golden crust all over; the process must be fairly slow, or the outside will be burnt. Serve on a long dish, with butter and cheese separately.

RISI E BISI
(*RISOTTO WITH GREEN PEAS*)

A Venetian dish.

2 lb. of green peas in the pod (or 12 oz. of shelled peas), 2 oz. of ham, a small onion, 1½ oz. of butter, 3 pints of chicken or meat broth, 2 teacupfuls of rice, Parmesan cheese.

VINCENZO CAMPI (1536-91)
THE KITCHEN (detail)
Milan, Pinacoteca di Brera

Put the chopped onion to melt in ½ oz. of butter. Add the chopped ham, which should be fat and lean in equal quantities. Let it melt slightly, add the shelled peas. When they are impregnated with the butter pour in a large cupful of hot broth, and when it is bubbling, add the rice. Now pour over more hot stock, about a pint, and cook gently without stirring; before it is all absorbed, add more. *Risi e bisi* is not cooked in quite the same way as the ordinary *risotto*, for it should emerge rather more liquid; it should not be stirred too much or the peas will break. It is to be eaten, however, with a fork, not a spoon, so it must not be too soupy. When the rice is cooked stir in an ounce each of butter and grated Parmesan, and serve more cheese separately.

To make a less rich dish cook the rice with water instead of stock, which will produce soothing food for tired stomachs.

SARTÙ DI RISO
One of the few Neapolitan rice dishes. It can be made in an expensive way with a great number of different ingredients, or more cheaply and simply, but even at its simplest it needs a good deal of preparation. Make it when there are chicken or turkey giblets available. The other elements to make a good *sartù* for six people are:

(1) A dozen *polpette*, little meat rissoles made from ½ lb. of minced meat, either raw or cooked, 2 thick slices of the crumb of white bread soaked in a little of the stock from the giblets, a large egg or 2 small ones, parsley, grated lemon peel, nutmeg, a crushed clove of garlic, salt, pepper. Mix the breadcrumbs with the minced meat, add the egg, the lemon peel, and the seasonings. Form the mixture into very small, round, flat rissoles, roll them in flour, and fry them brown in oil, dripping, or butter.

(2) Tomato sauce made from 1 lb. of peeled tomatoes, a small onion, 1 oz. of bacon or ham, garlic, basil, salt, pepper. Fry the bacon in a little butter, add the onion. When it is golden, add the peeled chopped tomatoes, then the garlic, the basil, and the salt and pepper. Let it cook fairly fast until the tomatoes are reduced to a pulp. The sauce must be thick and rather dry.

(3) The giblets. Cook them slowly for 2 or 3 hours, with an onion, a carrot, a bay leaf, a piece of celery, a slice of bacon, garlic, salt, pepper, and a pint of water. Add the liver at the end of the cooking, for 5 minutes only. Take the giblets and the liver out of the stock and slice into fairly large pieces.

(4) Mushrooms. Cut ¼ lb. of fresh mushrooms into thick slices and cook them in the giblet stock for 5 minutes. Take them out and put them with the cut-up giblets. When there are no fresh mushrooms use ½ oz. of dried mushrooms. Wash them in warm water and cook them 15 to 20 minutes with the giblets.

(5) A breakfastcupful of cooked green peas.

(6) 6 oz. of *Bel Paese* or gruyère or *Provolone* cheese (in Naples, of course, they use *mozzarella*) and 2 oz. of grated Parmesan.

(7) The rice. Boil 12 oz. of rice in a large quantity of boiling salted water for 12 minutes. Drain it.

(8) To make the *sartù*. Having assembled all the ingredients, butter a soufflé dish or large round cake tin. Spread the bottom with breadcrumbs. Put in half the rice. Over the rice arrange all the other ingredients, with a little of the tomato sauce. Cut the cheese into small squares and put these on the top of the giblets, mushrooms, peas, and *polpette*. Cover them with the rest of the rice. Pour on the remaining tomato sauce, and on the top of the sauce put the grated Parmesan, enough breadcrumbs to cover the whole surface, and a few squares of butter. Put the *sartù* in a medium oven for about 30 minutes, until there is a crusty brown coating of cheese and breadcrumbs on the top of the rice. Serve it in its own dish, with more cheese separately. To the stuffing inside can also be added hard boiled eggs, ham, kidneys, brains, pieces of cooked chicken or game. The initial cooking of the rice can be done in chicken or meat broth if you feel so inclined.

This *sartù* is perhaps a legacy from the days of Spanish rule in Naples.

BOMBA DI RISO
A dish of pigeons cooked with rice, a speciality of Parma.

2 pigeons, with their livers, hearts, and lungs, and the giblets of 2 chickens, a glassful of white wine, an onion, 1½ pints of meat or chicken broth, a dessertspoonful of concentrated tomato purée, ½ lb. of rice, a large handful of grated Parmesan, butter, breadcrumbs.

Brown the sliced onion in butter, then put in the pigeons whole, and the giblets, livers, hearts, and lungs, which altogether constitute what the Italians term the *rigaglie*, of the pigeons and chickens, cut into pieces. When they are all browned add the tomato purée; let it amalgamate with the butter before adding the white wine. Season the pigeons, and add some of the broth. Simmer gently, adding a little more broth from time to time, for 1½ hours.

Now cook a plain *risotto* with a small onion, butter, and water. Towards the end of the cooking add the sauce from the pigeons, all the giblets, a handful of grated Parmesan, and a good lump of butter, and take the *risotto* from the fire before it is completely cooked.

Now sprinkle breadcrumbs over the bottom of a large round mould or cake tin, about 2 in. deep. Put in half the rice, then the pigeons, each cut into four neat pieces. Add a little extra butter, and moisten with a small quantity of concentrated tomato dissolved in broth. Cover with the rest of the rice. Spread breadcrumbs over the top. Cook in a slow oven for 1-1½ hours.

RISO IN BIANCO
(BOILED RICE)
There are a dozen ways of doing this. The most reliable and satisfactory method is to invest in a really capacious pan (though not so heavy that it will make straining the rice a burden).

Fill your pan with water, bring it to the boil, salt it, and pour in your rice, allowing 2-3 oz. per person according to whether it is for a first or main dish. The rice need not, and in my experience should not, be washed first, but be careful to pick out any husks and small pieces of grit which it may contain. After the rice has been put into the boiling water and this is once more bubbling, any particles of dust will rise to the top and can be skimmed off, leaving the water clear. The rice is now boiling fast (a spoonful or two of olive oil floated on the top of the water helps to prevent it boiling over), with ample room to mill round so that the starch disperses into the water, which it cannot do if the pan is too small. Keep the pan uncovered, so that the steam escapes, and stir the rice occasionally with a wooden spoon. It is impossible to lay down an exact time-table for the boiling of rice, as it obviously varies according to the quality, the heat of the fire, and the thickness and size of the saucepan. The time to reckon is 14-18 minutes, and the last 3 or 4 minutes are the important ones; so until the process is familiar test it by tasting a grain or two, and be absolutely certain to keep the rice very slightly resistant. Once it has boiled too long all is lost; it will be irretrievably mushy, tasteless, and in fact unfit to eat. When it is ready, remove the pan at once from the stove and drain the rice through a large colander or, preferably, a sieve. It can then be put in a heated, shallow dish, so that the rice is spread out rather than piled up, and *without* a cover so that no steam falls back into it, into a warmed oven (the heat turned off) or over a pan of hot water for a few minutes, until it is quite dry. One of the nicest ways of eating plain rice is, it cannot be denied, with plenty of grated Parmesan cheese and an unlimited quantity of good fresh country butter, and this is a dish which may be eaten to perfection in northern Italy. The rice of Piedmont is so good and so full of flavour that it is almost a pity to pour a sauce over it, but if good butter and cheese are both lacking a sauce of chicken livers, or mushrooms, or tunny fish or green peas cooked in butter, or a meat *sugo*, can be served instead.

RISO IN BIANCO CON TARTUFI BIANCHI
(BOILED RICE WITH WHITE TRUFFLES)
One of the classic ways of eating white truffles. Prepare a dish of perfectly cooked boiled rice, pour over it a large quantity of the very best grated Parmesan cheese, an equally generous amount of fresh, cold, unsalted butter, and raw truffles cut in the finest of slices. A most exquisite dish.

RISO RICCO O RISO CON LA FONDUTA
(RICH RICE OR RICE WITH FONDUTA)
10-12 oz. of rice, a tumbler of milk, 4 oz. of gruyère cheese, 3 yolks of eggs, salt and pepper.

Put the grated cheese into a bowl with the milk and leave it for 2 hours.

As soon as you have put the rice on to boil, start making the cheese sauce, which is in fact a creamy *fonduta*. Put the milk and the cheese into the top of a double saucepan over hot water. When the cheese has melted, add the yolks of eggs and stir the sauce until it is creamy, seasoning it with ground black pepper and a little salt. When the sauce has to be left, so that the rice can be attended to, turn the flame very low so that the cheese does not coagulate or the eggs curdle; if the sauce is too thick, add a little more milk, warmed. Keep the rice very slightly undercooked, and instead of putting it in the oven to dry turn it into a buttered soufflé dish or cake tin and keep it hot for a few minutes over boiling water. As soon as the sauce is ready, turn the rice out on to the serving dish and pour the sauce all over and around it. This is a tricky dish. An easier alternative is to make it with a creamy béchamel richly flavoured with gruyère and with an egg yolk stirred in at the last minute. For the *fonduta* recipe see page 95.

RISOVERDI
(GREEN RICE)
Upon a foundation of spinach arrange a layer of boiled rice moistened with butter. Cover it with a thick cream of green peas and powdered pistachio nuts.

(Marinetti, *La Cucina Futurista*.)

RISO AI QUATTRO FORMAGGI
(RICE WITH FOUR CHEESES)
1½ oz. each of Provolone, Bel Paese, and gruyère, and 3 oz. of Parmesan; ½ lb. of rice, 2 oz. of ham or tongue.

Boil the rice, keeping it slightly underdone. Chop the Provolone, the Bel Paese, the gruyère, and the ham or tongue into small squares. Add half the grated Parmesan. Put a layer of cooked rice into a buttered mould or soufflé dish, on top of it a layer of the mixed cheeses and ham, a few small pieces of butter, then another layer of rice and cheese; finish with a top layer of rice, and over this spread the rest of the grated Parmesan and a little more butter.

Cook in a fairly hot oven, with the dish standing in a pan of water, until the top is golden. Meat sauce can be served separately, but with so rich a mixture is scarcely necessary.

SUPPLÌ
Supplì are rice croquettes containing in the centre a slice of *mozzarella* cheese and a piece of ham or *mortadella* sausage. They can be made most successfully with left-over *risotto*, and are so good that when making a *risotto* it is worth cooking enough to have about 2 cupfuls of rice left to make *supplì* the next day.

Stir 2 beaten eggs into the cooked rice to bind it. Take about 1 tablespoonful of the rice and put it flat on the palm of your hand; on the rice lay a little slice of ham and one of cheese. Place another tablespoonful of rice on the top of the ham and cheese and form it into a ball about the size of a small orange so that the ham and cheese are completely enclosed. Roll each *supplì* very carefully in fine breadcrumbs, then fry them in hot fat or oil, turning them over and round so that the whole of the outside is nicely browned. Drain them on to brown paper or kitchen paper. The cheese inside should be just melted, stretching into threads (to which the dish owes its nickname of *supplì al telefono*) as one cuts into the rice, so that a hard cheese such as gruyère is not suitable. An attractive dish for a first course at luncheon, and liked by everybody. But it needs a deft hand.

RISOTTO IN CANTINA
(RISOTTO OF THE WINE CELLAR)
This risotto, said to be native to the Veneto, is one I have not myself ever encountered. I wish I had. The recipe sounds authentic and its provenance is eminently respectable. It appeared in *Italy at Table*, a handsome volume published in 1967 by E.N.I.T., the Italian State Tourist Board. I quote it below to emphasise the elegant simplicity of the true north Italian risotto, so sharply in contrast with the elaborate and fanciful, not to say downright absurd, recipes so often published in English newspapers and magazines under that honourable name. As recently as April 11th, 1987 Mr

Michael Smith, writing in *The Daily Telegraph*, admitted that he had for long confused *pilaf* or *pilau* rice with the 'uniquely Italian risotto'. But having, as he disarmingly confessed, seen the error of his ways, he was now putting his record straight with a correct recipe for risotto. Unhappily for Mr Smith's laudable resolve, his new recipe called for 10 oz of 'pudding rice', plus soy or grapeseed oil for mixing with the butter in which the rice was to be fried, and, as liquid for cooking it in, the inevitable chicken stock made up from cubes. (Given the rest of the ingredients specified, real stock would have been wasted.)

How long, I wondered, as I read this extraordinary recipe, would it be before responsible cookery writers (Mr Smith is a television performer, author of several cookery books, and the entrepreneur behind a couple or more London restaurants) trouble themselves to discover that there is a world of difference between 'short-grain, round, Carolina or pudding rice' – I quote from Mr Smith's article – 'cooked in as much stock as it will absorb' and the large, round-grain Vialone, Arborio, and Arborio Superfino rices cultivated in Piedmont, Lombardy and the Veneto, and for which there is no, repeat no, substitute. The Superfino, by the way, is packed by the firm of Curti, and in England has been easily available in Italian shops for many years.

What then is that world of difference that I, and others who mind about such things, should be so insistent on the quality of the rice used for a true risotto? You might perhaps say what's in a name? But a great deal more than just a name is involved. Italian rice has large, round pearly grains with a clearly defined hard white core which, when cooked, remains visible and just slightly resistant to the teeth. It also possesses a pronounced aroma and flavour which the small round Carolina or so-called pudding rice simply does not have, and it cooks to a thick creamy mass, but not, unless you are unusually careless, to a mush. It is, in short, the rice itself and not the additions, the stocks, the flavourings, which make the northern Italian risotto unique.

In Italian restaurants in Italy, *risotti* are always listed on the menu with the soups, and invariably – with that one exception of the Milanese risotto habitually served with *ossi bucchi* – eaten as a first course. In a good and conscientious restaurant, say in Milan or Venice or Turin, you must wait for your risotto just as in a French restaurant you would expect to wait for your soufflé. (Don't by the way, look for good *risotti* in Florence and Tuscany. Tuscan cooks, at any rate in my experience, don't know how to make a correct risotto any more than do French or English ones.)

At Cipriani's Locanda on the island of Torcello in the Venetian lagoons it is the seafood *risotti* which are famous, and deservedly so, but the vegetable ones are if anything even more of a triumph. To make a fine shellfish risotto there in the lagoons should after all be easy enough, but to create something so subtle and original out of a handful of rice and a few spoonfuls of tender, chopped, fresh green vegetables plus a sprinkling of Parmesan and seasonings requires a very sure hand and great finesse of taste. But even in a busy trattoria in the heart of Venice, where at midday all is bustle and clatter, and where Venetians order and consume their copious midday meals at high speed, you may well be told that the last batch of risotto is finished and that you must wait twenty-five minutes for the next lot. Do you want it or not? There will be enough only for six portions. If you happened to be in the Trattoria all' Madonna, as from time to time I was in the 1960s and 1970s, it was wise to settle for both the long wait and the risotto. More often than not it would be a shellfish risotto, pale and creamy, as good in texture and taste as any at Cipriani's.

Of course it is not only in Venice and the islands of the lagoon that you find wonderful seafood risotti. I don't know what Ravenna Marina on the Adriatic is like nowadays, but I do remember one late autumn evening, perhaps in 1970, fetching up rather late and tired at a hotel there and being directed to a local restaurant called the Maddalena where Viola Johnson and I enjoyed a risotto which was quite extraordinary both for the intensity of the shellfish flavour – the very essence of the little local flat lobster, the *cicala* or *squilla* of this coast, and the perfection of the rice, which was on the brink, hovering on the very edge, but stopping just in time, of turning into soup.

What a fuss, you think, about a simple dish of rice? No, not at all. If one is to explain to others how a particular, unfamiliar, dish should be made, I think one must try to get it right, at least take the trouble to find out just what the correct ingredients are, and try to fool neither yourself nor your readers with phoney information. I should add that in 1963, when I wrote a new Introduction for the Penguin paperback edition of this book, I complained angrily about the irresponsibility of magazine and newspaper writers who made preposterous suggestions about heating up already cooked Patna rice in a tin of tomato soup and calling the result risotto, or using a scone-mix to make the base for a kind of tomato purée spread, topped with a slice of processed cheddar, the whole awful thing to be passed off as Neapolitan pizza. So it was saddening to find that a quarter of a century on so little has changed in the British attitude to authenticity in matters of the specialities of other countries.

Now I will get on with the *risotto in cantina*. The name means 'risotto of the wine cellar', and the recipe is brief and businesslike.

'First you prepare a simple risotto cooked in broth and enriched with Parmesan and butter. When the risotto is served, a glass of dry, slightly sharp, white wine is poured into each soup plate and the risotto put on top. The wine, heated by the risotto, takes on a slightly effervescent quality, extremely pleasant to the palate. The wine must not be *mixed* with the risotto; each forkful is dipped in as one eats it.'

I'm not sure why that sounds so enticing. Perhaps because those few lines do really transport one back to some very simple Venetian lagoon *cantina*, a place of refreshment something like a wine bar, where two or three basic dishes only are served. Apart from the risotto, you'd probably find a polenta of some kind, perhaps the white one, which on Fridays would accompany *baccalà mantecato*, the Venetian and Vicentina equivalent of the *brandade de morue* of southern France.

ANNIBALE CARRACCI (1560-1609)
THE BEAN EATER
Rome, Galleria Colonna

Haricot Beans, Chick Peas, Polenta etc.

TUONI E LAMPO
(THUNDER AND LIGHTNING)

A peasant recipe given to me by the Caprese writer Edwin Cerio. When the bottom of a sack of *pasta* is reached, there are always broken pieces, which are sold cheaply, by the kilo – all shapes and sizes of *pasta* mixed together. It is partly these broken pieces which constitute the charm of the dish, particularly for the children, who enjoy finding the different shapes on their plates. They are mixed with *ceci*, or chick peas, in about equal quantities. The chick peas, say ½ lb., must be soaked overnight, covered with water, and cooked slowly for 2 to 3 hours.* When they are all but ready, cook the *pasta* separately in boiling salted water; drain it and add it to the chick peas, which should by this time have absorbed most of their liquid. Stir grated Parmesan into the dish and serve it with butter, or oil, or tomato sauce. The nutty flavour and the slightly hard texture of the chick peas make a pleasant contrast to the softness of the *pasta*.

---

*See p. 30. Italian ready-cooked chick peas in tins can now be bought in England. They make a useful stand-by for the store cupboard.

FASŒIL AL FÙRN
(BEANS IN THE OVEN)

A Piedmontese country dish which is made with dried red haricot (*borlotti*) beans, cooked all night in a slow oven and eaten the following day at lunch time. The Piedmontese custom is to put the dish to cook on Saturday night so that it is ready to take out of the oven when the family return from Mass on Sunday at midday.

Put 1 lb. of haricot beans (white ones when red are unobtainable) to soak for 12 hours. Chop a good quantity of parsley with several cloves of garlic, and add pepper, cinnamon, ground cloves, and mace. Spread this mixture on to wide strips of pork rind, roll them up, put them at the bottom of a deep earthenware bean pot, cover them with the beans, and add enough water to cover the beans by about 2 in. Put the cover on the pot, and cook in a very slow oven, regulating the heat according to the time at which the beans are to be eaten. The slower they cook, the better the dish.

Serve in soup plates as a very substantial midday meal. A splendid dish when you are busy, hard up, and have hungry people to feed.

POLENTA

Polenta, yellow maize flour, is one of the staple foods of northern Italy, particularly of Lombardy and the Veneto, where boiled *polenta* very often takes the place of bread. There are different qualities of this *farina gialla*, coarsely or finely ground. Plainly boiled *polenta* is dull and rather stodgy, but left to get cold and then fried in oil, toasted on the grill, or baked in the oven, with meat or tomato sauce or with butter and cheese, it can be very good. In the Veneto it is the inevitable accompaniment to little roasted birds, and to *baccalà*. It can be made into *gnocchi* (as for semolina *gnocchi*, p. 79); into a kind of fried sandwich containing cheese and ham; and into a filling winter *pasticciata*, with a cheese sauce and white truffles.

Polenta can be bought in the Italian shops of Soho.

To cook it, boil about 2½ pints of salted water in a fairly large saucepan. Pour in 1 lb. of finely ground *polenta* (enough for at least ten people). Stir it round with a wooden spoon until it is a thick smooth mass. Now let it cook very slowly, stirring frequently, for 20 minutes. See that there is enough salt. Turn the *polenta* out on to a large platter, or wooden board, or marble slab. It can be eaten at once, with butter and cheese, or with a meat or tomato sauce, with boiled broccoli or with roasted quails or other little birds on the top; or it can be left until cold, cut into squares or rounds and cooked in any of the ways already mentioned.

For coarsely ground *polenta* use a little more water for the initial cooking.

In northern Italy every family has a special copper pot for cooking *polenta*, shaped rather like a cauldron, and it is stirred with a long stick. These implements figure over and over again in paintings of Venetian life, and the making of *polenta* will also be familiar to anyone who has read *I Promessi Sposi*,* Manzoni's famous novel of seventeenth-century Lombardy.

At the Locanda Cipriani on the island of Torcello I have eaten white *polenta* with creamy *baccalà*, a delicious combination.

*There is a fine translation by Archibald Colquhoun of *The Betrothed* (J.M. Dent).

POLENTA PASTICCIATA
(*POLENTA PIE*)

A Milanese dish. Cook ½ lb. of fine *polenta* in 1½ pints of water, as already described, and leave it to cool. In the meantime prepare a béchamel sauce with 1½ to 2 oz. of butter, 2 tablespoonsful of flour, and 1¼ pints of warmed milk. Season with salt, pepper, and nutmeg. When the sauce has cooked for a good 15 minutes, stir in 1½ oz. of grated cheese.

Wash ½ lb. of mushrooms and cut them into fine slices. Cook them for 3 or 4 minutes in a little butter. (In Milan white truffles are used, when in season; which is one way of turning a peasant dish into a rich man's feast.) Butter a wide shallow cake tin or fireproof dish. On top of a layer of *polenta* spread some of the béchamel, then some of the mushrooms. Two more layers of *polenta*, mushrooms and béchamel, and on top of the béchamel spread 1 oz. of grated Parmesan or gruyère. Bake in a fairly hot oven for about 30 minutes until there is a bubbling golden crust on the top of the dish. Serve as it is.

Enough for six to eight people.

PIETRO LONGHI (1702-85)
POLENTA
Venice, Ca'Rezzonico

ANTONIO DIZIANI (18th century)
WINTER (detail)
Padua, Museo Civico

POLENTA GRASSA
(*RICH POLENTA*)

Cook the *polenta* as already described and have ready a buttered fireproof dish. Spread it with a layer of *polenta*, and on this put slices of *fontina*, the rich buttery cheese of Piedmont, and small pieces of butter; then another layer of *polenta*, and more cheese and butter. Cook in the oven or under the grill until the top is browned.

LENTICCHIE IN UMIDO
(*STEWED LENTILS*)

12 oz. of brown lentils, a small onion, mint, garlic, olive oil.

Wash the lentils and pick out any pieces of grit. There is no need to soak them. Cover the bottom of a thick pan with olive oil, and when it is warm melt the sliced onion in it. Add the lentils, and as soon as they have absorbed the oil pour 2 pints of hot water over them. Add a clove of garlic and a sprig of fresh mint. Cover the pan and stew steadily for 1¼-1½ hours. By that time the lentils should be soft and the liquid nearly all absorbed. Now season with salt and pepper. Also good cold, with the addition of fresh olive oil and hard boiled eggs.

Enough for four or five people.

Brown lentils are whole (sometimes called German) lentils; they do not break up in the cooking as do red lentils, which are not suitable for this dish.

GIACOMO CERUTI (1700-68)
THE YOUNG PORTER
Milan, Pinacoteca di Brera

Eggs, Cheese Dishes, Pizze etc.

I T MUST BE ADMITTED THAT VERY FEW ITALIAN cooks have the right touch with egg dishes. They are particularly stubborn with regard to the cooking of omelettes, insist upon frying them in oil, and use far too much of the filling, whether it is ham, cheese, onion, tomatoes, or spinach, in proportion to the number of eggs, and in consequence produce a leathery egg pudding rather than an omelette. So instead of bewailing the legendary French omelette, the traveller bent upon eating eggs in an Italian restaurant is best advised to ask for *uova al burro*, the equivalent of *oeufs sur le plat*, which are usually well cooked in Italy. Scrambled eggs (*Uova Strapazzate or Stracciate*) are nearly always well cooked too; and when white truffles are in season a plate of plain scrambled eggs with *tartufi bianchi* sliced on the top is a lovely dish.

It is worth knowing that in the dining-cars of trains, where the food is neither notably good nor to everyone's taste, a dish of *uova al burro* may always be ordered instead of the set meal and will be brought rapidly and with perfect amiability by the dining-car waiter. So browbeating are the attendants in certain French and English railway dining cars over this question of ordering eggs or sandwiches instead of the dull, expensive, six-course meal provided that I have thought the matter worth mentioning.

The few egg dishes in the following chapter by no means exhaust the list of Italian ways of cooking eggs, but I have chosen them as being the best and most likely to contribute something to our own tables.

I have also included in this chapter some of the scores of cheese dishes which are so excellent a feature of the Italian kitchen and which provide good material for the cook's imagination in the confection of little luncheon and supper dishes.

The question of what cheeses to substitute for the originals is a matter of trial and error. *Bel Paese*, for example, melts to exactly the right consistency for croûtons of cheese done in the oven, whereas the French St Paulin, which appears to have about the same texture, becomes tough. A mixture of Gervais *demi-sel* and grated Parmesan or other hard cheese has a very good flavour, but naturally melts very quickly, so must be spread thickly. If gruyère is used for any of these quickly-cooked cheese dishes, it must be very fresh, or it will be found too hard. Provolone can be found in the Italian shops and has a mild flavour and semi-hard consistency very suitable for cooking.

About the *pizza* tribe, which also comes into this chapter, a whole book could be written. In its genuine form a primitive dish of bread dough spread with tomatoes and mozzarella cheese, baked in a very hot oven, the Neapolitan *pizza* is a beautiful thing to look at, and extremely substantial to eat; coarse food, to accompany copious glasses of rough wine. The *pizzeria*, a southern Italian institution, which has now spread farther north, is a place where you may eat a quick and cheap meal, prepared before your eyes. The variety of *pizze* is immense. The true Roman *pizza*, for instance, is made with onions and oil, no tomato. The Genoese *pizza* (also called *focaccia*) is a kind of bread, made with oil and salt, and is particularly good to eat with cheese. There are *pizze* made with mussels, with mushrooms, with ham; the Ligurian *pizza* closely resembles the Provençal *pissaladière*, with onions, black olives, and anchovies. A *pizza* in a private house will usually be made with pastry instead of bread dough as the foundation, and is rather more acceptable to anyone not blessed with the robust stomach of a Neapolitan. *Pizzette* are miniature *pizze*, about the size of a coffee saucer, and very thin, which are the speciality of certain cafés, bakeries, and *rosticcerie* of the big towns. (The best I have eaten were in Parma, where the pastry cooks are particularly gifted.) Anyone who wants a really cheap meal can go out to a bakery which has its own *pizza* oven and buy a large slice of *pizza* for a few lire, repair to the nearest *bottiglieria* or wine shop, and there drink a half litre of wine and eat his *pizza* for little more than a shilling (1953).

Another dish of the *pizza* family is the Neapolitan *calzone*, an enormous envelope of leavened dough with a slice of ham and wonderfully sticky cheese in the centre, the whole thing fried in smoking oil. It should perhaps be noted that the word *pizza* means a pie, and sometimes denotes what we should call a fruit tart or other pastry dish. A *pizza rustica* is another variety, a pastry case filled with a rich concoction of ham, cheese, eggs, and béchamel sauce.

UOVA AL TEGAME AL FORMAGGIO
(FRIED EGGS WITH CHEESE)
In china or metal egg dishes, one for each person, melt some butter. When it is hot put in a slice of *mozzarella* or *Bel Paese* cheese; break 2 eggs into each dish. Cover the pan while the eggs are cooking, but take care that the cheese does not blacken and burn. Serve in the dishes in which the eggs have cooked. A good slice of ham can be added to the dish; put it in first, underneath the cheese.

UOVA AL PIATTO CON POMIDORO
(EGGS AND TOMATOES)
Remove the skins from 1 lb. of tomatoes. Into a shallow, two-handled egg dish pour a small cupful of olive oil, and in this fry a sliced onion. When it is golden add the chopped tomatoes and stew them for about 15 minutes, seasoning with salt, pepper, garlic if you like, nutmeg, fresh basil or parsley. When the tomatoes are reduced more or less to a pulp break in the eggs and cover the pan. The eggs will take about 6 or 7 mintues to cook and should be left until you see that the whites are set and the yolks still soft. From the moment the eggs are put in, the dish can alternatively be put, covered, in a medium hot oven.

RENATO GUTTUSO (1913-87)
EGG AND CAN, 1980
New York, Acquavella Galleries

UOVA STRACCIATE AL FORMAGGIO
(SCRAMBLED EGGS WITH CHEESE)
A very nice variaton of scrambled eggs. For 4 eggs use 1 oz. of butter, 1 oz. of cream and 1 oz. of grated Parmesan. Melt the butter, add the beaten eggs, and, gradually, the previously warmed cream. Cook in the usual way for scrambled eggs, and sprinkle on the cheese when the eggs are in the serving dish.

UOVA CON PURÉ DI PATATE
(POACHED EGGS ON POTATO PURÉE)
Have ready a very creamy and very hot potato purée. On top put poached eggs, and over the eggs strew a fair amount of grated Parmesan cheese. Delicious invalid food.

FRITTATA AL FORMAGGIO
(CHEESE OMELETTE)
Beat 3 eggs in a bowl. Add a tablespoonful of water, a handful of grated Parmesan, or Parmesan and gruyère mixed, a seasoning of fresh herbs (either basil or marjoram, or parsley), a little salt, pepper.

Melt ½ oz. of butter in the omelette pan or frying pan, pour in the eggs, and cook for about 2 minutes. Put a plate over the pan, and turn the omelette on to it. Slide it back into the pan and cook it on the other side. Turn it out flat.

FRITTATA GENOVESE
(GENOESE OMELETTE)

Add a handful of chopped cooked spinach to 3 beaten eggs, and cook the omelette as in the preceding recipe.

UOVA MOLLETTE CON FUNGHI E FORMAGGIO
(EGGS WITH MUSHROOMS AND CHEESE)

Prepare 2 eggs for each person, putting them into boiling water and cooking them for 5 minutes only so that the yolks remain soft, while the whites are firm. Shell the eggs as soon as they are cool enough to handle. The operation is easier if you crack the shells gently all over with the back of a knife before starting to peel them. For 4 eggs wash and slice ¼ lb. of mushrooms and cook them in butter in a fireproof egg dish. When they are nearly ready put the shelled eggs into the pan, add more butter if necessary, and turn the eggs gently over two or three times so that they get hot, but they should cook as little as possible. Cover the eggs and the mushrooms with grated Parmesan, and serve as soon as this has melted, which should take about half a minute.

UOVA COL RISO
(EGGS WITH RICE)

Cook 4 eggs as in the above recipe. Boil a teacupful of rice, drain it, and fill 4 buttered china or glass egg ramekins with it, leaving enough room to put the shelled eggs in. Cover each egg with grated Parmesan and a little melted butter, and put the ramekins in a shallow pan of hot water; cover them with the lid and cook them for 5 minutes, until the cheese has melted. Can also be done with poached eggs.

UOVA SODE
(HARD BOILED EGGS)

Seven minutes' cooking for hard boiled eggs is quite sufficient. They are so much better if the yolks remain very slightly soft; if they are overcooked they become stodgy and acquire an unhealthy greenish hue. There is no necessity to plunge them into cold water; in fact they are easier to shell as soon as they are cool enough to handle, but do not leave them in the hot water or they will go on cooking.

RENATO GUTTUSO (1913-87)
TWO EGGS, 1980
New York, Acquavella Galleries

UOVA DIVORZIATE
(DIVORCED EGGS)

A purée of potatoes garnished with the yolks of hard boiled eggs; and a purée of carrots garnished with the whites.

(Marinetti, *La Cucina Futurista.*)

FONDUTA
(PIEDMONTESE CHEESE FONDUE)

One of the most famous dishes of Piedmont, this is not to be confused with Swiss fondue.

For each person allow an egg and 3 oz. of Fontina cheese. Cut the cheese into small dice and cover it with milk. Leave it to steep for at least 4 hours.

Put the cheese, any milk not already absorbed, the beaten eggs, and a nut of butter in a double saucepan, adding salt and pepper. Cook gently, stirring all the time. The minute the cheese and eggs have amalgamated into a thick cream pour it into an earthenware or porcelain dish and cover it with very fine slices of raw white truffles. The combination of the cheese and the truffles is so remarkably right that there is really no substitute.

MOZZARELLA IN CARROZZA

This dish, which means, literally, *mozzarella* in a carriage, is as common south of Rome as eggs and bacon in England. As with eggs and bacon, it is not easy to get it properly cooked.

Remove the crust from thin slices of sandwich bread. They should be about 3 in. long, 2 in. wide and ⅛ in. thick. Put slices of *mozzarella* cheese in between slices of bread. Beat 2 eggs in a large plate, with a little salt. Put the sandwiches to soak in the beaten egg, and leave them for about 30 minutes, turning them over once, so that both sides are saturated with the egg. Press the sides of the sandwiches firmly together so that the cheese is well enclosed. Fry them quickly in hot oil, and drain them on a piece of kitchen paper. Serve at once.

In England the same dish can be made quite well with *Bel Paese* cheese.

MOZZARELLA MILANESE
(CHEESE FRIED IN EGGS AND BREADCRUMBS)

Cut some slices of *mozzarella* (or *Bel Paese*) about ⅛ in. thick, 4 in. long and 2 in. across. Dust them with flour, dip them in beaten egg, then coat them with breadcrumbs.

Fry them in hot fat or oil. Turn them over once, and as the cheese appears to spread very slightly at the edges take them out and drain them on kitchen paper. Serve as quickly as possible.

TORTINI DI RICOTTA
(CHEESE CROQUETTES)
6 oz. of *ricotta*, 2 oz. of grated Parmesan, 2 eggs, a tablespoonful of flour, pepper, nutmeg, parsley or basil, breadcrumbs.

Beat together the white cheese, which failing *ricotta* can be either home-made milk cheese or *demi-sel*, the Parmesan, the flour, a scraping of nutmeg, about a teaspoonful of chopped basil or parsley, and an egg. The result should be a smooth paste. Form it into small croquettes (the amount given will make about 8), roll them in flour, the beaten egg, and breadcrumbs. Fry them in hot fat, butter, or, best of all, a mixture of oil and butter. There need not be a large quantity of fat, nor should it be boiling when the croquettes are put in.

The croquettes must be turned over once so that they are evenly fried, and then drained on to a piece of kitchen paper.

These croquettes make an excellent little luncheon dish, or can accompany a meat course, such as escalope of veal or roast chicken.

CROSTINI DI PROVATURA
(CHEESE CROÛTONS)
Provatura is a Roman cheese which has now almost disappeared from the market, and these *crostini*, a dish to be found in nearly every Roman *trattoria*, are now usually made with *mozzarella* cheese, although they still go by the name of *provatura*.

Cut rounds of bread from a small French loaf, rather less than ¼ in. thick. On each slice put a thick slice of cheese (*Bel Paese, provolone,* or gruyère). Arrange them in a long dish, each one slightly overlapping the other. Put the dish in a fairly hot oven and cook them about 7 minutes. The exact time and heat of the oven can only be ascertained by experience. This is a little dish so simple and excellent that it is worth making the experiment to get it right.

In the meantime, chop up 4 or 5 fillets of anchovies in oil. Heat them in 2 oz. of melted butter (for 6 to 8 crostini).

Pour this sauce over the crostini as soon as they come out of the oven, and serve at once. The bread should be fairly crisp, the cheese just melting but not spread all over the dish.

FRITTELLE
Make a paste in exactly the same way as described for the Caprese ravioli (p. 74).

Divide the paste into 2-in. squares. On one half of the squares lay small pieces of soft cheese such as *Bel Paese*. Cover with the other squares of paste, and see that the edges are well pressed down. Fry the *frittelle* in very hot oil or dripping. They puff out; and with the melting cheese inside, served *extremely hot*, they are excellent. If the fat is really hot they only need a minute or two in the frying pan.

FRITTATINE IMBOTTITE
(STUFFED PANCAKES)
Make a pancake batter with ¼ lb. of flour, a tablespoonful of olive oil, an egg, ¼ pint of milk, ¼ pint of water, salt.

Put the flour in a bowl, stir in a teaspoonful of salt, the olive oil, the egg, water and milk. Stir it very thoroughly and leave to stand for several hours. This amount makes 8 large pancakes.

Make the pancakes in the usual way and put them on a wooden board or a dish. On each put 1½ tablespoonfuls of any one of the stuffings described for *anolini, cappelletti,* or ravioli. Roll the pancakes up; arrange them in a well buttered fireproof dish. Put more butter on the top, a handful of grated cheese, and a ladleful of chicken or meat broth. Cook in a medium oven for 10-15 minutes. The broth,

STILL LIFE WITH EGGS AND GAME (Roman fresco)
Naples, Museo Nazionale

cheese, and butter amalgamate and make a sauce, and the pancakes should be tender and melting. Stuffed pancakes make a very excellent first course if carefully prepared, but they are too often made an excuse for using up any old remains.

The cheese stuffing as for *ravioli Caprese*, and the spinach and *ricotta* stuffing as for *tortelli di erbette* can both be put into pancakes with excellent results.

CRESPOLINI*
(SPINACH AND CHEESE PANCAKES)

For four people make 8 to 10 pancakes with ordinary pancake batter. Prepare a mixture of 4 oz. of cooked sieved spinach, the same of cream cheese, an egg, 1 oz. of grated Parmesan and 2 or 3 chicken livers cooked in butter and finely chopped.

Have ready a béchamel made with 2 oz. each of butter and flour, and 1½ pints of warmed milk.

Also have ready 2 oz. of grated Parmesan and 2 oz. of *mozzarella* or *provolone* cheese cut into thin slices; put a tablespoonful of the spinach mixture on to each pancake, and roll it up. Cut each filled pancake into three triangular pieces. Into well buttered earthenware or aluminium egg dishes, one for each person, put a layer of béchamel. On the top put the pieces of spinach-filled pancake; then the *mozzarella*, the grated Parmesan, and a few knobs of butter. Cook the *crespolini* in a hot oven for about 20 minutes, until the cheese on the top is melting, golden brown and crusty at the edges.

---

*According to Kettners *Book of the Table* (1877) in the English of Chaucer's time the word for pancake was 'crisp' or 'cresp'.

PIZZA NAPOLETANA
(NEAPOLITAN PIZZA)

This is the classic *pizza*, as made in the *pizzerie* of Naples and the south, freshly baked, in a specially constructed brick oven, for each customer.

¼ lb. of plain flour, a little under ¼ oz. of baker's yeast, a little tepid water, salt, 4 or 5

PELLICCIA (19th century)
THE PIZZA SELLER
Naples, Museo Nazionale di San Martino

fresh tomatoes, 6 anchovy fillets, *origano* or basil, 3 oz. of *mozzarella* cheese, olive oil.

Pour the flour on to a pastry board, make a well in the centre, put in the yeast dissolved in a little tepid water. Add a small teaspoonful of salt. Fold the flour over the yeast and blend well. Add sufficient water (about ⅛ pint, but the exact amount depends upon the quality of the flour) to make a stiff dough. Knead with the hands, pressing the dough out and away from you with the palm of one hand while you hold it with the other. When it feels light and elastic, roll it into a ball and put it on a floured

plate. Cover with a clean cloth and put in a warm place to rise. In 2-2½ hours the dough should have doubled in volume. Roll it out on a floured board into a large disc about ¼ in. thick, or divide it in half and make two smaller *pizze*.

Have ready the skinned and coarsely-chopped tomatoes, the cheese and the anchovies. Spread the tomatoes on top of the *pizza*, season with salt and pepper, put halves of the anchovy fillets here and there, and then the cheese cut in thin small slices. Sprinkle a liberal amount of *origano* or basil over the top, moisten with olive oil, pour more oil in a shallow round baking dish, which should be large enough to allow the *pizza* to expand during the cooking.

Bake in a hot oven for 20-30 minutes.

When no fresh tomatoes are available use peeled tomatoes from a tin, but not concentrated tomato purée. A few stoned black olives are sometimes added to the *pizza*.

The quantities given make a *pizza* of about 8 in. in diameter, which is sufficient for two or three people, although in an Italian *pizzeria* a *pizza* of this size constitutes one portion. It should be eaten almost as soon as it comes out of the oven, for it toughens as it gets cold.

This is robust food – to go with a corresponding appetite and plenty of rough red wine.

PIZZA ALLA CASALINGA

In private houses it is usual to serve a somewhat more elegant variety of *pizza*, made with a kind of yeast pastry instead of the classic bread dough, which is certainly more suitable when other courses are to follow.

Make a pastry dough with 6 oz. of flour, 2 oz. of butter, an egg, ¼ oz. of yeast dissolved in a little water, salt, and enough extra water to form a medium stiff dough. Let it rise for 2 hours.

Roll out the pastry, cut it into two rounds, and garnish them with the usual tomatoes, anchovies, *origano* or basil, and cheese, and allowing twice the quantities given for *pizza Napoletana*. Cook the *pizza* in oiled tins or fireproof dishes in a fairly hot oven for 25 minutes, adding the cheese only during the last 5 minutes.

PIZZA AL TEGAME
(FRIED PIZZA)

A dish which may be made in a hurry, baking powder instead of yeast being used in the dough, which is therefore cooked as soon as it is prepared, not left to rise.

¼ lb. of flour, a good teaspoonful of baking powder, a little water, salt. Tomatoes, cheese, and anchovies as for *pizza Napoletana*. Olive oil for frying.

Put the flour in a mound on the pastry board, make a well in the centre, put in the salt

COCKERELS
from *Theatrum Sanitatis* (14th century)
Rome, Biblioteca Casanatense

and the baking powder and 2 tablespoonfuls of water. Make into a dough, adding a little more water to make it the right consistency. Knead for a few minutes, then roll out into a thin round about 7 in. in diameter.

In a heavy frying pan, heat enough oil to come level with the top of the disc of dough. When it is hot, but not smoking, put in the ungarnished *pizza* and cook it steadily, but not too fast, for 5 minutes. When the underside is golden, turn it over. Now spread on it the prepared tomatoes, anchovies and *origano* or basil. After 2 minutes add the sliced cheese, and cover the pan until the cheese is melted. The entire process of cooking takes about 10 minutes.

An excellent variety of *pizza* if carefully made.

PIZZA ALLA FRANCESCANA
(FRANCISCAN PIZZA)

Make the dough in the same way as for *pizza Napoletana*. The garnish consists of about 2 oz. each of sliced mushrooms previously cooked in oil, 2 oz. of raw or cooked ham cut into strips, 2 or 3 peeled and chopped tomatoes, 3 oz. of cheese. Cook in the same way as *pizza Napoletana*.

PIZZA CON COZZE
(PIZZA WITH MUSSELS)

Add a teacupful of cooked and shelled mussels to the garnish for *pizza Napoletana* and leave out the anchovies.

PIZZETTE
(LITTLE PIZZE)

Make the same dough as for the *pizza casalinga*. The amounts given will make 8 *pizzette*, and for the garnish you need 7 or 8 tomatoes, 6 oz. of *Bel Paese* cheese, 8 fillets of anchovy, oil, and *origano*.

Cut the risen dough into rounds with a teacup, spread the tomatoes and anchovies and seasonings on them, and cook them for 15 minutes. Three minutes before they are ready, spread over them the cheese cut into small pieces.

PIZZA RUSTICA
(RUSTIC PIZZA)

A *pizza* made with pastry.

8 oz. of flour, 2 eggs, 4 oz. of lard, 1 cupful of sugar, a pinch of baking powder. Make a pastry with these ingredients, adding enough cold water to produce a soft paste.

For the filling of the *pizza* make a béchamel sauce with 1 oz. of butter, 2 tablespoonfuls of flour, a pint of milk. When the béchamel is cooked stir in the yolks of 2 eggs, 3 oz. each of grated Parmesan and white cream cheese, 4 oz. of *Bel Paese* cut in dice, 3 oz. each of cooked ham and *salame* sausage, and 2 hard boiled eggs, all cut in small pieces, and a handful of sultanas. Season with salt, pepper, and nutmeg, and fold in the beaten whites of the 2 eggs.

Line a tart tin with the pastry, fill with the prepared mixture, cover with a lid of pastry, and bake in a moderate oven for 30 minutes.

A hefty dish, this rustic pizza.

CALZONE

Another Neapolitan speciality. Make the same dough as for *pizza Napoletana*, and when it has risen roll it out very thin. Cut it into rounds about the diameter of a teacup; to one side of each lay a slice of ham and a slice of *mozzarella* (or *Bel Paese*) cheese; sprinkle with olive oil, salt, and pepper. Fold over into a half-moon shape, press down the edges so that the ham and cheese are well enclosed. Cook in an oiled baking dish in the oven for about 20 minutes, or fry in deep, very hot olive oil.

CRISPELLE

Add a generous amount of salt to some bread or *pizza* dough, roll out thin, and cut into rounds the size of a small crumpet. Leave to rise for 2 or 3 hours. Fry in very hot olive oil.

SARDENARA
(LIGURIAN PIZZA)

The method I use for this *pizza* is evolved from the Ligurian one called *Sardenara*, very similar to the Provençal *pissaladière*, and for which the traditional recipe was given me in 1952 by an old lady in the town of Sanremo. Both these varieties of *pizza* are better, at least to my taste, for being without the top dressing of rubbery cheese which always goes with the Neapolitan version.

For the dough: 5 oz. flour, 2 oz. butter, a whole egg, salt, ½ oz. yeast.

For the filling: 1¼ lb. ripe tomatoes, a medium-sized onion, olive oil, basil or origano (in Liguria called *curnieura*), seasonings, 12 small or 6 large black olives, 12 flat anchovy fillets.

Assemble all the ingredients and utensils for the dough before you start. You need scales, a mixing bowl for the flour, a cup, a glass of warm water and a wooden spoon for the yeast, and finally a big shallow bowl or dish, a light-weight cloth, and a knife.

First crumble the yeast into the cup and, using the handle of the wooden spoon, stir it to a paste with 2 tablespoons of the tepid water.

Weigh the flour and butter (which should be soft, so remember to take it out of the fridge well in advance) and crumble the two together, with a half-teaspoon of salt, in the mixing bowl. Make a well in the middle, break in the egg, add the yeast-and-water mixture, fold the flour over, and with your hands proceed to knead the mixture into a dough. If it is too dry add a little more water. The dough should come away quite cleanly from the bowl and should be a bit springy, neither too moist nor too dry. Form it into a ball.

Flour the second bowl, put the ball of dough in the centre, with the back of the knife make a cross right through it, cover it with the floured cloth. Transfer to a warm place, and leave for a minimum of 2 hours. (If my oven happens to be in use at a very low temperature, I put the dough in the plate drawer underneath; otherwise it goes near the boiler to rise.)

To make the filling, heat 2 tablespoons of olive oil in a frying pan; in this melt the thinly sliced onion, and when it is pale yellow add the skinned and roughly chopped tomatoes. Cook until most of the moisture has evaporated, seasoning with salt, freshly milled pepper, and a good teaspoon of dried basil or marjoram. (You can also add a crushed and chopped clove of garlic, if you like.) Stone the olives and have them ready – halved if they are large ones – on a separate plate with the anchovy fillets.

When the dough has risen – it should have doubled in volume and will look and feel very

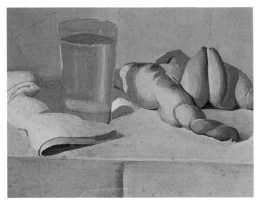

EDITA BROGLIO (mid-20th century)
BREAD, 1926
S. Michele a Moriano/Artist's collection

spongy and light – scoop it out of the bowl and knead it again.

Have ready an oiled 8- to 10-in. flan tin,* or simply a baking sheet. Put the ball of dough in the centre. With the heel of your palm, spread it out until it fills the tin or has formed a disc 9 to 10 ins. in diameter. If the dough is sticky, dust it with flour during the process.

Cover with the filling, on top put the anchovy fillets and olives arranged any way you please – throw on haphazardly as Italian and Provençal cooks do, or in a quadrille pattern if you want to make it look smart.

The filled pie can now be left to rise for another 15 to 30 minutes – anywhere in the kitchen – before you put it to bake in the centre of a pre-heated hot oven, Gas No. 6, 410° to 420° Fahrenheit, for 20 minutes. Then lower the temperature to Gas No. 4, 350° Fahrenheit, for another 20 minutes if you are using a flan tin, only 10 if a baking sheet.

The filling can of course be used on a basis of straightforward shortcrust pastry, instead of the yeast dough. But if you have a chance do try the yeast system – it is the way the aromatic filling partly sinks into the dough as it bakes, making the whole dish one entity instead of

two separate ones, which gives these pizza inventions their great charm.

Incidentally, a *pizza* of this kind makes fine cold food for a picnic – wrap it in plenty of grease proof paper for transport, and have some rough red wine to go with it.

---

*A removable-base tart tin or a flat round black iron baking sheet are the most satisfactory utensils for pizza-baking.

HOME-MADE CREAM CHEESE

Put 4 pints of very fresh milk in a large bowl. Stand it in a warm place (for example on top of the stove when the oven is alight) for 30 minutes. Now stir in 2 teaspoonsful of rennet, and go on stirring for a minute or two. Put the bowl back in the warm. In an hour a soft curd will have formed. Leave it another 2 or 3 hours, until the curd is separated from the whey. Put it in a muslin, tie it up, and hang it up to drain for 24 hours, during which time it should be taken down and the curd stirred once or twice, so that the cream is equally distributed and the whole mass evenly drained.

The cheese can now be salted and eaten at once or at a pinch can substitute for *ricotta* in cooked dishes, although its taste and texture are of course very different; or it can be eaten unsalted with sugar, or made into puddings. It can also be kept for 2 or 3 days. In this case, turn it into a clean muslin or cloth, and let it continue to drain either on a sieve or in a little rush basket or a pierced mould of glazed earthenware. Keep it in a cold place.

The quantities given yield about 1¼ lb. of fresh cream cheese.

BRUSCHETTA

Bake slices of white bread in the oven until they are crisp and golden. Rub them with garlic, and then pour olive oil over them. In the districts of Tuscany and Umbria which produce olive oil, the *bruschetta* are eaten with the newly made oil.

SCHOOL OF SARACENI (17th century)
THE FISHMONGER
Florence, Galleria Corsini

Fish Soups

 URELY IT IS CURIOUS THAT THIS ISLAND, WITH ITS vast fishing industry, has never evolved a national fish soup? It cannot be that the fish of northern waters are not suitable for soups and stews, for besides a large variety of molluscs and crustaceans which go so admirably into such dishes there are any number of white fish – skate, turbot, brill, bream, hake, halibut, haddock, plaice, to mention only the most obvious – which can make excellent soups. It is not, presumably, considering the way they are habitually served, out of consideration for the delicacy of their flavour that these fish are only steamed or fried. In any case, whatever the reason, there is a common notion in England that the only acceptable fish soup is a costly and troublesome lobster *bisque*. It seems to me that a study of Italian fish soups, of which there is a considerable variety, with ancient traditions, should have beneficial effects on our daily food.

Tomatoes, oil, onions, garlic, aromatic herbs, all the ingredients which go into a southern fish stew, we have. Obviously North Sea and Channel fish will produce a soup of different aspect and flavour from the *burrida* of Genoa, or the *brodetto* of the Adriatic, but, as we have no traditions to observe in these matters, this need cause no serious concern. Consider, for instance, the cheaper fish; the so called rock salmon is good for a stew, as it does not disintegrate; those smoked or frozen cod fillets which are sometimes the only alternative in the fishmongers' to expensive sole or lobster respond better to a bath of aromatic tomato and lemon flavoured broth than to a blanket of flour and breadcrumbs. . . . Why should cockles be confined to the pier at Southend, and soft roes to a slice of sodden toast, when these things are so cheap and make such a good basis for a fish stew? As for the vegetables, there is no need to restrict them, as the Italians do, to tomatoes and onions. Green peas and mushrooms, watercress and celery and cucumber, go admirably with fish. It is worth remembering that in the eighteenth century oranges were used as much for flavouring fish as are lemons today. Cider is not merely a substitute for white wine in cooking; the flavour it imparts to fish is excellent and original. People who like the taste of curry can use a scrap of curry paste or powder, or turmeric, in a fish stew instead of saffron; tarragon and fennel, mint and basil, nutmeg, mace, and coriander seeds (not all at once) are fine flavourings for fish. Garlic addicts will quickly perceive the charm of fried croûtons rubbed with garlic as an accompaniment to a fish broth. Here, then, in the devising of a really admirable English fish soup, is scope for inventiveness and imagination.

The last four fish soups in this section, recipes of my own, are made from ordinary English fish, and will, I hope, provide ideas on which others can base their own inventions. The two mussel soups (p. 104) can be made exactly as they stand; Dumas' clam soup (p. 105) can be made in England with mussels; and the soup with prawns (p. 105) is an easy one for this country.

BURRIDA
(GENOESE FISH STEW)

The fish the Genoese use for their *burrida* are the *scorfano* or *pesce cappone* (*scorpaena porcus*, the *rascasse* of the Provençal *bouillabaisse*); the *gallinella* (*trigla lyra*, sea-hen); the *pesce prete* (*uranoscopus scaber*, star-gazer); the *pescatrice* or *boldro* (*lophius piscatorius*, angler or frog-fish); eel or conger, the *scorfano rosso* (*scorpaena scrofa*, the *chapon* of Provence); octopus, inkfish, *nocciolo* or *palombo* (*mustelos laevis*, dogfish); *sugherello* (*trachurus*, a kind of mackerel). Clear outline drawings of all these fish, plus much other relevant information, are to be found in Alan Davidson's *Mediterranean Seafood* (Penguin).

To make the broth, heat about 2 oz. of olive oil in a wide saucepan. Put in a small chopped onion and let it brown slightly. Add half a carrot, a small piece of celery, a clove of garlic, and some parsley, all chopped small, and 2 or 3 anchovy fillets cut in pieces. After 5 minutes add 1 lb. of peeled and chopped tomatoes, or ¼ pint of freshly made tomato sauce, or a tablespoonful of tomato purée diluted with water, and ½ oz. of dried mushrooms which have been soaked a few minutes in water. Season with salt, pepper, and a little basil, and add a little water to the broth.

If octopus and inkfish are to be part of the *burrida* they should be put in while the broth is cooking and simmered a good 30 minutes. Now add a selection of the above mentioned fish, cut into thick slices, and cook for about 20 minutes.

BRODETTO ALLA RAVENNATE
(RAVENNA FISH SOUP)

In the Marche and on the Adriatic coast fish soup is known as *brodetto*.

Several towns of the Adriatic coast, where the fish is notably good, have their versions of *brodetto*; those of Ancona and Rimini are well known, and another good one comes from Ravenna Marina. It is worth while, when visiting Ravenna, to drive the five miles to the Marina and to eat *brodetto* a few yards from where the fish has been landed, in sight of the long stretch of white sand and the pine wood where Lord Byron used to ride. After luncheon, if it is a fine day, go down to the port

to see the fishing boats coming in with the day's catch; their sails are a fine patchwork of Adriatic colours, bright clear blues, rose reds, chrome yellow, faded green, cobalt violet; the nets are dyed black, and slung between the masts to dry.

Here is the recipe for fish soup as it is made at Ravenna Marina. It must be left to the imagination and resourcefulness of the reader to devise something as good and beautiful with North Sea fish.

GIUSEPPE RECCO (1634-95)
STILL LIFE WITH FISH (detail)
Florence, Galleria degli Uffizi

The fish to be used for the *brodetto* are two or three different varieties of squid (*seppie, calamaretti, calamaroni*), eel, red mullet, *spigola* (sea bass), sole, and *cannocchie* (*squilla mantis*), a flat-tailed Adriatic and Mediterranean crustacean with a delicate flavour and lilac marks on its white flesh. Also called *pannocchie* and *cicala di mare*.

First of all make the *brodo* or *sugo* (the broth, which is the basis of all Italian fish soups). Put the heads of the fish into a pan with parsley, pounded garlic, tomatoes, salt, pepper, *origano*, and a little vinegar. When the tomatoes and the fish are cooked, remove all the bones and sieve the broth. Keep aside this

broth, which should be fairly thin and of a deep red-brown colour.

Into a wide shallow earthenware pan put some olive oil and parsley and garlic pounded together. When the oil is hot add a fair quantity of sauce made from fresh tomatoes and thinned with a little water. Put in the prepared and cleaned *seppie* for they must cook for a good 30 minutes before all the other fish, which are to be added, at the appropriate moment, cut into thick slices. Cook them gently and without stirring or they will break - 30 minutes should be sufficient.

Remove them from their sauce, which will be nearly all absorbed by this time. Arrange them in a hot dish. Heat up the prepared *brodo*, and in this put rounds of bread either fried in oil or baked in the oven.

The broth and the fish are handed round at the same time but in separate dishes, so that each person may help himself to the variety of fish he chooses.

It will be seen that, owing to the variety of fish required, it is pointless to attempt this soup for fewer than six or eight people.

CACCIUCCO LIVORNESE
(LEGHORN FISH STEW)

Cacciucco, unlike most other Italian fish stews, is not considered as a *zuppa di pesce* but is eaten as a main course. Like all these dishes, it is probably of ancient origin.

It is made with the usual coarse fish which are too bony and spiny to be cooked in any other way, and with the addition of octopus, inkfish, sometimes crabs, and small lobsters.

For the broth, heat a generous amount of good olive oil in a large deep pan, throw in a few cloves of garlic, a sliced onion, a few sage leaves. Let these ingredients cook a little, but without browning, then stir in enough tomato sauce to make the broth of the consistency of a thin soup, a little white wine, and seasonings of salt, black pepper and red pepper, and a couple of bay leaves. In this soup cook first, for 30 minutes, some octopus cut into strips. Then add the other fish (the *scorfano, gallinella, pesce cappone*, all spiny brutes for which we have no equivalent in England, all cut into thick slices; some small tender inkfish, and a couple of small lobsters). Cook them all in the broth, which should be sufficient for the fish to bath in with ease, for about 20 minutes.

Prepare for each person at least 3 slices of bread either fried in oil or baked in the oven. Put these in the bottom of the soup tureen, put the fish on the top and then pour over the broth.

ZUPPA DI PESCE ALLA ROMANA
(ROMAN FISH SOUP)

The Romans are great eaters of fish soup; their recipes vary a good deal. Here is a particularly good one.

A *morena* (a kind of lamprey), a *pescatrice* (angler fish), *cappone* (the rascasse of the Provençal coast, a scaly fish of which there is no equivalent in northern waters), *scorfano* (much the same as the Provençal *chapon*; again, we have no such fish in England), ink-fish, octopus, mussels, clams, *scampi*.

First of all boil the cleaned octopus and the inkfish (see pp. 115 and 116). Make a fish stock with the heads and tails of the white fish, celery, garlic, and parsley. Strain it when it is cooked.

In another pan sauté a chopped clove of garlic and a fillet or two of anchovy in olive oil, and to this add 1 lb. of peeled and chopped tomatoes and a little chopped parsley. After 5 minutes put in the white fish cut into slices and the already cooked octopus and inkfish; let them cook a little and add the shellfish, cleaned and scrubbed very carefully, in their shells. Now add the prepared stock, and as soon as the shellfish have opened the soup is ready.

Serve it in a tureen with fried bread.

GIUSEPPE RECCO (1634-95)
MARINE LANDSCAPE WITH FISH AND OYSTERS
Besançon, Musée des Beaux Arts et d'Archéologie

ZUPPA DI PESCE CAPRESE
(*CAPRI FISH SOUP*)

Make a broth with olive oil, tomatoes, and white wine, as for the mussel soup below. In this put slices of cooked octopus or inkfish, mussels in their shells, *mazzancolle* (which are a kind of large prawn), and thick slices of *tonnetto*, a fat fish with dark blue and silver skin and pale pink flesh, not unlike a mackerel but much more delicate. (They come into season about the end of August, and are excellent fried or grilled.)

Serve the soup with slices of fried bread.

ZUPPA DI PESCE COI GAMBERI
(*FISH SOUP WITH PRAWNS*)

A soup which can be made in smaller quantities than most, as it contains only three kinds of fish: mussels, *totani* (p. 116), and prawns.

For four people, make about 2 pints of broth, as described below for mussel soup. In this cook 2 pints of mussels in their shells, a couple of *totani* previously boiled and cut in rings, and ½ pint of prawns. On the Mediterranean coast the prawns are cooked in their shells in the soup, and it is up to the eater to peel them – not only a messy business, but to my mind the shells give an unwelcome varnish-like taste to the soup. Ready cooked and shelled prawns can perfectly well be used. Instead of *totani* a few small scallops will be an improvement.

VINCENZO CAMPI (1536-91)
THE FISH SELLER (detail)
Milan, Pinacoteca di Brera

ZUPPA DI COZZE
(*MUSSEL SOUP*)

For four people, 5 pints of mussels, 2 lb. tomatoes, celery, parsley, garlic, herbs, lemon peel, white wine, and oil. Cover the bottom of a large and fairly deep pan with olive oil. When it is warm put in the onion, sliced very thinly. As soon as it begins to brown add a tablespoonful of chopped celery, 3 cloves of garlic sliced, some fresh marjoram, thyme, or basil, and ground black pepper (no salt). When this has cooked a minute or two put in the skinned and sliced tomatoes and let them stew 3 or 4 minutes before adding a glass of white wine (about 4 oz.). Let all bubble 2 minutes before covering the pan and turning down the flame. Cook until the tomatoes are almost reduced to pulp, then pour in a tumblerful of hot water, enough to make the mixture about the consistency of a thick soup, and leave to simmer a few more minutes. The basis of the soup is now ready. (It can be prepared beforehand.) The final operations must be carried out only immediately before serving. Heat the prepared soup and add the carefully cleaned and bearded mussels. Let them cook fairly fast until all are opened, which will take 10-12 minutes. Before serving sprinkle some cut parsley and a scrap of grated lemon peel over the mussels; have ready 3 or 4 slices of toasted French bread for each person, and a large bowl on the table to receive the empty shells as the mussels are eaten.

This is only one of the many ways of making a mussel soup. Other shellfish can be added, such as Dublin Bay prawns, allowing 2 or 3 for each person, but they should be bought uncooked, and the tails slit down the centre before adding them to the soup.

ZUPPA DI PEOCI
(*VENETIAN MUSSEL SOUP*)

In Venice mussels are known as *peoci*.

Warm a good quantity of olive oil in the bottom of a large saucepan. Add 3 or 4 cloves of garlic cut in small pieces and a good handful of chopped parsley. Put in the cleaned mussels, allowing at least a pint per person. As soon as all the mussels are opened, serve them in a soup tureen, with a little more parsley scattered over them.

GIUSEPPE RECCO (1634-95)
KITCHEN INTERIOR WITH A STILL LIFE OF FISH (detail)
London, Matthiesen Fine Art

SOUP OF PRAWNS AND SOFT ROES

Here is an example of an excellent fish soup which can be made with the most easily procurable and fairly cheap ingredients.

½ lb. of soft herring roes, 4 oz. of shelled prawns, 1 lb. of tomatoes, a glassful of white wine, garlic, parsley, olive oil, a pint of water.

Heat 2 tablespoonfuls of olive oil in a saucepan, put in the skinned and chopped tomatoes. Season with salt and pepper, add a little chopped parsley and a clove of garlic. Pour over the white wine, and when the tomatoes have softened add the water. Cook for 20 minutes and put through a sieve. In the resulting broth cook the soft roes for 3 or 4 minutes and add the prawns, seasoned with a little lemon juice, a minute or two before the soup is to be served. Serve with slices of bread fried in oil, and rubbed, if you like, with garlic.

SCALLOP SOUP

Another example of a fish soup which can be made in England.

6 or 8 scallops, 1 lb. of tomatoes, an onion, a clove of garlic, 2 oz. of cream, a glassful (4 oz.) of dry white wine, half a cupful (about 2 oz.) of cooked crab or prawns, a small piece of lemon peel, butter. Sauté the sliced onion in a little butter, add the chopped tomatoes, the garlic, and the lemon peel, salt and ground black pepper. Stew the tomatoes until they are completely melted, then add the white wine and let it bubble a couple of minutes. Put in 4 of the scallops (reserving the red parts) and the crab or prawns; cover with 2 pints of water and cook for 20 minutes. Put the soup through a sieve (but first removing the piece of lemon peel) and return the resulting thin purée to a clean pan, and 10 minutes before serving, heat it up, adding the remainder of the scallops cut into small pieces (but leave the red parts whole), the crab meat or prawns, and the cream, previously heated in a separate saucepan.

At the last minute stir in a little parsley, or any other fresh green herb (such as fennel, basil, celery, or chives) which may be available.

Enough for six helpings.

ZUPPA DI VONGOLE
(*CLAM SOUP*)

Alexandre Dumas gives this description of a vongole soup, '*la seule bonne qui j'aie mangée à Naples,*' in his *Grand Dictionnaire de Cuisine,* 1873.

'Into a saucepan put 4 dozen *vongole* or small clams [cockles or mussels can be used in England]. Pour over them three-quarters of a bottle of white wine and let them cook until they have opened. Drain them, setting aside the liquid in which they have cooked, and remove the empty half shells.

'Chop the white part of a leek with a small onion, add a clove of garlic, and sauté this mixture in a saucepan with good oil, add the liquid from the clams, and a litre [1¾ pints] of fish stock; add a peeled and chopped tomato, a bouquet of marjoram, and a few green leaves of celery. Let this bubble fast for 10 minutes, remove the bouquet and the garlic, stir the clams into the soup, and pour it into the tureen. Serve separately small croûtons of bread fried in oil.'

The following four recipes are not Italian; they are for fish soups which are based on Italian methods, but using ingredients easily obtainable in England. Being boneless, they will be more to English taste than most of the Italian fish stews.

FISHING (detail, Roman mosaic)
Desenzano, Villa Romana

the lemon sole, adding the prawns only for 2 or 3 minutes at the end of the cooking.

If you have some inkfish preserved in oil as described on p. 200, add a few slices at the same time as the halibut; a pint of mussels in their shells is another alternative. Cut a little fresh parsley over the soup before it is served.

Have ready 4 slices of a French loaf for each person, baked golden in a slow oven and afterwards rubbed with a piece of cut garlic. Put this prepared bread into each soup plate before serving.

Enough for three or four people.

One needs a fork for the solids, as well as a spoon for the broth.

SOUP OF SCALLOPS, PRAWNS AND COCKLES

1½ lb. of green peas, 6 scallops, 4 oz. of shelled prawns, ¼ pint of shelled cockles, ½ lb. of filleted brill or sole or other white fish, parsley, an onion, 2 tomatoes, garlic, olive oil, mint.

Slice the onion and let it turn faintly golden in the heated olive oil; add the chopped and skinned tomatoes, and after a minute or two the shelled peas; season with salt, pepper, and a few whole mint leaves; pour over 1½ pints of water and simmer until the peas are all but cooked. Add first the white fish and after 5 minutes the cockles (it is essential, having bought cooked cockles, to leave them under running cold water for at least an hour and then to make quite sure that all the grit has been washed away); then the scallops, each one cut into two rounds, then the red part of the scallops; then the prawns. Have ready a sauce made with the leaves of a small bunch of parsley, a clove of garlic, and salt, all pounded together to a paste, with the final addition of about 2 tablespoonfuls of olive oil. At the last minute stir this into the soup and serve quickly, with the usual fried or baked croûtons of bread.

Those who do not care for garlic can leave out the final addition of the prepared sauce and season the soup with lemon juice.

The cockles can also be left out, or mussels can be used instead – or indeed any fish you please.

Quantities sufficient for four or five large helpings.

A FISH STEW OR SOUP

2 fillets of lemon sole, ½ lb. of halibut, ½ lb. of smoked cod fillet, 2 oz. of shelled prawns.

For the broth: a small onion, ½ lb. of tomatoes, half a small cucumber, parsley, 2 oz. of olive oil, ¼ pint of water, mace, red and black pepper, bay leaves, thyme, 3 cloves of garlic, and a small glassful of white wine.

Heat the olive oil in a wide pan; melt the sliced onion; add the cloves of garlic, the chopped parsley, the cucumber unpeeled and cut into small dice, and the skinned and chopped tomatoes. Season with salt, the red and black pepper, and a little mace. Add the white wine, then the water. Simmer for 20 minutes. If the broth is too thick add a little water.

Cut the fish into thick slices, removing the skin if possible. Put the smoked cod first into the broth, and 5 minutes later the halibut; then

A LAST WORD ABOUT FISH SOUPS

Let those who cannot abide fish soups and detest extracting fishbones from their mouths take heart. They are not alone. For their benefit I quote what Norman Douglas had to say about *zuppa di pesce* when he wrote *Siren Land* in 1911 (it is true that a badly made fish soup is perfectly detestable, and it cannot be claimed that the cooking in Naples and roundabout is always very *soigné*. This does not alter my personal opinion that a *good* fish soup is lovely food). For the rest, Norman Douglas's triumphant warnings of the appalling fate which would certainly overtake anyone so foolhardy as to eat mussels, *aguglie*, *palombo* ('of course, if you *care* to eat shark, my dear') were repeated mainly to disconcert; he was himself the first to mock at the absurdity of food fads.

'We have a fish soup; *guarracini* and *scorfani* and *aguglie* and *toteri* and . . .

'Take breath, gentle maiden, the while I explain to the patient reader the ingredients of the diabolical preparation known as *zuppa di pesce*. The *guarracino*, for instance, is a pitch-black marine monstrosity, 1–2 in. long, a mere blot, with an Old Red Sandstone profile and insufferable manners, whose sole recommendation is that its name is derived from *koraxinos*. (*Korax* . . . a raven; but who can live on Greek roots?) As to the *scorfano*, its name is unquestionably onomatopœic, to suggest the spitting-out of bones; the only difference, from a culinary point of view, between the *scorfano* and a toad being that the latter has twice as much meat on it. The *aguglia*, again, is all tail and proboscis; the very nightmare of a fish – as thin as a lead pencil. Who would believe that for this miserable sea-worm with verdigris-tinted spine, which an ordinary person would thank you for not setting on his table, the inhabitants of Siren land fought like fiends? The blood of their noblest was shed in defence of privileges artfully wheedled out of Anjou and Aragonese kings defining the *ius quoddam pescandi vulgariter dictum sopra le aguglie*; that a certain tract of sea was known as the 'aguglie water' and owned, up to the days of Murat, by a single family who defended it with guns and man-traps? And everybody knows the *totero* or squid, an animated ink-bag of perverse leanings, which swims backwards because all other creatures go forwards and whose india-rubber flesh might be useful for deluding hunger on desert islands, since, like American gum, you can chew it for months but never get it down.

'These, and such as they, float about in a lukewarm brew of rancid oil and garlic, together with a few of last week's breadcrusts, decaying sea-shells and onion peels, to give it an air of consistency.

'This is the stuff for which Neapolitans sell their female relatives. But copious libations will do wonders with a *zuppa di pesce*.

'"Wine of Marciano, signore."

'"Then it must be good. It grows on the mineral."

'"Ah, you foreigners know everything."

'We do; we know, for example, that nothing short of a new creation of the world will ever put an end to that legend about the mineral.

'How unfavourably this hotch-potch compares with the Marseillese *bouillabaisse*! But what can be expected, considering its ingredients? Green and golden scales, and dorsal fins embellished with elaborate rococo designs, will satisfy neither a hungry man nor an epicure, and if Neapolitans pay untold sums for the showy Mediterranean seaspawn it only proves that they eat with their eyes, like children, who prefer tawdry sweets to good ones. They have colour and shape, these fish of the inland sea, but not taste. Their flesh is either flabby and slimy and full of bones in unauthorised places or else they have no flesh at all – heads like Burmese dragons but no bodies attached to them; or bodies of flattened construction on the *magnum in parvo* principle, allowing of barely room for a sheet of paper between their skin and ribs; or a finless serpentine framework, with long-slit eyes that leer at you while you endeavour to scratch a morsel off the reptilian anatomy.

'There is not a cod, or turbot, or whiting, or salmon, or herring in the two thousand miles between Gibraltar and Jerusalem; or if there is, it never comes out. Its haddocks (haddocks, indeed!) taste as if they had fed on mouldy sea-weed and died from the effects of it; its lobsters have no claws; its oysters are bearded like pards; and as for its soles – I have yet to see one that measures more than 5 in. round the waist. The fact is, there is hardly a fish in the Mediterranean worth eating, and therefore – *ex nihilo nihil fit*. *Bouillabaisse* is only good because cooked by the French, who, if they cared to try, could produce an excellent and nutritious substitute out of cigar-stumps and empty matchboxes. But even as a Turk is furious with a tender chicken because it cheats him out of the pleasure of masticating, so the Neapolitan would throw a boneless *zuppa di pesce* out of the window: the spitting and spluttering is half the fun.'

GIUSEPPE RECCO (1634-95)
STILL LIFE WITH FISH
Naples, Museo Nazionale di San Martino

ℱISH

FISH MARKETS

F ALL THE SPECTACULAR FOOD MARKETS IN ITALY, the one near the Rialto in Venice must be the most remarkable. The light of a Venetian dawn in early summer – you must be about at four o'clock in the morning to see the market coming to life – is so limpid and so still that it makes every separate vegetable and fruit and fish luminous with a life of its own, with unnaturally heightened colours and clear stencilled outlines. Here the cabbages are cobalt blue, the beet-roots deep rose, the lettuces clear pure green, sharp as glass. Bunches of gaudy gold marrow-flowers show off the elegance of pink and white marbled bean pods, primrose potatoes, green plums, green peas. The colours of the peaches, cherries, and apricots, packed in boxes lined with sugar-bag blue paper matching the blue canvas trousers worn by the men unloading the gondolas, are reflected in the rose-red mullet and the orange *vongole* and *cannestrelle* which have been prised out of their shells and heaped into baskets. In other markets, on other shores, the unfamiliar fishes may be vivid, mysterious, repellent, fascinating, and bright with splendid colour; only in Venice do they look good enough to eat. In Venice even ordinary sole and ugly great skate are striped with delicate lilac lights, the sardines shine like newly-minted silver coins, pink Venetian *scampi* are fat and fresh, infinitely enticing in the early dawn.

The gentle swaying of the laden gondolas, the movements of the market men as they unload, swinging the boxes and baskets ashore, the robust life and rattling noise contrasted with the fragile taffeta colours and the opal sky of Venice – the whole scene is out of some marvellous unheard-of ballet.

A very different kettle of fish, indeed, is the market of Genoa. Nothing will shake my conviction that Genova *la superba* is the noisiest city on earth. (This is nothing new; travellers have constantly remarked upon the fact.) The market-place will therefore be quite a rest; here one is oblivious of the uproar, spellbound by the spectacle of the odd fish which come up from these waters. Their names are descriptive enough: the angler or frogfish, the praying-fish, the sea-hen, the scorpion, the sea-cat, the sea-date, the sea-truffle, sea-snails, sea-strawberries, and a mussel with a hair-covered shell called *cozze pelose*. No wonder that anybody with a spark of imagination is prepared to put up with the ear-splitting din of Genoa, the crashing of trams and trains, the screeching of brakes, and even the agonized wailing of itinerant musicians in the taverns, in order to taste some of these sea beasts when they have been converted into *burrida*, the Genoese fish stew, or into the immense edifice of crustaceans, molluscs, fish, vegetables, and green sauce, which is known as *cappon magro*.

Along the coast at Santa Margherita the fish market is famous; here the fish are less forbidding and savage of aspect, but their brilliance of colour is phenomenal. Huge baskets are filled with what from a distance one takes to be strawberries but which turn out to be huge prawns (they are scarlet by nature, before they are cooked); dark green and grey *tonnetto*, gleaming silver with phosphorescence, are thrust head downwards, like so many French loaves, in a high basket; *moscardini*, brown and pale green, are arranged in rows, like newly washed pebbles; the tiny *calamaretti, fragoline di mare*, are black and grey (cooked in a wine sauce they turn a deep pink); the rose-coloured slippery little fish called *signorini* are for the *frittura*; the *scampi* are pallid compared to the brilliant prawns; an orange *langouste* is a tamed beast beside a black lobster, lashing furiously.

Another market with its own very characteristic flavour is that of Cagliari, in the island of Sardinia. Spread out in flat baskets large as cartwheels are all the varieties of fish which go into *ziminù*, the Sardinian version of fish soup: fat, scaly little silver fish streaked with lime green; enormous octopus, blue, sepia, mauve, and turquoise, curled and coiled and petalled like some heavily embroidered marine flower; the *pescatrice* again, that ugly hooked angler fish; cold stony little clams, here called *arselle*; *tartufi di mare*; silvery slippery sardines; rose-red mullets in every possible size, some small as sprats, like doll's-house fish; the fine lobsters for which Sardinia is famous. To eat the plainly grilled or fried fish in this island is an experience from which any town dweller, accustomed to fish which must have been in the ice at least a day or two, will derive great pleasure. The mullet, the thin slices of fresh tunny, the little clams, seem to have been washed straight from the sea into the frying pan, so fresh and tender is their flesh. In such conditions there is no necessity to create complicated sauces and garnishes; and, indeed, for the cooking of fish Italian cooks are mainly content to concentrate their skill on the arts of frying, grilling, and roasting.

PESCE FRITTO
(FRIED FISH)

The cleaned fish must be most carefully dried and then dredged with flour. There must be plenty of oil in the pan, enough to cover the fish, and it must be very hot, smoking slightly, not bubbling. When the fish is put in the oil, increase the heat under the pan so that the oil quickly regains the heat it has lost by having the fish plunged into it; but take care, if cooking on gas or an open fire, that the flame does not catch the oil.

To fry large fish cut them in slices about 1 in. thick, and flour them in the same way as a whole fish. Fried fish should be salted only when they come out of the pan. Drain them on kitchen paper and serve lemon with them. Allow about 7 minutes for frying a whole fish weighing 1 to 1½ lb., 5 minutes for sliced fish.

In Italy a green salad is often served at the same time as fried fish, cooked vegetables scarcely ever.

AN APULIAN COOK'S ADVICE ON THE FRYING OF FISH

'The chef then went into the question of how to fry fish; it was a more difficult accomplishment than it seemed to be. Fried fish must be crisp – not wet and flabby as they often were. Only barbarians used fat or butter. Olive oil, and nothing else, should be used; and Apulian oil was better for such purposes than the

GROEWENBROTH (18th century)
FISHERMAN
Venice, Museo Correr

famous Lucca oil, though not so good for salads and mayonnaise. Of course he was right. How many lovely soles are spoiled in England by frying them in fat; how sensible are the Jews, who only use olive oil!' (G. Orioli, *Moving Along*, Chatto & Windus, 1934.)

PESCE ARROSTO
(ROAST FISH)

Large fish, such as sturgeon, lamprey, grey mullet, *palombo* (a shark-like fish), sea bass, John Dory, large red mullet, are often roasted whole on the spit, basted with olive oil. They can also be baked in the oven. The result is not quite the same, however, for the skin of the fish does not acquire the crackle and slightly smoked flavour imparted by direct contact with the open fire.

To roast a big fish in the oven score it across on each side in three or four places, brush it with olive oil, and cook it on a grid standing in a baking dish in the top of a very hot oven, turning the fish over from time to time and basting it frequently with olive oil. Sprinkle with salt before serving.

The fish is cooked when the flesh is white right through, the average timing being about 10 minutes to the pound.

PESCE ALLA GRIGLIA
(GRILLED FISH)

Ai ferri and *alla graticola* also mean grilled fish. In Italy the grill may be a wire or iron grid placed over the top of a shallow, square, earthenware pot containing glowing charcoal, or it may be the top of a wood-burning range, a kind of flat iron griddle over charcoal or wood, or a modern electric grill. Domestic arrangements for grilling in England are not very adequate, although much improved since the advent of capacious eye-level grills on gas and electric cookers. A double wire grid, which can be turned over without the flesh or meat inside it being moved, is the best instrument for grilling over charcoal or wood.

Whatever grid is used should be brushed with oil and heated before the fish is put on to it, to prevent the skin from sticking. The fish should be scored across in two places on each side, brushed with oil or butter, and turned over once during the cooking. Apart from herring and mackerel, fish obtainable in England which are good grilled are trout, red mullet, salmon (cut in slices), sole, brill, small whiting (*nasello* in Italian), plaice, scallops (impaled on skewers), smelts, eels. Of these, whiting, plaice, brill, and scallops (*conchiglia dei pellegrini* or *capa santa*) are the better for being first marinaded in oil and lemon juice, as explained in the directions for marinaded fish (see below). Seven to ten minutes' grilling on each side is enough for the average fish weighing up to 1½lb. Scallops take only 5 minutes.

A *salsa verde* (p. 195) is often served with grilled or roasted fish.

PESCE IN BIANCO
(*BOILED FISH*)
The fish should be started off in cold water, salted, and with or without onions, pepper-corns, herbs, and lemon, as you please. It should be brought slowly to the boil and then kept barely simmering until the fish is cooked. Allow about 10 minutes per pound. A large fish should be cooked in a fish kettle with a draining grid; or wrapped in muslin (see the recipe for cooking *ombrina*, p. 121), to prevent its breaking when being taken out of the pot.

PESCE MARINATO
(*MARINADED FISH*)
In Italian cooking fish is sometimes marin-aded before being grilled or roasted. The fish is scored crosswise two or three times on each side. Oil, lemon juice, and fresh herbs usually constitute the marinade, and while grilling the fish are brushed over from time to time with

GROEWENBROTH (18th century)
MOLLUSC SELLER
Venice, Museo Correr

GROEWENBROTH (18th century)
CRAB SELLER
Venice, Museo Correr

the mixture, a treatment which is a consider-able help to a dry and flaky fish. Another way of serving fish is to fry them in oil, then marinade them for several hours in oil and white wine with the addition of chopped garlic, parsley, and whatever fresh herbs may be available – marjoram, origano, basil, or mint.

Both these Italian systems could be bene-ficially adopted in England for the treatment of otherwise uninteresting fish.

PESCE IN CARTOCCIO
(*FISH COOKED IN PAPER CASES*)
A good method of cooking fish such as salmon, trout, red mullet, and mackerel. Oil the paper and the fish, and add a *battuto* (p. 190) of onion, celery, parsley, garlic, and any other herbs you please. Close the edges of the paper by folding it over so that no juices escape.

Cook the fish in the oven at a moderate heat, and serve the fish in the paper so that each person can turn it out on the plate with its sauce intact. Fish in *cartoccio* can also be cooked very successfully under an electric grill; but not under a gas grill, because the paper is apt to catch alight.

PESCE ALL'AGLIATA
(*FISH IN GARLIC SAUCE*)
Slices of any coarse white fish, fried in oil, served in the following sauce:

In a mortar pound a clove or two of garlic, add a handful of breadcrumbs, enough oil to make a thick sauce, and a little vinegar.

COZZE AL VINO BIANCO
(*MUSSELS IN WHITE WINE*)
Allow about 1½ pints of mussels per person. When they are cleaned and scraped put them to open in a wide pan in which you have warmed enough olive oil to cover the bottom. Set the mussels going fairly fast, and as they start to open remove them into a bowl. They need watching at this stage, as the mussels at the bottom of the pan will be ready sooner than those at the top, and they must not be left to overcook. When they are all opened strain the liquid in which they have cooked through

a muslin and return it to a clean pan; to this add a glassful of white wine, 1 or 2 cloves of garlic chopped very fine, and a good handful of finely-chopped parsley. Let the mixture bubble fiercely until it has reduced and thickened; but take care it does not evaporate too much or the salt which has come out of the mussels will prove too much for the sauce. Remove the empty half shells from the cooked mussels, pour the sauce over them in the serving dish, and serve them cold.

VONGOLE ALLA MARINARA
(FISHERMAN'S CLAMS)
Wash and scrub the little clams (or mussels) and put them to open in a heavy pan over a fairly hot flame. They are to cook in their own liquid only. Cover the pan to start with, and take the lid off when the shells start to open. At this moment add chopped parsley and garlic.

Serve as soon as all the clams are opened, with their own juice.

A rough and ready dish, often served in seaport taverns. Even in London mussels cooked in this way preserve a good deal of their flavour of the sea.

VONGOLE CON CROSTINI
(CLAMS WITH FRIED BREAD)
Little clams, called *vongole* in the South, *arselle* in Genoa and in Sardinia, are cooked in exactly the same way as the mussels or clams described in the previous recipe, with oil, garlic, and parsley.

They are served in their own liquid, with an accompaniment of little croûtons of bread fried in oil, served in a separate dish.

DATTERI DI MARE
(SEA DATES)
Datteri (lythodomus lythophagus) are curious little shellfish, shaped like a date stone, which are found on the Genoese coast.

They have quite a delicate flavour, and make a good soup or stew in the same manner as mussels. This sea-date soup is a speciality of Porto Venere near Genoa. They are also good raw. Smollett describes how sea dates are found: 'Sometimes the fishermen find under

water, pieces of a very hard cement, like plaster of Paris, which contain a kind of muscle, called la datte, from its resemblance to a date. These petrifactions are commonly of a triangular form, and may weigh about twelve or fifteen pounds each; and one of them may contain a dozen of these muscles, which have nothing extraordinary in the taste or flavour, though extremely curious, as found alive and juicy, in the heart of a rock, almost as hard as marble, without any visible communication with the air or water. I take it for granted, however, that the enclosing cement is porous, and admits the finer parts of the surrounding fluid. In order to reach the muscles, this cement must be broke with large hammers; and it may be truly said, the kernel is not worth the trouble of cracking the shell.' (*Travels Through France and Italy*, 1766.)

Not a shellfish enthusiast, Tobias Smollett.

TARTUFI DI MARE
(SEA TRUFFLES)
A mollusc of the Venus family *Venus verrucosa*, with a ridged shell. Usually eaten raw – and very good, too. In Venice called *caparozzolo*, and in Genoa *tartufoli*. Identical with the French *praire*; the *clovisse* and *palourde* of Provence are also very similar, being either of two other molluscs of the same family, *Venus decussata* and *Venus edulis*.

MOLECCHE
(SOFT-SHELL CRABS)
Every year in Venice towards the end of April and the beginning of May a wholesale slaughter of these little animals takes place. It is the period when the crabs are changing their shells; they are then so light that they float to the surface and can be caught in shoals.

At this moment they are of a dull green colour, and only about 1½ in. across; they are flung, crawling helplessly, into frying batter and then into boiling oil.

The whole animal is consumed, claws and all, and it must be owned that, appalling as the treatment of these little creatures may seem, they are most delicious to eat.

At a banquet given by the Bolognese Senate in Castel Pietro to the Cardinal Legate Antonio

Barberini, nephew of Urban VIII (early in the seventeenth century), the *molecche* were served with fritters of dried figs.

ARAGOSTA, ARIGUSTA
(LANGOUSTE – CRAWFISH)
The *langouste*, crawfish, or rock lobster, (*palinurus vulgaris*), not the true lobster, is the one most commonly found in the Mediterranean.

ARISTOCRATS AT A LUNCH EATING GAMBERI
from *Theatrum Sanitatis* (14th century)
Rome, Biblioteca Casanatense

The Italians usually serve it freshly boiled, with butter or oil and lemon, and perhaps this is the best way. The Sardinian *langoustes* are among the best in the Mediterranean. Those from the waters round the island of Ponza also have a great reputation.

Put a live lobster in a deep pan of cold salted water and bring it slowly to the boil. Boil for 20-30 minutes according to the size. If it is to be served hot, take it out of the pan, cut it in half lengthways, and serve it with melted butter or a mayonnaise. If it is to be eaten cold, leave it to cool in the pan and cut it only just before it is to be served.

GIUSEPPE RECCO (1634-95)
FISH
Rome, Galleria Nazionale d'Arte Antica

FRITTELLE DI ARIGUSTA
(LOBSTER FRITTERS)

Cut the tail and claw meat of a lobster or crawfish into pieces about 1 in. in diameter. Season them and dip them in frying batter (see below). Fry them in very hot oil, drain them, and serve with mayonnaise.

PASTELLA
(FRYING BATTER)

¼ lb. of flour, 3 tablespoonfuls of olive oil, a pinch of salt, three-quarters of a tumbler (approximately ¼ pint) of tepid water, the white of one egg.

Stir the olive oil into the sieved flour, add the salt and the water, and stir to a smooth cream. Leave to stand for about 2 hours. Stir in the stiffly whisked white of egg when the batter is to be used.

There are many versions of batter for frying, but this is the lightest. If there is any left over, it can be kept a day or two in the refrigerator and will be perfectly satisfactory, although it will not be quite so crisp as when the egg has just been stirred in.

SCAMPI (NEPHROPS NORVEGICUS)
(NORWAY LOBSTERS)

Although the *scampi* of the Adriatic are almost identical in appearance with the Dublin Bay prawn (and the French *langoustine*), and are in fact, as far as I can ascertain, precisely the same crustacean, there is a world of difference in the flavour – those of the Adriatic being incomparably superior. They are larger, their tails are fatter, and they are much more meaty. In this country Dublin Bay prawns are usually sold ready boiled by the fishmonger, but they are nearly always overcooked, so whenever possible buy them uncooked.

Waiters in Italian restaurants have a habit of referring to any kind of prawns as *scampi*; whether this is done from ignorance or from a desire to please, it is bewildering to the tourist. If you want to be sure of getting *scampi* and not ordinary small prawns, ask to see them before ordering them; this is perfectly normal procedure in Italian restaurants.

(The above was written long before frozen scampi became almost a British national dish.

Now, in 1987, Dublin Bay prawns have all but vanished from British waters.)

SCAMPI LESSATI
(BOILED SCAMPI)

Boil the unshelled *scampi* tails in salted water for 10 minutes. Serve them hot with melted butter, leaving each person to shell his own. This is perhaps the best way of appreciating the delicate flavour of *scampi*.

SCAMPI FRITTI
(FRIED SCAMPI)

There are several ways of frying *scampi*.

The tails can be taken raw out of their shells, dusted with flour and plainly fried in oil, or they can be dipped in egg and breadcrumbs or in frying batter. They can also be first boiled, and then fried in any of these ways. They are best served plain, with no garnish but lemon.

SCAMPI IN UMIDO
(STEWED SCAMPI)

For this dish the *scampi* must be shelled raw, which is perfectly easy when they are as fresh as they should be.

Heat some olive oil in a thick, small pan. Cook the shellfish very gently in the oil. When they are nearly cooked (about 10 minutes) add some chopped garlic, a lot of parsley, a few capers, and a little lemon juice. Serve them with their own sauce.

Scallops are excellent cooked in the same way.

GIACOMO CERUTI (1700-68)
STILL LIFE
Milan, Pinacoteca di Brera

SCAMPI ALLA GRIGLIA
(GRILLED SCAMPI)

Rub the shells of the *scampi* with olive oil and salt. Put them on the solid hotplate of an electric cooker or on the grilling pan of an Aga cooker. They should cook gradually, being turned over and over, and from time to time removed so that they can be brushed with a little more oil. When they are nearly cooked, after about 15 minutes, flatten them gently with a rolling pin. In Venice they have a special little instrument for this operation. The flattening out ensures that they will cook evenly, and enables the shells to be peeled off easily when they are served. They will take about 20 minutes altogether to cook. The idea is that the scampi should be cooked by heat from *underneath*, rather than from above, so the most successful utensil for the purpose is a ridged cast iron grill plate which is heated over gas or electricity.

MAZZANCOLLE
(IMPERIAL PRAWNS)

A variety of very large prawn (Lat. *Penaeus Caramote*) also called *Gambero Imperiale, Spannocchio, Mazzacuogno*. They are cooked in the same way as *scampi*, and are every bit as good, if not better.

CALAMARETTI E SCAMPI ALLE STECCHE
(INKFISH AND SCAMPI ON SKEWERS)

The smallest, tenderest little *calamaretti*, soft as butter, are used for this Adriatic coast dish, which is perfectly delicious.

The cleaned *calamaretti* and the shelled raw *scampi* are coated with egg and breadcrumbs, impaled longways, end to end on green twigs, and fried golden in butter. Try it with scallops, the white parts cut into two rounds, alternated with the red. They only take 5 minutes to cook.

RICCI
(SEA-URCHINS)

Sea-urchins were eaten by the Greeks and the Romans, served up, according to Macrobius, with vinegar and hydromel, with the addition of mint or parsley. When Lentulus feasted the priest of Mars, this formed the first dish at supper. Sea-eggs also appeared at the marriage feast of the goddess Hebe.

Sea-urchins (there are several edible varieties) are a menace to bathers on the shores of the Mediterranean, for they cluster by the hundred in shallow waters, hidden in the rocks, and anyone who has ever trodden on a sea-urchin with a bare foot knows how painful and tedious a business it is to remove their sharp little spines from the skin. They are, however, delicious to eat for those who like food redolent of the sea, iodine, and salt. They are served cut in half, and the coral flesh so exposed is scooped out with a piece of bread; they are at their best eaten within sight and sound of the sea, preferably after a long swim, and washed down with plenty of some cold local white wine. Figuier says that they are sometimes also 'dressed by boiling, and eaten from the shell like an egg, using long sippets of bread; hence the name of sea-eggs, which they bear in many countries'.

Sea-urchins are wrested from their lairs in the rocks with wooden pincers, or can be picked up by hand provided you wear gloves.

OSTRICHE
(OYSTERS)

The culture of oysters has been practised in Italy since Roman times. The original system of oyster beds was invented by Sergius Orata in the fifth century B.C.

Never having tasted Italian oysters I am not in a position to express an opinion as to their merits. Cavanna (*Doni di Nettuno*, 1913) gives a recipe for *Ostriche alla Veneziana*. Prepare a mixture of finely chopped parsley, celery, aromatic herbs, garlic, and breadcumbs; put a little of this preparation over each oyster in its deep half shell. Add a few drops of olive oil to each, and cook them a few moments on the grill over a wood fire. Sprinkle with lemon juice before serving.

POLIPI, SEPPIE, CALAMARI
(OCTOPUS, SQUID, CUTTLE)

'Although usually termed cuttle-*fish*, it is not a fish at all, but a mollusc, and is allied to the slugs, snails, and bivalves, being by far the most highly organized class of mollusca.

'There are three varieites known in our seas: the cuttle, the squid, and the octopus.

'The octopus has eight limbs, as its name suggests, but the squids and the cuttles have in addition two long tentacles with spoon-like extremities (one might call them arms and hands); the latter are also furnished with suckers on the under-sides (palms).

'The shell of the cuttle is reduced to a supporting "bone" inside the animal. This is the cuttle-bone of our bird fanciers, and used also to be greatly in demand for grinding into

GIOVAN BATTISTA RUOPPOLO (1629-93)
STILL LIFE WITH CRAB AND FISH (detail)
Naples, Private Collection

pounce-powder before the era of blotting paper. The presence of so many of these cuttle bones on our shores is eloquent of the effects of the conger and other large fish in keeping the cuttles within limits of numbers, for the conger has no fear of the cuttle, his slippery skin gives no hold to the suckers of the mollusc, and his sharp teeth make short work of the succulent tentacles. In the squids, the shell is also internal, and is reduced even further than in the cuttles, being only a long, thin, semi-transparent horny "pen" . . . .

'The octopus is common along our southern shores and round the Channel Islands.' (W.A. Hunter, *The Romance of Fish Life*.)

Enormous quantities of squid and cuttlefish are eaten in Italy. They vary in size, shape, colour, flavour, and most especially in degrees of toughness. The very small variety with eight tentacles called *polipetto* or *moscardini*, or *fragoline di mare*, found both on the Genoese and Adriatic coasts, are exquisitely tender and have a delicious flavour. There is a way of cooking them in Genoa, in wine and oil, with their tentacles turned back so that they look like open flowers of a deep pink colour, which would surely tempt even the most nervous or prejudiced. *Calamari* and *totani* are the long-bodied varieties, with eight tentacles and two more longer arms; these are the kind which are stewed, or cut into rings and fried, or put into soups. Very often they are tough and rubbery because they have been cooked with insufficient care. *Seppie* have the same eight short tentacles and two long ones as *calamari* and *totani*, but a shorter rounder body. They are cooked in the same way as the *totani*, and can also be stuffed, a good dish if carefully cooked; or stewed in their own ink to make a dish called *seppie alla Veneziana*, which is usually accompanied by *polenta*.

Polipi are octopus, which must be bashed a good deal before cooking to make them tender, and stewed or boiled slowly. The inkfish to be obtained in England are *seppie* and *calamari*. They are nearly always a fairly good size, too big to be fried without being first boiled, but many are the good inkfish stews which may be made from them, and they can be preserved in the way described on p. 200; and the smaller ones can be very successfully grilled.

Diogenes the Cynic, it is said, died from trying to eat a raw inkfish.

CALAMARI IN UMIDO
(STEWED INKFISH)

1 lb. of inkfish, 2 large onions, 3 cloves of garlic, 2 or 3 tomatoes, tomato paste, red wine, oil, herbs.

To clean the inkfish, remove the insides from the pocket-like part of the fish, and pull out the thin transparent spine bone. Remove also the purplish outside skin, which comes off very easily in warm water.

From each side of the head remove the little ink bag (the whole operation is carried out in a bowl of water and is very quickly done) and take out the eyes and the hard beak-like object in the centre of the tentacles, of which Dumas remarks that it is *'non pas un nez, mais l'anus (au milieu du visage!)'*. Rinse the inkfish in running water until it is quite free of grit. When clean they are milky white.

Cut the body of the inkfish into rings, about ¼ in. wide, and the tentacles into strips. Season them with salt and lemon juice. Now put the onions, cut into rings, into a pan in which you have warmed enough olive oil to cover the bottom. Let them turn golden and add the inkfish. After 2 minutes put in the chopped tomatoes, some marjoram and thyme, and the garlic, and after 2 more minutes pour in a small glassful of red wine; let this reduce a little and add a dessertspoonful, not more, of tomato purée. Add enough hot water to reach the level of the ingredients in the pan, put on the lid, and cook very slowly for 1½ hours. Serve with rice or with toasted French bread.

SEPPIE E CALAMARI IN ZIMINO
(CUTTLE-FISH AND SQUID IN ZIMINO)

Zimino is a Genoese stew of fish. The same kind of dish is also found in Sardinia, where it is called *ziminù*.

MARINE FAUNA (detail, Roman mosaic)
Naples, Museo Nazionale

Make a *soffritto* (p. 190) of oil, onion, parsley, celery, and fennel, all chopped fine. When it has cooked a minute or two, add chopped beet leaves from which the middle rib has been removed, or spinach. Let the mixture simmer a few minutes in the covered casserole, and then add the cuttle-fish or squid, or octopus and *moscardini*, salt, pepper, and tomatoes, and continue cooking until the fish are tender, which will take between 30 and 45 minutes. Some people prefer the dish without tomatoes, and in this case increase the quantity of parsley, celery, and other green stuff. (G. Cavanna, *Doni di Nettuno*, Firenze, 1913).

FRITTO MISTO DI MARE
(MIXED FRIED FISH)

One of the most common fish dishes in all sea-coast restaurants.

Small red mullet, inkfish or squid, prawns. The inkfish, if at all large, must first be boiled, otherwise they will be tough. Prepare them in the way described for *calamari in umido* (p. 116) and boil them until they are tender; it may be 30 minutes or it may be an hour, according to size. Cut them into rings. The prawns are fried raw and unshelled, the red mullet cleaned in the usual way. All the fish are lightly dusted with flour and fried in very hot oil. Drain on kitchen paper.

Allow 2 small red mullet, half a dozen rings of inkfish, and half a dozen prawns per person. Serve halves of lemon with the fish.

FISH (detail, Roman mosaic)
Rome, Museo Nazionale

TRIGLIE ALLA GRIGLIA
(GRILLED RED MULLET)

Medium-sized red mullet are the best for grilling, and grilling is the most delicious way of cooking these fish. Make a couple of incisions crosswise on each side of the fish, which should have its liver left in. Brush it with oil. Cook it under a hot grill for about 7 minutes on each side – it will be golden and crackling. If the fish is absolutely fresh, it has such a marvellous flavour of the sea that it is absurd to serve any sauce with it. Town fish can do with a little melted butter and parsley, or a *salsa verde*.

TRIGLIE ALLA VENEZIANA
(RED MULLET MARINATED IN WHITE WINE)

Put two leaves of fresh mint and a small piece of garlic inside each red mullet, medium-sized ones being best for the dish. Roll them in flour and fry them gently in oil; drain them and arrange them on a long dish. Prepare the following sauce. In a little oil sauté a small onion finely chopped; let it melt but not turn brown, then pour in about 6 oz. of white wine and a tablespoonful of wine vinegar. Simmer the sauce for 10-15 minutes, until it has reduced by one third. When it has cooled, pour it over the red mullets. Serve them cold, garnished with a little parsley and slices of lemon or orange. Instead of frying the mullets, they can be scored across twice on each side and grilled, and the sauce then poured over them. They can also be eaten hot cooked in this way, and are excellent.

GASPARO DIZIANI (1689-1767)
THE FESTIVAL OF SANTA MARTA
Venice, Ca' Rezzonico

TRIGLIE COL PESTO
(RED MULLET WITH PESTO)

A medium-sized red mullet per person; ½ lb. of tomatoes for 4 mullet, olive oil, 3 or 4 anchovy fillets, garlic, basil, or parsley, vinegar, salt.

First prepare a simplified *pesto* (p. 193) with pounded garlic, (1 or 2 cloves according to taste), a bunch of basil or parsley, and finally a tablespoonful of olive oil.

Peel the tomatoes and chop them. Wash the anchovy fillets in water and vinegar. In a capacious frying pan, heat the olive oil and cook the tomatoes in it for 5 minutes, seasoning them with salt and pepper and adding the chopped anchovies. At the last minute stir the prepared *pesto* into the sauce and pour it very hot over the mullets, which have been grilled 5-7 minutes on each side.

ALICI, ACCIUGHE
(ANCHOVIES)

Fresh anchovies and fresh sardines are two of the most delicate fish of the Mediterranean. Anchovies in particular are difficult to get hold of. They are caught only at the time of the waning moon. Most of them are immediately salted and put into barrels or tins. The few which find their way to the market are snatched by the early risers. The restaurants rarely serve them, considering them, like so many cheap foods in Italy, insufficiently *signorile* or elegant.

Also they involve a good deal of labour, for most people like them boned. They are then fried in oil and served with lemon.

ALICI AL GRATIN
(ANCHOVIES AU GRATIN)

A particularly good way of cooking fresh anchovies. Several hours before they are to be cooked prepare a cupful of breadcrumbs mixed with a cupful of chopped parsley, 2 or 3 cloves of garlic, salt, pepper, and enough olive oil to moisten the mixture.

Arrange the boned anchovies in a shallow oiled fireproof dish. Put the breadcrumb mixture lightly on the top, add more oil, and cook them a few minutes in a fairly hot oven.

Try this recipe with sprats or, better still,

with herrings, boned or not, as you please. They take about 15 minutes to cook.

ALICI ALL'ISCHIANA
(ISCHIA ANCHOVIES)

Split fresh anchovies, bone them, and arrange them in circles in a round baking dish. Pour olive oil and lemon juice over them and sprinkle them with fresh wild marjoram (*origano*). Bake them a little under 10 minutes.

GIOVANNI BELLINI (1432-1516)
SUPPER AT EMMAUS (detail)
Venice, San Salvatore

SARDE RIPIENE
(STUFFED SARDINES)

'Wash and split fresh sardines (or pilchards) and remove backbones and heads. Have ready a forcemeat consisting of grated bread and Parmesan cheese in equal parts, a little chopped parsley, and an egg. Stuff your fish with this. Season each sardine with salt and pepper, then roll them up lightly, beginning with the neck. Place them beside each other in a shallow saucepan greased with butter and let them fry; add a little water and let them simmer for ten minutes more, then squeeze a few drops of lemon juice over them. Serve hot.

'I have eaten this dish in Sicily and elsewhere, but never so well cooked as at Cosenza and Cotrone. In Tuscany they use oil instead of butter. This is a mistake, as the sardine has enough grease of its own; even with butter one must not be too generous.' (G. Orioli, *Moving Along*, Chatto & Windus, 1934.)

SOGLIOLE ALLA PARMIGIANA
(SOLE WITH PARMESAN CHEESE)

Have medium sized soles, one for each person, skinned on both sides. Lay them in a buttered flame-proof dish, well seasoned with salt and pepper, and with more butter on the top. Let them brown gently, and turn them over so that they brown on the other side. Spread a thin layer of grated Parmesan over the top of each, and add a tablespoonful of chicken or fish broth for each sole. Cover the pan, and simmer slowly for 5 minutes, until the soles are cooked through and the cheese melted. Serve in the dish in which they have cooked, with halves of lemon and a green salad. The cooking can be done in the oven instead of on top of the stove. Made with fillets instead of the whole fish, this recipe produces a splendid quick and unfussy little dish.

SOGLIOLE AL MARSALA
(SOLE WITH MARSALA)

The combination of sole and Marsala is unfamiliar but rather good. Simply cook fillets of sole, lightly dusted with flour and seasoned with salt and pepper, in a little bubbling butter. Pour over them 3 or 4 tablespoonsful of Marsala and the same quantity of broth made from the bones of the fish. (Cream instead of the broth is equally good.) Let the fillets cook gently until they are tender and the sauce reduced.

SOGLIOLE ALLA VENEZIANA
(SOLE WITH VENETIAN SAUCE)

A medium-sized sole per person, mint, parsley, garlic, onions, white wine, butter.

Mash 1 oz. of butter (for 2 soles) with a tablespoonful of parsley, 2 of chopped mint, and a small piece of garlic; season with a little salt and pepper. Make two crosswise incisions on each side of the soles (which should be skinned on both sides); press the prepared butter mixture into the incisions.

Now prepare the sauce. In a little butter melt a thinly sliced large onion; let it cook very gently so that it turns yellow but not brown; add a small glass of white wine and cook for 10 minutes; now add a small glass of water, and salt and pepper. Let it continue to simmer while you grill the soles, allowing about 7 minutes for each side. Serve them on a hot dish, with the sauce poured over.

TONNO
(TUNNY FISH)

The best fresh tunny fish I have ever come across was in Sardinia. It was *ventresca* (stomach) cut into thin slices, brushed with oil, and grilled. It was tender and delicate, and bore no relation to the boot-like slabs of tunny stewed in tomato sauce which one gets on the south coast of France – and in Italy, too. To have good tunny fish, it is essential to ask for *ventresca*.

TONNO ALLA LIVORNESE
(TUNNY FISH IN TOMATO SAUCE)

Fry slices of *ventresca* (see above) of fresh tunny in oil. Drain them. Stew them for 30 minutes in a fresh tomato sauce flavoured with garlic. Garnish with plenty of parsley.

CEFALO O MUGGINE
(GREY MULLET)

This fish has been much maligned owing to the fact that unless it is very carefully cleaned and washed in plenty of running water it has a muddy taste. Grilled or roasted whole it is very good, and can also be most successfully cooked in the Provençal fashion for grilling red mullet or *loup* (sea bass); that is, placed on a bed of dried wild fennel branches (see p. 25) and brushed with oil or butter. When it is cooked heat some brandy in a soup ladle, set light to it, and pour it flaming over the fish.

LUIGI MONTEVERDE (19th century)
STILL LIFE WITH HERRING
Brescia, Galleria d'Arte Moderna

AGUGLIE
(GARFISH)

These are long thin fish with a needle-like beak and green bones.

In spite of the hard words in which Norman Douglas was in the habit of referring to them (quoted on p. 107), many people eat them with pleasure, and to me, at any rate, their veridian-green bones add to their charm. They can be fried in oil or stewed in a sauce made with tomatoes and onions and flavoured with *origano*.

MORENE
(LAMPREYS, OR SEA-EELS, OR MURRY)

Although *morene* or *muroena Helena* are probably the lampreys of the Romans, there is, in fact, another distinct species of lamprey,

petromyzon marinus, which also inhabits the Mediterranean. 'Full-grown,' according to Figuier, 'it is about three feet long, marbled brown upon yellow. In the spring it ascends the rivers, when it is sometimes caught in abundance . . . the lamprey feeds on worms, molluscs, and small fishes . . . the flesh is fat and delicate . . . . In the twelfth century one of our Kings, Henry I, surfeited himself at Elbeuf by partaking too royally of the lamprey . . . .'

Muroena Helena Figuier describes as 'serpent-like fishes, of cylindrical form and delicate proportions, but strong, flexible, and active, swimming in waving, undulating movements in the water, just as a serpent creeps on dry land . . . it attains the length of forty to fifty inches. It loves to bask in the hollows of rocks, approaching the coast in springtime. It feeds on crabs and small fishes, seeking eagerly for polyps. The voracity of these fishes is such that when other food fails they begin to nibble at each other's tails....

'Those who have studied the classics will remember the passionate love with which the Roman gourmet regarded these fishes. In the days of the Empire enormous sums were expended in keeping up the ponds which enclosed them, and the fish themselves were multiplied to such an extent that Caesar, on the occasion of one of his triumphs, distributed six thousand among his friends. Licinius Crassus was celebrated among wealthy Romans for the splendour of his eel ponds. They obeyed his voice, he said, and when he called them, they darted towards him in order to be fed by his hands. The same Licinius Crassus and Quintus Hortensius, another wealthy Roman patrician, wept the loss of the *muroenas* on one occasion, when they all died in their ponds from some disease. ... It was thought among the Romans that *muroenas* fed with human flesh were the most delicately flavoured.... In the present day sea-eels are little esteemed in a gastronomic point of view. Nevertheless they are still sought for on the coast of Italy, and the fishermen avoid with great care the bites of their acrid teeth.' (Figuier, *The Ocean World.*)

Platina (*Platine De Honesta Voluptate et Valitudine,*) reproached the popes and noblemen of Rome for feasting their guests on lampreys for which they paid as much as twenty gold pieces and which they slaughtered by plunging them into Cyprus wine, a nutmeg in the mouth and a clove in each opening of the gills; after this preparation they were put in a casserole and cooked with pounded almonds and all kinds of spices. Smollett (*Travels Through France and Italy,* 1766) noted the lamprey on the coast of Nice 'a very ugly animal of the eel species, which might pass for a serpent ... the Italians call it *Murena* ... the murena of this country is in no esteem, and only eaten by the poor people'.

Orioli found *morene* in the market at Crotone in Calabria. 'Were it not for all those bones, they would be one of the best fish in the world; and the bigger the better. From a modern Italian cookery book I learn that lampreys have lost some of their flavour and fallen into disrepute because they are no longer fed

on the flesh of slaves. ...' (*Moving Along*, Chatto & Windus, 1934.)

In Rome *morene* are sometimes put into the *zuppa di pesce* (p. 103). At a restaurant in the end of the world Calabrian village of Agropoli I have eaten *morene* of a lovely flavour, the flesh milky white, melting, and tender. At its best roasted rather than fried.

SPIGOLA
(SEA BASS)
One of the finest flavoured Mediterranean fishes (the *loup* of Provence). At its best roasted or grilled.

On the Adriatic coast it is called *branzino*.

PESCATRICE
(FROGFISH OR ANGLER-FISH)
This brute owes its Italian name (the angler fish – also called *rana* or frogfish) to the fact that it has long filaments attached to its head, which, while the fish itself lurks in the sand, wave above its head and act as bait to smaller fish. Its eyes are so placed that it can see its prey overhead and so snap the small fish into its ever open jaws. In France it is called *baudroie* or *lotte*.

On the Mediterranean coast of Italy *pescatrice* used to be considered of no account and was always used for *zuppa di pesce*. On the Adriatic, and particularly in Venice, the tails only are sold, and are eaten grilled or roasted. The local name of the *pescatrice* on this coast is *rospo*, while in Tuscany it is sometimes called *boldro*.

ORATA
The Daurade of Provence (Lat. *chrysophrys aurata*).

A large Mediterranean fish with, in spite of its name which implies gold-fish, silvery scales. The nearest approach to it to be found in England is the sea bream, which can be used for the recipe below.

There are two good ways of cooking this fish, in *cartoccio* (p. 111), and with a sauce of white wine and sultanas, which can be applied very successfully to carp and also to fresh haddock.

ORATA AL VINO BIANCO
(ORATA COOKED IN WHITE WINE)
A fish weighing about 2 lb., a tumbler of white wine, an onion, half a carrot, a clove of garlic, parsley, a bay leaf, 1 oz. of butter, 2 tablespoonsful of sultanas or raisins.

Melt the butter and in it fry the chopped onion, carrot, garlic, parsley, and bay leaf. Put in the fish, pour over the white wine, add enough water to cover it, and poach the fish gently for about 25 minutes. When the fish is cooked, remove it to a heated serving dish, and reduce the sauce over a fast flame. When it has bubbled away to half its original volume season it with salt and pepper and stir in the sultanas, which should have been soaked in warm water while the fish is cooking. Let the sultanas get thoroughly heated, and pour the sauce over the fish.

DENTICE
(DENTEX)
A Mediterranean fish of which there is no equivalent in northern waters. At its best grilled or roasted.

PESCE SAN PIETRO
(JOHN DORY)
Not a prepossessing fish, but a fine one, and especially highly regarded in Venice. The fillets can be cooked in any of the ways applicable to fillets of sole.

The head and carcase make fish stock for soup. But take care when handling the bones; they can give you a nasty jab.

PESCE SPADA
(SWORDFISH)
There is a considerable swordfishing industry in Sicilian waters. The flesh of the swordfish is white and fat, and is good grilled.

OMBRINA
(OMBRINA LECCIA)
A Mediterranean fish with firm delicate white flesh; it is something like the sea bass but very much larger. It is usually cooked *in bianco* (poached).

Wrap the cleaned fish in a cloth or muslin

and tie it round and round with string. This method keeps the fish from breaking during the cooking. Simmer it in water containing a plentiful amount of slices of lemon, carrots, bay leaves, peppercorns, and, if you like, some fennel.

Leave the fish to cool in the liquid, and unwrap it only when it is cold. Serve quite plain with a mayonnaise separately.

This is also an excellent way of cooking a piece of salmon or a large trout. The fish can be wrapped in grease-proof paper instead of a cloth.

STORIONE
(STURGEON)

Sturgeon is fairly common on the Adriatic coast. It is a fine-looking beast, but, probably because so much is expected of the fish which produces caviar, its flavour is disappointing. It is usually roasted over a charcoal fire or in the oven, and makes an imposing appearance on the table.

Boiled sturgeon, cut into thin slices, marinaded in oil and served cold, makes a very excellent *antipasto*; it should be cooked in as little water as possible, or, better still, steamed.

In the seventeenth century sturgeon was cooked with candied citron, turbot with dried cherries and mirabelle plums.

TROTA
(TROUT)

Excellent trout are fished in the Italian lakes and northern rivers. They are usually cooked *in bianco* (boiled), or fried, or grilled. The last method seems to me to be preferable.

Wash the trout carefully to get rid of any possible muddy taste. Score them across once or twice on each side, brush them with melted butter, and grill them as explained on pp. 110-11. Serve them with plenty of melted butter.

PESCE PERSICO
(PERCH)

Perch is fished in the Lake of Maggiore. It is fried in slices or fillets, or grilled whole.

CARPIONE
(CARP)

Of the famous French dish of *carpe à la Chambord* (in which the carp is stuffed with veal or whiting forcemeat, larded with bacon, and braised in white wine) Kettner, in his *Book of the Table* (Dulau & Co., 1877), tells the following story: '. . . it [the castle of Chambord] is most widely known throughout the world for one little detail of cookery which was first practised in its kitchen. Before the time of Francis there was no special merit in French

ANNIBALE CARRACCI (1560-1609)
LANDSCAPE WITH FISHING SCENE (detail)
Paris, Musée du Louvre

cookery. It was no better than English or Flemish. The French, with all their strength, were barbarians as compared with the Italians. It was in the Italian cities that the arts revived and that all the refinements of wealth and commerce were best cultivated. Francis the First married his son to Catherine of Medici, who brought with her to Paris and to Chambord all the graces and muses of Florence. Through her the Italians taught the French manners, enlightened them in critic-

ism, schooled them in art, showed them how to cook. They brought the fricandeau with them from Italy, and when they were installed in the kitchen at Chambord they applied the principle of the fricandeau to the fish which abounds in the neighbourhood. The commune of Chambord has more than a dozen considerable ponds, all abounding in carp, a fish which is sometimes poor in flavour. But veal also is apt to be insipid, though it adopts and appropriates extraneous flavours with rare docility and with beautiful results. The Italian artists determined to lard the carp as they larded the cushion of veal to make a fricandeau. The effect was so good that the method of dressing carp à la Chambord spread over France, thoroughly established itself in the French kitchen, and is celebrated over the world as among the triumphs of French art. Unhappily the later French cooks made the most dreadful blunders in the application of the Chambord method. Some are quite ignorant of what the method really is; and those who seem to be aware of it are weak enough to apply it to fish which are not of the same character as the carp and which do not need to be larded.'

ANGUILLE
(EELS)

Comacchio, on the east coast of Italy, is the centre of the Italian eel-fishing industry. Comacchio eels are usually very large, and they are very good, especially when cut into thick slices, sandwiched between bay leaves, and roasted on the spit.

George Augustus Sala (*The Thorough Good Cook*, 1895) has the following to say about eels: 'Some people are prejudiced against eels. Combat the prejudice; subdue it.'

GIUSEPPE RECCO (1634-95)
STILL LIFE WITH FISH BY A POOL
Derbyshire, Locko Park,
Collection Capt. P. Drury-Lowe

VINCENZO CAMPI (1536-91)
THE FISH SELLER
Kirchheim Castle

ANGUILLE ARROSTO
(*ROAST EELS*)

'Cut large eels into slices 8-10 centimetres thick [3-4 in.], and impale them on the spit, alternating them with sage, bay leaves, or sprigs of rosemary, basting them from time to time with oil and with the fat which has collected in the pan underneath them, and with a generous quantity of salt. Towards the end of the cooking the fire should be very hot.

'In some provinces of northern Italy this dish is accompanied by *mostarda di Cremona* (p. 197). The association may seem strange, but is truly felicitous, and those who do not care for it may accompany these eels with a simple mustard sauce. Instead of cooking the eels on a spit the slices can be threaded on to skewers, two or three on each, and cooked on the grill.

'The eels need not be skinned for this dish, as the skin forms a protective crust which prevents the flesh itself from hardening during the cooking and which can be easily peeled off by each person.

'Another way of roasting the eels is to marinade the slices for a good hour in oil, salt, pepper, and lemon; baste them repeatedly with this mixture while they are cooking, and turn them over carefully.' (Recipe from *Doni di Nettuno* by G. Cavanna.)

ANGUILLE IN UMIDO
(STEWED EELS)

Orioli gives this recipe for stewing eels in his book *Moving Along* (Chatto & Windus, 1934).

'For a kilogramme [approximately 2 lb.] of eels take 2 big onions, a small celery, a carrot, and some parsley. Chop these vegetables into pieces not too small and boil them in ½ litre [a little over ¾ of a pint] of water together with the rind of half a lemon, pepper, and salt. When nearly cooked, strain them and throw away the lemon peel.

'Cut your eels into 3-in. pieces and put a layer of them at the bottom of an earthen stew-pan, cover them with a layer of the vegetables, and so on. Then add the liquor in which the vegetables have been boiled.

'Put the stew-pan into the glowing embers of a wood fire. It must be kept covered and the contents never stirred, but it should be moved round from time to time in order to ensure an equal heat. Let it boil gently for 3 hours, then add 1 good tablespoonful of strong wine vinegar, and boil a few more minutes before serving.'

ANGUILLE IN UMIDO AL VINO BIANCO
(EELS STEWED IN WHITE WINE)

1¼ lb. of eels, 3 tablespoonfuls of oil, 1 oz. of butter, a clove of garlic, 2 or 3 sage leaves, the rind of a quarter of a lemon, a teaspoonful of concentrated tomato purée, a wineglassful (4 oz.) of white wine.

Clean the eels and cut them in slices about 1 in. thick. Melt the oil and butter in a pan, put in the fish and let it brown a little on each side. Add garlic and lemon peel, the purée dissolved in a little water, the white wine, salt, and pepper. Simmer gently for 30 minutes.

Enough for four people.

ANGUILLES MARINÉES FAÇON D'ITALIE
(EELS MARINADED IN THE ITALIAN WAY)

Take some large eels, which you cut in thick slices, and three-quarters fry them in oil. Boil some red wine with salt and a piece of sugar. Put into it the oil which has been used to fry your fish, with a few bay leaves.

Put your fish into a pot with all its marinade. It will preserve a long time. Different sorts of fish can be conserved in this fashion. (Recipe from *Les Dons de Comus*, 1758.)

BOCCONE SQUADRISTA

Cutlets of fish between 2 large slices of apple; the whole sprinkled with rum and set alight as it is served. (Marinetti, *La Cucina Futurista*.)

CAPPON MAGRO

This celebrated Genoese fish salad is not a work to be lightly undertaken. Shopping for the ingredients, preparing and cooking them, making the sauce, and finally the construction of the salad itself, is a lengthy and costly proceeding. On the other hand, for those who have the time to devote to cooking, the preparation of such a dish is an entertainment in itself, allowing plenty of stimulus for the imagination both in the choice of ingredients and in the final arrangement of the dish.

Since the diversity of fish and vegetables in a *cappon magro* constitutes its chief beauty, it is a dish to be made for not less than eight people.

The ingredients as the Genoese make it are potatoes, carrots, artichoke hearts, celery, beetroot, cauliflower, French beans, anchovies, olives, a white fish such as *spigola* (sea bass), lobster, prawns, crabs, and oysters, all arranged upon a base of ship's biscuit previously soaked in oil and vinegar. The sauce poured over the top is compounded of parsley, garlic, eggs, capers, anchovies, fennel, breadcrumbs, olives, oil and vinegar.

The following recipe, using ingredients to be found in England, and leaving out the oysters, which would make the cost out of all proportion, is enough for eight to ten people and makes a very splendid appearance upon the table for a buffet supper. Although no more indigestible than an elaborate fish mayonnaise, guests should perhaps be warned of its garlicky flavor and filling qualities.

A crawfish or lobster of 2-2½ lb., 1½ lb. of rock salmon, 3 or 4 large scallops, a medium-sized dressed crab, 2 oz. of peeled prawns, a small head of celery, 1 lb. of potatoes, ½ lb. of mushrooms, a medium-sized cauliflower, ½ lb. of French beans, ½ lb. of carrots, 2 beetroots, 4 or 5 eggs, 2 oz. each of black and green olives.

For the sauce: a large bunch of parsley, a clove of garlic, a tablespoonful of capers, 2 anchovy fillets, the yolks of 2 hard boiled eggs, 6 green olives, half of a small fennel heart, or a bunch of fennel leaves, a handful of breadcrumbs, a large cupful of olive oil, a little vinegar.

For the basis of the dish, get a large sandwich loaf instead of ship's biscuit, and see that there is a supply of olive oil, garlic, and lemons in the kitchen, and a handsome oval or round platter upon which to serve the *cappon magro*.

Start by preparing the bread. From the sandwich loaf cut two fairly thick slices, lengthways, without the crust, and let them harden in a gentle oven. Rub them well on both sides with garlic, then pour oil over them, and a little vinegar, and leave them overnight.

All the vegetables, with the exception of the celery and the mushrooms, must be cooked, but take great care not to *over*cook them, for if they are sodden they will be tasteless and will also ruin the appearance of the dish. This also applies to the cooking of the rock salmon (a fresh haddock or a whiting will do equally well, but rock salmon has a particularly good consistency for this kind of dish, and is very easy to bone). All these ingredients (not forgetting the scallops, which can be poached for 5 minutes with the white fish), when cooked, should be seasoned with olive oil, salt, and lemon juice, and left to cool. Clean the mushrooms, slice them, and season them in the same way, and wash the celery.

To make the sauce, remove the thick stalks from the parsley, wash it, put it into a mortar with a little salt and the clove of garlic. Pound until it is beginning to turn to a paste (this does not take so long as might be supposed). Then add the capers, the anchovies, the stoned olives, and chopped fennel. Continue pounding; add the breadcrumbs, which should have been softened in a little milk or water and pressed dry. By this time there should be a thick sauce. Pound in the yolks of the hard boiled eggs. Now start to add the olive oil,

slowly, stirring vigorously with a wooden spoon as if making mayonnaise, and when the sauce is the consistency of a thick cream add about 2 tablespoonfuls of vinegar.

Now arrange the prepared bread on the bottom of the dish, so that it constitutes a platform for the other ingredients. Spread it with a little of the prepared sauce. The vegetables, cut into slices, and the white fish are to be built up pyramid-wise, and can be arranged in layers according to fancy, but keep the olives and perhaps a few slices of carrots and beetroot to decorate the finished work. About halfway add some more sauce. The arrangement of the flaked crab, the lobster, prawns, scallops and eggs must be left to the taste of the cook, but obviously the decorative pieces such as the red part of the scallops and the coral of the lobster should go on the top, after the rest of the sauce has been poured over the pyramid. The salad can also be studded with a few unshelled prawns, or with the quartered hard-boiled eggs, halves of lemon, and slices of beetroot threaded on little skewers. The final operations should be left as late as possible, so that each ingredient retains its own flavour and fresh glowing appearance as the dish is brought to the table.

The word *cappon* presumably has the same origin as the French *chapon*, the piece of oil and garlic soaked bread upon which a green salad is sometimes mixed. *Magro* denotes a *maigre* or fasting dish.

BACCALÀ
(SALT COD)

Baccalà, or *stoccafisso*, the *morue* of the French, is a common Friday and fast day dish all over Italy. I doubt whether salt cod will ever be popular in this country; it requires to be soaked, preferably under running water, for at least 24 hours, and needs skinning, boning, and slow and careful cooking if it is to be an acceptable dish. In Italy the initial soaking in running water is often carried out by the grocer who sells salt cod, and the Italians have several excellent ways of cooking it. English residents in Italy, and those staying in self-catering holiday villas, may find the recipes useful.

BACCALÀ ALLA VICENTINA
(VICENZA SALT COD)

For this dish the cheaper pieces of the salt cod are used. Soak 2 lb. of it for 48 hours, if possible under a running tap.

Drain the fish; skin and bone it. In a braising or sauté pan, heat a good deal of olive oil with a little butter. In the mixture put a sliced onion, and when it is soft add the prepared fish. Pour over sufficient boiling milk to cover the fish. Stew slowly for 2 to 3 hours, until the cod is quite tender and the sauce very much reduced and thick.

Polenta, boiled, cut into slices when cold, and toasted, or fried, goes with this dish; or croûtons of fried bread, or boiled potatoes.

BACCALÀ MANTECATO
(CREAM OF BACCALÀ)

This dish, a speciality of Venice, and one of which the Venetians are very proud, is almost identical with the *brandade de morue* of Provence. Possibly the Nîmois cook who claimed to have invented it borrowed the idea from Venice – perhaps the origin of both dishes is Spanish.

For *baccalà mantecato* you need about 1½ lb. of the best quality Bergen salt cod, cut from the middle, and fattest, part of the fish, which before being put to soak has been beaten until it has lost some of its toughness. (In Venice the bashing of the *baccalà* against the stone mooring-posts alongside the canals and in the market place is a familiar sight.)

Leave the cod under running cold water for 24 hours. Steam it in a double pan for about an hour, then remove all skin and bone. Put the pieces of fish into a heavy mortar and pound and pound, with the addition of a few tablespoonfuls of olive oil, until a thick creamy mass results. (*Baccalà mantecato* is rather less liquid than the *brandade*.) If the fish is not sufficiently fat, and so does not turn to a soft purée, add a little warmed milk.

Slices of *polenta* are served with *baccalà mantecato*.

Smoked cod fillets make a good dish cooked this way. They should be soaked for about 6 hours, when the skin will come off easily. Cook as described for the *baccalà*. The pounding takes about 10-15 minutes, and the amount of olive oil added should be about 6 tablespoonfuls, and half that quantity of milk or, better, cream. The dish will not come out beautifully white as does *baccalà*, but the combination of the fish and the olive oil is unfamiliar and good.

Serve piled up in a mound, surrounded with squares of fried bread. Enough for four.

The fish can be reheated in the double saucepan without coming to harm.

POLPETTINE DI BACCALÀ
(LITTLE RISSOLES OF SALT COD)

To use up any fish there may be left over from the foregoing recipe, stir an egg or two into the fish purée, add a little parsley, and form into small *polpettine* not larger than a half-crown in diameter and fairly flat. Roll them in flour, fry them in oil or dripping. Serve with lemon.

BACCALÀ ALLA LIVORNESE
(LEGHORN SALT COD)

Cut 2 lb. of salt cod, already soaked for 24 hours and skinned, into large pieces about 6 in. by 4 in. Remove as many bones as possible without breaking the fish. Flour the slices and brown them gently in oil, drain them, and then stew them for an hour in a freshly made tomato sauce flavoured with garlic. Before serving stir in a handful of parsley.

LUMACHE
(SNAILS)

'The ancients held snails in especial esteem for the table. The Romans had many species served up at their feasts, which they distinguished in categories according to the delicacy of their flesh. Pliny tells us that the best were imported from Sicily, from the Balearic Isles, and from the Isle of Capri. The largest came from Illyria. Ships proceeded to the Ligurian coast to gather them for the tables of the Roman patricians. The great consumption led to the establishment of parks in order to fatten the animals, as is now done with oysters. They were fed for this end upon various plants mixed with soup; when it was desired to improve the flavour a little wine and some-times laurel* leaves were added.

'At Naples a soup made from *Helix memoralis* is sold publicly to the strange population with which the streets of that city swarms, for the King's pavement is their bed-chamber, dining-saloon, and workroom.' (Figuier, *The Ocean World*, 1868).

---

*Figuier means bay leaves, I fancy.

LUMACHE IN ZIMINO
(*STEWED SNAILS*)

Before snails are cooked, they must be starved for about a fortnight so that all the slime and scum comes out of them. Keep them wrapped loosely in a cloth, in a basket. The cloth must be changed at frequent intervals, or it will be smelly and dirty beyond endurance.

Now soak the snails in salted water to which a little vinegar has also been added for 3 hours. Wash them under running cold water until the last traces of scum have disappeared. Cook them in plenty of water, with salt and herbs, for 1½ hours. Strain them, and take the snails out of their shells, removing from each one the hard little black piece on the end of the body. The snails are now ready to be prepared in whatever fashion is chosen.

For snails *in zimino* heat some olive oil in a casserole; add a small sliced onion, 2 or 3 cloves of garlic, rosemary, parsley, fresh or dried mushrooms, salt and pepper. In this sauce cook the shelled snails for 10 minutes.

I think it would be perfectly possible to try this recipe with French ready-prepared snails packed in tins, now widely distributed and appreciated in this country.

GIOVANNA GARZONI (1600-70)
DISH WITH GRAPES, PEAR AND SNAIL (detail)
Florence, Palazzo Pitti, Galleria Palatina

JACOPO CHIMENTI DA EMPOLI (1551-1640)
STILL LIFE
Florence, Galleria degli Uffizi

MEAT

 HERE ARE PLENTY OF PLAINLY ROASTED AND GRILLED meat dishes in Italian cookery. The beef of Tuscany, the pork of Emilia and Romagna, the veal of Lombardy, and the lamb and kid of Rome are all first class. Italians are very appreciative of the true flavour of a leg of pork or veal, roasted with butter and herbs, of steaks grilled absolutely plain over a charcoal fire, and delicate little fried veal cutlets; sometimes you will be told in a restaurant that a steak is made from *vitellone*; this is misleading for the foreigner, who naturally supposes that *vitellone* means veal. The explanation, in the lucid words of an Italian friend, is as follows:

'*Vitello* is the animal that has never been fed on anything but milk and is slaughtered when only a few weeks old.

'*Vitellone* is the older animal, generally from one to three years, but which has never been made to work. As you know, oxen are used in Italy for work in the fields, and that is the reason for so much tough meat on the market. It would be too costly to keep animals which are reared solely for consumption gorging themselves and loafing after they are fully grown, so they are slaughtered young in this country, which explains why the only really good, tender meat to be found is *vitellone*, that is to say young beef.'

There are a number of interesting beef stews (made from the meat of those hard-worked oxen), and excellent ways of cooking pork.

Although in Italy mutton is not considered *signorile*, and seldom appears, baby lamb and kid are delicacies.

There are some highly original cold meat dishes, notably the Genoese *cima*, *vitello tonnato*, and some of the rolled veal or beef dishes with beautiful yellow and green stuffings. Pork cooked in milk is quite new to us in England. The sauces of Italian meat dishes have an entirely individual flavour, owing to the herbs used, to the fact that ham is a predominant ingredient instead of salt pork* which is more usual in French cooking, and to the oil or butter which are the main cooking mediums. White wine is used more often than red, but Marsala more commonly than either. The tomato and garlic flavoured meat dishes, which conform most nearly with the English notion of Italian cooking, nearly all come from the south, where the meat is of poor quality (although at one time Sorrento was celebrated for the excellence of its veal) and is best cooked in some highly-flavoured manner; even so, these dishes are very different from what might be supposed; fresh tomatoes, basil, *origano*, anchovies, and pine nuts combine to give the sauces an original taste which has nothing to do with the thick mass of tinned tomato purée indiscriminately spread over meat, poultry, and fish alike in restaurants which advertise what is now ominously known as 'continental cuisine'.

---

*The French *petit salé* is not smoked, and tastes very different from our bacon.

COSTOLETTE MILANESE
(MILANESE VEAL CUTLETS)

The genuine Milanese veal cutlets are, as the name should indicate, a cutlet on the bone. Any fat and gristle is cut away and it is flattened out with the cutlet bat, coated with beaten egg which has been seasoned with salt and pepper, then with fine breadcrumbs, and fried in a plentiful amount of very good clarified butter so that the outside is crisp and golden. The cutlets are garnished with halves of lemon and parsley. Accompaniments are either a green salad or sauté potatoes.

It will be seen that this dish is very different from the slice of nondescript meat encased in a sodden jacket of bread and blotting paper and fried in synthetic lard which so frequently masquerades as a Milanese cutlet in this country. Some Milanese cooks marinade the cutlets in milk for an hour before coating them with the egg and breadcrumbs, which whitens and softens the meat.

SCALOPPE MILANESE
(MILANESE VEAL ESCALOPES)

Escalopes are slices from the fillet, or inside cut of the leg. Each should weigh approximately 3 oz. and should be cut on the bias, without seam or sinew. Otherwise they buckle during cooking. They are cooked in the same way as the Milanese cutlet. It is hard to get an English butcher to cut escalopes in the proper way, so that it is best to buy the meat in one piece and cut it oneself, but a sharp butcher's knife is essential for this operation; should a cutlet bat not be among the kitchen utensils, an empty bottle is quite effective for flattening out escalopes. But envelop them in greaseproof paper before flattening them.

Cold Milanese escalopes, drained of all fat on a piece of kitchen paper, make a first class picnic dish.

PICCATE AL MARSALA
(VEAL WITH MARSALA)

Piccate, also called *scaloppine*, are very small squares of veal, sliced exceedingly thin, each weighing not more than 1 oz. and measuring roughly 3 in. square. Allow 3 or 4 little slices to each person; beat them out flat, season

them with salt, pepper and lemon juice, and dust them lightly with flour. In a thick frying pan put a good lump of butter, enough to cover the bottom of the pan when it is melted. Put in the slices of veal and brown them quickly on each side; add 2 tablespoonfuls of Marsala (for 8 pieces), let it bubble, then add, if possible, a little meat or chicken stock, not more than a tablespoonful. Stir the sauce, so that the wine, the butter, and the stock are

THE BUTCHER'S SHOP
from *Theatrum Sanitatis* (14th century)
Rome, Biblioteca Casanatense

well amalgamated; turn down the flame and let the contents of the pan simmer another minute or two, until the sauce begins to turn syrupy. The whole process of cooking should take only 5 minutes. Serve immediately. Mushrooms are a good vegetable to serve with this dish.

COSTOLETTE BOLOGNESE
(BOLOGNESE VEAL CUTLETS) (1)

This is a typical Bolognese fashion of treating veal. The mixture of cheese with meat appears at first an odd one, but since veal is so often

merely a texture rather than a taste it soon becomes apparent that the idea is intelligent. The foundation of the *costolette Bolognese* is a veal escalope cooked in the Milanese fashion – that is, beaten out thin, coated with beaten egg and fine breadcrumbs, and cooked gently in butter. For each escalope allow a fine slice of Parma ham of the same size and about 2 dessertspoonfuls of grated Parmesan. When the veal is golden on both sides place a slice of ham over each escalope, then the cheese, then a tablespoonful of just melted butter. Cover the pan and cook for 3 or 4 more minutes, until the cheese has melted.

The original *costolette Bolognese*, according to the Bolognese cooks, was made with thinly sliced fillets of pork, which has more flavour than veal. Presumably pork made too heavy a dish. But yet another method, which could only have originated in a region where extravagance is the rule rather than the exception, is to combine the flavour of fresh pork with the light texture of veal by pressing a slice of one on top of the other and then finishing the dish with ham and cheese in the way already described.

COSTOLETTE ALLA BOLOGNESE
(BOLOGNESE VEAL CUTLETS) (2)

A good escalope of veal and ½ oz. of grated Parmesan per person, butter, stock, Marsala.

Cut the escalopes from a fillet of veal or from the boned leg; they should be about ¼ in. thick and weigh about 3 oz. each. Season them with salt and pepper, flour them lightly, and brown them in plenty of butter on a fairly fast flame; add 2 tablespoonfuls of Marsala, stirring it into the butter. On top of each escalope spread a generous amount of grated Parmesan, and then moisten each with a few drops of stock; at the same time add a tablespoonful of stock to the sauce. Turn down the flame, cover the pan, and cook gently for another 5 minutes, until the meat is tender and the cheese melted. In Bologna, the region of rich and delicious cooking, they would add, in season, some sliced white Piedmont truffles to this ingenious dish.

A dish of French beans goes well with these escalopes; so do braised endives, with their slightly bitter aftertaste which counteracts the richness of the cheese and wine mixture.

SCALOPPE FARCITE
(STUFFED ESCALOPES)

Veal and cheese again. This recipe was given me by Signor Bolognini, who cooked at his restaurant Bolognini in the Via Mazzini in Bologna, and was also President of the Società dei Cuochi d'Avviamento di Bologna, where in 1953 he was teaching cooks of the future.

For each person you need 2 small and very thin slices of veal, a piece of ham the same size as the veal, 2 tablespoonfuls of grated Parmesan or gruyère, a slice of gruyère, a tablespoonful of sliced truffles or mushrooms, a little meat glaze or stock, butter.

First cut the cleaned truffles or mushrooms very thinly and sauté them in butter – 2 minutes for truffles, 5 or 6 minutes for mushrooms. Now make a sandwich, the veal on the outside, and the ham, mushrooms, and grated cheese inside. Melt ½ oz. of butter in a thick sauté or frying pan, put in the veal, and let it brown 2 or 3 minutes on each side; put a thin slice of gruyère on top of each veal sandwich, pour over either a tablespoonful of melted meat glaze or 2 tablespoonfuls of ordinary meat stock and cook, with the cover on the pan, 2 or 3 more minutes, until the butter and the stock have formed a syrupy sauce.

SALTIMBOCCA

Literally 'jump into the mouth'.

2 or 3 thin slices of veal per person, the same number of slices of raw or cooked ham, the same size as the slices of veal, sage leaves, salt, pepper, butter, Marsala.

Flatten out the slices of veal until they are as thin as possible. On each one lay a slice of ham and a leaf of fresh sage. Make each one into a little roll and secure them with a toothpick. Cook them gently in butter until they are well browned all over, then pour a small glassful of Marsala (or white wine) over them. Let it bubble for a minute, cover the pan, and simmer until the meat is quite tender: 10-15 minutes should be long enough. Serve with croûtons of fried bread. Thin slices of beef can be used instead of veal, but they will, of course, take a good deal longer to cook.

BOCCONCINI

Thin slices of veal and ham as for the *saltimbocca*, a finger of gruyère cheese for each slice of meat, butter.

Make little rolls of the veal and the ham, with the cheese in the centre. Cook them in butter. A little fresh tomato sauce can be added halfway through the cooking. Veal must be used for *bocconcini*, as the cheese in the middle would be melted long before the meat were cooked if beef were used.

BRACIOLETTE RIPIENE
(STUFFED VEAL ROLLS)

Take 8 or 10 small slices of veal, a large bunch of parsley, 2 oz. of pine nuts, 2 tablespoonfuls of sultanas, 8 or 10 small slices of Parma ham, white wine, 2 tablespoonfuls of grated cheese. Lay a slice of ham or bacon on top of each flattened out slice of meat, then a spoonful of the stuffing, which consists simply of the pine nuts, the chopped parsley, the cheese, and the sultanas mixed together. Roll up the meat, put a toothpick through each, brown them in oil, and add a glassful of white wine. Cook them slowly for 15-20 minutes. If beef is used instead of veal cook the *braciolette* for at least 40 minutes.

VITELLO ALLA GENOVESE
(VEAL WITH WHITE WINE AND ARTICHOKES)

Cut small thin slices of veal as for the *piccate* (p. 130). Prepare 2 or 3 artichokes as described for the raw artichoke salad on p. 46. Cook these artichoke slices very gently in butter, and

BREAD AND BUTCHER'S SHOPS (detail, late 15th-century fresco)
Val d'Aosta, Castello d'Issogne

when they are half cooked (about 5 minutes) put in the slices of veal. Brown them on both sides. Add a small glassful of white wine. Let it bubble, then turn down the flame and cook another minute or two.

The combination of veal with the artichokes and white wine is a particularly good and refreshing one.

SCALOPPINE ALLA PERUGINA
(VEAL ESCALOPES WITH CHICKEN LIVER CROÛTONS)

Prepare small veal escalopes as for *piccate* (p. 130). Cook them in butter, and serve them accompanied by the *crostini di fegatini* described on p. 153, but the bread need not necessarily be fried – the chicken livers can be served on plain slices of bread.

SCALOPPINE DI VITELLO BATTUTO
(ESCALOPES OF MINCED VEAL)

½ lb. of fillet or leg of veal, a shallot or very small onion, garlic, parsley, 2 eggs, salt and pepper.

Mince the veal, the shallot, the garlic, and the parsley. Beat in the eggs. Season with salt and pepper. Make the mixture into *polpettine* (round flat rissoles) and leave them for 1 or 2 hours. When the time comes to cook them roll each *polpettina* out flat into the shape of an escalope. Flour them on each side, and cook them gently in butter, adding a little Marsala when they are browned on each side.

A very good way of dealing with veal which may be tough.

Some butchers sell ready-minced veal which is good value for this dish and which will cost half the price of true escalopes.

FESA COL PROSCIUTTO
(LEG OF VEAL LARDED WITH HAM)

A piece of leg of veal weighing about 2 lb., ½ lb. of raw ham, 2 carrots, 2 oz. of butter, a tablespoonful of olive oil, a tumblerful of white wine, sage leaves.

Cut the ham into strips about ¼ in. wide and ⅛ in. thick. Make incisions lengthways in the meat, through the centre, and then above and below, so that there will be 3 layers of strips of ham, forming irregular stripes in the meat. Put the ham into the incisions, and here and there a strip of carrot (*per la coreografia*, as I was told by the cook in Parma, where the dish is a speciality). Tie the meat up with string, brown in the heated butter and oil, add a leaf or two of sage, then pour over the white wine. Cook gently on the top of the stove, with the cover on the pan, for 2½ hours. Serve cut into slices, with the sauce poured over.

OSSI BUCHI MILANESE
(STEWED SHIN OF VEAL)

2 lb. of shin of veal (if from a full-grown calf allow 4 lb.) sawn into pieces 2 in. thick, ¼ pint each of white wine and stock, ¾ lb. of tomatoes, parsley, a lemon, a clove of garlic, 2 oz. of butter.

In a wide shallow pan, brown the slices of shin of veal in the butter. Once browned, arrange them in the pan so that they remain upright, in order that the marrow in the bone may not fall out as the meat cooks. Pour the white wine over them, let it cook for 10 minutes, then add the skinned and chopped tomatoes; let them reduce; add the stock. Season. Cook for 1½ to 2 hours keeping the pan covered for the first hour.

Prepare a handful of chopped parsley, a clove of garlic chopped, and the grated peel of half a lemon. The Milanese call this mixture *gremolata*, and it is an essential part of the traditional *ossi buchi Milanese*. It is to be sprinkled on the top of the *ossi buchi* before serving.

To make the dish as it should be, very tender veal from an animal not more than three months old should be used. A dish of *risotto Milanese* (see p. 81) always accompanies *ossi buchi*.

Incidentally, I have seen it asserted that *ossi buchi* means drunken bones. It doesn't. It means bones with holes, or hollow-bones.

SPEZZATINO DI VITELLO
(VEAL STEW)

A dish in which to use up the pieces of meat left when escalopes have been cut from a leg of veal. You need about 1 to 1½ lbs.

Cut the meat into 2-in. pieces. Fry a sliced onion in a mixture of pork fat and butter, and then brown the meat. Pour in a small glassful of white wine and let it bubble 2 or 3 minutes. Add 2 skinned and chopped tomatoes and 2 or 3 pimentos cut into strips, and season with salt. Usually no pepper is needed, as the pimentos are strong enough. Simmer the stew slowly for 1½ hours. Serve with it a dish of fine green peas (these can also be added to the stew if preferred).

ROLÉ DI VITELLO
(A VEAL ROLL) (1)

A piece of lean veal weighing about 1½ lb., 2 eggs, parsley, 2 or 3 slices of *mortadella* sausage, a handful (about 1½ oz.) of Parmesan, butter, oil, a tumblerful of milk.

Make a *frittata*, or flat omelette, with the eggs, the grated Parmesan, the chopped parsley, and the *mortadella* sausage, also chopped.

Beat the meat out as flat as possible. Cover it with the omelette. Roll up the meat and tie it with string. In a mixture of olive oil and butter fry a chopped onion. Brown the meat all over. Pour in the heated milk. Cover the pan and simmer very gently for 2 hours. Can be served hot or cold. The appearance of the stuffing, yellow, pink, and green, is particularly attractive. For a party at which cold food is to be served a dish of this veal roll, another made according to the recipe which follows, and a third of the stuffed beef described on p. 141, make a fine display.

ROLÉ
(ROLL OF BEEF OR VEAL) (2)

1 to 1½ lb. of lean veal or beef (a piece of rump steak does very well), a large thin slice of uncooked ham, 2 or 3 hard boiled eggs, butter, white wine.

Flatten out the meat. Season it. Place the raw ham on top of it (a slice of mild bacon and one of cooked ham together will give approximately the right flavour), then the eggs, whole. Roll up the meat, tie it with string, and brown it in butter and oil. Add a leaf of sage. Pour a good glassful of white wine over the meat and cover the pan. Cook it very slowly on the top of the stove for 2-2½ hours. Serve it cut into slices,

MARCELLO FOGOLINO (1480-1548)
BANQUET
Malpaga, Castello

with the sauce poured over. Good cold, but the sauce must be left to cool separately, so that the fat can be taken off the top. A dish from Parma. It can also be cooked in a very moderate oven.

POLPETTONE
(MEAT ROLL)

2 lb. of raw minced veal, beef, or pork, 4 eggs, garlic, an onion, a handful of parsley, pepper and salt.

For the stuffing: 2 hard boiled eggs, 2 oz. of cooked ham, 2 oz. of Provolone or gruyère cheese, seasoning.

Mix the meat, the eggs, the chopped garlic, onion, and parsley together, and season them. Flatten the mixture out on a floured board. In the centre put the stuffing of hard-boiled eggs, ham, and cheese, all coarsely chopped.

Roll the meat up into a large sausage. Enclose it in a buttered paper. Melt some butter in a fireproof dish and cook the *polpettone* in a very slow oven or on top of the stove for 1½ hours. If the fat dries up, add a little water or stock, and keep the pan covered. Serve hot. Enough for eight people. The *polpettone* is also very good cold.

Nowadays I cook this dish in rather the same way as a meat loaf, in a rectangular tin or terrine.

POLPETTE

The only English translations of *polpette* would be rissoles, or meat balls, both of which have a rather sinister connotation. *Polpette* are usually made from raw meat. For six people you need 1 lb. of beef or veal, minced (buy the meat in the piece, butchers' minced meat is seldom good), 1 egg, 2 or 3 cloves of garlic, a thick slice of white bread, milk, parsley, salt, pepper, nutmeg, lemon peel, flour, dripping or oil for frying.

Put the garlic and the parsley and a strip of lemon peel through the mincer with the meat. Stir in the bread, which should have been steeped for at least 15 minutes in a little milk, and the liquid then pressed out in the hands. Beat in the whole egg, add the flavourings. Flour a board – and your hands. Form little flat cakes, no larger in diameter than 1¼ inches. Don't squeeze them too hard or work them too

PIETRO FABIUS (18th century)
ARISTOCRATIC PICNIC BY LAKE POSILLIPO (detail)
Naples, Museo Nazionale di San Martino

much. Roll them lightly in the flour on the board. Make a little dent in the top of each; this makes them lighter. Fry them in hot oil or dripping and leave them to drain 1 or 2 minutes on brown paper or on a wooden board.

Serve with them a green salad, or a potato or tomato salad. Made like this, *polpette* are not at all dull; in fact they make a most excellent little luncheon dish.

VITELLO TONNATO
(VEAL WITH TUNNY FISH SAUCE) (1)

This is one of the summer dishes to be found in all parts of Italy; it is excellent and original.

2 lb. of boned leg of *vitello di latte* (sucking calf), 2 anchovy fillets, an onion stuck with 2 cloves, a bay leaf, a piece of celery, a carrot, a few sprigs of parsley, salt. Remove the skin and the fat from the meat. Make a few incisions in it, and in these put small pieces of the anchovies. Roll up the meat, tie it with tape, and put it into a pan of boiling water with the vegetables. Simmer it for 1½ hours. When cooked, remove from the pan and leave to cool. Untie the meat, cut it in thin slices, and put it in a narrow *terrine*, where it is to marinade for a day or two in the following sauce.

4 oz. of tunny fish in oil, 2 anchovy fillets, the juice of 1 or 2 lemons, 5 oz. of olive oil, a

handful of capers. Pound the tunny fish and the anchovies; add the olive oil gradually so that it amalgamates with the tunny, as for a mayonnaise. Squeeze in the juice of the lemons and add the capers, from which the vinegar has been strained. The sauce should be fairly liquid. Pour it over the meat and leave in a cold place. Serve as it is, garnished with slices of lemon.

This is the classic recipe for *vitello tonnato*, as given by Artusi in *l'Arte di Mangiar Bene (circa 1890)*.

Another way of cooking it, and it seems to me a better one, is given below.

VITELLO TONNATO
(*VEAL WITH TUNNY FISH SAUCE*) (2)

Roast a 2 lb. piece of boned leg of veal or fillet. Leave it to cool. Having poured the fat from the pan, make a little stock from the juices in the pan with the addition of a cupful of water. (No flour).

Make a tunny fish mayonnaise as described on p. 195, thinning it to the consistency of thick cream with the prepared stock. Pour the mayonnaise over the sliced veal, and serve next day with a green salad.

CIMA
(*STUFFED COLD VEAL*)

One of the excellent specialities of Genoa, where the cooking does much to compensate for the incredible noise and bustle of that city.

A piece of breast of veal weighing about 1 lb. when boned, ¼ lb. each of veal brains and sweetbreads, 3 oz. of lean leg of veal, 4 eggs, an artichoke heart, 2 oz. of shelled green peas, 1 oz. of butter, 1 oz. of Parmesan, marjoram.

Put the brains to soak in warm salted water, clean them of skin, filaments, and blood. Blanch them in boiling salted water. Flatten out the breast of veal until it is about ¼ in. thick. Fold the meat in two, and sew it up on two sides so that you have a bag in which to put the stuffing.

Cut the piece of lean veal into pieces and put it in a pan with the butter and the sweetbreads cut up small. Cook for 10 minutes, and then mince the meat, or chop it finely with the *mezzaluna*. Add the prepared brains, and un-

cooked green peas, the raw artichoke heart in small pieces, marjoram, salt, pepper and the grated Parmesan cheese, and the beaten eggs.

With this stuffing fill the prepared breast of veal and sew up the opening very carefully. Put in a large saucepan, cover with salted water, bring gently to the boil, and let it cook with the water just moving for 1½-2 hours. Let it cool in the liquid. Take it out, put it on a board, cover it with a greaseproof paper, and put a heavy weight on it to compress the meat and the stuffing.

ANON (18th century)
STREET VENDOR OF MEATS AND SAUSAGES
Naples, Museo di San Martino

Before serving remove the thread and cut the meat into slices. The green of the peas and the artichokes makes a delicious contrast to the cream colours of the meat and eggs in the stuffing.

This dish will not be found in the grand restaurants or hotels of Genoa, for it is considered a dish of the people. It can be bought by the pound in a *rosticceria*, and is also often served in the small *trattorie*.

QUAGLIETTE DI VITELLO
(*VEAL OLIVES ON SKEWERS*)
Literally 'little veal quails'.

Season some thinly cut squares of veal with salt, pepper, and lemon juice. On each slice lay a piece of ham the same size; roll them up, and round each little roll place a very thin piece of bacon; thread them on to small skewers, alternating each one with a slice of raw onion, a leaf of sage, and a small square of stale bread about ½ in. thick. Put the skewers on to a fireproof dish, and pour over them a little melted bacon fat or dripping. Cook them in the top of a hot oven for 7 or 8 minutes, turning them over and basting them two or three times. Serve them on a dish of white rice. Those who find the scent of sage overpowering can replace it with mint or basil, or simply sprinkle the meat with marjoram or thyme before cooking it. Can also be made with pork or lamb.

SFORMATO DI VITELLO E ZUCCHINE
(*A PIE OF VEAL AND SMALL MARROWS*)

1 lb. of lean veal, 2 oz. of butter, 3 oz. of Parmesan cheese, 1¼ lb. of small marrows, salt, pepper, nutmeg.

Cut the veal into thin small escalopes, and slice the unpeeled marrows into rounds. Salt them and leave them to drain for an hour. Butter a deep pie dish and put in a layer of *zucchine*; season with pepper and nutmeg, and cover with slices of the meat. Sprinkle cheese and butter over the meat, and continue with alternate layers of *zucchine* and meat, butter, and cheese, until all are used up. The last layer should be *zucchine*, with cheese and butter on the top. Cook in a moderate oven for 40 minutes. Serve hot. Cucumbers or aubergines can be used instead of small marrows, and lamb or pork instead of veal; for these allow at least an extra 20 minutes' cooking time.

FRITTO MISTO

A *fritto misto* (literally 'mixed fry') is a very variable dish and may consist of two or three ingredients or as many as half a dozen. The most usual are very thin escalopes of veal, brains, artichoke hearts, small slices of aubergine or *zucchine*, mushrooms, cauliflower.

Each item is dipped in frying batter, fried in deep oil, and served with halves of lemon. When composing a *fritto misto* the essential point is that all the ingredients should be of very good quality, the meat tender, the vegetables young, all carved into delicate slices, and the batter light and crisp. Equally important a consideration is the immediate serving of the *fritto misto*; like any food fried in batter, these little mouthfuls are not worth eating if they have been kept waiting.

FRITTO MISTO ALLA FIORENTINA

Chicken breasts, brains, sweetbread, artichoke hearts, *mozzarella* cheese.

Cut the breast of a roasting chicken into 8 little fillets: clean and blanch 2 veal brains and 4 sweetbreads. Prepare 4 artichoke hearts, as explained on p. 46, and 4 little slices of *mozzarella* or *Bel Paese* cheese. Have ready a frying batter, as described on p. 114. Dip the chicken breasts and the artichoke hearts into it, and put these first into the very hot oil. They will take about 5 minutes to cook. After 3 minutes add the sweetbreads, the brains prepared as for croquettes (p. 146), and lastly the cheese, which takes only a minute in the hot oil. Drain all the ingredients, as they are ready, on kitchen paper, and serve them piled up in a hot dish, garnished with lemon.

FRITTO MISTO MILANESE

Escalopes of veal, calf's liver, brains, cockscombs, artichokes, cauliflower, small marrow (*zucchine*), eggs, breadcrumbs, clarified butter.

The veal and the liver are very thinly sliced as for *piccata* (p. 130). The cockscombs, which in England are apparently always thrown away, must be cooked for an hour in salted water and skinned, the cooked artichoke hearts sliced into rounds, the partly cooked cauliflower divided into flowerets, the *zucchine* cut into chips (see *zucchine fritte*, p. 168), and the brains prepared as for croquettes (p. 146).

For a Milanese *fritto* all the ingredients are coated with egg and breadcrumbs and fried in clarified butter.

STUDIO OF LONGHI (18th century)
BANQUET IN THE PALAZZO NANNI ON THE GIUDECCA
Venice, Ca' Rezzonico

course, if the boiled beef of the place, always excellent, is too serious an undertaking, or if the *frittura mista* is too light, let me recommend the *rognoni trifolati*, veal kidney stewed in butter with tomatoes and other good things, including a little Marsala wine. The white Piedmontese truffles served as a salad, or with a hot sauce, must on no account be overlooked; nor the *cardoons*, the white thistle, served with the same sauce; nor, indeed, the *zucchini ripieni*, which are stuffed pumpkins:† and some *fonduta*, the cheese of the country, melted in butter and eggs and sprinkled with white truffles, will form a fitting end to your repast, unless you feel inclined for the biscuits of Novara, or *gianduiotti*, which are chocolates or nougat from Alba or Cremona, where they make violins as well as sweets. You should drink the wine of the country, Barbera or Barolo, *Nebbiolo* or Freisa; and I expect, if you really persevere through half the dishes I have indicated, that you will be glad of a glass of Moscato with the fruit. Take your coffee at the Café Romano if you long for 'local colour'. (Lt. Col. Newnham-Davis, *The Gourmet's Guide to Europe*, Grant Richards, 1911).

---

*No. They are sweet peppers or pimentos.

†No. Small marrows.

GABRIEL BELLA (18th century)
DINNER AT THE THEATRE SAN BENEDETTO FOR THE NORTHERN DUKES
Venice, Galleria Querini

A PIEDMONTESE MEAL

'You will be fed well enough at your hotel whether you are at the Grand, or Kraft's, or the Trombetta. But if you want to test the cookery of the town I should suggest a visit to the Ristorante del Cambio, which is in the Piazza Carignano, where stands a marble statue of a philosopher and which has a couple of palaces as close neighbours; or to the Lagrange and Nazionale, both of which are in the Via Lagrange. Or, best of all, perhaps, go to the Ristorante della Meridiana, which is in the Via Santa Teresa. The proprietor, who is a mine of knowledge on all subjects regarding Turin, will serve at request not only the dishes of Lombardy, which he cooks admirably, but all the southern dishes as well. The *barolo vecchio*

of the house, generally only brought to your notice when you have established yourself as a regular patron, is well worth asking for on the earliest opportunity. The prices of the Meridiana are quite moderate.

'If you, wherever you happen to dine, wish to commence with hors d'oeuvre, try the *peperoni*, which are large yellow or red chillies* preserved in pressed grapes and served with oil and vinegar, salt and pepper. The *grissini*, the little thin sticks of bread which are made in Turin and are famous for their digestible quality, will be by your plate. Next I should suggest the *busecca*, though it is rather satisfying, being a thick soup of tripe and vegetables. And then must come a great delicacy, the trout from the Mont Cenis Lake. For a meat

BOLLITO

The great dish of northern Italy, especially of Piedmont. Visitors often ignore it, supposing that boiled meat must be dull. This is a great mistake. Served in the proper way, with a variety of different meats, vegetables, and sauces, it is extremely good, the equivalent, in fact, in a more lavish way, of the French *pot au feu*. It is obviously not a dish for a small household, for to be really good the quantity and variety of the meats cooked in a *bollito* must be considerable.

A large piece of lean beef or a fillet of veal, a calf's head, calves' feet, a capon, and on special occasions a turkey, are all cooked in the same pot, the calf's head being put in first, as it takes longest to cook, the other elements being added at intervals according to the time they need. A *cotechino* sausage is cooked in a separate pot.

often intractable and this way of cooking it gives it an opportunity to become a little less tough.

Allow a piece of rump steak for each person, and for four people 1½lb of ripe tomatoes, salt, pepper, *origano* or basil or parsley, oil, garlic.

Beat the steaks (the dish can also be made with slices from a round of beef, but they must be cooked longer), season them with salt and pepper, and brown them in a pan with a little olive oil. Have ready in another pan a sauce made by cooking the peeled and chopped tomatoes with a small amount of olive oil, salt, pepper, and 3 or 4 sliced cloves of garlic. The tomatoes must not be allowed to turn to pulp and should retain their fresh flavour. The Neapolitans add a liberal flavouring of *origano* (p. 23) or fresh basil; failing either of these herbs, good fresh parsley, not finely chopped but cut with scissors, will do instead. Spread this *pizzaiola* sauce thickly over each beef steak, put the lid on the pan and cook for another 5 minutes.

Serve the steaks, each one covered with its sauce, on a large hot dish. No additional vegetable is necessary.

ANNIBALE CARRACCI (1560-1609)
THE BUTCHER'S SHOP
Oxford, Christ Church

All these different meats are served hot on the same huge dish; very splendid they look, pink and brown and cream coloured, and I have never tasted veal with more savour than that of the Piedmontese *bollito*. The accompaniments are boiled white haricot beans, potatoes, stewed cabbage, *salsa verde*, and a tomato sauce spiced with vinegar and mustard.

There is, of course, a lovely broth from the cooking of the *bollito*, to be dealt with at another meal.

A genuine *bollito* is rather expensive, but a similar dish can be made with cheaper ingredients. A piece of gammon, for instance, with tongue, and a boiling chicken, would be a very good combination. A calf's head, a pig's head, silverside of beef and calves' feet could go in too. Cook the accompanying cabbage as described for *cavoli in agrodolce* on p. 171, or have sauerkraut instead. Serve different kinds of mustard as well as the sauces.

BISTECCA ALLA FIORENTINA
(FLORENTINE BEEF STEAK)
The true Florentine beef steak is a huge rib steak, similar to an American T-bone steak, from an animal not more than two years old. Nowhere in Italy are the steaks so good, so full of flavour and at the same time so tender as in Tuscany.

The steak is grilled over a charcoal fire and seasoned with salt after cooking. It has no need of any adornment except perhaps a little good butter placed on the top as it is served, and it is so large that there is no room, nor any necessity, for a vegetable on the plate with it.

BISTECCA ALLA PIZZAIOLA
(STEAK WITH TOMATO AND GARLIC SAUCE)
A Neapolitan dish, evolved presumably for the reason that in southern Italy the meat is

FILETTO CASANOVA
(FILLET STEAKS WITH BRANDY AND MARSALA)
For 4 fillet steaks the ingredients are a little oil, 1 oz. of butter, 3 oz. of brandy, 2 oz. of Marsala, 4 oz. of good goose-liver pâté.

Season the steaks with salt and ground black pepper, rub them very lightly with olive oil, and leave them for an hour or two. They are then to be grilled, or fried in a very hot pan, for a minute only on each side, so that they are browned.

In a pan large enough to accommodate the 4 steaks, melt the butter and in this cook the goose liver pâté so that it turns to a thick purée; add the Marsala. Cook for a minute and put the grilled steaks into this sauce. In a small pan or a soup ladle, warm the brandy; set it alight and pour it over the steaks. Shake the pan so that the flames spread and burn as long as possible. By the time the flames are extinct the meat should be cooked.

VINCENZO CAMPI (1536-91)
THE COOK
Rome, Galleria Doria Pamphili

MANZO STUFATO AL VINO ROSSO
(BEEF STEWED IN RED WINE)
Cuts suitable for this *stufato* are chuck steak or top rump, but it is hardly worth cooking it with less than 2-3 lb. The meat should be lean and can be cut into large pieces, although to my mind it is preferable to leave it in one piece. Marinade it for 4 or 5 hours in a tumbler of coarse red wine and the usual flavourings – a sliced onion, 3 or 4 cloves of garlic, salt, pepper, herbs.

To cook the meat, take it out of the wine and remove any of the herbs or vegetables which may have stuck to it. In a sauté pan or earthen casserole brown a sliced onion in a mixture of oil and pork or bacon fat. Now brown the piece of meat nicely on both sides. Add some chunks of bacon or raw ham (3 or 4 oz.) and pour on the marinade, through a strainer. Let the liquid bubble fiercely for 3 minutes or so. Add half a cupful of water (or beef stock); cover the pan, and let it simmer for 3 hours. At the end of this time the meat should be tender, but not cooked to rags, and the sauce reduced. If it is too liquid turn up the flame and let it bubble until it has thickened somewhat. A piece of *cotenna* (pork rind) cooked with the meat is a help.

This stew is equally extremely successful when carried out with a piece of lean veal, without bone. Green peas go nicely with it, or *crocchette di patate* (p. 162), or the carrots described on p. 166.

STUFATO DI MANZO ALLA GENOVESE
(GENOESE BEEF STEW)
2 lb. of lean beef, such as topside or rolled rib, 1 lb. of onions, 2 tomatoes, a carrot, a piece of celery, butter, white wine.

Melt the sliced onions in butter; they should not brown, only turn pale yellow. Put in the beef, in one piece, and brown it on each side. Add the peeled and sliced tomatoes, the sliced carrot, and the celery; season with salt, pepper, and basil. Pour a wineglassful of white wine over the meat, cover the pan, and cook gently for 2-3 hours.

Like all such dishes in which only a small quantity of liquid is used, this stew should be cooked in a pot in which the meat just about fits, for if the liquid is spread over a wide area it gets dried up in the cooking.

SPIT-ROASTING
from *De Sphaere* Codex (15th century)
Modena, Biblioteca Estense

COSTA DI MANZO AL VINO ROSSO
(RIB OF BEEF MARINADED IN RED WINE)
Choose, if possible, a thick piece of rib of beef weighing about 3 lb. and with the bone. It will need rather a large, shallow casserole or braising pan, but if this is not available the bone can be removed. Put the meat into an earthenware dish or bowl and over it pour a good half bottle of strong red wine. Add a small sliced onion, a sliced carrot, a piece of celery, a couple of bay leaves, a clove or two of garlic and a little ground black pepper. The meat is to marinade for about 24 hours, being turned over three or four times so that each side is well soaked in the wine. When the time comes to cook it, take it out of the marinade and dry it very carefully. In a casserole which will conveniently hold the meat melt a little butter or dripping; brown the meat on both sides. Add salt. In the meantime, in another pan, reduce the strained marinade to half its original volume; pour it over the meat. Cover the pan, and simmer very slowly for about 3 hours, or longer if the meat is very tough. At the end of the cooking there should be just sufficient sauce, thickish, to moisten each person's helping. Should the meat used be on the fat side some of the fat will have to be skimmed off the sauce.

I have adapted this excellent recipe from Ada Boni's *Talismano della Felicità*. Even an impossibly tough and coarse piece of meat cooked in this way (so long as it has simmered in the most leisurely way) emerges tender, full of flavour, and not in the least stringy. Potato *gnocchi*, moistened with butter and a little grated Parmesan, make a nice accompaniment.

STUFATINO ALLA ROMANA
(ROMAN BEEF STEW)
A traditional Roman dish. It is made with the lean part of shin of beef, cut off the bone into thinnish slices. For six people allow about 2½ lb. of meat, minus bone and fat. In dripping or butter sauté a small sliced onion and 2 sliced cloves of garlic. When this has slightly browned add 1½ oz. of bacon, in strips; give this a stir and add the pieces of meat seasoned with salt and pepper and a little marjoram. Let the meat brown on both sides, and pour in a tumbler of strong dry red wine; let this bubble until it has reduced by at least half. Now stir in a tablespoonful, not more, of concentrated tomato purée (or 4-6 large peeled and chopped tomatoes). Let this cook for 3 to 4 minutes, then pour in enough boiling water to barely cover the meat. Cover the pan, and simmer the *stufatino* very slowly for 2-3 hours. By the time it is cooked, the sauce should be thick, of a fine dark colour and rich savour. As an accompaniment, stewed celery is a favourite with the Italians.

STRACOTTO
(BEEF STEW)
1 lb. of lean beef, a piece of Italian pork sausage (*not* an English pork-and-breadcrumb sausage) weighing about 3 oz., or the same weight of fresh lean pork meat, a carrot, an onion, a small piece of celery, 1 oz. of butter, a small glassful (about 3 liquid oz.) of white wine, salt and pepper, a cupful of meat broth, a tablespoonful of concentrated tomato purée.

Brown the sliced onion, carrot, and celery in the butter. Add the beef, in one piece, and the sausage or pork. Cook gently for 10 minutes. Add the tomato purée, stir it well into the juice in the pan, add the white wine, let it bubble a little, then pour in the broth. Season with salt and pepper. (A couple of cloves are sometimes added at this stage.) Cover the pan with a thick layer of paper, then with the lid, and cook in a very slow oven for several hours – anything from three to five.

When the *stracotto* emerges the beef should be soft enough to cut with a spoon, and the sauce thick. This is the way beef is cooked to make the filling for *anolini*, the delicious ravioli of Parma. The recipe for making them is on p. 76.

Stracotto also makes a very good dish to serve as it is, perhaps increasing the quantities, as it is hardly economical to cook a small amount of meat for such a very long time.

MANZO RIPIENO ARROSTO
(STUFFED ROAST BEEF)

1 lb. of lean beef, either rump or shoulder, cut in a thick slice. For the stuffing, 2 chicken livers (or 1½ oz. of liver paste), 2 oz. each of cooked ham and tongue, 1 oz. of grated Parmesan, an egg, a thick slice of white bread, a small onion, a small piece of celery, half a carrot, parsley, salt, pepper, herbs, and seasoning.

Chop the onion, carrot, celery, parsley, and the chicken livers. Stir in the bread, which should have been soaked a few minutes in water and pressed dry, the ham, tongue (cut in strips), the cheese, the beaten egg, some thyme or basil, salt and pepper. Flatten out the slice of beef (it will be easier if it has first been plunged into cold water for a minute) and spread the stuffing on to it. Roll it up into a sausage shape, tie it with string, and cook it in a little oil, either in a heavy pan on top of the stove, very slowly, or in the oven. If cooked in the oven, it can be done at the normal slow-roasting temperature (provided the meat is not too tough).

Like most of these stuffed meat dishes, this one is at its best when cold. With care, even a piece of tough stewing steak can be made into a good dish, cooked in this way. Having browned the prepared and stuffed meat in oil or dripping, add about 2 in. of water to the fat in the roasting pan, cover the meat with a greased paper and cook at a very low temperature for about 4 hours.

Nowadays, it is more satisfactory to make this dish in larger quantities.

LESSO RIFATTO
(RÉCHAUFFÉ OF BOILED MEAT)

To make a good dish from cold boiled beef, slice ½ lb. of onions very thinly and put them to stew very gently in 1 oz. of butter. When they have turned yellow add the finely chopped cold meat, a clove of garlic, salt and pepper. If the onions get too dry add a little meat stock. Before serving stir in a small handful of chopped parsley and the juice of half a lemon.

THE ART OF ROASTING MEAT IN SARDINIA

'The Sardinians, but chiefly the shepherds, and, generally speaking, all the country people, excel in the art of roasting meat on the spit and of cooking it beneath the flames.

'For the first operation, they use a long wooden or iron spit which they turn, crouched meanwhile close to a fierce fire; for the second, they dig a hole in the ground. After having levelled and cleaned it, and lined it with branches and leaves, they place therein the meat, even the entire animal as it is killed, without gutting it; they then cover it with a light layer of soil, upon which they burn a big fire for several hours.

'This fashion of cooking meat owes its origin to the necessity of the cattle and sheep thieves to hide their booty while cooking it. Thus more than once the owner of a stolen animal going out to search for it has sat round the fire under which his sheep was cooking, without dreaming that the people who had invited him to join them were precisely those who had robbed him.

'I have been assured that not only are whole sheep and pigs cooked in this fashion, but calves and mules, and that nothing can equal the excellence of their flesh when so prepared.

'It is even claimed that for festive occasions the mountain shepherds sometimes take a sucking pig, enclose it in a gutted sheep, which in its turn is put into a calf, and then cook the whole in the manner described; the different meats, they say, cook evenly and acquire an exquisite flavour.' (Chevalier Albert de la Marmora, *Voyage en Sardaigne 1819-1825*, 1826.)

This Sardinian brigand cooking is very reminiscent of the original *klephti* or robber cooking of Greece, where the system of flavouring meat or game with aromatic herbs, wrapping it in paper and cooking it slowly in an oven has come to be generally known as *klephti* cooking. I am told that for a country *festa* in Sardinia a whole sheep or kid is still occasionally cooked in an underground oven, wrapped in myrtle branches, which give the meat a marvellous flavour. (See *Porceddù*, p. 142).

ABBACCHIO AL FORNO
(ROAST SUCKING LAMB)

Into an incision made near the bone of a leg of sucking lamb put a few cloves of garlic, salt and pepper, and a few leaves of rose-

SANO DI PIETRO (1406-81)
KILLING THE PIG (detail)
Siena, Biblioteca Communale

mary. Roast the meat with butter or oil, and see that it is well done. Carve it in good thick slices.

Sometimes a little white wine is poured over the lamb about 15 minutes before it is ready; and this, with the juices which have come out of the meat, after the fat has been strained off, makes a sauce.

The season for this famous speciality is Easter time. A leg of baby lamb as known in Italy is just about large enough for two people.

COSTOLETTE D'AGNELLO ALLA MARINETTI
(MARINETTI'S LAMB CUTLETS)

Lamb cutlets cooked with bay leaves, rosemary, garlic, pepper, white wine, and lemon, and served with dates stuffed with salted pistachio nuts. (F. Marinetti, *La Cucina Futurista*, 1932.)

CAPRETTO AL FORNO
(ROAST KID)

Cook a *gigot* of kid in exactly the same way as described for *abbacchio* (roast lamb) above.

Kid is just as good as, and very often better than, lamb. Serve it with small roast potatoes and a green salad.

CAPRETTO AL VINO BIANCO
(KID IN WHITE WINE)

About 2 lb. of kid (or lamb) cut in one piece from the leg, 2 carrots, 3 tomatoes, an onion, a turnip, a piece of celery, an orange, coriander seeds, garlic, a small glassful each of white wine and Marsala, olive oil, herbs.

Put a few pieces of garlic into the meat and rub it well with salt, pepper, and marjoram or *origano*. Fry the sliced onion in oil; then brown the meat. Add the tomatoes, peeled and chopped, and when these are soft, the other vegetables, add the garlic, orange peel, the crushed coriander seeds (about a teaspoonful), and the white wine. After 5 minutes add the Marsala and the seasonings and salt. Cover the pan and simmer gently for 2 hours. The sauce should be reduced and fairly thick. Squeeze the juice of half the orange over the meat.

MONTONE USO CAPRIOLO
(MUTTON TO TASTE LIKE ROEBUCK)

For a medium-sized leg of mutton, prepare the following marinade: warm a small quantity of olive oil in a saucepan and into it put an onion, a carrot and a stick of celery, all finely chopped; let them brown very slightly and add 2 cloves of garlic, a sprig each of rosemary and thyme, about 8 peppercorns and 12 juniper berries, 2 bay leaves, and a very little salt. Over the vegetables and herbs pour half a bottle of red wine and 2 tablespoonsful of vinegar. Simmer the marinade for 15 minutes. Leave it to cool, then pour it over the leg of mutton in a deep dish. Leave it to marinade for 3 days, turning the meat over two or three times so that it is well impregnated with the wine.

To roast the mutton. Dry the meat carefully, removing any pieces of vegetables which are adhering to it. Put it in a roasting pan and start it off on a good heat in a previously heated oven. Lower the heat after 15 or 20 minutes, and finish the cooking in a moderate oven.

To make the sauce. Strain the marinade, put it into a small pan, and reduce it by half; stir into it a tablespoonful of red currant jelly, a tablespoonful of Marsala, a few strips of candied orange peel and a handful of pine nuts (p. 29). Stir the sauce over a low flame until it is thickish. Serve it separately. It must be admitted that mutton treated like this in no way resembles roebuck, but it has an excellent flavour and thus was a good method of dealing with a piece of the elderly ewe mutton which we had to cope with while I was writing this book in 1953.

ARISTA FIORENTINA
(FLORENTINE ROAST PORK)

Remove the rind and, should there be an excessive amount, some of the fat from a piece of loin of pork weighing about 3-4 lb.

Press 2 or 3 cloves of garlic into the meat, with a few leaves of rosemary and 2 or 3 whole cloves. Rub the meat with salt and pepper and put it into a roasting pan with water, about 2 in. deep. Cook it in a moderate oven in an open pan.

It will take somewhat longer than the normal method of roasting; allow about 45 minutes to the pound. The meat emerges tender and moist. Let it cool a little in its own juice, then pour off the liquid (don't throw this away – there will be good pork fat on the top when it has set) and serve the pork cold.

ARISTA PERUGINA
(PERUGIA ROAST PORK)

The method is the same as for the *arista fiorentina*, but instead of rosemary flavour the pork with fennel leaves and garlic, or if there are no fennel leaves available a few pieces of the fennel bulb or some fennel seeds. Although it is not orthodox, I find the flavour of the meat is greatly enhanced by rubbing the clove of garlic in a few crushed coriander seeds before putting them into the meat. One of my favourite recipes.

A nice accompaniment is a potato salad flavoured with a very little fennel.

PORCEDDÙ
(SARDINIAN ROAST SUCKING PIG)

Sardinian sucking pig has the best flavour and consistency of any I have ever tasted; it is divided in two lengthways, each half cooked on a spit over a wood fire and basted with dripping until the skin is crackling; then both pieces are put on to a dish spread with a bed of myrtle leaves. More myrtle leaves are put on the top, the dish covered with another dish, and the pork left to inhale the aroma of the myrtle.

COSTA DI MAIALE ALLA GRIGLIA
(GRILLED PORK CHOPS)

For 2 large pork chops, chop a handful of fennel (bulb and leaves) and a clove of garlic; season with salt, pepper, and about 8 crushed juniper berries.

Put a clove of garlic into each pork chop near the bone; score them lightly across and across on each side, and coat them with the fennel mixture. Pour a thin film of olive oil over each, and leave them to marinade for 3 or 4 hours, turning them over once or twice so that the oil penetrates both sides.

should have reduced to about a small cupful, full of all the delicious little bits of bacon and onion, and the meat should be encased in a fine crust formed by the milk, while it is moist and tender inside. It is at this moment that any meat or bird cooked in milk should be carefully watched, for the remaining sauce evaporates with disconcerting rapidity, leaving the meat to stick and burn.

To serve, pour the sauce, with all its grainy little pieces, over the meat. Can be eaten hot or cold. But best cold, I think.

Whatever the weight of the piece of meat to be cooked in this fashion, allow roughly a pint of milk per pound.

One or two readers have told me they find this recipe very tricky. It can be made easier by transferring the dish, uncovered, to a moderate oven, after the web has formed. When the meat is cooked, return the pan to the top of the stove and reduce the sauce.

CASOEULA
(MILANESE STEWED PORK)

1½ lb. lean pork, ½ lb. of Italian pork sausage (*cotechino*, for example, p. 146), a piece of pork or bacon rind, a white cabbage weighing 2-3 lb., 3 oz. of fat bacon, ½ lb. of carrots, an onion, a stick of celery, a bay leaf, salt, pepper, a tumblerful of white wine, a tablespoonful of flour, 1 oz. of butter.

Melt the butter in a large and heavy pan and in it brown the chopped bacon, the sliced onion, the carrots cut into rounds, and the celery into short lengths. Now add the pork cut into thick slices, the sausages (whole if they are small, and cut into chunks if it is a *cotechino*), and the slice of pork rind.

Season with salt and pepper, add the bay leaf, and sprinkle with the flour. Pour over the white wine. Cover the pan and cook very slowly. If there is too little liquid add a little stock or water.

While the meat is cooking clean the cabbage and cook it for 10 minutes in boiling salted water. Drain it, cut it into quarters, and add it to the *casoeula* 30 minutes before it is to be served. The whole process should take 1½-2 hours, according to the quality of the meat. Slices of plain or fried *polenta* are served with the *casoeula*. Plenty for four people.

JANUARY (detail, 15th-century fresco)
Trento, Castello di Buonconsiglio

Cook them under the grill exactly as they are, preferably in a dish in which they can be served, for about 20-25 minutes. They must be turned over at least twice. If the chops are tender, this is one of the most excellent ways possible of cooking them. The fennel and the juniper berries give a most original, but not at all violent, flavour, and the oil does not, as might be supposed, make the meat greasy.

Serve plenty of bread to soak up the delicious liquid in the pan.

Another much-used recipe.

MAIALE AL LATTE
(PORK COOKED IN MILK)

About 1½ lb. of loin of pork, or boned leg, without the rind, rolled into a sausage shape, 1½ pints of milk, 1½ oz. of butter, 1½ oz. of ham, salt and pepper, an onion, garlic, coriander seeds; marjoram, basil, or fennel.

Melt the butter, brown the finely chopped onion in it, then the ham, also finely chopped.

Stick a clove of garlic inside the rolled meat, together with 3 or 4 coriander seeds and a little marjoram, basil, or fennel. Rub it with salt and pepper and brown it in the butter with the onion and ham. In the meantime heat the milk to boiling point in another pan. When the meat has browned pour the milk over it. Add no more salt or pepper. Keep the pan steadily simmering at a moderate pace, uncovered. Gradually a golden web of skin begins to form over the top of the meat while the milk is bubbling away underneath. Don't disturb it until it has been cooking for a good hour. At this moment break the skin and scrape the sides of the pan, stirring it all into the remaining milk, which will be beginning to get thick. In about another 30 minutes the milk

ROMAN HAM

The book of Apicius (see p. 9) gives a recipe for cooking ham with 'a good many dried figs and 3 bay leaves, remove the rind, and make small incisions in the flesh, which you fill with honey; wrap it in a paste of flour and oil, when it is cooked, take up the ham, and serve as it is.'

PROSCIUTTO DI PARMA
(PARMA HAM)

The unique flavour of Parma hams, so the people of Parma claim, is due not only to the feeding of the pigs (partly upon the whey left from the making of Parma cheeses) and the methods of curing but more especially to the dry and airy climate of the hill country of the province of Parma. The region is well watered by the rivers Parma, Baganza, and Taro, and in the months during which the hams are maturing is not subject to any violent changes of temperature. Thousands of ready salted hams are sent every year by the pig farmers of Lombardy to be matured in the good air of the Parmesan country, and especially to Langhirano. The Parmesans will tell you, however, that neither these hams nor those produced in the more extreme climate of the mountains have the delicacy or flavour of the genuine hams from the pigs fattened on their own Parma hillsides.

The districts mainly responsible for the production of these hams are Langhirano, Felino (known also for its white wine and its wonderful salame), Sala Baganza, Noceto, and Moderno.*

The season for curing the hams is from September to March. After the pigs have been killed the hams are kept in the cold for 4 days; they are then salted, with approximately 1-1½ kilos of salt according to the size of the ham, plus 20 grams of nitrate, which preserves the pink colour of the hams, to every 100 kilos of salt; the hams are laid in wooden trays, and every 6 or 7 days are moved round so that the salt penetrates thoroughly. They are salted from 30-50 days, according to the weight, which may vary from approximately 8 to 11 kilos. The surplus salt is then washed from the hams and they are hung up to dry, in a warm draught, for 6 or 7 days, after which they are transferred to a cooler temperature for 6 or 7 months – for the first month at 20°, the second

GIACOMO·NANI (1698-1770)
STILL LIFE WITH PROSCIUTTO AND BIRDS
Naples, Museo Nazionale di San Martino

month at 15°, and for 3 to 6 months at 10°. The important factor during this period is that air should circulate freely round the hams. Given every care and the most modern and scientific treatment it is still by no means certain that the hams will turn out perfectly. Even in districts where these hams have been turned out for generations, a certain percentage of them, owing partly to the relatively light proportion of salt used in the curing process, still prove unsatisfactory for the market, a factor which accounts both for the high price and comparative rarity of a first-class Parma ham, and this in spite of the fact that something like 150,000 hams are produced yearly in the province of Parma.

A description of how Parma ham† is eaten, with figs, melon, or butter, is on p. 50.

Other famous specialities of the province of Parma are the *culatello di Zibello* (p. 50), *bondiola* or *coppa* or *capocollo*, and *spalla di San Secondo* (which are all made from cured shoulder of pork), *pancetta* (made from the stomach), and *Salame di Felino*.

---

*For further information about Parma hams consult *Le Conserve di Carne* (Ghinelli; ed. Casanova, Parma, 1950), and *Gastronomia Parmense* (Ferrutius, Parma, 1952).

†Although Parma ham is often described on English restaurant menus as smoked, it can be seen from the foregoing that this is incorrect – *E.D. 1963*.

VINCENZO CAMPI (1536-91)
THE FRUIT SELLER (detail)
Milan, Pinacoteca di Brera

SALAME

Nearly every province in Italy has its own traditions and opinions as to the preparation of *salame*, determined by agricultural conditions, the climate, and the tastes of the inhabitants. The differences are in the kinds of meats used and the proportions of lean to fat, in the way the meat is chopped and mixed, in the size and shape of the sausage, in its seasoning, salting, and maturing; and although the production of such foods has become largely industrialized, local traditions regarding these details are respected, so that mercifully there are always dozens of different kinds of *salame* to be tasted and enjoyed.

Crespone, or *salame Milano*, the one most easily to be found in Italian shops abroad, consists of equal proportions of lean pork, beef, and pork fat, seasoned with pepper, garlic, and white wine. The rice-like grainy appearance of the fat is characteristic of this *salame*. Although the most widely exported, Milan *salame* is regarded by Italian connoisseurs as too mass produced to have a really fine flavour.

Salame Fiorentina is a larger sausage, made of pure pork, in which the meat and fat are cut in fairly big pieces. *Finocchiona* is a variation of the Florentine *salame*, flavoured with fennel seeds. *Salame* made entirely of pork is usually more delicate and tender than that made from a mixture of pork and beef or veal.

Salame di Felino. The village of Felino near Parma is known for its white wine and has given its name to the *salame* made in the district. Felino *salame* does occasionally appear in Soho shops; it is recognizable by its irregular shape and hand-made appearance, and the label, usually, of Luigi Boschi, one of the best producers.

Anyone visiting Parma should not fail to ask for Felino *salame*. It is infinitely more delicate than the ordinary commercial *salame*, being made from pure lean pork meat, with 15-20 per cent of fat, flavoured with white wine, whole peppercorns, and a very little garlic. Owing to the delicacy of its curing it does not keep very well, although the difficulty is being overcome by the system of encasing the *salame* entirely in a wax covering for export. Even in Italy Felino *salame*, which is more expensive than Parma ham, is found only in luxury grocers.

Salame Fabriano, from Ancona and the Marche region, was at one time also a pure pork *salame*, but is now made on a commercial scale from a mixture of pork and *vittellone* (see p. 129).

Salame Genovese is 20 per cent pork, 50 per cent *vittellone*, 30 per cent pork fat; a fairly strongly-flavoured sausage which makes a delightful combination with *sardo* cheese and raw broad beans for the favourite Genoese *antipasto* (see p. 44).

Soppresse is the pork and beef *salame* common in Verona, Padua, and the Veneto.

Salame Napoletano is made with pork and beef in the same proportions as the Milanese *cresponi*, but with a more powerful flavouring of both black and red pepper.

Salame Sardo, the local Sardinian product, is a very excellent countrified pork *salame* flavoured with red pepper, which the Sardinians claim is 'more healthy' than black pepper – on exactly what grounds they seem none too sure.

Salame Ungherese, or Hungarian *salame*, is now very popular in Italy. The meat (pork and beef, and pork fat) is chopped very finely and flavoured with pepper, paprika, garlic, and white wine. It is mostly Italian-made, not imported from Hungary.

Cacciatori are small *salame*, each weighing about ½ lb., made in the same way as Milan *salame.* Less salt is used in the curing, and they are matured for a far shorter period.

Mortadella. There are dozens of different varieties of the famous Bologna sausage; the best are made with pure pork, but the cheaper *mortadella* of commerce may be a mixture of pork, veal, tripe, pig's head, donkey meat, potato or soya flour, and colouring essence. Coriander and white wine are always used in the flavouring. *Mortadella* is not cured in salt but cooked by a steam process. In Bologna there is good *mortadella* to be found, but on the whole it is a pasty sausage lacking the bite and stimulating character of the raw salt-cured *salame.*

COTECHINO

Cotechino is a large pork *salame* salted only for a few days, weighing between 1 and 2 lb. A speciality of the whole of Emilia and Romagna, and especially of Modena.

Make a few incisions in the skin of a *cotechino* (they can usually be found in Italian delicatessen shops*) with a fine skewer or a knitting needle. Wrap it in a muslin or linen cloth. Put it in a pan, lying longways, and cover it with cold water. Simmer it slowly for 2-3 hours according to the weight. Serve it hot, cut into thick slices and accompanied with stewed white haricot beans, lentils, and mashed potatoes.

---

*Buy imported ones whenever possible. Those made in England are not generally as good.

ZAMPONE DI MODENA

Zampone is made from the same pork mixture as *cotechino*, the difference being that the meat is stuffed into the skin of a pig's trotter. It is to be found in Italian shops.

Soak the *zampone* for 12 hours in cold water. Loosen the strings which are tied round it, and make two incisions with a sharp knife in the form of a cross between the trotters. Wrap the *zampone* in a cloth, put it in a pan in which it will lie flat, and cover it with cold water.

Cook it very slowly for 3 hours, or for 4 hours if its weight exceeds 4 lb.

Serve it very hot, accompanied by the same vegetables as the *cotechino.*

GROEWENBROTH (18th century)
SAUSAGE SELLER
Venice, Ca' Rezzonico

SALSICCE ALLA ROMAGNOLA
(*ROMAGNA SAUSAGES*)

1 lb. of pure pork sausages, freshly made tomato sauce or ½ lb. of raw tomatoes, sage, olive oil.

The sausages used for this dish are the northern Italian country sausages called *luganeghe*. We have no English equivalent, but they can be obtained in Italian shops.

Fry the sausages very slowly in olive oil, adding a couple of sage leaves. When they are browned all over pour off excess fat, cover them with the tomato sauce or the raw skinned and chopped tomatoes. Simmer for 15 minutes.

CROCCHETTE DI CERVELLA
(*BRAIN CROQUETTES*)

2 calf's brains, an egg, flour, butter, vinegar.

Clean the brains, freeing them from the skin and blood. Put them into a pan and cover them with water, to which is added a thread of vinegar. Let them simmer for 20 minutes. Drain them well, pound them into a paste. Season with salt and pepper, and when they are cold form them into small croquettes. Dip them in beaten egg and then flour. Fry them gently in butter, turning them over several times so that they brown evenly. They will be cooked in 5 minutes.

FEGATO ALLA VENEZIANA
(*VENETIAN CALF'S LIVER*)

A dish to be found all over Italy, but at its best in Venice.

2 lb. of onions, 1 lb. of calf's liver, olive oil. Slice the onions very finely. Cover the bottom of a thick shallow pan with oil. When it is warmed, not smoking, put in the onions. They are to stew very gently, turning soft and golden yellow, not brown. Salt them lightly. When they are ready (about 30-40 minutes, cooked with the cover on the pan) add the prepared liver. This should ideally be the very tenderest calf's liver, so soft that you could put a finger through it as if it were bread. It should be cut in the thinnest possible slices, like little scraps of tissue paper, and it needs only a minute's cooking on each side. Serve as quickly as possible.

When obliged to use tough liver for this dish, have it cut as thinly as possible, but cook it slowly with the onions, for 10-15 minutes. It will still make an excellent dish, although it will not have the finesse of genuine *fegato alla Veneziana.*

FEGATO DI VITELLO ALLA MILANESE
(*MILANESE CALF'S LIVER*)

Cut the liver into slices about ¼ in. thick. Season them with salt, pepper, and lemon juice, and leave them for about an hour. Dip them in beaten egg, coat them with breadcrumbs, and fry them in butter.

Before serving them add a little cut parsley to the butter, and garnish the dish with halves of lemon.

CARLO MAGINI (1720-1806)
STILL LIFE OF SAUSAGES
Campione di'Italia, Silvano Lodi Collection

FEGATO DI VITELLO AL MARSALA
(CALF'S LIVER WITH MARSALA)

Cut the liver in very thin slices, and cook as for *Piccate al Marsala* (p. 130).

ROGNONI TRIFOLATI
(STEWED KIDNEYS)

½ lb. of veal or sheep's kidneys, parsley, olive oil or butter, a small glassful of Marsala, half a lemon.

Skin the kidneys and cut them in halves. Plunge them into boiling water to which the lemon juice has been added. Leave them a minute or two. Drain them, cut them into thin slices, and cook them gently in the heated olive oil or butter. Add a scrap of grated lemon peel, salt and pepper. When the kidneys are tender add the Marsala and let it bubble until it has reduced to half its volume.

Serve the kidneys sprinkled with plenty of parsley.

Enough for two people.

ROGNONI CON CIPOLLE E VINO BIANCO
(KIDNEYS WITH WHITE WINE AND ONIONS)

Clean some veal kidneys and plunge them into boiling salted water; leave them for 5 minutes, drain them, and then marinade them for a couple of hours in a glass of heated white wine.

Slice some onions, about 1 lb. for ½ lb. of kidneys, and stew them very gently in butter until they are quite soft but not browned (as for the onions in *fegato alla Veneziana*, p. 146). Remove the kidneys from the wine, cut them into fine slices, and add them to the onion mixture; add a little of the white wine, cover the pan, and cook gently for another 20-30 minutes, adding more white wine from time to time. Serve with croûtons of fried bread.

JOACHIM BEUCKELAER (c. 1530/5-1573/4)
PILATE SHOWING JESUS TO THE PEOPLE
(detail)
Florence, Galleria degli Uffizi

TRIPPA
(TRIPE)

I do not myself greatly care for tripe, but it cannot be denied that Italians cook it in the most delicious ways. *Trippa alla Romana, alla Fiorentina* and *alla Parmigiana* should not be missed by the visitor in Italy.

The tripe used for these dishes comes from veal, and is naturally much more delicate than the ox tripe to be found at English butchers. Nevertheless with careful cooking even this coarse tripe can be converted into excellent dishes.

TRIPPA ALLA FIORENTINA
(FLORENTINE TRIPE)

1 lb. of tripe, ½ pint of freshly made tomato sauce (sieved), marjoram, Parmesan cheese.

Buy the tripe ready soaked and boiled by the butcher. Boil it for an hour, then drain it and cut it into strips about 2 in. long and ½ in. wide. Simmer it for another hour in the prepared tomato sauce, heavily seasoned with marjoram, and before serving strew a thick layer of Parmesan cheese over it. An important point about tripe is that it should remain very slightly resistant, *al dente*, like *pasta*. Overcooked tripe turns to a repellent slithery mass.

TRIPPA ALLA PARMIGIANA
(PARMESAN TRIPE)

1 lb. of tripe, butter, Parmesan cheese.

Cook the tripe as for the preceding recipe, cut it in strips in the same way, and heat it in

VINCENZO CAMPI (1536-91)
THE KITCHEN (detail)
Milan, Pinacoteca di Brera

butter, then add a large handful of grated Parmesan cheese and let it melt a little before serving.

PHOENICIAN TRIPE
(FOR ONE PERSON)

A recipe given by G. Orioli in *Moving Along*. 'My own invention,' he says, 'and I call it "Phoenician" because the tripe is flavoured with saffron. Phoenicians could not live without this condiment; they took it with them on their voyages, and I dare say you might trace old Phoenician settlements like Marseilles and Cornwall by their still existing cult of saffron.' Here is the recipe.

'½ lb. of tripe. Wash it well, put it to boil with plenty of water till cooked. Drain it and cut it into thin slices. Put 1 tablespoonful of olive oil into a saucepan. When it boils, put into it a piece of bread not larger than two walnuts; take it out as soon as it is fried, since it serves only to remove the greasy flavour of the oil. Now put the tripe into the oil in the same saucepan with 2 cloves and let it absorb the oil and get rid of its own moisture. Add little by little some hot broth, and let it boil gently for at least an hour. After this, add a good pinch of saffron and leave the tripe to cook for another 15 minutes.'

Orioli also describes seeing a woman at Genazzano in Calabria at the public fountain, washing what appeared to be a large white fur or woollen blanket; it was an entire ox tripe, and she was bashing it against the marble basin of the fountain.

SCHOOL OF CARAVAGGIO (*c.* 1600)
STILL LIFE WITH BIRDS
Rome, Galleria Borghese

POULTRY AND GAME

 HE BEST CHICKENS IN ITALY COME FROM TUSCANY. A young plump chicken of the Valdarno grilled in butter on a charcoal fire is a lovely dish of the simplest kind. Both the Florentines and the Bolognese have a number of ways of cooking chicken breasts which are unique. For boiling chickens there are also some original recipes, although I have not included the rather uninspiring series of chickens cooked in a frying pan (*pollo in padella*) with tomatoes, pimentos, or other vegetables, as they are invariably disappointing.

A small roast turkey is a favourite *signorile* Italian dish for a dinner party. The Bolognese dish of turkey breasts fried with ham and cheese is perfectly delicious, even if rather over-rich.

Italian game is not equal in quality to our own, but there is a great deal of it. Any and every kind of bird, great or small, familiar or strange, is done to death both for the fun of the chase and for the benefit of the table.

Orioli recounts how he and Norman Douglas saw a rare migratory bird, a spotted eagle, hanging outside a butcher's shop in Reggio di Calabria. Would people eat this bird? 'Some gentlemen prefer it to turkey,' was the reply. In the market place at Crotone, he also records, there were three storks for sale. In Sardinia 'there are people who eat the *gente rubia*, or red-folk, as the Sardes call the flamingoes; but they are not considered very tasty. The epicures of Cagliari, like the old Romans, are fonder of larks and nightingales, and consume thousands of these little birds year by year.' (*Sardinia and the Sardes*, Charles Edwards, Richard Bentley & Son, 1889.)

Although game birds are almost invariably roasted in Italy, there are interesting recipes for hare, venison, and wild boar. (The Sardinians make a ham from wild boar, but it is becoming rare.)

Sour-sweet sauces for these animals are characteristic of Italian cookery; they are well worth a trial.

POLLO ALLA DIAVOLA
(GRILLED CHICKEN)

One of the nicest ways of cooking small chickens, when they are as plump and tender as they are in Tuscany, where this dish is most often to be found. When a simply cooked meal for two people is required a grilling chicken weighing 1-1½ lb. (weighed when plucked and cleaned), accompanied by a green salad or a few potatoes, will be excellent, provided the grilling is carefully attended to. In Tuscany a charcoal or wood grill is always used. Electric grills are perhaps better than gas grills as a substitute, as there is no flame to catch the fat and blacken the food to be grilled. There are a number of portable electric grills on the market, and people who like grilled food would do well to invest in something of the kind in addition to the grill provided on the normal-sized household cooker.

To grill a small chicken cut it lengthways in two pieces. Brush it over with melted butter or good olive oil and put it under the grill. As soon as it starts to brown season the cooked side with salt and pepper and brown the other side. It must not dry up, so baste it frequently with more oil or butter and turn it over two or three times. Given a fairly fast and even heat, it should take about 20 minutes.

PETTI DI POLLO ALLA BOLOGNESE
(CHICKEN BREASTS WITH HAM AND CHEESE)

In principle the same as the *costolette Bolognese* (p. 130), using fillets of chicken instead of veal. Cut each side of the breast of a young and tender chicken into two slices. Instead of coating them with egg and breadcrumbs, flour them very lightly and cook them slowly in butter for 15-20 minutes, turning them over and over. Add the ham and cheese and finish cooking them as for the veal cutlets. In the season, white truffles in thin slices are put on top of the ham before the cheese is added. There is nothing to prevent one adding a few sliced mushrooms instead, particularly when field mushrooms are in season. But of course they are in no way a substitute for white truffles.

PETTI DI POLLO ALLA FIORENTINA
(CHICKEN BREASTS FRIED IN BUTTER)

Allow one small roasting chicken for two people; the other ingredients are salt, pepper, a little flour, butter.

Cut each side of the breast of a tender roasting chicken cleanly from the bone, having first lifted away the skin. (With a sharp knife the process is perfectly easy.) Cut right along the breastbone down to the rump of the bird. The meat from the breast divides naturally into two fillets on each side, one large and one small. Flatten these fillets out a little, season them with salt and pepper, and dust them very lightly with flour. Heat a good lump of butter in a thick frying pan, and as soon as it has melted put in the fillets. Let them cook quite fast for the first 2 or 3 minutes, until one side is brown. Turn them over, lower the heat and cover the pan. (At this stage, if it is more convenient, the cooking can be continued in a gentle oven.) The fillets should be cooked in 15-20 minutes. Serve them in a hot dish, with the rest of the butter from the pan poured over, and scrape the delicious brown juicy scraps from the pan over them too.

This is a lovely way of cooking a good chicken, and has a nice extravagant air. Obviously the rest of the bird can be used for any one of a dozen dishes – the *risotto* (p. 83) perhaps, or the rice and chicken salad (p. 153), or *pollo tonnato* (p. 153).

With the chicken breasts serve some very effortless garnish, a few sauté potatoes or mushrooms, or a green salad – nothing too powerfully flavoured to detract from the delicacy of the chicken.

MICHAELANGELO MERISI DA CARAVAGGIO (1573-1610)
THE SUPPER AT EMMAUS (detail)
London, National Gallery

POLLO IN PORCHETTA
(CHICKEN STUFFED WITH HAM)

Stuff a chicken with thickish fingers of cooked ham (about 6 oz. for a 3-4 lb. bird), a clove or two of garlic, and a few strips of fennel (either bulb or stalks and leaves), with the addition of black pepper but no salt.

Cook the chicken in butter in a closed casserole in the oven.

If a boiling chicken is to be used for this dish, cook it in a roasting pan in the oven with 2 or 3 inches of water or stock, as for the *arista Fiorentina* (p. 142), with the breast of the bird upwards, until it has browned a little. Then turn it over and keep the oven at a moderate heat. It should cook in 3-3½ hours. A Tuscan dish.

POLLO AL LATTE
(CHICKEN COOKED IN MILK)

Cook a chicken in the same way as pork cooked in milk (p. 143). The time will depend upon the quality of the bird. For a boiling fowl allow at least 2 hours' gentle simmering, and have enough milk to cover it; for a tender bird an hour should be enough. Can be eaten hot or cold.

POLLO TONNATO
(COLD CHICKEN WITH TUNNY-FISH SAUCE)

Divide a cold boiled chicken into six pieces, or if a dish for two is required use only the breast. Cover the chicken with a tunny-fish mayonnaise (p. 195) thinned to the consistency of cream with a little of the chicken broth.

INSALATA DI RISO E POLLO
(CHICKEN AND RICE SALAD)

Boil a breakfastcupful of rice, and while it is still warm season it liberally with oil, nutmeg, and ground black pepper. Add a little lemon juice or white wine vinegar.

Having prepared the basis of the salad, add to it rather more than its volume of cold cooked chicken cut into long pieces, 3-4 oz. of raw mushrooms prepared as for the mushroom salad on p. 45, and some raw fennel or celery cut into strips. The salad should be prepared a good 2 hours before it is to be eaten.

PIETER AERTSEN (1508/9-1575)
THE COOK
Genoa, Palazzo Bianco

CROSTINI DI FEGATINI
(CHICKEN LIVER CROÛTONS)

For two people you need 6-8 oz. of chicken livers, a slice of ham, butter, 4 slices of French bread, lemon juice, a little flour, a few tablespoonsful of stock.

Clean the chicken livers, taking great care that the little greenish piece which is the bile is removed. If any is left in it will ruin the flavour of the livers. Chop them up into dice and dredge them with flour. Cut the ham into small pieces, brown it a little in butter (use a small pan), then put in the chicken livers. Cook them gently. They must not be fried. After a few minutes add a teaspoonful or two of meat or chicken stock, salt, pepper (very little), and a drop of lemon juice. Cover the pan. The livers will be perfectly cooked in about 10 minutes.

In plentiful butter (clarified, if possible) fry the croûtons of bread from which the crusts have been removed. They should be crisp outside but still soft inside. Arrange them on a dish and pour the chicken mixture over them.

A quickly made and very excellent little dish, to be found usually in Tuscany and Umbria, where the consumption of chickens is perfectly enormous. The *crostini* are generally served at the beginning of a meal.

FILETTI DI TACCHINO BOLOGNESE
(TURKEY BREASTS FRIED WITH HAM, CHEESE, AND WHITE TRUFFLES)

In principle the same as the Bolognese veal cutlets (p. 130).

Cut the two sides of the breast of not too large a turkey into fillets. This is a very easy operation, described in the directions for the *petti di pollo Fiorentina* on p. 152. From an 8-lb. turkey you get 8-10 good-sized fillets. Flatten them out a little on a wooden board, season them with salt and pepper, and dust them very lightly with flour. Melt a generous amount of butter in a frying pan (if they are all to be done at once you will probably need to keep two pans going at the same time). Cook the fillets on both sides, gently, for the butter must not blacken or burn. When they have cooked for 10 minutes place a slice of cooked ham on each fillet, a thin layer of mushrooms (instead of the white truffles which would be used in Bologna*) finely sliced and previously cooked for 5 minutes in butter, and then a layer of grated Parmesan cheese of the best quality obtainable. Over each fillet pour a tablespoonful of chicken or turkey broth. Cover the pan. Proceed to cook very gently for another 7-10 minutes. Some of the cheese spreads, amalgamates with the butter and the stock in the pan, and forms a sauce. Serve quickly, for if the dish is kept waiting the sauce will dry up and the cheese will become hard.

*Tinned white truffles are obtainable. They are very expensive, and I think that anyone not familiar with the fresh ones would wonder, eating the tinned version, what all the fuss is about.

FILETTI DI TACCHINO AL MARSALA
(TURKEY BREASTS WITH MARSALA)
The initial preparations are as for the preceding recipe. Cook the fillets in butter, and when they are nearly done pour over them first a small glassful of Marsala, and after it has bubbled and amalgamated with the butter the same quantity of broth. Cook in the open pan for another 2 or 3 minutes.

FILETTI DI TACCHINO IN PASTA SFOGLIA
(TURKEY BREASTS IN FLAKY PASTRY)
First prepare a flaky pastry with 6 oz. each of butter and flour. Divide it into the same number of pieces as you have fillets of turkey, as if making *vol-au-vent* cases, but long and rectangular, to hold the fillets of turkey. Bake them for about 15 minutes, and on taking them out of the oven slip a knife through the centre of each one, so that you have a long narrow pastry case.

Now cook your turkey fillets as described for *filetti di tacchino Bolognese*, but only as far as the stage before adding the ham, mushrooms, cheese, and stock. Let them cool. Fifteen minutes before they are to be served place each fillet, with its covering of ham, mushrooms and cheese inside its pastry case, with the butter in which the fillets have been cooked, and a little extra if necessary. Put them in a quick oven for a few minutes, long enough for the cheese to melt and for the rest of the ingredients to get hot.

This is a dish so rich and cloying that I would not have described it here had I not been asked a number of times for the recipe. At the Pappagallo restaurant in Bologna, where this is a speciality (christened *Tacchino Margaret Rose* in honour of Princess Margaret's visit), they advise an ice cream to finish

JACOPO CHIMENTI DA EMPOLI (1551-1640)
THE POULTRY SELLER
Pesaro, Museo Civico

the meal. They are quite right, for their ice creams are so remarkably good and refreshing that they prove exactly the right digestive after such food.*

The dish can also be made with the turkey breasts cooked in Marsala, without the addition of cheese and mushrooms; or with chicken breasts.

*Written in 1953.

TACCHINO STUFATO AL VINO BIANCO
(TURKEY STEWED WITH WHITE WINE)
A dish to make with the legs and wings of a turkey when the breast has been used for *filetti di tacchino Bolognese* (p. 153). The other ingredients are 2 carrots, an onion, butter, flour, a small turnip, ½ lb of fresh mushrooms or ½ oz. of dried ones, half a teacupful of breadcrumbs, ½ pint of white wine, garlic, salt, pepper, herbs, water or stock, a small slice of ham or bacon, half a lemon.

Fry the onions in butter in a capacious pan. Salt and pepper the pieces of turkey and flour them lightly. Brown them in the butter with the onion. Put in the carrots, the turnip, the lemon, the garlic, the ham or bacon, and the herbs. Pour the white wine over and let it cook, not too fast, for 10 minutes, stirring from time to time. Add 1½ pints of hot water, or broth from the giblets if you have it. Cover the pan and cook for about 1½ hours – longer if the turkey is a tough one. Strain off all the liquid and keep the pieces of turkey hot in the oven. Put the liquid and the vegetables, bacon, and lemon through the sieve. To this purée add the breadcrumbs and the mushrooms (if dried ones are used they should have been

VINCENZO CAMPI (1536-1591)
THE POULTRY SELLER
Milan, Pinacoteca di Brera

soaked for 10 minutes in warm water). Cook the sauce for 10 minutes, stirring it so as to amalgamate the breadcrumbs, which thicken the sauce. Pour it back over the turkey, and let it get thoroughly well heated before serving. A white *risotto* goes nicely with it.

TACCHINO ARROSTO RIPIENO
(*STUFFED ROAST TURKEY*)
1 lb. of minced veal, 1 lb. chestnuts, a dozen prunes, 4 pears, a glassful of white wine, the liver of the turkey, 10z. of butter, salt, pepper, nutmeg.

Soak the prunes, and cook them until they are soft enough for the stones to be taken out. Score the chestnuts across, boil or bake them for 10 minutes, and shell and skin them; then boil them until they are tender. Chop the prunes and chestnuts, cut the peeled pears into squares. Heat the butter in a saucepan, put in the liver of the turkey, add the minced veal, the prunes, chestnuts, and pears, a seasoning of salt, pepper, and nutmeg, and pour over a small glassful of white wine. Cook for 5 minutes, and stuff the turkey with the mixture. Cover with slices of fat bacon and roast in the usual way.

ANITRA IN AGRODOLCE
(*DUCK IN SOUR-SWEET SAUCE*)
A duck weighing 4-5 lb., 2 large onions, 2 tablespoonsful of sugar, a little fresh mint, 2 oz. of butter, 2 tablespoonsful of wine vinegar, a pinch of ground cloves, ¾ pint of meat or chicken broth or water, flour.

Slice the onions very thin and melt them in the heated butter and dripping. Season the duck with salt and pepper, roll it in flour, and put it to brown with the onions. Add the ground cloves. When the duck is well browned pour over the heated broth or water, cover the pan, and cook gently for 2-3 hours. Turn the duck over from time to time so that it cooks evenly. When it is tender remove it from the pan and keep it warm in the oven. Pour off as much fat as possible from the sauce and stir in the chopped mint (about 2 tablespoonsful). Have the sugar ready caramelized – that is, heated in a pan with a little water until it turns toffee coloured. Stir this into the sauce and add the vinegar. See that the seasoning is right and

serve the sauce separately as soon as it has acquired a thick syrup-like consistency.

This dish is also excellent cold. Instead of pouring off the fat before adding the mint, sugar, and vinegar, make the sauce as directed and remove the fat – it makes the most delicious dripping – when the sauce is cold.

PICCIONI COI PISELLI
(*PIGEONS WITH PEAS*)
'Much anger arose from a Piedmontese officer giving the name of *Spirito Santo* to a dish of stewed pigeons.'*

2 pigeons, 2 oz. of cooked tongue, 2 oz. of ham or bacon, an onion, a glassful (4 oz.) of white wine, the same of stock, 1 lb. of shelled green peas, basil, salt and pepper, 1 oz. of butter. Brown the onion in the melted butter, add the tongue and the ham cut into squares, then the pigeons. Brown them all over. Season

with salt, pepper, and basil. Pour the wine over the pigeons, and when it has bubbled a little pour in the stock. Cover the pan and simmer steadily for 1½ hours. Put in the peas and cook until they are tender (about 20 minutes). See that the seasoning is right. A couple of chicken livers, added during the last 5 minutes of cooking, make a good addition to this excellent way of cooking pigeons.

---

*Smyth's *Sardinia*, John Murray, 1828.

PALOMBACCI ALLA PERUGINA
(*WOOD PIGEONS IN THE FASHION OF PERUGIA*)
The wood pigeons should be roasted on the spit before a wood fire until they are three-quarters cooked. Have ready a tumblerful of good red wine, a plate of juicy olives, a few juniper berries, and 2 or 3 sage leaves.

GIUSEPPE MARIA CRESPI (1655-1747)
STILL LIFE WITH GAME
Bologna, Collezione Cassa di Risparmio

A deep incision is cut in the pigeons so that the insides, which have not been removed, fall out of the birds, which are then put into a pan with the wine, the olives, the sage, and the juniper berries and simmered until they are tender.

An easy recipe to adapt.

PERNICI ARROSTO
(ROAST PARTRIDGES)

For 4 partridges prepare a stuffing of 4 oz. each of unsmoked bacon, cooked ham, and mushrooms and a dozen juniper berries, all chopped together with the livers of the birds.

Wrap the stuffed partridges in slices of back pork fat or bacon and roast them in butter in the oven.

When they are cooked keep them hot in the serving dish while 4 slices of bread are fried in the fat left in the baking dish, with the addition of more butter (clarified) if necessary.

PERNICI IN BRODO
(PARTRIDGES COOKED IN BROTH)

Cook stewing partridges in a light stock with soup vegetables (an onion, a carrot, celery) and some basil leaves, salt, and pepper. When the partridges are tender (they should cook gently, and if they are old birds will take about 2 hours) take them from the broth, cut each one in half, and pour over them a sauce composed of olive oil, lemon juice, and chopped parsley. Serve them cold.

FAGIANO FUTURISTA

Marinetti's directions for cooking pheasant from *La Cucina Futurista* (Futurist Cooking, 1932):

'Roast a carefully cleaned pheasant, then keep it hot for an hour in *moscato di Siracusa* (a heavy white Sicilian wine) in a *bainmarie*, and for another hour in milk, by the same method. The pheasant is then to be stuffed with *mostarda di Cremona* (see p. 197) and candied fruit.'

The pheasant, it seems, is a bird which inspires endless fantasies in the kitchen. Norman Douglas gives a recipe (*Venus in the Kitchen*, Heinemann, 1952) for cooking it with cinnamon, dried apricots, prunes, cherries, pine nuts, saffron, cloves, chopped mushrooms, white wine, vinegar, and sugar.

In *Away Dull Cookery* (Lovat Dickson, 1932) T. Earle Welby describes an elaborate pheasant dish served with four different condiments: walnuts, orange salad, peeled grapes, and salted almonds. Alexandre Dumas (*Grand Dictionnaire de la Cuisine*, 1873) has a pheasant cooked on the spit to be served with a *ragoût de pistaches*.

Faisan à la Géorgienne, described in *La gastronomie en Russie* (A. Petit, Paris, 1860), is stewed with walnuts, grapes, orange juice, Malmsey wine, and green tea.

Although Marinetti's cooking technique seems to have been rather sketchy, he clearly knew something of the history of gastronomy and was not always being as original as he pretended....

His pheasant recipe can be adapted in several ways. A pheasant is very often dry, so the baths in sweet wine and milk are not such foolish ideas.

BECCAFICHI AL NIDO
(FIGPECKERS IN THEIR NESTS)

These little birds are usually grilled on a skewer, the whole bird being eaten. This is a variation, an old country recipe from Liguria. Each little bird is roasted on one of the large beautiful wild red mushrooms common in the district.

On the underside of a large mushroom, from which the stalk has been cut, place a figpecker; season with salt; cover with a tablespoonful of olive oil. Put all the little birds and mushrooms so arranged in a covered baking dish and cook them in the oven. (Originally they were cooked on top of the stove in a heavy iron pan with a lid specially constructed so that glowing charcoals could be placed on the top, and the birds were thus cooked *fra due fuochi*, between two fires.)

Snipe or plover can be cooked in the same way, when large mushrooms are obtainable; cover the pan with a greaseproof paper until halfway through the cooking. For snipe and plover allow 20-30 minutes in a rather low oven.

UCCELLETTI
(SMALL BIRDS)

All kinds of small birds, thrushes (*tordi*), larks (*allodole*), robins (*pettirossi*), blackbirds (*merli*), bullfinches (*monachine*), as well as quails, ortolans, snipe, woodcock, figpeckers – in fact almost anything which flies is killed and eaten in Italy.

These small birds are usually roasted or grilled. In the north of Italy they are served on a bed of *polenta*, or occasionally with rice. In central and southern Italy the more usual accompaniment is slices of bread fried in the fat in which they have cooked. In the *rosticcerie*, the shops which sell cooked food, little birds are impaled on skewers, with a bay leaf and a small slice of bread between each, and roasted. In England snipe or plover can be cooked in this way, which is successful as long as the birds are well basted and are not dried up in the cooking.

'Over the fire a large wheel revolves, on which are trussed rows of fowls, thrushes, and larks, the latter alternated with bits of bread, pork, and sage leaves. In the frying pans are savoury messes of yellow *polenta*, made from the maize flour, frying in oil, and of brown *migliaccio*, a cake of chestnut flour, and piles of nicely cooked *fritto*, the materials for which are endless, ranging the vegetable and animal kingdom.' (Leader Scott, *Tuscan Scenes and Sketches*, T. Fisher Unwin, 1888.)

CONIGLIO AL MARSALA
(RABBIT COOKED IN MARSALA)

Cut a rabbit into six or eight pieces. In a braising pan put 1 oz. of butter and 1 oz. of ham or bacon cut into small chunks, and a small stick of celery cut into ¼-in. lengths, then the pieces of rabbit. Let them brown. Add 4 chopped tomatoes, crushing them with a wooden spoon as they start to cook. Stir in a chopped clove of garlic, some fresh marjoram, salt, and black pepper. Now pour in a small glassful of Marsala and let it bubble until it is reduced by half. Add hot water or stock, enough to barely cover the pieces of rabbit; cover the pan and simmer slowly. Halfway through the cooking put in a small aubergine, unpeeled but cut into inch squares which should have been sprinkled with salt and left to drain for an hour; ten minutes before the rabbit is ready add a red or green pimento cut into strips. The sauce of this dish should be thickish, sufficient, but not too copious, and the pimento still a little bit firm. The whole dish will take about an hour to cook, providing the rabbit is a reasonably tender one.

A chicken can be cooked in the same way, but if it is a boiling fowl it will need 2 good hours of slow cooking.

LEPRE IN AGRODOLCE
(HARE IN SOUR-SWEET SAUCE)

¼ lb. of ham, half a tumblerful each of Marsala and stock or water, 2 oz. of sugar, flour, vinegar, thyme or marjoram, a medium-sized hare, 2 oz. of butter.

Cut the hare into the usual six or eight pieces and lard with little strips of the fat part of the ham, then put them to marinate for several hours in a mixture of equal parts vinegar and water. In a large pan melt the butter, put in the rest of the ham cut into squares and the pieces of hare, which should have been dried and dredged with flour. Season with salt, pepper, and a little thyme or marjoram. Pour over them the heated Marsala, then the stock, and cook over a moderate fire, adding a little more stock from time to time if necessary. When the hare is all but cooked (about 1½ hours) prepare the sauce.

Put the sugar to caramelize in a heavy pan with 2 tablespoonsful of water. When it is golden add 4 oz. of red wine vinegar and stir very quickly so that the sugar does not turn to toffee. When the mixture is smooth stir it into the sauce from the hare and let it all cook together a few minutes. The sauce should be about the consistency of thick cream, and shiny.

LEPRE ALLA MONTANURA
(HARE STEWED WITH PINE NUTS AND SULTANAS)

Put the liver, lungs, and heart of the hare to marinate in a tumbler of coarse red wine, with a tablespoonful each of pine nuts and sultanas, the chopped peel of half a lemon, a saltspoonful of powdered cinnamon, 4 cloves, and 2 dessertspoonsful of sugar. Leave to marinate for at least 4 hours.

GIOVANNI MICHELE GRANERI (active 1770)
DEER HUNTING IN SARDINIA
Turin, Museo Civico

The hare itself is to be cut up into six pieces – the four legs, and the back into two. Sprinkle with flour, and brown in butter or dripping in which a sliced onion and 2 or 3 oz. of ham or bacon have already been gently fried. Season with pepper and salt, and when the pieces of hare have browned on each side add the entire contents of the marinade. Cover the pan, simmer gently, and from time to time add a little stock or water, as the sauce will reduce as it cooks.

In the Trento and the Veneto, where this

way of cooking hare is popular, it is served with an accompaniment of *polenta* and a green salad. Instead of *polenta* a few slices of fried bread go well with it; the dish is really too rich to need accompanying vegetables.

LEPRE DI CEPHALONIA
(CEPHALONIAN HARE)
A dish from the Ionian Islands, but of Italian origin.

Cut up a hare and put it in a deep earthenware pot. Pour over it the juice of half a dozen lemons, add a little salt and pepper. Leave it to marinate for at least 12 hours.

When the time comes to cook it cover the bottom of a capacious and heavy pan with about ¼ in. of fruity olive oil. When it is hot, put in a sliced onion. Let it brown slightly, then add the pieces of hare. Brown them on both sides. Add about a dozen cloves of garlic,* salt, pepper, a generous amount of *origano*, and a wineglassful of red wine. (If the hare is being cooked in an earthenware pot heat the wine before pouring it in, or the pan may crack.) Cover the pan and simmer for 2½-3 hours.

This may sound an outlandish dish, but try it. The lemon flavour, the garlic, and the olive oil have an excellent effect upon the cloying and dry qualities of hare. It is not, of course, a refined dish, and the wine to go with it should be chosen accordingly.

---

*Do not be frightened by the quantity. In the cooking the garlic becomes transmuted. Try. You will see.

CINGHIALE
(BOAR)
'Here, then, we ate wild boar, shot in the precincts of the mine that very morning, and baked in a ground oven by a Sarde cook. With lettuces, bread, cheese, olives, oranges, wine of Tortoli, and the mountain air, it was a feast for an alderman.' (Charles Edwards, *Sardinia and the Sardes*, 1889.)

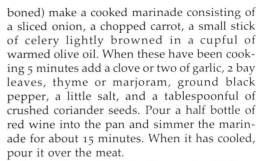

CINGHIALE ARROSTO
(ROAST WILD BOAR)
Marinate a leg of boar for 24 hours in a marinade composed of olive oil, lemon juice, an onion, a piece of celery, rosemary, 2 cloves of garlic, 2 cloves, 2 bay leaves, salt and pepper.

To roast it, remove the meat from the marinade and dry it carefully. Put it in a roasting pan with pork fat, cover it with paper, and cook it as for roast pork.

Serve boiled chestnuts with it, and red-currant jelly. Smollett says that the wild boar of Piedmont has 'a delicious taste, not unlike that of the wild hog in Jamaica'. Sardinian wild boar, although a little dry, certainly has a most excellent flavour.

CINGHIALE ALLA CACCIATORA
(HUNTER'S WILD BOAR)
Lard a leg of boar with strips of ham. Brown it in butter, with a sliced onion, a carrot, a piece of celery, and parsley; season with salt and pepper. Pour over a tumblerful of white wine, and 2 minutes later a tumblerful of stock. Cover the pan and simmer very gently for 3 hours.

CINGHIALE IN AGRODOLCE
(WILD BOAR WITH SOUR-SWEET SAUCE)
Put a saddle of boar into a marinade as described for venison with cherry sauce (see the following recipe). Leave it for 3 days. Take it out and lard with strips of fat ham. Roast it in a mixture of oil and butter. To make the sauce, strain the marinade, reduce it to half its original volume by fast boiling, and add it to 2 oz. of sugar which has been caramelized in another pan with 2 tablespoonfuls of water. Stir in 4 tablespoonfuls of red wine vinegar, a few pine nuts, and some candied orange peel cut into strips. Serve the sauce separately.

CERVO CON SALSA DI CILIEGIE
(VENISON WITH CHERRY SAUCE)
For a piece of venison weighing about 3 lb. (preferably from the shin of the animal, and

boned) make a cooked marinade consisting of a sliced onion, a chopped carrot, a small stick of celery lightly browned in a cupful of warmed olive oil. When these have been cooking 5 minutes add a clove or two of garlic, 2 bay leaves, thyme or marjoram, ground black pepper, a little salt, and a tablespoonful of crushed coriander seeds. Pour a half bottle of red wine into the pan and simmer the marinade for about 15 minutes. When it has cooled, pour it over the meat.

Leave the venison in the marinade for 2 days. To cook the meat, take it from the marinade and free it from any pieces of vegetables sticking to it. Brown it in hot fat, put it in an earthenware pot into which it will fit without too much space to spare. In the same fat fry a sliced onion and a sliced carrot. Put these into the pot, pour over the strained marinade, and add 2 teacupfuls of water, a few dried mushrooms, pepper, plenty of herbs (no rosemary or sage), a little salt, and a clove of garlic. Over the top of the venison put a thick slice of fat ham or bacon. Cover the pan with a tight-fitting lid and let the liquid just come to the boil. Thereafter let it cook very slowly, preferably in the oven, for about 3½ hours.

While the meat is cooking prepare the cherry sauce. Take the stones out of a breakfastcupful of bottled cherries. In a small pan dissolve 2 tablespoonfuls of red-currant jelly. Add the cherries and a little of their juice, a scrap of black pepper, a teaspoonful of wine vinegar, a dessertspoonful of crushed coriander seeds. Simmer for 5 minutes.

Fifteen minutes before serving press all the liquid and the vegetables from the venison through a sieve. Keep the meat hot in its covered pan. Reduce the sauce obtained from the venison to two thirds of its volume by rapid boiling. Add it to the cherry sauce and pour the whole thing back over the meat. Cut the slice of bacon into large squares, put it round the meat, and return the pot to the oven for a few minutes.

The coriander seeds are important to the dish – they give an aromatic orangey flavour.

Brown lentils go well with stewed venison.

JACOPO BASSANO (c. 1510-1592)
THE ELEMENT OF EARTH
Baltimore, Walters Art Gallery

Vegetables

S AN ACCOMPANIMENT TO MEAT, CHICKEN, or game Italians rarely serve vegetables. 'Two or three little potatoes', as they usually express it, and a green salad are indeed quite sufficient with a steak or roast lamb after a first course of *pasta* or hors d'oeuvre. An exception is the traditional accompaniment to *bollito*, *cotechino*, and *zampone*, which consists of a selection of haricot beans, stewed lentils, cabbage, spinach, and potato purée.

Many vegetables are treated as a separate dish, usually as a first course rather than coming after the meat as in France. Into this category come artichokes, all the stuffed vegetables such as aubergines, pimentos, onions, small marrows; the *sformato*, a kind of vegetable pudding described further on in this chapter, and all the tribe of vegetables cut into slices or chips and fried.

French beans, spinach, and broccoli very often appear, seasoned with oil and lemon, as a salad. There are numerous vegetables of the radish family – *radicchie, ravanelli*, etc. – of which the leaves are made into salads; some of them are a very decorative bright red colour and look very fine on the market stalls, but their flavour does not come up to their appearance. Beet leaves and chard (*bietole, biete*) are used in stuffings for ravioli and for soups.

Broad beans are delicious eaten raw as an hors d'œuvre. Fennel may appear at the beginning of a meal or at the end, with the fruit; or it may be cooked *al gratin* like celery, but is then apt to be stringy, whereas raw it is crisp and crunchy. Fried in very hot oil, with a light coating of

batter, it is extremely good. Of celery I have already written in the chapter on herbs.

The Italians, who do not idolize the potato as we do, cook it far better. It is true that the potato baked in its jacket is unknown to them, but they make lovely creamy purées of potatoes and excellent croquettes flavoured with Parmesan cheese, and their roast and fried potatoes are always delicious. This is partly due to the good quality of the vegetables themselves, and partly to the fact that the cooking medium is always oil or butter, never a vegetable substitute; the potatoes emerge from the oven golden and tasting of herbs.

As for the green peas, those bigots who will not hear of an eatable green pea anywhere but in England (because they have probably refused to try them anywhere else) would think otherwise if they had eaten the sugary, brilliant little peas from the Roman countryside.

When Italian *petits pois* were brought for the first time (in 1660) to France from Genoa and presented to Louis XIV himself, they created something like a furore at the French court. A dish of these imported peas became a luxury such as would be an equivalent quantity of truffles today. Over thirty years later, in 1696, when their cultivation in France had been established, they had lost nothing of their value. From Madame de Sévigné we have the information that 'impatience to eat them, the pleasure of having eaten them, the joy of eating them again, are the three questions which have occupied our princes for the last four days. There are ladies who, having supped, and well supped, with the King, go home and there eat a dish of green peas before going to bed . . . it is a fashion, a fury . . . .'

Of the most marvellous and remarkable vegetable (if so it can be called) of the Italian kitchen, the white truffle, I have written elsewhere in this book (pp. 11 and 30). There is also a variety of mushrooms unknown, or at least completely neglected, in this country. *Funghi porcini*, the *boletus*, is the most common in Italy; these fungi are gathered in vast quantities in the early autumn, and dried for the winter.* Both the *porcini* and *funghi ovoli*, the spectacular scarlet and orange *amanita Caesarea* are, in restaurants, either grilled or roasted, or cooked *in umido* (cut in thin slices and stewed in oil with garlic and herbs). There are other and most interesting ways of cooking them in the old traditional country cookery of northern Italy, and these recipes can be most successfully applied to English cultivated or field mushrooms. In the autumn markets of the north there are all manner of wild, dubious, enticing little mushrooms and toadstools displayed in great baskets by the old women who have brought them in from the country: the rubbery yellow *gallinaccio (cantharellus cibarius)*, the *chanterelles* of the French, some irresistibly unhealthy looking green fungus which I have been unable to identify, clusters of little toadstools which the Piedmontese call *famiole*, and most lovely fat apricot coloured mushrooms called, in Piedmontese, *trun*, which means thunder.

'Then there are certain red flat-topped *funghi* with yellow rays beneath, called by the mountaineers *famiglioli*, and the *claviari*, which look like branches of coralline; the *grifole*, a mass of fan-shaped fungus, of a dark or grey colour – this is so hard that it is not eatable unless it is first boiled and then baked. But the species which most suggests poison to our English minds are large yellow masses of soft substance, called

also *grifole*, or, more correctly, *poliporo*, some of which are yellow of the most brilliant colour, and others which the peasants call *Lingua di castagno* (chestnut tongues), of a bright carmine. All the last four species grow on chestnut or oak trees, springing from the bark.' (Leader Scott, *Tuscan Scenes and Sketches*, 1888.)

Mushrooms are cultivated in Italy, but apparently on a very small scale, for one seldom finds them in the market, neither have I ever come across any fungi at all resembling our own field mushrooms. What these may lack in spectacular colouring they make up for in flavour. The consistency is quite different, but that need be no deterrent to the cooking of them by some of the excellent Italian methods. The quality of cultivated mushrooms has so vastly improved in the last few years that one can pick and choose among the different varieties for any given dish. For example, for the dish described in the chapter on game, in which a little bird is roasted inside a large mushroom, choose the shaggy-looking brown variety, which takes time to cook; for deep fried mushrooms, a method most highly to be recommended, the medium-sized round white variety is best; and for grilling, the flat ones. Raw mushrooms for salads, several of which I have described in the *anti-pasto* chapter, will be new to many people. They are perfectly delicious, with a consistency and flavour unlike any other food.

---

*If Leader Scott (*Tuscan Scenes and Sketches*, 1888) is to be believed, the inhabitants of one village alone, called Piteglio, in the Appennines, in which there was neither butcher nor baker, gathered between them in the season 3,000 lb. of mushrooms a day.

PATATE AL LATTE
(POTATOES COOKED IN MILK)
Cut raw yellow potatoes into thick rounds. In a saucepan put enough milk to cover the potatoes and bring it to the boil. Put in the potatoes and cook them gently until they are tender. Strain them (the milk can be used to make soup), put them into a wide fireproof serving dish, season them with salt, pepper, and nutmeg, garnish them with some cut parsley or fresh basil, and add 2 or 3 table-spoonfuls of the milk. Heat them a few minutes more.

A good way of cooking old potatoes.

CROCCHETTE DI PATATE
(POTATO CROQUETTES)
Boil 1 lb. of potatoes and put them through a sieve. Stir in 1 oz of butter, 1 oz. of grated

Parmesan or gruyère, an egg, salt, pepper, and nutmeg.

When it is cooled form the mixture into croquettes, roll them in egg and breadcrumbs, and fry them in plenty of very hot oil.

TORTA DI PATATE
(POTATO PIE)
2 lb. of potatoes, 3 oz. of cheese (gruyère or *Bel Paese*), 3 oz. of cooked ham or ham sausage, or *mortadella*, 2 eggs, 3 tablespoonsful of bread-crumbs, 3 oz. of butter, 4 tablespoonsful of milk.

Sieve the boiled potatoes, add milk and 2 oz. butter; season with salt, pepper, and nutmeg. Line an 8 in. pie tin with butter and half the breadcrumbs. Spread a layer of potatoes smoothly into the tin. On top arrange the cheese and the ham cut into squares, and the 2 eggs, boiled for 6 minutes, shelled, and cut

into quarters. Cover the ham, cheese, and eggs with the rest of the mashed potatoes. Spread the remaining breadcrumbs on the top, pour over a little melted butter, and cook the pie for about 40 minutes in a fairly hot oven.

FUNGHI ALLA GRATICOLA
(GRILLED MUSHROOMS)
Choose large mushrooms (in Italy it is usually the *funghi porcini*, or boletus, which are cooked on the grill).

Pour a teaspoonful of oil on each mushroom, a little salt, a little chopped garlic and a season-ing of *origano* or marjoram. Cook them, the underside nearest the flame, under the grill, slowly, adding more oil if they threaten to dry up. Before serving turn the mushrooms over and leave them for a minute or two so that the undersides become thoroughly impregnated with the oil, but do not cook them any more.

FUNGHI FRITTI
(FRIED MUSHROOMS)

Make a frying batter according to the recipe on p. 114.

Cut fairly large firm mushrooms, with their stalks, into slices about ¼ in. thick. Dip them in the batter* and fry them in very hot oil for about 2 minutes only. Take them out as soon as they are golden. Drain them and sprinkle them with salt.

*When I published this recipe in a Sunday paper some years ago a venerable French professional chef expressed outrage that there were no directions to blanch the mushrooms first. Which only goes to show that the French still have something to learn from the Italians.

FUNGHI IN UMIDO
(STEWED MUSHROOMS)

1 lb. of mushrooms, garlic, mint, olive oil.

Wash the mushrooms (there is no necessity to peel the cultivated ones), drain them, cut them in thin slices (with their stalks). Warm some olive oil in a pan, put in the mushrooms, add 2 or 3 whole cloves of garlic, salt, black pepper, and a little chopped mint. Cover the pan and stew gently for about 20 minutes.

FUNGHI RIPIENI
(STUFFED MUSHROOMS)

1 lb. of mushrooms, 2 oz. of ham or bacon, garlic, parsley, breadcrumbs, 2 tablespoonfuls of grated Parmesan cheese, oil.

Choose rather large cup-shaped mushrooms. Wash them and remove the stalks. Chop the bacon or ham with the parsley, the garlic, and the mushroom stalks, and add the grated cheese and 2 tablespoonfuls of breadcrumbs. Spread the mixture on the mushrooms, season them with salt and pepper, pour a little oil over them and cook them, covered with a greaseproof paper, in a moderate oven for about 30 minutes. From time to time add a little more oil so that the mushrooms do not dry up.

CÈPES À LA GÉNOISE
(BOLETUS OR MUSHROOMS STEWED IN VINE LEAVES)

A recipe given by Edmond Richardin in *L'Art du Bien Manger* (Paris, 1913).

'This method, simple, devoid of difficulties, is applicable not only to *cèpes* (*boletus*), but to all mushrooms, *oronges* (*amanita Caesarea*), field mushrooms, etc.

'Cut off the stalks of the mushrooms level with the heads, salt them liberally with *gros sel* so that the water drains out, and put them an instant in the oven, simply to dry them. While they are draining and drying, put in a fireproof dish (porcelain or heavy earthenware, but avoid hammered iron, as it heats too quickly) some washed and dried vine leaves, arranged so that they line the bottom of the dish.

'You then pour over sufficient olive oil to cover the vine leaves by 1 centimetre, and heat them on a slow flame, so that the vine leaves absorb the oil without turning up at the edges. When the oil is hot but not boiling place the mushrooms on the vine leaves in even layers, the stalk sides uppermost, and put them in a good oven for about 30 minutes. At the end of this time, during which the reserved stalks have been cut into rounds the thickness of a five-franc piece, remove the dish from the oven, garnish it with the stalks, and in each of the four corners of the dish put a half clove of garlic, so that *amateurs* can crunch them and others can put them easily aside. Return the dish to the oven for 10 minutes, and serve boiling, after having sprinkled it with ground black pepper. The mushrooms thus protected by the vine leaves conserve all their consistence and flavour. Exquisite.' And so it is.

PAOLO VERONESE (*c.* 1528-88)
FEAST IN THE HOUSE OF LEVI (detail)
Venice, Galleria dell'Accademia

GIOVANNA GARZONI (1600-70)
CHINESE DISH WITH ARTICHOKES, ROSE AND STRAWBERRY
Florence, Palazzo Pitti, Galleria Palatina

CARCIOFI
(ARTICHOKES)

'Everything here [Civitavecchia] falls like manna. Twelve hundred artichokes cost twenty-one sous, twenty-five figs cost a sou ...' (Stendhal, Letter to di Fiore, 12 June 1832.)

Globe artichokes are almost one of the staple vegetables of Italy. There are several different varieties and they are cooked in a good many different ways. The large green ones, which are so tender that the whole vegetable can be eaten, are at their best in the famous Roman dish *carciofi alla Giudea* (fried whole in oil), or *alla Romana*, stewed in oil and garlic. They can be cut into slices and fried, sometimes in batter, and served as part of a *fritto misto*. Very tiny artichokes are preserved in oil. The medium-sized ones with violet-coloured leaves are perfectly delicious stewed in oil and white wine, and equally good cut in papery slices and either cooked in butter as an accompaniment to veal or served raw with a seasoning of oil and lemon. Hearts of artichokes are often combined with eggs in a *frittata*, also in a kind of omelette cooked in the oven, and are an important ingredient of the excellent *torta pasqualina*, Genoese Easter pie. The French and English way of eating artichokes plainly boiled, and dipping them leaf by leaf in butter or oil and lemon, is quite unknown to the Italians.*

Decorative bouquets of artichokes, with their stalks and leaves, are one of the characteristic sights of Roman markets. In England artichokes are so expensive and so rarely fresh and tender that probably few people will feel like trying Italian ways of cooking them. Nevertheless some of the recipes are worth recording.

---

*A reader living in Italy tells me I am wrong about this, and that it is just a coincidence that in Italy I have never come across artichokes so served.

TO PREPARE ARTICHOKE HEARTS FOR COOKING
In some parts of Italy artichoke hearts are sold ready prepared for cooking. You take off the outside leaves and with a sharp knife cut off two thirds of the top of the artichoke. Take out the choke and trim round the outside so that only the heart and a few of the inside leaves are left. As each one is ready throw it into cold water in which you have squeezed lemon juice.

CARCIOFI ALLA GIUDEA
(JEWISH ARTICHOKES)

One of the famous specialities of Rome. Roman artichokes are so tender that the whole vegetable, leaves and all, can be eaten. Quite large artichokes are used for this dish. Leave a good 2 in. of the stalk on the artichoke, remove the outside leaves, and, holding the artichoke in the left hand, turn it slowly round, gently opening out the leaves with the right hand and cutting off the tips of the leaves with a sharp knife. This operation completed, drop the artichokes in water to which a good quantity of lemon juice has been added. When all the artichokes are ready, turn them upside-down on a board and press them down so that they become slightly flattened out.

Have a deep pan nearly full of very hot oil. (Traditionally, the pan is earthenware.) Plunge the artichokes into the oil, stalks uppermost. Keep the oil at a steady heat, and turn the artichokes over and round, so that they cook evenly, eventually returning them to their original position with the stalks uppermost, and with a wooden spoon press them gently down on the bottom of the pan, so that the leaves spread out. In less than 10 minutes they should be golden bronze all over. Now dip your hand in cold water and, keeping as far away as possible from the stove, to avoid the spluttering oil, shake a few drops of water over each artichoke. This operation has the effect of making the artichokes crisp and crackling. Take them out of the pan, drain them on kitchen paper, and serve them upside-down on a hot dish.

They have a very spectacular appearance, like a large inverted sunflower.

Carciofi alla Giudea will hardly be a practical dish for English kitchens, but no one visiting Rome round about Easter time, when the new artichokes are in season, should fail to eat them in one of the *trattorie* near the old ghetto where this dish originated. In more sophisticated restaurants these artichokes are seldom as good, as they are often boiled first and then fried, and their point is lost.

CARCIOFI RIPIENI ALLA MAFALDA
(*MAFALDA'S STUFFED ARTICHOKES*)

Prepare the artichokes by removing the outside leaves, cutting off about an inch of the top of the leaves and scooping out the choke.

Make a stuffing (for 6 artichokes) with 2

SCHOOL OF CARAVAGGIO (*c.* 1600)
STILL LIFE WITH FLOWERS AND FRUIT (detail)
Rome, Galleria Borghese

ITALIAN SCHOOL (17th century)
TWO ARTICHOKES
Trustees of the Chatsworth Settlement

tablespoonfuls of breadcrumbs, 4 chopped anchovy fillets, and 2 chopped cloves of garlic. Cover the bottom of a small deep pan with olive oil, and when it is warm put in the stuffed artichokes. Add a glassful of white wine. Simmer very gently for about an hour. Serve hot.

CARCIOFI ALLA VENEZIANA
(*VENETIAN ARTICHOKES*)

For this dish the small dark violet-leaved artichokes are used. Put 6 or 8 of them, with only the outer leaves cut away, into a braising pan, covered with equal parts of olive oil, white wine, and water. Stew them gently, with the cover on the pan, for an hour, then take off the lid, turn up the flame, and let the liquid reduce until only the oil is left.

ASPARAGI
(*ASPARAGUS*)

The wild asparagus (*asparagi di campo*) of the Roman countryside are exquisite. They need to be cooked for a few minutes only and served with plain melted butter.

The gigantic asparagus of Pescia, near Pistoia in Tuscany, are highly regarded by Italians, but they have not the flavour of our own or of the French asparagus of Lauris or Cavaillon. The Italians are fond of cooking asparagus with Parmesan cheese. They are first boiled, then cooked a minute or two in a pan with butter and the grated cheese. It is a good way of serving asparagus which have not a notably fine flavour. A sauce of oil and lemon juice is another classic accompaniment to asparagus.

BROCCOLI
(*BROCCOLI*)
Cook the broccoli for 5 to 7 minutes in boiling salted water. Serve with melted butter, or cold with oil and lemon.

FAVE AL GUANCIALE
(*BROAD BEANS AND BACON*)
1½ lb. of broad beans, 2 oz. of bacon, 1 oz. of butter, a small onion.

Put the chopped onion to melt in the heated butter. Add the chopped bacon. After 2 minutes add the shelled broad beans. Simmer for 5 minutes. Barely cover with water. Cook gently for 15-20 minutes. Add salt if necessary and a little pepper.

A favourite Roman dish.

CAROTE AL MARSALA
(*CARROTS WITH MARSALA*)
Clean about 1½ lb. of carrots and cut them in half lengthways, and then in half again. Cut out the woody part in the centre, if they are old carrots. Melt 1 oz. of butter in a sauté pan and put in the carrots. Turn them over and over so that they become impregnated with the butter. Season with pepper, a little salt, a little sugar, and a minute or two later pour in a small glassful of Marsala. Simmer for 5 minutes and then just cover the carrots with water. Put the lid on the pan and stew gently until the carrots are tender. Turn up the flame and let the liquid, which should already be considerably reduced, all but bubble away. The carrots should be shiny, with a little syrupy sauce. Garnish them with a scrap of cut parsley.

Marsala with carrots may sound an unsuitable combination. Try it and see. It is one of my favourite vegetable recipes. Good by itself, or with any kind of lamb.

CROCCHETTE DI SPINACI
(*SPINACH CROQUETTES*)
To 1 lb. of cooked, drained and chopped spinach add 1½ oz. of grated Parmesan, nutmeg, salt, pepper, and 1 beaten egg. Form the mixture into small croquettes on a floured board, roll them in breadcrumbs, and fry them in hot oil or dripping.

GIOVANNI MARTINELLI (1610-59)
STILL LIFE WITH ASPARAGUS
Florence, Palazzo Pitti

SPINACI CON UVETTA
(*SPINACH WITH SULTANAS*)
2 lb. of spinach, 1 oz. of sultanas, 1 oz. of pine nuts, a clove of garlic, 1 oz. of butter, olive oil, salt and pepper.

Clean the spinach and put it into a large saucepan with a little salt but no water. Plenty of moisture comes out as it cooks. When it is cooked drain it, pressing it hard so that as much of the moisture as possible is removed. In a wide saucepan or frying pan warm the butter and 2 tablespoonfuls of olive oil. Add the spinach, the chopped garlic, and a little pepper. Turn the spinach over and over; it should not fry, and neither should the garlic. When it is thoroughly hot put in the sultanas, which should have soaked for 15 minutes in a cup of warm water, and the pine nuts. Cover the pan, and continue to cook very gently for another 15 minutes.

SPINACI ALLE ACCIUGHE
(*SPINACH WITH ANCHOVIES*)
Heat 1 lb. cooked, drained, and chopped spinach in butter, adding a little lemon juice and 2 or 3 chopped anchovy fillets.

PISELLI AL PROSCIUTTO
(*GREEN PEAS AND HAM*)
The green peas which grow round about Rome are the most delicious I have ever tasted anywhere. Small, sweet, tender, and very green, they are really best simply stewed in butter. Cooked in this way they make a most delicate sauce for finely-cut home-made *pasta*, or for *riso in bianco*. The Romans adore these green peas cooked with ham. Try this method with young English green peas before they become wrinkled and floury.

2 lb. of peas, a small onion, lard or butter, 3

oz. of very good cooked ham cut into strips.

Melt the chopped onion in the lard or butter, and let it cook very gently, so that it softens without browning. Put in the shelled peas and a very little water. After 5 minutes add the ham. In another 5-10 minutes the peas should be ready.

SFORMATO DI PISELLI FRESCHI
(*SFORMATO OF GREEN PEAS*)

A *sformato*, a dish which figures largely in Italian home cooking but never in restaurants, is a cross between a soufflé and what we should call a pudding. It is a capital way of using green peas, French beans, spinach, fennel, or any vegetables which are plentiful but no longer in the tender stage when they may be eaten simply with butter. A *sformato* is a trouble to prepare, but requires fewer eggs than a soufflé and is not at all exacting to cook. It may be served as a separate course with some kind of sauce, or as a background to meat (*scaloppine*, for example), or lamb cutlets, or small pieces of veal grilled on a skewer.

For a *sformato* of fresh green peas you need about 3 lb. of peas, 3 eggs, 1½ oz. of butter, 1½-2 oz. of cooked ham, a small onion, 1 oz. of grated Parmesan, a tablespoonful of flour, a cupful of milk.

First sauté the chopped onion very lightly in half the butter; add the shelled peas and cover them with water. Season them with salt and let them simmer until they are completely cooked.

While the peas are cooking, prepare a little very thick béchamel with 1 oz. of butter, a tablespoonful of flour, and the cupful of milk previously heated. Season it well, add to it the ham cut into small strips and the grated cheese. When the peas are cooked, strain them and put them through a sieve, keeping a few apart. Return the purée to the saucepan with a nut of butter, and add the béchamel and the whole peas. Give it a stir or two so that the mixture is well amalgamated. Leave it to cool, and then stir in the yolks of the eggs, and lastly the beaten whites. Pour the whole mixture into a buttered cake tin or soufflé dish, and steam it, with a cover on the pan, for about an hour. Turn the *sformato* out on to a dish, or

serve it in its own dish, and either pour a sauce over it or arrange round it whatever meat it is to accompany. (Apart from meat, prawns or scallops cooked in butter go nicely with the green pea *sformato*, or a mushroom sauce, or poached eggs.)

This *sformato* may be made very successfully with frozen green peas.

SFORMATO DI FAGIOLINI
(*SFORMATO OF FRENCH BEANS*)

1 lb. of French beans, a tablespoonful of flour, ½ oz. of butter, a cup of milk, 2 eggs, 2 oz. of Parmesan.

Boil the French beans, strain them, and chop them. Make a little thick béchamel with the flour, butter, and milk, and add the cheese. Stir the beans into the prepared sauce (off the fire), add the eggs. Put into a buttered soufflé dish and steam for 40-60 minutes. Turn out on to a hot dish and pour over a *fonduta* sauce made as for *Riso Ricco* on p. 86.

ZUCCHINE
(*SMALL MARROWS OR COURGETTES*)

I think it worth recording here that, when I was writing this book in 1954, marrows meant zeppelin-shaped harvest-festival-size gourds, swollen and watery. *Zucchine* or courgettes were rare and expensive luxuries, imported from France. However, by 1957 Poupart's, the well-known nursery gardeners of Walton-on-Thames, Surrey, had initiated the cultivation of courgettes for the British market and before

GIOVAN BATTISTA RUOPPOLO (1629-93)
STILL LIFE WITH FLOWERS AND VEGETABLES (detail)
Oxford, Ashmolean Museum

long they were to be found in many enterprising greengrocers' shops. The Poupart courgettes were small, delicate, and to most people at the time a novelty. It is to that firm that we owe the general acceptance today of this attractive and versatile vegetable, although it is not until July or August that our home-grown courgettes reach the shops. In spring and early summer they are imported from Kenya, Israel, and possibly even further afield.

Zucchine are usually cooked unpeeled, cut into thin rounds, fried in butter or oil. They can also be stuffed, stewed, used in a sauce for *pasta*, fried in batter, added to vegetable soups, and cooked with tomatoes and cheese in the same way as aubergines. Very thin strips of *zucchine* fried crisp in hot oil, piled up on the dish like potato straws, are sold in every Roman *rosticceria* in the summer. In some country districts marrow flowers are stuffed with rice, cooked in oil, and served cold.

A Neapolitan gourmet told me he considered that every dish containing *melanzane* (aubergines) would be far better if *zucchine* were used instead.

ZUCCHINE FRITTE
(*FRIED SMALL MARROWS*)
Cut ½ lb. of small unpeeled marrows into little strips, like very small chips. Salt them and leave them to drain for an hour.

Shake them in a cloth with flour and fry them in deep oil. They will only take about 3 minutes to cook. Lift them out of the pan with a perforated spoon and drain them on kitchen paper.

ZUCCHINE IN AGRODOLCE
(*SMALL MARROWS IN SOUR-SWEET SAUCE*)
Cut the unpeeled *zucchine* into rounds, salt them lightly, and leave them to drain for an hour.

Cook them gently in a little olive oil with a cover on the pan; when they are nearly cooked, season with ground black pepper, a little powdered cinnamon, salt if necessary, and (for 1 lb. of *zucchine*) 2 tablespoonsful of mild wine vinegar and a tablespoonful of

sugar. Cook them a few minutes more. There should be a small amount of sauce, rather syrupy.

ZUCCHINE IN STUFATO
(*STEWED SMALL MARROWS*)
1 lb. of very small marrows, 1 lb. of onions, olive oil.

Slice the onions and put them with the whole marrows, unpeeled, into a small pot with a coffee-cupful of olive oil. Stew them very slowly for an hour to an hour and a half with the cover on the pan. Season with salt and pepper before serving.

ZUCCHINE RIPIENE
(*STUFFED MARROWS*)
Cut unpeeled small marrows into 2 in. lengths, scoop out the flesh, and mix it with any stuffing which happens to be to hand, made from minced cold meat, or rice, or cheese, breadcrumbs, and parsley, or the stuffing described for the beef dish on p. 141. Stuff the marrows, but don't fill them too full. Cook them slowly in oil or butter for 20 minutes.

PUMPKINS, from *Tacuinum Sanitatis* (14th century)
Paris, Bibliothèque Nationale

MELANZANE
(*AUBERGINES, OR EGG PLANT*)
Considering that aubergines have been cultivated in Italy since the fifteenth century, it is odd that the Italians should never have evolved a dish of aubergines half as good as the Balkan *moussaka* or the Greek purée of aubergines with oil and garlic, or the Turkish *imam bayeldi*, or the Provençal *ratatouille*. Neapolitans think a great deal of a kind of solid cake of *melanzane* interspersed with layers of *mozzarella* and a gratin of Parmesan on the top called *Parmigiana*, which is quite good when eaten immediately it comes out of the oven, although I do not myself think that cheese and aubergines are an ideal combination. There are one or two ways of stuffing aubergines which are good if done with a light hand.

MELANZANE A FUNGHETTI
(*SAUTÉ OF AUBERGINES*)
Funghetti is a term applied to certain vegetables fried in small pieces with their skins on. It does not mean that there are mushrooms in the dish.

Cut 3 or 4 unpeeled aubergines into half-inch squares. Put them into a bowl, sprinkle them with salt, and leave them for an hour, then drain off the liquid. Heat a good quantity of olive oil in a large frying pan, and when it is hot put in the aubergines and let them fry rather gently, turning them over from time to time. They will take about 15 minutes to cook. About 5 minutes before they are to be served add some chopped garlic (about a couple of cloves), and at the last minute a little chopped parsley. By the time the aubergines are ready they will have absorbed the oil, but if there is too much, drain it off before serving. Cooked in this way aubergines make a very good accompaniment to any meat or chicken dish, or can be served as a separate vegetable. They are also good cold.

PARMIGIANA
(*AUBERGINE PIE*)
2 lb. of aubergines, ½ lb. of *mozzarella* cheese, 2 oz. of Parmesan, ¼ pint of freshly made tomato sauce, olive oil, salt, pepper, flour.

Peel the aubergines and cut them into long thin slices. Salt them and put them into a colander to drain for an hour or two. Dust them with flour, fry them gently in olive oil, and drain them on kitchen paper. Put a little oil in the bottom of a china soufflé dish or a deep cake tin. Put in a layer of the aubergines, cover it with thin slices of cheese and then the tomato sauce. Continue in this way until the aubergines are all used up. Cover with the grated Parmesan and sprinkle oil over the top. Cook in a moderate oven for 20-30 minutes.

MELANZANE RIPIENE
(STUFFED AUBERGINES)

For the stuffing for 4 large aubergines you need about 4 oz. of white bread without the crust, 8 anchovy fillets, a dozen black olives, a handful of parsley, 2 or 3 cloves of garlic, a tablespoonful of capers.

Cut the aubergines in half and scoop out about half the flesh. Chop this with all the rest of the ingredients, having first softened the bread with a little milk or water. Season with pepper and marjoram or *origano*, but salt will probably not be necessary. Put the stuffing

AUBERGINES, from *Theatrum Sanitatis* (14th century)
Rome, Biblioteca Casanatense

lightly back into the aubergines and arrange them in a baking dish. Pour a generous quantity of oil over them, cover the pan, and cook in a slow oven for about an hour.

CAPONATA*

Edmond Richardin gives this recipe in *L'Art du Bien Manger*, claiming that it is a Sicilian dish (which it is) and that it came from the chef of the German Ambassador in Rome.

'Peel 4 or 5 aubergines, cut them in large dice, salt them, and when most of the water has come out of them fry them in oil.

'Prepare 1½ oz. of capers, 3 oz. of olives, a head of celery blanched in salted water, 4 anchovies soaked in warm water to rid them of the salt; all these are to be cut in *julienne* strips. Slice a white onion; melt it in oil; add 1½ oz. of sugar, ¼ pint of tomato purée. Reduce, and let it take on a dark colour; after which add half a glassful of vinegar. Simmer for a few minutes. Season highly, add chopped parsley, and stir in the prepared capers, celery, anchovies, olives, and the aubergines.

'Arrange in a dish in a dome shape, and garnish around the base with tunny fish in oil, or lobster, or tunny fish roe (*botargue*).

'It is necessary to prepare this dish in advance so that all the ingredients become impregnated with the flavour of the sweet-sour tomato.

'Served in summer as a vegetable, or as an hors d'œuvre.'

---

*No translation. An interesting dish, though. Try it in half quantities.

FRITTO MISTO DI VERDURE
(MIXED FRY OF VEGETABLES)

Aubergines, *zucchine* (small marrows), *mozzarella* cheese.

Peel the aubergines, cut them into slices lengthways, salt them and leave them to drain for 2 or 3 hours. Cut the unpeeled small marrows also into long slices and salt them in the same way as the aubergines. Cut the cheese into slices about ⅛ in. thick. When the time comes to cook them dip each ingredient into frying batter (p. 114) and fry them in very hot

oil. To make the dish even for two or three people, two frying pans will be necessary (unless you have a really capacious deep-frying pan), as it is essential that the vegetables should not be kept waiting for more than a minute or two. Drain them on kitchen paper and serve them in a large flat dish.

SCAROLE RIPIENE
(STUFFED BATAVIAN ENDIVE)

This dish is made with very small *scarole* (the French *escarole*). In England the Batavian endive is found usually only in a very large size and rather tough, so it is best to use small round lettuces instead.

For the stuffing mix a handful of breadcrumbs with 12 stoned and chopped black olives, 6 chopped anchovy fillets, a few capers, 1 oz. each of pine nuts and sultanas, 2 or 3 cloves of garlic and a handful of chopped parsley. Stir a coffee cupful of olive oil into the mixture. Season with pepper and a very little salt. Wash the lettuces and open out the leaves; put some of the stuffing in the centre of each, fold the leaves back again, and tie up each lettuce with string.

In a heavy saucepan heat some olive oil with a *battuto* (p. 190) of 2 chopped anchovy fillets, a clove of garlic, and a tablespoonful of capers. Put in the lettuces and add a very little water. Cover the pan and cook as slowly as possible for about an hour. Now add a small glassful of white wine and cook for another 10 minutes.

Heavy, oily cooking, but good and typically southern Italian.

PEPERONATA
(SWEET PEPPER AND TOMATO STEW)

8 red pimentos, 10 good ripe tomatoes, a large onion, butter, and oil.

Brown the sliced onion very lightly in a mixture of oil and butter. Add the pimentos, cleaned, the seeds removed, and cut into strips; season them with salt. Simmer them for about 15 minutes, with the cover on the pan. Now add the tomatoes, peeled and quartered, and cook another 30 minutes. There should not be too much oil, as the tomatoes provide enough liquid to cook the pimentos and

GIORGIO DE CHIRICO (1891-1952)
STILL LIFE WITH PEPPERS
Florence, Galleria Nazionale d'Arte Moderna

the resulting mixture should be fairly dry. Garlic can be added if you like. These quantities make enough for six or seven people, but *peperonata* is so good when re-heated that it is worth making a large amount at one time.

To store for a few days in the refrigerator, pack the *peperonata* in a jar, and float enough olive oil on the top to seal the contents.

PEPERONI RIPIENI
(STUFFED PIMENTOS)

For 4 large red or yellow pimentos prepare the same stuffing as for stuffed aubergines (p. 169).

Cut the pimentos in half lengthways and remove the seeds and the stalks. Fill them with the prepared stuffing (not too much or they become too solid and heavy), moisten them

with olive oil, and cook them in a covered dish in a slow oven for an hour. From time to time pour a little more oil over them.

CIPOLLINE IN AGRODOLCE
(SWEET-SOUR ONIONS)

1 lb. of small onions, 2 tablespoonfuls each of olive oil and vinegar, a tablespoonful of sugar, 2 cloves, a bay leaf, salt.

Choose small pickling onions, as much as possible of the same size. Put them unpeeled into boiling water and cook them for 10 minutes. When they have cooled peel them, put them in a pan with the heated olive oil, the bay leaf and cloves. Simmer them very gently for 5 minutes, and add the vinegar and the sugar. Cook until the sauce turns to a syrup.

Can be served hot or cold.

CIPOLLE RIPIENE
(STUFFED ONIONS)

Make a stuffing of chopped parsley, garlic, anchovies, a little ham, half a dozen black olives, and a handful of breadcrumbs. Cook the unpeeled onions in boiling water for 15 minutes. Peel them, cut them in half, and take out the centre, leaving a ring of three or four layers. Fill these with the stuffing, pour a little oil in the top of each, and bake them in a slow oven for an hour. A typically southern Italian dish.

SCIULE PIENE
(PIEDMONTESE STUFFED ONIONS)

6 medium-sized onions, 4 macaroons (about ¼ lb.), a slice of white bread about 1 in. thick, without the crust, a little milk or stock, butter, a tablespoonful of sultanas, 3 tablespoonsful of Parmesan, salt, pepper, nutmeg, ground cloves, cinnamon, 1 egg.

Boil the onions for 15 minutes, without peeling them. When they have cooled peel off the skins. Extract the core of the onion, and then working from the outside proceed to separate the onion into layers, so that you have a number of hollow rings of different sizes. The process is perfectly simple, provided the onion is sufficiently soft.

To make the stuffing, crumble the maca-roons and pound them with the bread which has been softened in milk or stock, add the seasoning and spices (not too heavily) and the cheese, the chopped cores of 2 or 3 of the onions, the sultanas, and the beaten egg.

Put a little of the stuffing into each onion ring (not too much, or they will be stodgy) and add a little piece of butter to each one. Bake them in a moderate oven for about 45 minutes. They can be eaten either hot or cold. If very large onions are used cut them into half cross-wise before separating them into rings. Made with small onions, so that each little ring is merely a mouthful, this is good food with drinks.

The ingredients for the stuffing sound a very odd mixture, and the dish is obviously a sur-vival from the days when a mixture of sweet and savoury, with plenty of spices, was per-fectly normal. The resulting flavour is rather good. *Sciule piene* is the Piedmontese for *cipolle ripiene* (stuffed onions).

CAVOLI IN AGRODOLCE
(*SOUR-SWEET CABBAGE*)

Wash a large green cabbage and cut it into thin strips, discarding the hard parts of the stalks in the centre of the leaves.

In a roomy saucepan, heat a little olive oil or bacon fat, or a mixture of the two. In this sauté a small onion. When it is golden add 2 or 3 large ripe peeled tomatoes (or a small spoonful of concentrated purée diluted with a little water). When the tomatoes are soft, add the cabbage. Stir it round; add salt and pepper and a large tablespoonful of wine vinegar. Let it simmer for 20 minutes, stirring frequently with a wooden spoon. Five minutes before serving stir in a tablespoonful of soft white sugar.

VERZE RIPIENE
(*STUFFED CABBAGE LEAVES*)

Blanch white cabbage leaves in boiling salted water for 5 minutes.

On each leaf put a small spoonful of any stuffing you fancy, as for the stuffed *zucchine* (p. 168); roll up the leaves, squeeze them in the hand so that they remain firmly rolled up, and cook them in oil or broth for about an hour.

Stuffed cabbage leaves and stuffed *zucchine* are often served together as a way of using up cold meat.

DE PISIS (20th century)
STILL LIFE, 1933
Venice, Galleria d'Arte Moderna de Ca'Pesaro

GIOVAN BATTISTA RECCO (1615-60)
STILL LIFE WITH SWEETMEATS
London, Matthiesen Fine Art

SWEETS

T WAS LARGELY THROUGH THE MEDIUM OF Venetian traders that cane sugar was brought to Europe from the East, where it had first been seen some time in the eleventh century by the crusaders at Tripoli. For three or four hundred years sugar was a luxury, and honey continued to be the medium of sweetening food for all but the very rich. Nevertheless the Italians seem rapidly to have made use of the new discovery in the invention of all kinds of sweetmeats, and Italian pastry-cooks and confectioners acquired a great reputation. As late as the nineteenth century it was the custom for those English noblemen who kept sumptuous tables to employ Italian confectioners as well as French chefs.

Italian pastry-cooks are still famous. Their pastries – *pasta frolla* (a kind of short pastry made with the addition of sugar and eggs) and *pasta sfoglia* (flaky pastry) – are first class, but most of their confections require quantities of butter, sugar, almonds, eggs, and cream. The amount of cakes consumed by Italians is prodigious; a crowd of men eating cream cakes is a familiar sight in the coffee bars of any big town, and it is perfectly usual in Italy to eat several little sweet biscuits or macaroons with the lunch-time apéritif. Curiously, in a country where most of the food is so beautiful in appearance, the decoration of the cakes and pastries to be seen in the shops is in terrible taste; nothing could be more spectacularly gaudy than the displays in the Roman confectioners' shops at Easter time.

There are for the traveller in Italy, however, any number of interesting traditional sweetmeats to be tried, such as the famous *panforte* of Siena, rich and spicy and oddly reminiscent of plum pudding; also to be found in Siena are *copate*, delicious little wafer-like cakes, and *ricciarelli*, almond biscuits (such things must be looked for in pastry-shops, not restaurants). In Milan there is the *panettone*, a kind of spiced brioche containing sultanas which in every size from a small bun to an enormous cottage loaf is a traditional Christmas gift. *Pastiera Napoletana* is another festive sweet, originally made specifically at Easter. It is an elaborate pie made with buttery *pasta frolla* filled with a rich mixture of *ricotta*, sugar, eggs, candied fruit and *grano duro*, whole wheat grain lengthily simmered in milk until the grains soften and burst. *Pastiera* is no longer an exclusively Neapolitan speciality; like the *pizza Napoletana* it has spread to Rome and other regions of Italy. I believe that the original *pastiera* was descended from the medieval frumenty or *formentata*, the wheat pottage common to most European countries. At one time the ready-prepared *grano* was sold from big bowls in shops and market stalls. Nowadays prepared *grano* can be bought in tins. Every feast day has its traditional dish, usually something sweet such as the *zeppole di San Giuseppe*, which are a species of ring-shaped doughnut, cooked and sold on street stalls which are set up for the occasion, and charmingly decorated with flowers and branches. Some sort of *torrone* or nougat invariably appears for a *festa*, and *frittelle* or fritters. It was the Italians who invented *amaretti*, or macaroons, and they are to be found all over Italy in dozens of different forms, one of the best being the little macaroons no larger than an almond in its shell, which are a speciality of Salsomaggiore in the province of Parma; sometimes they are made with pine nuts, as in *pinoccate*, the Christmas and Epiphany cakes of Perugia.

The town of Parma is well known for its pastry-shops, where a variety of excellent little cakes are presented with rather more sobriety of decoration than is customary in Italy; curiously enough this town is also one of the rare places in Italy where savoury pastries, such as the anchovy or cheese *allumettes* which are common in France,* are found in the coffee shops.

Ricotta, the ewe's milk white cheese which is so enormously used in Italian cooking, is also a great feature in sweet dishes; the Neapolitans have a beautiful looking pastry called *sfogliatelle*, flaky pastry in the shape of a small fan or scallop shell, filled with a mixture of sweetened *ricotta* and candied fruit. Spices still play a large part in Italian confectionery, and the *ricotta* in a *torta* or pie is heavily flavoured with cinnamon, cloves, and nutmeg.

All these things belong to the province of the professional pastry-cook. The sweet dishes for which I here give recipes are dishes which can be made at home; they would never be found in an Italian restaurant, for the sharp division which exists between restaurant and home-cooked food in Italy is never more apparent than in the domain of the sweet course. The *dolce* in a restaurant consists almost invariably of a great slice of some very showy cake, drenched in a sweet liqueur, or it may be a chestnut purée resting heavily on a basis of meringue and smothered in cream; or it may be that exuberant joke the *Zuppa Inglese*, a Trifle much glorified, it is true, but still a Trifle.

The composition of sweet dishes in an Italian household is considerably more restrained. I have confined the selection of recipes to those which can be successfully made outside Italy, at a modest cost in money, time and labour, and which have at the same time some originality and character.

---

*French culinary influence in Parma is usually attributed to French cooks brought there by the Austrian ex-Empress of France, Marie-Louise, Napoleon's widow and Duchess of Parma.

CREMA DI MASCHERPONE
(SWEET CREAM CHEESE)
Mascherpone is an unsalted cream cheese made from thick cream, chiefly in Lombardy. It is used for many sweet dishes, although it is also eaten with salt, or quite plain with strawberries. Home-made cream cheese (see p. 99), very fresh and unsalted, can be made into a very delicious sweet on the same lines as *crema di mascherpone*.

Allow about 2 oz. of cream cheese per person (4 pints of milk will give about 1 lb. of cream cheese). For 1 lb. of cream cheese allow 4 oz. of sugar, 4 yolks of eggs, and 2 or 3 table-spoonsful of brandy, rum, or, best of all, kirsch.

Put the cream cheese through a sieve and stir it until it is quite smooth. In another basin beat up the eggs and sugar, then add the liqueur. Add this mixture gradually to the cream cheese until it is a thick cream. Put it on the ice for 2 or 3 hours.

A pint of cream, left to go thick and slightly sour, drained in a muslin, then beaten up with sugar and liqueur, produces something very like the original *crema di mascherpone*.

RICOTTA AL CAFFÉ
(CREAM CHEESE WITH COFFEE)
Again, home-made milk cheese (p. 99) can be used for this sweet. For four people allow 8-10 oz. of cream cheese, 4-6 oz. of caster sugar, 4 dessertspoonsful of freshly roasted coffee, very finely ground (as for Turkish coffee), and 2 oz. of rum. Put the cream cheese through a sieve; add the sugar, the coffee, and the rum, and stir it until it is smooth and thick. Make the cream at least 2 hours before serving, so that the coffee flavour has time to develop. Keep it in a cold place. Serve it with fresh cream and thin wafer biscuits.

BUDINO TOSCANO
(TUSCAN PUDDING)
¾ lb. of *ricotta* or unsalted home-made cheese (p. 99), 2 oz. of ground almonds, 1½ oz. of candied orange peel, 4 oz. of sugar, 1 oz. each of raisins and sultanas, 4 yolks of eggs, vanilla sugar, the grated peel of a lemon.

Put the cream cheese through the food mill. Stir in the beaten yolks of eggs and all the other ingredients.

This pudding *should* be cooked in a buttered mould in the oven for 30 minutes, but as a matter of fact it is very much better in its natural state, as a kind of thick cream. When cooked it is more like cake. In either case, sprinkle the top with vanilla sugar (p. 27).

BUDINO DI RICOTTA
(CREAM CHEESE PUDDING)
10 oz. of *ricotta* or home-made unsalted cream cheese, 3 oz. of sugar, 3 oz. of ground almonds and 2 or 3 crushed bitter almonds, 5 egg whites, lemon peel, breadcrumbs.

Sieve the cream cheese, add the sugar, the almonds, the beaten whites of eggs, and the grated peel of a lemon. Pour into a buttered, 2-2½ pint shallow cake tin, spread breadcrumbs on the top, and cook for 30 minutes in a moderate oven.

Enough for six or seven people.

TORRONE MOLLE
Torrone is the Italian name for all kinds of nougat. This sweet, literally 'soft nougat', is an

ingenious invention, for it needs no cooking and can be successfully turned out by the least experienced of cooks. For six to eight people, the ingredients are 6 oz. each of cocoa, butter, sugar, ground almonds, and plain biscuits such as Petit Beurre or Osborne, plus 1 whole egg and 1 yolk.

Work the butter and the cocoa together until you have a soft paste, then stir in the ground almonds. Melt the sugar in a saucepan with a little water over a gentle flame and add it to the cocoa mixture. Stir in the eggs, and finally the biscuits cut into almond-sized pieces. This last operation must be performed gently so that the biscuits do not crumble. Turn the whole mixture into an oiled turban mould* and put it in the refrigerator or the coldest part of the larder. Turn it out on to a dish to serve. The *torrone* is infinitely better when prepared the day before it is to be eaten.

The combination of the plain biscuits with the chocolate mixture is reminiscent of that most admirable picnic food, a slab of bitter chocolate accompanied by a Petit Beurre biscuit.

---

*That is what was used by Lina, the Tuscan cook who introduced me to this delicious recipe, rather different from the one usually known under this name in Italy. The *torrone* is easier to turn out from a rectangular loaf tin, or a cake tin with a removable base. The oil should be sweet almond oil (to be bought from chemists).

AN ITALIAN PUDDING

'Take a pint of cream and slice therein as much French roll as will make it thick; beat up 5 eggs; butter the bottom of a dish, slice 8 pippins into it, and add thereto some orange peel, sugar, and half a pint of port wine. Pour in the cream, bread and eggs, lay a puff paste over the dish, and bake for 30 minutes.' (G.A. Sala, *The Thorough Good Cook*, 1895.)

BUDINO DI MANDORLE
(*ALMOND PUDDING*)
For using up whites of eggs.

4 oz. of ground almonds, 4 oz. of sugar, 4 whites of eggs, 2 tablespoonsful of brandy or rum.

Melt the sugar in a pan with 2 or 3 table-spoonsful of water. Sitr in the ground almonds

PIETRO MARUSSIG (1879-1937)
LADIES IN A CAFÉ
Milan, Galleria Nazionale d'Arte Moderna

and continue stirring until the whole mixture has turned a pale biscuit colour. Beware of this operation; once the mixture starts to take colour it burns very easily. Leave to cool, then pound in a mortar, adding the brandy or rum. Fold in the beaten whites, pour into a buttered mould or soufflé dish, and steam for about 40 minutes, until the pudding looks spongy right through. Serve cold. Enough for three or four people.

TORTA DI ALBICOCCHE
(APRICOT TART)

Make a pastry with 7 oz. of flour, 3½ oz. of butter, 3½ oz. of vanilla sugar (p. 27), the yolks of 2 eggs, the grated peel of a small lemon, ½ teacupful of water.

Knead the pastry very lightly and roll it out as little as possible.

Spread it on flat buttered pie tins. Two 6-inch tins are about right. Or use 5 oz. flour to 2½ of butter, and about 1 lb of apricots, to fill one 8-inch tin.

On top of the pastry arrange 2 lb. of apricots which have been cooked with a little sugar, cut into halves, and stoned. There should not be too much juice or the pastry will be sodden.

Cook for 25 minutes – the first 15 minutes in a hot oven, and the last 10 with the heat diminished. Serve cold.

A most delicious sweet. The vanilla sugar is important to the flavour.

CASTAGNE AL MARSALA
(CHESTNUTS WITH MARSALA)

For four people 1 lb. of chestnuts is sufficient. Score them across the rounded side with a sharp knife. Put them into a baking tin in a moderate oven for 15 minutes. Drain them. Both skins should peel off quite easily, but the operation must be done while they are still warm. Get them out of their skins without breaking them, if possible.

Put them into a pan and cover them with three quarters Marsala and a quarter red wine. Add 2 or 3 tablespoonfuls of sugar. Simmer them gently until they are quite tender and the wine has turned to a thick syrup. They can be served hot or cold, with cream.

MONTE BIANCO
(MONT BLANC)

1 lb. of chestnuts, ½ lb. of sugar, 4 oz. of cream, salt.

Score the chestnuts across the rounded sides and either boil them for 10 minutes or roast them in a slow oven for 15 minutes. While they are still hot (but not *red* hot – there is no necessity for burnt and bleeding fingers) remove the shells and the inner skins. Cover the chestnuts with plenty of water and simmer them for about an hour until they are perfectly tender. Strain off the water and mash the chestnuts with the sugar and a good pinch of salt. Put them through a potato ricer or a food mill with fairly large holes, held over the dish in which they are to be served. As the sieved chestnuts come out of the ricer they are to fall lightly into a cone-shaped mound.

Over the prepared chestnuts pour the whipped cream (flavoured, if you like, with a little brandy or Marsala or rum), but do not press it down or attempt to put the pudding into shape, or it will lose its lightness. If possible, prepare the *Monte Bianco* only a short while before it is to be served. Enough for 4.

TARTUFI DI CIOCCOLOTA
(CHOCOLATE TRUFFLES)

¼ lb. of bitter chocolate, 1½ oz. of butter, 1 egg yolk, a tablespoonful of milk, 1 oz. of cocoa.

Melt the chocolate in a *bain-marie* with the milk, and when it is a smooth cream take it off the fire and work in the butter and the yolk of egg. Leave the mixture for 4 or 5 hours. Form it into small walnut shapes, coated with the cocoa. To be eaten within 48 hours. To vary the flavour, a tablespoonful of black coffee can be used instead of the milk when melting the chocolate.

ANON (19th century)
CHOCOLATE MAKER'S SIGN
Milan, Museo di Milano

PIETRO LONGHI (1702-85)
THE MORNING CUP OF CHOCOLATE
Venice, Ca' Rezzonico

DOLCE MAFARKA

One of Marinetti's inventions from *La Cucina Futurista*.

'2 oz. of coffee, 3½ oz. of rice, 2 eggs, the peel of a lemon, a pint of milk, 1½ oz. of orange-flower water, sugar to taste.

Cook the ground coffee in the milk, and sugar it to your taste; strain it, then pour in the rice and cook it (in a steamer) *al dente*. Remove from the fire; when it is cold grate into it the lemon peel, and stir in the orange-flower water and the eggs, mixing well. Pour into a mould and put it on the ice. When it is well iced serve with fresh biscuits.'

ROSE DIABOLICHE
(DIABOLICAL ROSES)

Marinetti again.

'2 eggs, 3¼ oz. of flour, the juice of half a lemon, a tablespoonful of olive oil.

Mix the above ingredients into a not too thick batter; throw into it some velvety red roses, with the outside petals pruned away and the stalk cut off at the calyx, and fry them in boiling oil, as for *carciofi alla Giudea*.'

Indicated for brides to eat at midnight, in January, and especially good if covered with *dolce mafarka*, according to Marinetti.

TORTIGLIONE
(ALMOND CAKES)

1 lb. of ground almonds, a tablespoonful of flour, 4 whites of eggs, 1¼ lb. of sugar.

Mix the almonds, sugar, and flour together in a basin; add the beaten whites of eggs. Make the mixture into small coils resembling a curled snake, and in each put 2 coffee beans for eyes and a little piece of red candied fruit for a tongue.

Bake in a slow oven.

PESCHE RIPIENE
(STUFFED PEACHES)

6 yellow peaches, 3 oz. of macaroons, 1 yolk of egg, 2 tablespoonsful of sugar, 1 oz. of butter.

Cut the peaches in half, take out the stones and a little of the pulp to make a deep space for the stuffing. Add this pulp to the pounded macaroons and stir in the other ingredients.

Stuff the peaches with this mixture, spreading it in a smooth mound over each half. Put them in a buttered fireproof dish and bake in a moderate oven for about 30 minutes.

PESCHE IN VINO BIANCO
(*PEACHES IN WHITE WINE*)

Into your last glass of white wine after luncheon slice a peeled yellow peach. Leave it a minute or two. Eat the peach and then drink the wine.

(I do not suggest that this should be applied to a valuable Rhine wine or a cherished white Burgundy.)

ARANCI CARAMELLIZZATI
(*CARAMEL ORANGES*)

This way of serving oranges is a speciality of the Taverna Fenice in Venice, a restaurant where the colours of Venetian painting are translated to the kitchen. Saffron-coloured *polenta* is cooking in copper pans next to an immense dish of artichokes, purple and dark green, stewing in a bath of white wine and olive oil. On the other side of the stove is a deep pot of red-brown Venetian bean soup, and simmering in a *bain-marie* is an orange and umber sauce of tomatoes, clams, and onions. Translucent little squids sizzle on the grill; on a marble table are rose-coloured *scampi* and vermilion Adriatic crabs, and coils of pale-gold *fettuccine* are drying in plaited baskets. In the coolest part of the larder the oranges shine, luminous with their sugary coating. A particular variety of Sicilian oranges, without pips, is used for the confection of these caramel oranges, but even with the ordinary kinds, where the pips must be extracted as the fruit is eaten, the dish is well worth a trial.

Now, in 1987, caramel oranges have long ago become a cliché of London Italian restaurants, but they are better when made at home.

Peel 4 oranges extremely carefully with a very sharp knife, so that not one scrap of pith is left on them. Now prepare a syrup with 6 oz. of sugar to a teacupful of water. When it is thick, dip the oranges into the syrup, turning them over so that the whole orange may be

PANFILO NUVOLONE (1581-1631)
STILL LIFE WITH PEACHES ON A TAZZA
Campione d'Italia, Silvano Lodi Collection

well coated with the sugar. They should be in the syrup for only 2 or 3 minutes. Take them out and arrange them on a large dish. Now cut the peel, as thin as possible (this can be done very successfully with a potato peeler), from two other oranges. Cut this peel into fine strips about the length of matches. Plunge into boiling water and cook for about 7 minutes, to rid the peel of its bitter taste. Drain, then cook in the syrup until the strips have begun to take on a transparent look and are becoming caramelized. Becoming is the operative word. Don't let them turn to toffee.

Put a spoonful of this caramelized peel on top of each orange. Serve the oranges very cold. The addition of a little kirsch to the syrup is, I consider, an improvement.

INSALATA DI FRUTTA
(FRUIT SALAD)

Peaches, apricots, plums, and fresh purple figs, all peeled and cut up into rather small squares. Make it in the morning for the evening, add a little sugar and lemon juice, which will dissolve to a syrup, and serve it very cold.

ZABAIONE

For each person allow the yolks of 2 eggs, 2 teaspoonfuls of sugar and 1 small sherry glassful of Marsala.

Beat the yolks and the sugar together until they are white and frothy. Stir in the Marsala, and put the whole mixture into a thick pan* over a slow fire. Stir continuously, as for a

FOLLOWER OF CARAVAGGIO
STILL LIFE – FRUIT AND FLOWERS, *c.* 1630
Hartford, Connecticut, Wadsworth Atheneum

custard, taking great care that the *zabaione* does not curdle. It must not boil. As soon as it thickens, pour it into warmed glasses and serve it immediately. In Italian restaurants *zabaione* is not often served as a sweet dish, but it is much recommended by Italian doctors as a restorative.

*An untinned copper sugar-boiling pan is the best utensil for zabaione.

FRUTTA
FRUIT

'Philemon, a Comick Poet, died with extreme laughter at the conceit of seeing an asse eat figs.' (Thomas Nashe, *The Unfortunate Traveller*, 1594.)

'BROWN TURKEY. Undoubtedly the best Fig both in or out of doors, flesh red, very delicious and extremely fertile.' (From Bunyard's *Catalogue of Fruit Trees.*)

'Peel a fig for your friend, a peach for your enemy.' (Italian proverb.)

To eat figs off the tree in the very early morning, when they have been barely touched by the sun, is one of the exquisite pleasures of the Mediterranean.

There are wonderful figs to be found all over Italy. The figs of Sicily are celebrated. There is a certain garden in Anacapri where the fig trees bear round purple figs which are not much to look at; their skins are mapped with fine lines, but the fruit cracks gently as it is picked, disclosing rose madder flesh which is sweet with a dry aftertaste, and these are the most lovely of all figs to eat with Parma ham.

BARTOLOMEO BIMBI (1648-1730)
CHERRIES
Florence, Palazzo Pitti

GIOVANNA GARZONI (1600-70)
CHINESE BOWL WITH FIGS, BIRD AND CHERRY
Florence, Palazzo Pitti

I GELATI
ICES

The first ices and ice creams were frozen in metal containers set in wooden pails filled with crushed ice and salt, initially also with the addition of saltpetre or nitre. It was the method of artificial freezing discovered in the second half of the sixteenth century, probably in Naples, but not applied to sherbets and creams until the 1650s or 1660s. So it was not Catherine de Medici who introduced ices to France when she arrived there in 1533 to marry the Duke of Orleans who later became Henri II, any more than it was Marco Polo who discovered them in China in the thirteenth century. Those are legends which are apparently central to the credo of the ice cream trade, particularly in Italy, and which I believed myself when I wrote this book in 1954. Later, I discovered that Catherine, who was born in 1519, couldn't have known about ices because no method of artificial freezing had been evolved until just about the time of her death in 1589. Even then, it was only some seventy years later, in the early 1660s, that *acque gelate* or *eaux glacées*, the frozen aromatic waters which were the first ices, became known in Naples, Florence, Paris, and in Spain.

It was still a long while, about thirty years, before instructions for making and freezing ices found their way into print, in Italy as in France.

Appropriately, it was in Naples that the earliest Italian recipes for *sorbetti* were published. They appeared in the second volume of Antonio Latini's *Lo Scalco alla Moderna, The Modern Steward*, published

No two figs are alike. That is one of the joys of figs, for it makes the perfect one far to seek. For me, the best figs are not Sicilian, nor the flavoury little figs of the Abruzzi. They are the figs from one particular tree in a garden on the Greek island of Euboea – figs with fine skins of a most brilliant green, the fruit itself of a deep rich purple, with more body, less honey sweet, but with a more intense flavour than figs anywhere else in the world.

Perhaps the only other fruit in Italy with a flavour and character intense as those of the fig is the wood strawberry. Through the long Italian summer there are always *fragole dei boschi*; they are best eaten simply with sugar, possibly a little lemon or orange juice, but not cream, which does not combine very successfully with their grainy texture.

Fruit is an integral part of every Italian meal, no matter how many courses may already have been eaten. It is cheap, and piled carelessly up in market stalls, without cotton-wool wrappings or paper frills to make peaches, pears, figs, and grapes ridiculous. The skins of oranges and lemons fresh from the trees have a penetrating aromatic scent. Just occasionally you come across the apricot with its true magic flavour. Every street stall all over Italy is festooned with bananas. In Venice one of the most charming sights is the display of coconuts. Cut into slices, they are arranged on a kind of tiered cake-stand, and a little jet of water on the summit bubbles over and keeps them fresh and cool.

GIOVANNA GARZONI (1600-70)
STILL LIFE WITH POMEGRANATE
Florence, Palazzo Pitti

in 1694. (The first volume had appeared in 1692, confusingly also reprinted in 1694.) Latini, a native of the Marche, who was steward to the Spanish Prime Minister of Naples, Don Stefano Carrillo y Salcedo, commented, not perhaps without a note of sarcasm, that 'in the city of Naples a great quantity of sorbette is consumed, they are the consistency of sugar and snow, and every Neapolitan, it would appear, is born knowing how they are made'. From that remark, I take it that by the 1690s ices were already being sold in the streets of Naples, perhaps from those picturesquely decorated stalls from which lemonade and iced water were dispensed or perhaps by street vendors in a category distinct from that of the water sellers.

The instructions given by Latini for making ices were deliberately sketchy. He was being careful not to impinge on the preserves of professional colleagues, nor to reveal the secrets of the *ripostieri*, the shopkeepers. It is possible however to judge from his quantities that the *sorbetti* of Naples as he described them were semi-frozen and very sweet sherbets, in contrast to the hard and glassy water ices of Paris at the same period. Apart from fresh fruit such as strawberries, bitter cherries, and lemons, Latini's ingredients were pine nuts, milk, candied fruit, cinnamon – still a favourite in Naples and Scily three hundred years later – and chocolate, made into a frozen *scomiglia* or mousse, early for its time, and no doubt evolved by the chocolate-addicted Spaniards. Also early were the ices frozen in *tavolette*, tablets, the bricks which were to become synonymous with Neapolitan ices all over the world and already familiar in Naples by the 1690s.

LUCA FORTE (c. 1600/15-1670)
STILL LIFE WITH ROSES, ANEMONES, POMEGRANATES AND LEMONS
WITH BIRDS (detail)
London, Matthiesen Fine Art

BARTOLOMEO BIMBI (1648-1730)
APRICOTS AND PEACHES (detail)
Florence, Palazzo Pitti

In Latini's world of Spanish administrators, Neapolitan noblemen and their families, government officials and high-ranking naval officers, ices were invariably prepared for early evening collations, very often alfresco ones served in the grounds of great seaside palaces, and made in quantity. In the shade of lemon and orange groves, among the scented roses for which the gardens of Naples were then famous, the richly-dressed ladies and gentlemen and their children would stroll and talk and play, the sea shimmering below in the evening sunlight, the islands of Ischia and Capri scarcely visible in the hazy distance, in the foreground the plume of smoke rising from Vesuvius to remind them of the ever-present menace of the volcano.

Also published in Naples at about the same time as Latini's grandiose volumes was an obscure little twelve-page booklet, undated, anonymous, and unrecorded in Italian national collections, entitled *Brieve e Nuovo Modo da farsi ogni sorte di Sorbetti con facilita*, meaning *Short New and Easy Method of making every kind of sherbet*. Full of Neapolitan terms, measurements, and ingredients, the little booklet gave twenty-three recipes for ices, and was perhaps intended as a sales brochure to be given away with equipment such as freezing pots and moulds. Several different types of these are called for in the recipes, a favourite being *ricottelle*, the fluted log-shaped individual moulds later well-known in France as *canelons* or tubes. It was very often in *ricottelle* moulds that the clotted cream, fresh curd cheese, or egg-thickened ices

BARTOLOMEO BIMBI (1648-1730)
CITRONS AND LEMONS
Florence, Palazzo Pitti, Galleria Palatina

RENATO GUTTUSO (1913-87)
HOMAGE TO ZURBARAN
London, Marlborough Fine Art

called *stracchini gelati* in Naples and *fromages glacés* in France were frozen, although in Italy the nomenclature of the various categories of ices changed as time went on, and also, as might be expected, from region to region. In Florence water ices were not at first called *sorbetti*, but *acque gelate*, corresponding to the French *eaux glacées*, and at the same time were also known as *neve*, in Paris *neiges*. In Neapolitan usage an egg-enriched ice was a *candito d'ova*, frozen in bricks, while in the 1680s the Florentine Count Lorenzo Magalotti, who as Secretary to the Cimento Academy in the 1660s had recorded all the freezing experiments carried out by the Fellows of the Academy, evolved a version of frozen *zabaglione* which he called a *candiero*. In Naples fancy ices with names to match started early. An ice with a scalded and sweetened milk base heavily flavoured with pulverised cinnamon was partly frozen in the usual freezing pot before being embellished with finely chopped pieces of the much-loved Neapolitan candied pumpkin, then trans-

ferred to a variety of individual moulds such as pyramids, *ricottelle*, and other shapes. This ice was picturesquely called *sorbetta d'aurora*, sunrise sherbet.

The two stages of freezing carried out in the case of the aurora ice, and others given in the same booklet, was probably the *nuovo modo* referred to in the title, and represented an advance in the technique of making ices. The stirring of the half-frozen sherbet and the breaking down of the ice crystals was at least a step toward the achievement of a smoother, less grainy ice.

In the early days ices in Italy and in France were always served in two-handled goblets called *giarre*, and were required to be sufficiently frozen to stand up in peaks, or as the late seventeenth-century Tuscan poet Francesco Redi charmingly phrased their appearance, in a poem called *Arianna Infirma*, 'finest frozen snow rising from the rims of the goblets in hillocks'.

GRANITA AL CAFFÉ
(COFFEE GRANITA)

6oz. of coffee, 3 oz. of sugar, 2 pints of water.

Put the finely ground coffee and the sugar into an earthenware jug, pour the boiling water over it, and put the jug in a saucepan of hot water. Leave it, with a very gentle flame underneath, and let the coffee infuse for 30 minutes.

Leave it to get cold, strain it through a very fine muslin, and freeze in the ice tray at the usual temperature for making ice. Stir it from time to time. It will take 2½-3 hours to freeze. Fresh cream may be served with it.

The addition to the *granita* of ¼ pint of cream, *after* it has frozen, produces the best and simplest made iced coffee I know.

GRANITA DI LIMONE
(LEMON GRANITA)

6 or 7 lemons (enough to produce ½ pint of juice), ¼ lb. of sugar, 1 pint of water.

Make a syrup of the sugar and water by bringing them to the boil and boiling for 5 minutes. When the syrup is cold mix it with the lemon juice and freeze in the ice-tray of the refrigerator at the normal temperature for making ice. On account of the sugar the freezing will take about an hour more than the usual time taken for making ice.

Enough for six helpings.

GRANITA DI FRAGOLE
(STRAWBERRY GRANITA)

2 lb. of fresh strawberries, ½ lb. of sugar, the juice of half a lemon and half an orange, ¼ pint of water.

Put the strawberries through a sieve (2 lb. should yield about a pint of pulp). Add the lemon and orange juice. Boil the sugar and water together for 5 minutes. When cool, add it to the strawberry mixture. Freeze as for the lemon water-ice.

Enough for six to eight helpings.

CUSTARD FOR ICES

'Take 1 pint of good fresh cream and mix it slowly in a small copper pan with 8 yolks of eggs, which must be quite fresh. Cut a very thin slice of lemon peel, just the surface of the

RENATO GUTTUSO (1913-87)
GIRL EATING ICE CREAM
Milan, Collezione De Ponti

rind of a lemon, and put it in the cream. Put your pan on a slow fire, and stir the cream constantly with a whisk, taking care not to let it boil, for it will turn to curds; this you will easily perceive, as it then begins to form small lumps. You will know when it is done by the cream becoming of a thicker consistence, and instead of turning round the pan, it at once stops; then immediately take it from the fire, add to it 6 oz. of pounded sugar, more or less, according to taste. Strain it through a sieve over a basin, and give it what flavour you choose.

'In case of necessity, you may use half milk and half cream, by adding the yolks of 2 more eggs, but it is better with newer cream and fewer eggs.' (G.A. Jarrin, *The Italian Confectioner*, 1837.)

GELATO DI CAFFÉ
(COFFEE ICE CREAM)

Make the custard as above, but using two thirds of the quantities; that is ¾ pint of cream, 6 yolks, and 4 oz. sugar; add 4 oz. of

freshly roasted coffee beans before cooking the mixture; once cooked, leave the beans in the custard for several hours before straining it. Then freeze as explained below. This method gives the perfect coffee flavour – mild but true.

GELATO DI ALBICOCCHE
(APRICOT ICE CREAM)

To the original mixture of 4 yolks, ½ pint of cream, and 3 oz. sugar, add, when it is cold, a teacupful of apricot purée, made by stewing ¼ lb. of dried apricots in water until they are soft. Strain off the juice and put the fruit through a sieve. If it seems rather liquid put it in a pan over a gentle fire and let it dry out a little. When fresh apricots are in season, 1 lb. is needed to produce the required amount of purée. But no extra sugar. Freeze as explained below.

GELATO DI FRAGOLE
(STRAWBERRY ICE CREAM) (1)

Add the pulp from 1 lb. of fresh strawberries to ½ pint of cream, 4 yolks of eggs and 3 oz. of sugar prepared as already described, and freeze as explained below for 2½-3 hours. Enough for six helpings.

GELATO DI FRAGOLE
(STRAWBERRY ICE CREAM) (2)

Add the pulp from 1 lb. of fresh strawberries to ½ pint of fresh cream, whipped with 3 oz. of sugar. Freeze as explained below for 2-2½ hours. Makes a very deliciously flavoured ice, but not such a smooth mixture as the one made with eggs. It must be stirred three or four times during the freezing.

GELATO DI FRAGOLE
(STRAWBERRY ICE) (3)

To the preparation as for strawberry water-ice add ¼ pint of fresh whipped cream, and freeze at maximum freezing temperature for 2½ hours. This is perhaps the best of all.

The foregoing chapter on the early ices of Italy was written in 1987 for the new edition of *Italian Food*, and replaces all that I wrote on the

MICHAELANGELO MERISI DA CARAVAGGIO (1573-1610)
BASKET OF FRUIT
Milan, Pinacoteca Ambrosiana

subject – much of it erroneous I'm afraid – when the book first appeared in 1954. I have also eliminated footnotes and other matter no longer relevant to conditions in Italy, or to the making of ices at home. In the 1950s we used the old hand-cranked wooden pail freezers, with their metal inner containers fitted with churning devices which beat the cream throughout the freezing process. The ice and the salt essential to that traditional method of freezing weren't always easy to come by, and when an obliging fishmonger *was* able and willing to supply the ice it still had to be wrapped in a sack and broken up small – the finer the ice, the quicker the freezing – more often than not resulting in a kitchen awash with melting ice. One pound of salt to every three of ice used in the freezing pail was supposed to be the proper proportion, but getting it just right was tricky and the three pounds of salt to every nine or ten of ice needed for a six to eight pint freezer pail seemed a hefty amount. The alternative method was to freeze ices in refrigerator trays. That was reasonably successful, but involved turning the thermostat to maximum freezing point as well as a good deal of tedious surveillance for a partially satisfactory result and a rather small yield.

Then came the time when nearly everybody had a freezer of some kind, and given care and the occasional vigorous stir, sorbets and ice creams could be produced with fair success. But again it was a slow process, and given that timing was important, required a good deal of attention. Then there were various small sorbettières which went into the freezer and even into the ice-making compartment of fridges, taking up much space and only spasmodically working as their manufacturers intended. On the whole they were more trouble than they were worth. At last, in the early 1980s came the first small-scale, electrically powered ice cream churners with their own built-in freezing units. Evolved in and imported from Italy, the new machines made, and still make, ices as smooth and fine in texture as any from a high class professional *gelatiera*. The simultaneous churning and

FILIPPO NAPOLITANO (1595-1630)
COOLING BOWL
Florence, Palazzo Pitti

freezing action of these machines mean that the basic mixture, whether a rich egg and cream custard, or a simple fruit and sugar syrup preparation for a water ice, is frozen smooth, free of ice particles and grainy patches, in twenty to twenty-five minutes. The *granita*, so-named because of its characteristically grainy texture, will soon have to be re-christened.

For the benefit of those who do not freeze their ice creams in a freezer, an old fashioned churn, or the new *gelato* machines, my original instructions may still be of interest. Summarised, they were as follows: The refrigerator should be turned to its maximum freezing point, the filled ice tray or trays covered with aluminium foil, and the cream stirred after the first hour of freezing. Return immediately to the refrigerator. Rich mixtures such as that for the coffee ice cream took 2½-3 hours to freeze, and needed only one stir. They did not freeze hard, and remained creamy. The most inconvenient aspect of freezing ice creams in the refrigerator was that everything else in it got far too cold. The extra formation of ice also meant much more frequent defrosting of the refrigerator. For sorbets, as distinct from ice creams, I found that it was quite satisfactory to freeze them in the ice trays at the normal temperature for making ice. But it was still necessary to cover the filled trays with foil.

CHRISTIAN BERENTS (1658-1720)
ROMAN VEGETABLES AND FRUIT
Rome, Galleria Nazionale di Arte Antica

ᎦAUCES

 ITH THE EXCEPTION OF BÉCHAMEL (FOR WHICH THE Italians share with the English an unbounded admiration) and mayonnaise, Italian sauces are quite unfamiliar and quite unlike any French sauce. They are of a far less evolved and elegant nature, there are no *fumets* or meat glazes, and very little in the way of sauces thickened with eggs and butter such as *béarnaise* or *hollandaise*. Cream is rarely used except for sweet dishes.

The foundations of many Italian sauces are olive oil and wine, and they are given consistency with breadcrumbs, cheese, tomato purée, pounded herbs, and spices. They are simpler to cook than French sauces, there are fewer traps for the unwary; and though they are not so impressive, Italian sauces lack neither variety nor originality, and some of them have great freshness of flavour. Tomato sauce is most erroneously supposed by people who have eaten Italian food only in Italian restaurants abroad or in southern Italian holiday resorts to be the unique sauce of the country. It does, of course, play a large part in Italian cookery, but the good cooks use it in only very small quantities,

and there are as many ways of making it as there are cooks in Italy. The principles are always the same, but the flavourings and the time taken to cook it determine its character. Perhaps the best are both Neapolitan, *alla marinara*, in which the tomatoes are barely cooked at all, and *alla pizzaiola*, richly flavoured with garlic and herbs.

Sugo usually, but not invariably, denotes a meat sauce (the word has no English equivalent, since gravy has such an unfortunate connotation, but it corresponds to the French *jus*). The best known is the Bolognese meat sauce called *ragù* in its native town; but there are plenty of other variations to choose from.

Agrodolce, or sweet-sour sauces, have an ancient splendour about their composition, with their candied fruit, pine nuts, wine, raisins, vinegar, and sugar. The green sauces of Liguria; the basil and cheese *pesto*; the walnut and parsley sauce for *pasta*; the fennel, capers, parsley, olives, and oil of the sauce for *cappon magro* are aromatic, garlicky, exuberant with all the smells of the Mediterranean.

A number of sauces not actually in this chapter are described with the dish of which they are part, but are listed under sauces in the index.

BATTUTO

A *battuto* is the initial preparation of soups and stews which is used particularly in Roman cooking. It consists usually of an onion, a carrot, celery leaves, parsley, and garlic, all finely chopped, and browned in oil, butter, or dripping. Sometimes bacon or ham, cut into small dice, are added. On this foundation goes the meat to be stewed, or the broth and vegetables for a soup.

Soffritto is another word for *battuto*.

RAGÙ

This is the true name of the Bolognese sauce which, in one form or another, has travelled round the world. In Bologna it is served mainly with *lasagne verdi*, but it can go with many other kinds of *pasta*. The ingredients to make enough sauce for six generous helpings of *pasta* are 8 oz. of lean minced beef, 4 oz. of chicken livers, 3 oz. of uncooked ham (both fat and lean), 1 carrot, 1 onion, 1 small piece of celery, 3 teaspoonfuls of concentrated tomato purée, 1 wineglassful of white wine, 2 wine-glassfuls of stock or water, butter, salt and pepper, nutmeg.

Cut the bacon or ham into very small pieces and brown them gently in a small saucepan in about ½ oz. of butter. Add the onion, the carrot, and the celery, all finely chopped. When they have browned, put in the raw minced beef, and then turn it over and over so that it all browns evenly. Now add the chopped chicken livers, and after 2 or 3 minutes the tomato purée, and then the white wine. Season with salt (having regard to the relative saltiness of the ham or bacon), pepper, and a scraping of nutmeg, and add the meat stock or water. Cover the pan and simmer the sauce very gently for 30-40 minutes. Some Bolognese cooks add at the last 1 cupful of cream or milk to the sauce, which makes it smoother. Another traditional variation is the addition of the *ovarine* or unlaid eggs which are found inside the hen, especially in the spring when the hens are laying. They are added at the same time as the chicken livers and form small golden globules when the sauce is finished. When the *ragù* is to be served with spaghetti or *tagliatelle*, mix it with the hot *pasta* in a heated dish so that the *pasta* is

thoroughly impregnated with the sauce, and add a good piece of butter before serving. Hand the grated cheese separately.

This is the recipe given me by Zia Nerina, a splendid woman, titanic of proportion but angelic of face and manner, who in the 1950s owned and ran the Trattoria Nerina in Bologna. Zia Nerina's cooking was renowned far beyond the confines of her native city.

SUGO DI CARNE
(*MEAT SAUCE*)

½ lb. of lean minced beef, 1 onion, 1 carrot, 1 small piece of celery, ½ oz. of dried mushrooms, parsley, ½ wineglassful of white wine, 1 teaspoonful of concentrated tomato purée, salt and pepper, ½ oz. of butter, stock, flour.

Brown the onion in butter. Add the other vegetables, finely chopped, the chopped parsley, and the previously soaked dried mushrooms. When these are browned put in the meat. Stir it well so that it is all browned, then sprinkle in a tablespoonful of flour; now add the concentrated tomato, the heated white wine, and about ½ pint of meat stock. Simmer for 40 minutes, uncovered. The sauce can be either sieved or left as it is. Excellent with potato *gnocchi* or any kind of *pasta*.

It should have sufficient body for the meat and the liquid not to separate when it is poured over the *pasta*, but should not be too thick. Makes 10-12 oz. sauce, enough for four to six helpings of *pasta*.

SALSA GENOVESE
(*GENOESE SAUCE*)

½ lb. of veal, 1 carrot, 1 onion, celery, 1 tablespoonful of dried mushrooms, 2 or 3 tomatoes, 1 tablespoonful of flour, 1 large cupful of stock, 1 wineglassful of white wine, butter.

Brown the sliced onion in butter; add the other vegetables (the dried mushrooms previously soaked for 15 minutes in warm water), and the chopped or minced veal. When it has browned, put in the skinned and chopped tomatoes, then stir in the flour. When the flour has thickened add the heated white wine; let it bubble a few minutes and then add the stock, also heated. Season the sauce and let it cook for

30 minutes. It can be either sieved or left as it is. For *pasta*.

In Italy the veal used for this would be trimmings left from the joints from which escalopes have been cut.

SALSA DI FEGATINI
(*CHICKEN LIVER SAUCE*)

½ lb. of chicken livers, a few dried mushrooms, flour, Marsala, stock, butter.

Clean the chicken livers, flour them lightly, and cut them into small pieces. Soak the dried mushrooms in warm water for 15 minutes and chop them.

Cook the chicken livers in butter with the mushrooms. Season them with salt and pepper, pour over 1 sherry-glassful of Marsala (or white wine). When this has reduced, add 1 cupful of chicken or meat stock, and simmer the sauce until it is thick. Serve with potato *gnocchi*.

SALSA DI POMIDORO
(*TOMATO SAUCE*) (1)

Chop 2 lb. of ripe tomatoes. Put them into a saucepan with 1 small onion, 1 carrot, 1 piece of celery, and a little parsley, all finely chopped. Add salt, ground black pepper and a pinch of sugar. Simmer until the tomatoes have turned almost to a purée. Put the sauce through a sieve.

If a concentrated sauce is needed put the purée back in a saucepan and cook it again until the watery part of it has dried up. Before serving it with meat, fish, or any kind of *pasta*, add, when they are obtainable, a couple of fresh basil leaves.

SALSA DI POMIDORO
(*TOMATO SAUCE*) (2)

1 onion, 1 carrot, 1 piece of celery, 3 or 4 oz. of raw minced veal or beef, or a mixture of meat and Italian ham (but fresh meat gives the best results), a few mushrooms either fresh or dried, 1½ lb. of tomatoes, oil or butter, garlic.

Fry the onion, the carrot, the celery, and the mushrooms in the oil or butter. Add the chopped meat and the garlic, then the chopped tomatoes. Season with salt, pepper, and a little sugar. Simmer until the tomatoes

GIOVANNA GARZONI (1600-70)
THE OLD MAN OF ARTIMINO
Florence, Palazzo Pitti

are completely cooked, and sieve the sauce. Season it with salt, pepper, and any fresh herb you please.

Makes approximately 1 pint of sauce.

SALSA DI POMIDORO
(TOMATO SAUCE) (3)

When tomatoes are or not very ripe make a sauce according to either of the foregoing recipes, but use half the quantity of fresh tomatoes plus 1 tablespoonful of concentrated tomato purée diluted with 2 tablespoonsful of water or stock. This makes an excellent sauce, but it must be cooked a little longer to diminish the sharp flavour of the concentrated purée.

SALSA DI POMIDORO AL MARSALA
(TOMATO SAUCE WITH MARSALA)

1 lb. of fresh tomatoes, 1 small onion, 1 oz. of lean ham or bacon, 1 clove of garlic, butter, Marsala.

Fry the chopped onion in butter, add the ham or bacon cut into small pieces, then the peeled and quartered tomatoes and the garlic. Season with salt and pepper, and let the sauce cook rapidly for 5 minutes. Pour in a sherry-glassful of Marsala and cook 2 or 3 more minutes.

For *pasta*, rice, fish, meat. Use tinned peeled tomatoes when fresh ones are not sufficiently ripe.

SALSA PIZZAIOLA

This Neapolitan sauce, made from fresh tomatoes, flavoured with garlic and basil or *origano*, is usually spread on to steaks or some kind of meat cut into steaks; it can also be used for fish or for *pasta*. It is described in the recipe for *bistecca alla pizzaiola* on p. 138.

BESCIAMELLA
(BÉCHAMEL)

To make 1 pint of béchamel the ingredients are 1½ oz. of butter, 2 tablespoonsful of flour, 1¼ pints of milk, salt, pepper, and in some cases nutmeg or a bay leaf.

The right amount of butter is essential to the making of a good béchamel. Melt it in a thick pan. When it bubbles but before it starts to turn brown, put in the flour, through a wire sieve. Stir it gently with a wooden spoon until you have a thick creamy mass. Now add a little of the *hot* milk. Stir vigorously, and as soon as it is absorbed by the flour add more, and go on adding it gradually until it is all used up. By this time the sauce should be quite smooth, but it must be cooked for another 15-20 minutes or it will taste of flour. See that it is well seasoned with salt, pepper, and a little nutmeg; or if the flavour of bay leaf is preferred, put the bay leaf in the milk while it is being heated and remove it before adding the milk to the sauce or the flavour will be too strong.

These quantities make a béchamel of the right consistency for most dishes, but it can be made thicker or thinner according to necessity by using more or less milk.

However successfully béchamel is made, it is always an improvement to sieve it before serving. The sauce may be made in advance and heated up, but to prevent a skin forming as it cools, pour a little melted butter over the top.

SALSA DI LEPRE
(HARE SAUCE)

An alternative to the hare sauce for *pappardelle* (fresh noodles) described on p. 66.

GIOVANNA GARZONI (1600-70)
BOWL WITH PEACHES AND PLUMS
Florence, Palazzo Pitti

Marinade the pieces of hare (the legs will be sufficient, the back being used for another dish) in red wine, onions, garlic, bay leaves, pepper, rosemary, and sage, with a carrot cut into dice and some celery leaves. Leave for 2 days. Brown the meat in lard or oil, add some fresh herbs and vegetables, a few dice of ham or bacon, and pour over them 1 tumblerful of red wine. Stew the hare very slowly until the meat is falling off the bones; these must all be removed and the meat put through a sieve so that a thick purée is obtained. Reheat the sauce in a *bain-marie* and pour it over the cooked *pappardelle*.

SALSA DI PROSCIUTTO
(HAM SAUCE)

A sauce to make when good chicken stock is available. In a small pan melt 1 oz. of butter. In this sauté 3 or 4 oz. of cooked ham cut into thin matchlike strips. Do not let it frizzle - it must cook slowly. Stir in 1 teaspoonful, not more, of concentrated tomato purée. Add 2 good cupfuls of stock, and simmer for about 5 minutes. The sauce should reduce a little. Serve with plain rice and grated Parmesan.

LA BAGNA CAUDA

One of the famous specialities of the province of Piedmont.

3 oz. each of olive oil, butter, anchovies, and garlic. In Piedmont they use salted whole anchovies from the barrel. Fillets tinned in oil are less overpowering.

Heat the butter and the oil, put in the anchovies cut in pieces and the garlic finely sliced. Simmer for 10 minutes. The sauce is served in a dish kept hot over a spirit lamp, and with it goes a dish of raw cardoons (celery can replace them), raw sliced cabbage, and pimentos both cooked and raw. Sliced white truffles are sometimes added to the sauce, and occasionally even cream as well.

The Piedmontese do not usually serve the *bagna cauda* at meals, but at any time of the night or day they may feel hungry and thirsty, for it is a dish which essentially needs the accompaniment of plenty of strong coarse red wine, such as the local Barbera. It is also excessively indigestible, and is indicated only for those with very resistant stomachs. For garlic eaters it is, of course, a blissful feast.

SALSA AGRODOLCE
(SWEET-SOUR SAUCE)

This characteristic Italian sauce must have descended from the Romans. In the so called book of Apicius there is a recipe for a sauce containing 'pepper, mint, pine nuts, sultanas, carrots, honey, vinegar, oil, wine and musk'.

The components of an *agrodolce* vary according to the meat which it is to accompany. For venison, hare, and boar the basis is usually the wine in which the meat has been marinaded. Pine nuts, sultanas, and vinegar are nearly always a part of the sauce. Sugar has taken the place of honey. Grated bitter chocolate is a later addition, which, extraordinary as it sounds, merely gives body and colour to the sauce and an indefinable, curious, but not at all obtrusive flavour. Candied peel and cherries, and sometimes red-currant jelly, are often added as well.

The instructions for making these sauces will be found in the recipes for hare and boar, and a simplified, perhaps the best, version in the recipe for duck on p. 156. The mint gives it a particularly engaging flavour.

SALSA DI TONNO
(TUNNY FISH SAUCE)

6 oz. of tinned tunny fish in oil, 1 cupful of meat or chicken stock, olive oil or butter, parsley, pepper.

Heat the oil or butter. Add the tunny broken up into small pieces, and some chopped parsley. Let it cook gently. After 5 minutes add the hot stock, season with ground black pepper, and cook for another 5 minutes.

To serve with spaghetti or *risotto*.

SALSA DI GAMBERI
(PRAWN SAUCE)

1 small onion, parsley, 4 oz. of cooked shelled prawns, ½ oz. of pine nuts, oil, and butter.

Chop the onion and melt it in 1 tablespoonful each of oil and butter. Add 1 tablespoonful of chopped parsley and the prawns. Roast the pine nuts, pound them in a mortar, and add them to the prawns. Add 5-6 tablespoonfuls of warm water and simmer very slowly for 15 minutes. The sauce can be either sieved or served as it is, with rice, eggs, or fish.

½ lb. of shelled prawns is equivalent to approximately a pint unshelled.

SALSA DI FUNGHI ALLA VERONESE
(VERONESE MUSHROOM SAUCE)

In a mixture of butter and olive oil fry a small chopped onion, a handful of chopped parsley and a little garlic.

Sprinkle this *battuto* with flour and then stir in ½ lb. of mushrooms, washed and sliced. Season with salt and pepper, and simmer until the mushrooms are cooked. The liquid which comes from the mushrooms should be sufficient to amalgamate with the flour and so make a slightly thickened little mushroom stew rather than a sauce. Before serving the sauce, which is excellent for *pasta*, for chicken, steak or veal as well as the Veronese *risotto* on p. 83, add a generous lump of butter.

PESTO

1 large bunch of fresh basil, garlic, a generous ounce each of pine nuts and grated Sardo or Parmesan cheese, 1½-2 oz. of olive oil.

Pound the basil leaves (there should be about 2 oz. when the stalks have been removed) in a mortar with 1 or 2 cloves of garlic, a little salt and the pine nuts. Add the cheese. (Sardo cheese is the pungent Sardinian ewe's milk cheese which is exported in large quantities to Genoa to make *pesto*. Parmesan and Sardo are sometimes used in equal quantities, or all Parmesan, which gives the *pesto* a milder flavour.)

GIOVANNA GARZONI (1600-70)
STILL LIFE WITH CHERRIES
Florence, Palazzo Pitti

When the *pesto* is a thick purée start adding the olive oil, a little at a time. Stir it steadily and see that it is amalgamating with the other ingredients, as the finished sauce should have the consistency of a creamed butter. If made in larger quantities *pesto* may be stored in jars, covered with a layer of olive oil.

This is the famous sauce which is eaten by the Genoese with all kinds of *pasta* (see *trenette col pesto*, p. 67), with *gnocchi*, and as a flavouring for soups. The Genoese claim that their basil has a far superior flavour to that grown in any other part of Italy, and assert that a good *pesto* can only be made with Genoese basil. As made in Genoa it is certainly one of the best sauces yet invented for *pasta*, and 1 tablespoonful of *pesto* stirred in at the last minute gives a most delicious flavour to a *minestrone*. Try it also with baked potatoes instead of butter.

Since basil is not easy to find in England except for people who grow it themselves, an imitation of this sauce can be made with parsley, and although the flavour is totally different it is still very good indeed – although it cannot of course be called *pesto*.* Walnuts can be used instead of pine nuts.

The quantitites given will make enough *pesto* for six helpings of *pasta* if served as a first course; four helpings if the chief part of the meal.

*Two or three brands of Italian tinned pesto are imported. They are reminiscent of the original, but I would not recommend them to anyone not already familiar with the real thing. They could give a false impression.

JACOPO LIGOZZI (1547-1627)
MOUSE AND WALNUT
Florence, Galleria degli Uffizi, Gabinetto Disegno

MAIONESE
(*MAYONNAISE*)

Italian mayonnaise is made only with eggs and olive oil, and sometimes a little lemon juice. Italians think it exceedingly comical that mustard should be added, as it often is in France. They may well be right, for the mayonnaise in Italy, when really good oil is used, is perfectly delicious, and the cooks are, as always, prodigal with the eggs.

To make a really good mayonnaise for four or five people use 3 yolks of eggs, about 8 oz. of olive oil, and salt.

Put the yolks of the eggs into a heavy bowl or mortar which will not slide about on the table (or stand the bowl on a newspaper or cloth). Stir the yolks with a wooden spoon for about a minute before adding 1 teaspoonful of salt, then start putting in the oil. It must be stirred in drop by drop until the mayonnaise starts to attain its characteristic consistency, so it is easier to have it in a small jug with a narrow lip rather than in the bottle. After a few minutes several drops can go in at a time, and gradually more and more until in the end the oil is being poured in in a thin but steady stream.

Stir all the time; the mayonnaise should be very thick, with a consistency almost like thick paint. If it starts to lose its shiny gloss it is a sign that the eggs have absorbed enough olive oil. The mayonnaise will not necessarily curdle, but it will become a creamy sauce rather than the jelly-like substance which sticks to the spoon and falls with such a delicious plop on to the plate. A very few drops of lemon juice can be added at the last moment. Should the oil have been added too recklessly or the mayonnaise curdle (that is, when the oil separates from the eggs), break another yolk into a clean bowl, stir it, add a little of the curdled mayonnaise, and then the rest, a spoonful at a time.

There is no necessity whatever to stand the bowl on ice when making mayonnaise, to keep the kitchen at some special temperature, or in any way to consider its confection as a mystery, a conjuring trick, or a technical achievement to be attempted only by highly skilled cooks.

MAIONESE VERDE
(*GREEN MAYONNAISE*)

To a plain mayonnaise add a handful of pounded parsley or basil, pine nuts, and pistachio nuts.

MAIONESE TONNATA
(TUNNY FISH MAYONNAISE)

Make a stiff mayonnaise with 2 yolks of eggs, a little salt, 4 oz. of olive oil, and a very little lemon juice.

Pound or put through a sieve about 2 oz. of tinned tunny fish in oil. Incorporate the purée gradually into the mayonnaise.

Excellent for all kinds of cold dishes, particularly chicken or hard-boiled eggs, for sandwiches, or for filling raw tomatoes for an hors d'œuvre.

SALSA DI NOCI
(WALNUT SAUCE)

2 oz. of shelled walnuts, 1 coffee-cupful of oil, 2 tablespoonfuls of breadcrumbs, 1½ oz. of butter, 1 large bunch of parsley, salt and pepper, 2 tablespoonfuls of cream or milk.

Take the skins off the shelled walnuts after pouring boiling water over them. Pound them in a mortar. Add the parsley, after having picked off all the large and coarse stalks. Put a little coarse salt with the parsley in the mortar – this will make it easier to pound. While reducing the parsley and the walnuts to a paste add from time to time some of the butter, softened or just melted by the side of the fire. Stir in the breadcrumbs, and, gradually, the oil. The result should be a thick paste, very green; it need not be absolutely smooth, but it must be well amalgamated. Stir in the cream or milk. Season with a little more salt and ground black pepper. A bizarre sauce, but excellent with *tagliatelle*, or with fish, or as a filling for sandwiches.

PEPERATA

A Veronese sauce to be served with *bollito* (p. 137) or any plainly cooked meat or poultry, hot or cold.

ABULCASSIS (15th century)
PRESSING OLIVE OIL
Paris, Bibliothèque Nationale

1½ oz. each of beef marrow and butter, or 3 oz. of butter, about 3 oz. of fresh white breadcrumbs, 1½ oz. of grated Parmesan, salt, ground black pepper, enough stock to moisten the mixture. Melt the butter and the beef marrow together; the butter should not cook. Stir in the breadcrumbs and the cheese, add a little stock, enough to make a smooth paste. Season with salt and a generous amount of ground black pepper. To be served cold.

SALSA DI POMIDORO CRUDO
(SAUCE OF RAW TOMATOES)

Plunge 1 lb. of very ripe tomatoes into boiling water and skin them. Chop them up, adding a little finely cut onion, garlic, parsley or fresh basil, and as much good olive oil as you care for. Make it an hour or two before it is to be served.

SALSA VERDE
(GREEN SAUCE)

Oil, lemon juice, parsley, capers, garlic, salt, and pepper, all mixed together as for a *vinaigrette*. There should be plenty of parsley and the sauce should be rather thick. Chopped anchovy fillets are sometimes added.

SALSA PER INSALATA
(SALAD DRESSING)

To an oil and lemon dressing add a crushed clove of garlic and 2 crushed fillets of anchovies. No salt.

SALSA VERDE AL RAFANO
(GREEN SAUCE WITH HORSERADISH)

1 large bunch of parsley, a few sprigs of mint, 1 tablespoonful of grated horseradish, 2 tablespoonfuls of breadcrumbs, 2 ripe tomatoes, olive oil, salt, pepper.

Peel and chop the tomatoes and mix them with the finely chopped parsley and mint. Add the horseradish, the breadcrumbs, and about 3 tablespoonfuls of olive oil – enough to make a sauce of the consistency of a thin mayonnaise. Season with salt and pepper.

To serve with cold meat.

GIOVAN BATTISTA RUOPPOLO (1629-93)
FRUIT AND FLOWERS
Naples, Museo di Capodimonte

PRESERVES

VISITED BENEDETTO ORFEI ON A SOFT MAY AFTERnoon . . . . He received me most civilly and served in my honour some old flagons of *vino santo* and certain Roman and Sicilian confections: walnuts preserved in honey, a sort of *fondant* paste perfumed with rose, mint and lemon, in which were buried pieces of candied fruit (orange peel, citron, pineapple), a very sweet quince paste called *cotognata*, another paste called *cocuzzata*, and a variety of wafers of peach paste known as *persicata* . . . . He stretched out his right hand, seized a wafer of *persicata* which he rolled carefully, and swallowed in one mouthful . . . .' (Guillaume Apollinaire, *L'Hérésiarque & Cie*, Paris, Stock, 1910.)

Perhaps the most remarkable of Italian preserves is the fruit mustard, *mostarda di frutta*, of Cremona. Made of whole fruits, pears, cherries, little oranges, figs, plums, apricots, and slices of melon and pumpkin, preserved in sugar syrup flavoured with mustard oil, this confection has an absolutely original flavour. Its origin goes back to the honey, mustard, oil and vinegar condiments of the Romans, who also preserved roots such as turnips in these mixtures.

It is eaten as an accompaniment to cold boiled meat and ham, and goes marvellously also with tongue, with cold roast pork, and even with chicken, turkey and pheasant. Cavanna (p. 124) suggests it should be eaten with eels. In Milan the grocery shops sell it from huge wooden pails. Although unfamiliar in this country, I have rarely known the *mostarda di frutta* not to meet with the approval of those to whom it has been offered.

Unhappily, *mostarda di frutta* has today become a dishonourable travesty of that ancient and beautiful preserve so often noted by travellers in Italy, from Michel de Montaigne in the 1580s and the Reverend John Ray FRS in the 1660s down to the 1950s when I myself was so beguiled by its shining appearance in those big wooden pails in the Milan provision stores. By 1970, a Cremona firm called Fratelli Sperlari was exporting a brand of mustard fruits packed in bucket-shaped tins with the list of ingredients – in Italian and English – printed on the label. The contents of that latter-day fruit relish included 'pear, apricot, cherry, fig, citron, plum, peach, sugar, corn syrup, mustard oil, and Agar Agar with certified colour and preservatives (sulphur dioxide) added'.

Where were the honey and the grape must, the wine and vinegar, the quinces, the green almonds and walnuts, the cloves and ginger, the turnip-rooted parsley and mustard seeds which at least as far back as Apicius in the 4th century AD had gone into successive versions of that ancestral Italian confection? Weird some of the Roman and medieval mixtures, called *compostes*, surely were, but could any of them have been as weird as the latter-day product evolved by the Sperlari Brothers of Cremona? Well, I tasted it and – why mince words – it really was downright horrible.

A very different version of fruit mustard, and one which I think has not been debased, is a Venetian speciality, a mustardy quince marmalade, called *mostarda vicentina*, Vicenza mustard. This conserve I have bought now and again in Venice, in the autumn, but only then, for it is a seasonal product and is sold out by Christmas or even before. It tends to ferment, or so I have been told by the shopkeepers who sell it in the

Rialto market. It must have been something like this version which Michel de Montaigne remarked upon in October 1581 when he was in the region of San Secondo (now in the province of Parma), where 'they put upon the table for me an assortment of condiments in the form of excellent relishes of various kinds. One of these was made with quinces'. Only a few days later, at Borgo San Donnino, in the Cremona region, there was another variation: 'they put on the table a mustard-like relish made with apples and oranges cut in pieces, like half-cooked quince marmalade.'

Italian preserved and candied fruit is spectacular. Whole pineapples, melons, citrons, oranges, figs, apricots, red and green plums, pears, even bananas in their skins, are sugared in the most skilful way, and make marvellous displays in the shops of Genoa and Milan.

Fichi mandorlati, the dried figs of Bari, are incomparably the best dried figs I have ever come across. Packed in square straw boxes, they are large, moist and dark, with a slightly roasted flavour, spiced with almonds, fennel seeds and bay leaves. Another interesting and delicious dried fruit to be eaten as a dessert are the *uva passolina* of the south, sultanas soaked in brandy and wrapped up in little parcels of lemon leaves.

CONSERVA DI POMIDORO
(*PRESERVED TOMATOES FOR SAUCE*)

At the moment when tomatoes are at their ripest and reddest, cut several pounds into quarters. Pack them into sterilized bottles or jars, adding 1 teaspoonful of salt and a leaf or two of fresh basil to each jar. Screw down the jars. If bottles are being used the corks must be either put in with a corking machine or securely fastened with a network of string. Wrap each jar or bottle in a cloth or in newspaper so that they will not touch each other and place them lying on their sides in a large pan filled with cold water. Bring it gently to the boil and then let them cook for 20 minutes.

This is the tomato preserve which is used in the winter for making sauce, for soups, for all *pizze*, and for almost any dish requiring tomatoes.

CONSERVA DI PEPERONI
(*PRESERVED PIMENTOS*)

3 lb. of red and yellow pimentos, salt, fresh basil.

Put the pimentos, whole, under the grill and leave them until the skins are quite black. They must be turned round from time to time. This process will take from 15-20 minutes according to the size of the pimentos and the heat of the grill. In Italy they are put directly on to a glowing charcoal fire. The smell of roasting pimentos is delicious.

Rub off the blackened skins, removing every speck, after having extracted the seeds and the cores. Wash them in cold water.

ANON (17th century)
STILL LIFE WITH ARTICHOKES AND LILIES
Florence, Palazzo Pitti

ANON (17th century)
STILL LIFE WITH GRAPES AND PUMPKINS
Florence, Palazzo Pitti

Divide them into strips and drop these strips into sterilized wine bottles or preserving jars. When the bottles are full add 1 teaspoonful of salt to each and a few leaves of basil (this is not essential).

Cork the bottle, tie down the corks with string, or screw down the tops of the preserving jars. Wrap each one in a cloth or in sheets of newspaper to prevent them touching each other during the cooking. Lay them flat in a large pan of cold water so that they are quite covered. Bring to the boil and continue boiling for 15 minutes.

3 lb. of pimentos will fill two 75 cl. wine bottles.

Pimentos preserved in this way should keep for months, make a most excellent hors d'œuvre, and can be used for most dishes requiring pimentos. Once opened a jar or bottle must be used up fairly quickly.

A year or two ago (1987) I read in a book somewhere that if the charred peppers are put into a paper or a plastic bag and left there for ten to fifteen minutes, the blackened skins will peel away without the slightest difficulty and there will be no need to wash the peppers under the tap. I tried the method and it works. A tip so successful I wish I had known of it long ago.

PEPERONI ALL'ACETO
(PIMENTOS PRESERVED IN VINEGAR)
First remove the stalks and the pips of the pimentos, but do not peel them. Drop them into boiling water for a minute or two only. Drain them very carefully. Arrange them in wide jars, and cover them completely with good white wine vinegar (uncooked). On top of the vinegar put a layer, a good 2 in. deep, of olive oil. To serve them, wash them in cold water to remove some of the vinegar and pour a little olive oil over them. Treated like this, the pimentos are free from the excessively acid taste which one finds in the commercial *peperoni all'aceto*.

BASILICO CONSERVATO ALL'OLIO
(BASIL PRESERVED IN OIL)
Pick all the leaves from the stalks of a large quantity of basil when it is plentiful and very

fresh. Wash them and dry them in a cloth. Put them into a preserving jar, completely cover them with good olive oil, and screw down the jar.

Preserved in this way the basil retains more of its flavour than when it is dried, but acquires a rather seaweed-like consistency.

TOTANI ALL'ANACAPRESE
(SQUID PRESERVED IN OIL AS IN ANACAPRI)
Totani, which are a variety of the inkfish family, usually about 6 in. long, are probably preserved in this way in other parts of the Mediterranean, but Anacapri is the only place I have actually come across them. The height of the *totani* season in the Bay of Naples is in August; they are caught in vast quantities at the full moon.

Clean the *totani* as directed for the inkfish on p. 116, and cut them into rings. Drop them into boiling vinegar, and cook them for a few minutes only. Strain off the vinegar. When they are cold put them into jars, cover them completely with olive oil, and into each jar put 1 tablespoonful of fresh *origano* (or thyme or marjoram). Cover the jars and leave them for six weeks at least.

The fish gradually lose the acid taste imparted by the vinegar and become tender as they absorb the oil. They make a good addition to an hors d'œuvre. The Anacaprese like to serve them on Christmas Eve. Anyone who is addicted to inkfish could lay in a supply, prepare them in this way, and use them for fish soups, for a mixed fry of fish, or for garnishing fish salads.

PERSICATA
(PEACH PRESERVE)
5 lb. of peaches, about 3 lb. of sugar.

GIOVANNA GARZONI (1600-70)
PLUMS, JASMINE AND CONVOLVULI
Florence, Palazzo Pitti

Drop the peaches in boiling water for a minute so that the skins come off easily. Remove the stones. Sieve the fruit, and for every pound of pulp add ¾ lb. of sugar. Boil until the mixture turns to a paste, like quince cheese. Spread in flat dishes, with the jelly about ¼ in. thick. Dry in a warm oven, or in the sun, until it is sufficiently firm to be turned over and dried on the other side. Cut into squares and store in tins. If preferred, the paste can be put straight into jars and used as a jelly.

CONFETTURA DI FICHI
(FIG JAM)

2 lbs. of green figs, ¾ lb. of sugar, the grated peel and juice of 2 lemons.

Put all the ingredients into a pan together and cook for about 1½ hours.

GIOVANNA GARZONI (1600-70)
FIGS
Cumpione d'Italia, Silvano Lodi Collection

THE CANDIED WALNUTS OF TURIN

It was the autumn of 1963. With my old friend Viola Johnson I had been on a brief visit to Alba to eat the famous white truffles, and now we were due to return to London. In those days there were direct flights between London and Turin, and that circumstance provided a good opportunity for Viola to see her father who still lived in his native city, where she had herself been born and brought up. But at this moment we were shopping for small gifts to take home to England.

Strolling down the Via Roma, where the confectioners' shops were at the time famous, we stopped to admire a particularly tempting display of fondants, pink and white, coffee and lemon and lilac-coloured, and alluring chocolates made in imitation of chestnuts, truffles and hazelnuts. (Turin is the home of the delectable *gianduia*, those celebrated chocolates filled with a soft, melting, rich and buttery hazelnut paste.) Also in the window was something unfamiliar. A box of black, sugared fruit. Were they prunes, we asked the lady in charge of the shop. No, they were *noci candite*, candied walnuts. Gathered green, we were told, they turn black and soft when preserved – like our own pickled walnuts, but there the resemblance ends – and as we saw them there in their frilly paper cases they looked like nuggets of onyx, sugar-dusted. They were about the size of damsons, soft, clove-scented;

and, we learned, they were a speciality unique to this one particular Turin sweetshop. To this day I remember that it was called Cotto, and was – I hope still is – at No 68. The lady, who turned out to be the owner, told us that the recipe for the *noci candite* had long ago been brought to Cotto's by a confectioner from the Asti region of Piedmont – perhaps as far back as the days when Turin was the capital of the old Duchy of Savoy.

That year I took home several boxes of Cotto candied walnuts for Christmas presents – surprisingly, I found that this fascinating speciality had escaped the notice of the Touring Club Italiano's *Guida Gastronomica* – and every autumn for several years to come I wrote to Turin for a new supply of the Cotto candied walnuts. So did at least two of the friends to whom I had introduced this curiously addictive sweetmeat. Then one year the walnuts failed to arrive. No explanation was forthcoming. Eventually, after a lapse of three or four years, I asked Viola Johnson, who by this time had moved to Switzerland, but still visited Italy regularly, to investigate the disappearance of those walnuts.

When Viola's answer came I realised that I should have known all along that our little black nuggets were doomed. The explanation was so obvious. A question of labour. It was essential to harvest the walnuts at precisely the right stage of ripeness, when the shells were still soft enough to be pierced with a needle. Alas, that crucial period, which lasts only a few days, coincides with that of the compulsory paid holidays which had only recently been decreed by Italian law. The owner of Cotto's had told Viola that she could not afford to pay extra labour both for the gathering of the nuts and the immediate initiation of the lengthy process of candying the nuts, for that too is essential to the success of the entire operation.

So the unique candied walnuts vanished. It was a familiar story, but none the less sad for that. I believe that they had been a survival from the seventeenth century, perhaps from its earliest decades when every available fruit, aromatic seed, leaf, nut, sweet-scented flower, from carnations and roses to violets and primroses, not forgetting citrus peels, cooling angelica and lettuce stalks, quince, pumpkin, and peach pulp, were all subjected to the then recently evolved process of crystallising and candying with sugar, or more simply to the marginally less complex one of preservation in sugar syrup.

Curiously, although I have searched many relevant books, I have never yet found a recipe for precisely those candied walnuts. For walnuts preserved in syrup there are dozens – white walnuts, black walnuts, walnuts with their tender young shells, and walnuts without. But for the dry, candied walnuts, with a whole clove stuck into one end, no formula. Probably it wouldn't be too difficult to work one out. In seventeenth-century England it was quite common for the ladies of prosperous households and their housekeepers to put up whole fruits in syrup with a view to candying or crystallising them later as a dry preserve to add to the spread of sweetmeats offered at the dessert or banquetting course at the end of dinner. A great deal of patient work and time are involved in making candied fruits in syrup, and no fewer than eight separate operations are required. (More if you count the initial needle-piercing, water-steeping and sun-drying stages.) For the candying, a further process of gradual drying out in a special sweet-meat-drying stove or cupboard would be needed. Anyone who has ever read instructions for the making of *marrons glacés* will recognise the similarity to the first eight stages involved in the following eighteenth-century directions for *noci confette* given in *Il Confetturiere Piemontese* (Milan 1792). I quote the recipe here simply as a matter of record.

GIACOMO CERUTI (1700-68)
STILL LIFE WITH MARROW
Milan, Pinacoteca di Brera

NOCI CONFETTE
(CANDIED WALNUTS)

'Take some fresh and still-tender walnuts, peel them, then cut a cross in each one and plunge them into a pan of cold water, put them on the fire, and when they are so tender that they can be easily pierced with the eye-end of a needle, transfer them to a bowl of cold water, which must be changed twice daily, so that it remains clear. The walnuts are then to be left to dry in the sun for three days. You then stick them with little pieces of cinnamon, and cloves, put them into a thin cold syrup and leave them until next day, when you remove them and give the syrup a boil-up or two, leave it to cool, then plunge the nuts into it.

'For four days running you repeat the process. On the fifth day you set the walnuts and the syrup on the fire just long enough for it to come to the boil, you skim carefully, take out the walnuts, leave the syrup to boil a little more, then let it cool and pour it over the walnuts. Thus leave them for two days before once more repeating the process. Having removed the walnuts you complete the sixth operation by boiling the syrup to the 'pearl' stage and pouring it over the walnuts.

For the seventh process, you again boil up the syrup, this time leaving the walnuts in it as you let it boil two or three times. Skim well, extract the nuts. Again bring the sugar to the pearl stage and pour it over them. Or to finish the candying, you can omit part of this seventh stage and instead let the syrup cook slowly all day, leave it to cool, then pour it over the walnuts.

'On the eighth day you now put all, syrup and walnuts, on the fire, let the syrup boil two or three times, extract the nuts, and boil the syrup to the 'large pearl' stage.'

Here, none too soon, the recipe ends. Judging by many similar recipes for candying fruit, I think that you could finally pot up the walnuts in the syrup, or you could pour the latter one more time over the nuts, and finally, extract them, leaving them to dry out, well-coated with the syrup, on wire stands.

It is not difficult to see what the lady of Cotto's confectionery business meant when she explained about the labour involved in the preparation of her *noci candite*.

I should add that these candied walnuts of Turin were not at all like the crystallised fruits of Milan, Nice and Provence. They were neither tough nor sticky, but soft as fresh plums or damsons would be, sweet of course, a little crunchy with their dusting of sugar, and with that haunting scent and taste of cloves. The Cotto walnuts had no cinnamon as was prescribed by *The Piedmontese Confectioner* of 1792.

ALESSANDRO MAGNASCO (1677-1749)
THE MARKET
Milan, Museo Castello Sforzesco

CHEESES

HE ORIGINS OF *GRANA*, OR PARMESAN, CHEESE MUST be very remote. The Parmesans claim that it has been made in the district for two thousand years. In any case it was already well known in the fourteenth century, when one of Boccaccio's characters, mocking the ignorance of one Calendrino, tells him that at Bengodi (in the province of Parma) 'there is a mountain consisting entirely of grated Parmesan cheese ... on which live people who do nothing but make maccheroni and ravioli, and cook it in capon broth'.

The fame of Parma cheese as a condiment for *pasta* and rice and all cooked dishes is due to the fact that it does not form elastic threads as it melts, an almost unique property amongst cheeses; it will keep for years, and the older it is the better.

Parma cheese is made from skimmed milk, mixed with rennet and cooked for about 30 minutes until the curd has separated. (The whey is turned into foodstuffs for Parma pigs, the cream into first-class butter.) The curd is put into forms holding about 30 kilos each. After going through various processes of draining and drying, after six months the cheeses are given the black coating of *fumo nero*, which seals them from the air and gives them their characteristic appearance. The maturing of Parma cheeses is attended by all the care and expert attention devoted in France to a valuable wine. Thousands of cheeses stored in wooden racks are tested by men who have been at this work all their lives. By the sound they hear when the cheeses are tapped with a special little hammer and by the smell of a skewer thrust into the solid mass these men will predict how a cheese will turn out. A good Parma cheese should be pale yellow, honeycombed with pinpoint holes, finely and closely grained; from this graining comes the name *grana*, by which the cheese is commonly known in Italy, *grana Reggiana* indicating that the cheese comes from the district of Reggio Emilia, and *grana Lodigiana* from Lodi in Lombardy; in Parma it is called *Parmigiana*. *Grana* is also made in the neighbourhoods of Modena, Piacenza, Ferrara, and Bologna, but the Parmesans consider their own product by far the finest. Parma cooking is rich with cheese and with the creamy local butter. Special dishes have been devised to make use of the new cheeses which, delicious as they are, are considered not good enough to justify the long maturing process. (One of these dishes, *fonduta alla Parmigiana*, is made with alternate layers of *sliced* Parmesan, white truffles, and grated Parmesan, melted in a small pan in the oven.)

A good *grana* cheese should be at least two years old, the stage at which it is know as *vecchio*. At three years it is sold as *stravecchio*, at four years as *stravecchione*; and the price varies according to its age.

It is rare to find good Parmesan in this country; instead of being yellow and rocky-looking, it is more often grey and waxy, lacking both the typical honeycombing and the aromatic pungent savour. Whether this is because people are not prepared to pay the price for good Parmesan, or whether both the exporters and the importers are only too aware of the fact that the British public is uncritical in the matter of cheese, I do not know. Whatever the reason, it makes almost impossible the eating of Parmesan as a cheese, broken off in chunks, at the end of a meal. With a glassful of good red wine there is nothing more delightful when one is in the mood for a cheese to bite into rather than a soft cheese.

GIOVANNI SEGANTINI (1858-99)
AT THE BAR
Rome, Galleria Nazionale di Arte Moderna

Gorgonzola and *Bel Paese* are the other two Italian cheeses known all over the world; both are made in Lombardy, country of good butter and dairy produce. Gorgonzola is in no way, as French gastronomic writers are fond of asserting, an imitation of Roquefort, which is made from sheep's milk, whereas gorgonzola is made from cow's milk, and the blue veining is produced in a different way. In the maturing of Roquefort mouldy breadcrumbs are spread between the layers of prepared curd, and the cheeses are matured in limestone caves. The curd for gorgonzola is left until a natural mould starts to form and the cheeses are then turned at frequent intervals and tested continually, until the mould has penetrated right through. (Nowadays the mould is frequently induced with the aid of copper wires.) Roquefort is essentially a crumbly cheese, gorgonzola a creamy one. Both are fine strong cheeses. Which one may prefer is a question of mood; neither is a cheese for every day.

Bel Paese is a reliable soft cheese, much appreciated by those who like only mild cheeses, which is presumably the reason it is always to hand in every Italian restaurant, while far more interesting cheeses are never seen. It is a good cheese for cooking, and can often be used as a substitute for *mozzarella*, as I have explained elsewhere in this book. *Pastorella*, frequently to be found in this country, is a version of *Bel Paese*, made in smaller sizes. Most of the good creamy cow's milk cheeses of Italy also come from Lombardy. *Taleggio, robiola, taleggino* and *robiolina*, the last two being more powerful versions of the first, are delightful cheeses, runny and soft. *Stracchino* is another of the same kind, but varies a good deal in quality. *Pannerone* is a white version of gorgonzola, a curious cheese, well worth trying. *Mascherpone* or *mascarpone* are the fresh little double-cream cheeses sold in white muslin parcels, to be eaten with sugar or fruit.

Asiago is a mountain cheese from the Veneto, made from partially skimmed cow's milk. It somewhat resembles the *Cantal* of Auvergne in consistency and flavour, and when old can be used for grating.

Fontina, the famous Piedmontese cheese, is a fat, creamy kind of gruyère, with very small eyes, rather sickly if one eats it often, but ideal for the Piedmontese *fonduta* for which it is always used. Italian *groviera* or gruyère is almost indistinguishable from *emmenthal*.

Italian sheep, buffalo, and goat's milk cheeses have a good deal of character and variety. Innumerable are the different versions of *pecorino*, hard sheep's milk cheese, used in country districts instead of Parmesan. The Romans are particularly fond of it, so are the Abruzzesi, the Sardinians, and the Genoese. In the neighbourhood of Siena it is made in small sizes, covered with a red rind. I always buy *pecorino* when I see it in London, for its taste evokes memories of good country food, of meals eaten in the open air: garlic sausages and black olives, coarse bread and coarse red wine.

Ricotta (see also p. 30) is the soft ewe's milk cheese beloved of the Romans, eaten with sugar or salt or cinnamon and used so enormously in cooking throughout Italy. There are also salted and smoked versions of *ricotta*, real peasant cheeses. Today (1987) *ricotta* is largely made from cow's milk.

Mozzarella, the leavened buffalo milk cheese so dear to the Neapolitans, must be eaten absolutely fresh and dripping with its own buttermilk, for by the time this has drained away it is already dry and stodgy, the spring has gone out of it, and off it goes to the kitchen to be fried or baked or to adorn a *pizza Napoletana*. As a matter of fact genuine *mozzarella* is becoming increasingly rare, for the simple reason that every year there are fewer and fewer buffaloes in Italy. It is being replaced by *fior di latte* ('eaten only by servants,' a Neapolitan aristocrat once told me) and *scamorza*, the same kind of cheeses made with cow's milk but with much less flavour. Smoked *mozzarella*, with its golden skin, has great charm for anyone who likes the flavour of smoked food. *Uova di bufalo* are egg-shaped *mozzarella* cheeses, *treccia* is plaited *mozzarella*. All these *mozzarella* cheeses are made in the province of Campania, at Aversa, Agerola, Battipaglia, Salerno, and also in Apulia, Calabria, and the Abruzzi.

Provola is another buffalo cheese from the Campania, which is also sometimes smoked (the cheeses are put in a wooden tub and hung in the smoke from burning straw). *Provolone* has a dozen different forms and sizes, and may be buffalo or cow's milk, made in anything from pear-sized cheeses to a large sausage shape; it must either be eaten very fresh, when it has a soft but firm texture, a pale yellow colour, and a good earthy tang, or it must be kept for cooking.

Cacio a cavallo, so called because of the way two of them are strung together as if astride a horse, is the same kind of cheese as *provolone*; Paul Valéry found *cacio a cavallo* cheese 'parfait, le meilleur du royaume' (one wonders which other Italian cheeses he had tasted). *Buttiri*, also called *burrini*, one of the Calabrian versions of *cacio a cavallo*, enclose an egg of butter which astonishingly remains fresh in its wrapping of cheese; you cut it in slices across so that you get butter and cheese in one slice, like a sliced hard boiled egg with its white and yolk – a typically ingenious Italian trick.

The Sardinians, apart from their beloved *pecorino sardo*, have a fondness, which they share with the Greeks, for that salty white cheese called *fetta*, and also make particularly good yoghurt, called *gioddù*. In every part of Italy there are cheeses of purely local manufacture made from cow's, goat's, or sheep's milk according to agricultural con-

PREPARING CHEESE (detail, 15th century fresco)
Trento, Castello del Buonconsiglio

ditions. *Caciotta* is made from both cow's and sheep's milk in the Marche, from sheep's milk in Umbria and Tuscany, from goat's milk in Capri. *Raviggiolo* is another Tuscan and Umbrian sheep's milk cheese; *paglierino* is a purely local Piedmontese cow's milk cheese; *tomini del talucco* is a goat's milk cheese made at Pinado in Piedmont; *Bitto* is a Lombard country cheese made from a mixture of cow's and goat's milk; Sicilian *canestrato* is a sheep's milk cheese, sometimes mixed with goat's milk; at S.Lazzaro in the mountains above Sorrento there is a *provola di pecora* (*provola* made with sheep's milk instead of buffalo's or cow's milk) and in Piedmont a *robiola* made with goat's milk. Such local cheeses should be looked for on market stalls and in village shops, and are nearly always worth trying when they can be found.

The Abruzzesi have a most excellent custom of serving pears to eat with their local *pecorino* cheese.

BACCIO MARIA BACCI (20th century)
AFTERNOON IN FIESOLE
Florence, Galleria degli Uffizi

NOTES AND BOOKS ON ITALIAN WINES

HAT ENCHANTING NAMES THEY HAVE, THESE WINES of Italy that roll off the tongue like poetry: Lacrima Christi, Albana, Chianti, Capri, Montepulciano, San Gimignano. Not always so beautiful to taste, but some distinctly good, and a few fine.'

Those carefully chosen words are quoted from a book of light-hearted gastronomic reminiscences entitled *Food and other Frailties* by Romilly Fedden, an English painter who died in the early 1940s. The book, put together and seen through the press by the author's son Robin, was published by Seeley Service, London, in 1948. Writing myself about Italian wine in 1954 I found Romilly Fedden's opinion of the subject pleasingly summed up, and used his lines to open my own short chapter on the wines I had lately encountered in Italy and those available at the time in England. In fact I found that there weren't all that many, and that those on offer in restaurants were very overpriced compared to their approximate equivalents from France. The price discrepancies at that time were mainly due I think to the fact that while the French exported a good deal of sound and even classy wine in cask for bottling in England, nearly all the better-class Italian wines we imported were bottled in Italy and, when it came to a comparison of prices, suffered accordingly. There were also, and inevitably, those which were just plain overpriced to start with, and which by the time restaurant proprietors had added their hefty mark-ups seemed like very poor buys indeed.

In Italy I had often been the guest of Viola and Arthur Johnson who lived in a flat in Rome and moved in summer to a villa in Anacapri. Both Arthur, a distinguished international lawyer, and Viola, who was half

Torinese and half British by birth, were knowledgeable about wine and owned a vineyard at Grottaferrata outside Rome. The Johnson Grottaferrata, red and heady, was one of the treats of the months I spent in Rome in 1952, and another was a white wine, fresh and *frizzante*, from the Veneto estate of Franco Marinotti, a personal friend of the Johnsons. That sparkling white wine, dry, well-chilled, made a refreshing pre-lunch draught on warm June mornings in Rome. Both the Johnsons, from whom I learned much about Italian wine and food, and to whom I dedicated this book, are now, alas, dead, and it is many years since I have drunk red Grottaferrata. (I remember a bottle from some other vineyard close to the Johnson property drunk in a Frascati restaurant in the late 1960s, and that too was excellent. Yet the wine appears to be very little known.)

In the summer of 1952 I made a little excursion to Sorrento, Salerno, Paestum and down to the coastal village of Agropoli, in company with Arthur and Viola Johnson. There was a good deal of indifferent food and some pretty poor wines, but diverting up to the hill town of Ravello, far above Amalfi and the coast, we came on an unusual red wine with a picturesque label and indeed a picturesque name. It was Gran Caruso, made by the Caruso Brothers of Ravello. The same family owned the comfortable hotel where we stayed, and there we found attractive food as well as good wine, both sufficiently uncommon on that trip to have lodged firmly in my memory. In particular there were *crespolini*, delicate little pancakes filled with a mixture of spinach, ricotta and chicken livers for which the chef kindly gave me the recipe (it is on p. 97), and the dish has been a lasting favourite of my own, as well as being much taken up by later cookery writers. The three cheeses in the dish, ricotta in the filling, mozzarella and Parmesan added just before the *crespolini* are consigned to the oven for their final cooking, made the light red Gran Caruso a truly happy choice to accompany this stylish regional speciality. (But beware clumsy and stodgy versions executed – the right word I'm afraid – by inept cooks who dip deep into their tomato sauce pots and lose control when it comes to the mozzarella.) In the 1960s red Gran Caruso turned up on the wine list of a small London trattoria on the Chelsea Embankment, and for years afterwards it was the wine I ordered every time I lunched there. Some time in the 1970s there came a sad day when I was told there was no more Gran Caruso because it was no longer imported. Whether that was so, or whether the proprietors of the restaurant had merely changed their suppliers, I never did ascertain, but I've not felt quite the same about that trattoria since, and I still advise anyone looking for interesting Italian wine to remember Gran Caruso. There's a good rosé made by the same people, and I believe there is also a white, although I have no recollection of it. I see that Burton Anderson, in his admirable pocket wine guide published in the Mitchell Beazley series, considers the Ravello table wines the best of the Amalfi coast and mentions 'a fish wine of more than usual character' made by Episcopio from a blend of grapes which includes the famous Greco cultivated on the slopes of Vesuvius.

There were several other wines which I found especially enjoyable in the Italy of the early 1950s, and more in later years, on visits to Alba in the white truffle season, a visit I described in a 1963 *Spectator* article reprinted in 1984 in *An Omelette and a Glass of Wine* (listed below), to San Gimignano, the little Tuscan town of towers and Ghirlandaios, to Venice, to Modena, to the Chianti country, to Parma. But during the past twenty or so years Italian vine cultivation, wine-making and wine production have changed so much, become so complex a subject that it is not really very useful to pick out the odd favourite here and there and highlight it by describing its characteristics, the grape or grapes from which it is made, the good vintages of the past decade, the food with which it goes best. In short, to attempt to cover Italian wine in a brief chapter, as in 1954 I did, is now out of the question. Personally, when I'm in Italy, I try to keep to the wines of the region, at the same time bearing in mind the DOC laws (the initials stand for *Denominazione di origine controllata*, the equivalent of the French *Appellation Contrôlée*) according to which a given wine made from specified grape varieties grown in a particular zone and vinified according to methods meeting the required standards of alcohol content, colour, acidity, flavour and the rest have had a widespread and, on the whole, beneficial effect on Italian wine production and have also, in many cases, changed it very substantially since they were first applied in 1966. I should add that out of some two thousand different wines produced in Italy, some fifteen hundred still, in 1987, remain outside the DOC, and that among the outsiders plenty of excellent ones are to be found. Then, there is a further elaboration in that a few very choice wines have been elevated to a status superior to DOC and known as DOCG, the G indicating that the wine concerned is *garantita* as well as *controllata*.

Among wines accepted into the exalted category of DOCG are two famous ones from Piedmont: Barbaresco and Barolo, both made from the Nebbiolo grape, and two from Tuscany, Vino Nobile di Montepulciano and Brunello di Montalcino. Both these Tuscan wines are made from Sangiovese grapes and of late years Brunello has acquired a quite astonishing reputation, with prices in accordance. Brunello is one of those rare wines which in good years is exceptionally long-lived, and according to Burton Anderson, already referred to above, 'is capable of grandeur with great age'. Where wine is concerned grandeur and great age are attributes which come expensive, so much so that according to a report published in the *Independent* in March 1987, the Biondi-Santi family's 1964 Brunello was priced at £400 a bottle. Yes, you read that aright.

Biondi-Santi, it should be explained, is the company which initiated the making of Brunello in the late nineteenth century, and Victor Hazan, author of a fine book, *Italian Wine*, published in the USA and in England, remarks of this wine that if one is in doubt about how the terms austere, big, and full are applied to wine, then 'a mouthful of it will provide a forceful demonstration of their meaning', and he perhaps would not have been surprised to learn the price the 1964 had achieved by 1987. It is one of the seven great vintages he lists, starting with 1945, the others being 1955, 1961, 1970, 1975 and 1982. Perhaps one shoud try to catch the 1982 or the 1975, while they are still relatively young and cheap.

The Sangiovese grape which makes Brunello and Vino Nobile di Montepulciano – don't confuse this wine with other Montepulcianos from the Abruzzi and Apulia – is also the main one of Chianti, but it is not the only one. Trebbiano, a white grape cultivated in Italy for centuries – Michel de Montaigne, in Florence in the summer of 1581, noted that the Trebbiano wine had given him a headache – and the Malvasia or Malmsey, also white, and the red Canaiolo are the four grapes which go into Chianti, or rather are supposed to go into it. But this is where the non-expert runs into trouble. The making of Chianti is a vastly complex subject, and the laws relating to its production forever, apparently, in process of change. There is a great host of Chianti producers, and agreement between a majority is hardly to be expected. The name Chianti has in fact been protected by Italian law for decades, and may apply only to those wines which come from a certain district lying roughly between Siena and Florence. These are the wines entitled to be sold as Chianti Classico, their bottles bearing the *marca gialla* or yellow seal which is the official government stamp. The emblem for these wines is the famous black cockerel. Six additional zones are also controlled by the Chianti Classico consortiums, and these are known as Chianti Putto, the latter word meaning a cherub, the distinguishing mark on the seal of these wines.

How much the black cockerels and the cherubs actually mean these days in terms of quality is hard to say, and there is in addition the age of the wine to be taken into account when you buy a bottle of DOC Chianti or order one in a restaurant. If the label tells you the wine is *vecchio*, that means it is a minimum of two years old, if *riserva*, three. But as Burton Anderson puts it, 'Chianti is not one wine, but many,' adding cheerfully that 'as with Bordeaux, it would take a lifetime to get to know all the names, places and tastes'. If you are in the Chianti country a good place to head for is the attractive little town of Greve (pronounced gravy) where there is an *Enoteca Gallo Nero*, an establishment selling a very large choice of Classico Chiantis.

When it comes to the white wine of the Chianti region, officially there is none – because legally the name may apply only to red wine. That doesn't alter the fact that quite a deal of white wine is made in the Chianti area. One I remember from the early 1970s was a *bianco di Coltibuono*, an agreeable, dryish wine made on the estate of Badia a Coltibuono (Badia means Abbey), better known for its red wine, and with a restaurant serving authentically robust Tuscan food without pretention. Another good white Tuscan bought well chilled from a café to take into the country for a midday picnic one warm autumn day at about the same period was one which came from the hill-top town of Pitigliano in southern Tuscany (Pitigliano was a thriving and happy little community of Jewish and Christian families until Mussolini forcibly dispersed the Jews during the 1939-45 war), but a better known white wine is Villa Antinori Bianco made from Trebbiano and other noble grapes grown on the Antinori family estates in the Classico country.

One white wine of Tuscany which is a curiosity, although one which has been known in the region since Dante's day, is the Vernaccia of San Gimignano. The vernaccia grape cultivated on the hillsides around San Gimignano makes deep straw-coloured wine with a flavour which has always seemed to me rather odd, and a taste for it is one which I have never quite acquired. At one time I went often to San Gimignano, where the hotel waiters expect you to drink Vernaccia all through every meal. Personally, I find that a little goes a long way and no amount of reflection that this was the wine Chaucer knew as *vernage*, and that Dante too was familiar with it, could quite convince me that it goes well with modern Italian food. But you cannot go to San Gimignano of the Beautiful Towers and not try its very own and very famous wine. Incidentally, *vernage* was a wine quite often called for in our own early English recipes, although whether that means that in the fourteenth and fifteenth centuries it was exported from Florence to England, or whether the recipes were, I'm not at all sure. One point, though, should be made clear. Now that Sardinia has become a popular place for rather up-market villa holidays, many visitors to the island will have encountered the local Vernaccia of Oristano, a wine just as well known as the San Gimignano version. Sardinian Vernaccia, however, is a very different wine from its Tuscan namesake, with a distinctly sherry-like flavour. Burton Anderson, I see, calls it 'the glory of Sardinia', and confirms that its vinification resembles the solera system on which sherry is made. He commends it as a wine to drink with that oddity among Mediterranean fish specialities, the salty dried grey mullet roes pressed into flat sausage-like slabs encased in wax, and which in Italy is called *bottargo*. In Sardinia the mullet in question are fished around Oristano. In France, where it is a speciality of Martigues, west of Marseilles, the same product is called *boutargue*; and as *botargo* it was known as an imported delicacy in England at least as long ago as the seventeenth century. It is thinly sliced and eaten with toast and plenty of lemon juice. An ancient Mediterranean taste.

Now, after this briefest of essays incorporating a few personal memories of wines drunk in Italy during many visits, from 1952 up to 1983, here is a short list of books, British, American, Italian, which should surely be enlightening to anyone inclined to find out more about this complex subject, whether by sampling the wines in their native air, by the acquisition of a few bottles from a wine merchant, or by visiting Italian restaurants in Britain or America.

In restaurants, try something other than the Soave, so often flabby and insipid, almost automatically suggested by the wine waiter, and venture on one of the newer of the Italian whites made from the Chardonnay grape now cultivated in north-east Italy, or try perhaps a Lagrein Rosato, a pink wine of much charm also from a northern province, Trentino-Alto Adige, once known as the Sudtirol. This rosé is one of character, and goes well with the *prosciutto* of San Daniele or of Parma. When it comes to red, instead of the everlasting Valpolicella, try the attractive Venegazzu, a wine from the Veneto which was one of the welcome alternatives which in the 1980s began appearing on London trattoria lists. Burton Anderson talks of 'the eloquent bouquet and austere breed' of Venegazzu, and mentioned '71, '76, '78 and '79 as recent good vintages when in 1982 he compressed his really remarkable knowledge of Italian wines and winemaking into the pocket book from which I have quoted. By an alphabetical accident, Anderson's two books head my list. But I think they would in any case have come first.

Anderson, Burton. *Vino: the wines and winemakers of Italy*. Little, Brown, Boston 1981 and Macmillan, London 1980. Papermac edition 1982.

Anderson, Burton. *The Mitchell Beazley Pocket Guide to Italian Wines*. Mitchell Beazley International, London 1984.
Laws and labels explained, grape varieties, regional maps, recent vintages, brisk details of wines of all regions from the Abruzzi – or Abruzzo as some have it – Apulia and the Alto Adige via Basilicata, the Campania, Emilia-Romagna and Friuli to Sicily, Tuscany, Umbria, the Valle d'Aosta, the Veneto, not forgetting the Marches, Lombardy, Liguria, Piedmont. Most people have heard of the famous wines of the latter region, among them Barolo and Barbaresco, but even an obscure wine called Ansonica made on the tiny island of Giglio off the Tuscan coast gets a mention. Well, if you happen to be planning an excursion to Giglio, the isle of lilies, that's just the kind of thing you need to know about. At the end of each regional section there is a short list of local dishes, with a suggestion of a suitable wine to accompany each. These suggested combinations of wine and food are rarely banal or obvious, and so make good reading. In addition there's a glossary. Altogether this little book is a marvel of brevity, with no sacrifice of clarity.

Asher, Gerald. *Gerald Asher on Wine* with an Introduction by Elizabeth David. Random House, New York 1982. Jill Norman and Hobhouse, London 1983. Paperback edition, revised and updated, Vintage Books, a Division of Random House, New York 1986. Gerard Asher is British and was for about twenty years a successful London wine merchant, importing many lesser-known French regional wines. Now he lives in San Francisco, has run a wine business for a large corporation there, and has for several years contributed a monthly wine article to *Gourmet* magazine. The two lively chapters on Italian wine in his book include one on the intricacies of Chianti production and appellation.

Belfrage, Nicholas. *Life beyond Lambrusco*. Sidgwick and Jackson, London 1982. The jocular title is misleading. Belfrage is a serious writer and takes Italian wine seriously. His book is very informative and worthwhile.

Dallas, Philip. *Italian Wines*. Faber & Faber, London 1983.

Hazan, Victor. *Italian Wine*. Alfred A. Knopf, New York 1982. Penguin Books, London 1984. Victor Hazan is Italian-born, but now lives in the USA. His book is comprehensive and sympathetic. A fine reference book.

Ray, Cyril. *The Wines of Italy*. McGraw Hill, New York and London, 1966. Penguin Books, London 1971.
A prize-winning book when it first appeared, and although much has changed since the author revised it for publication in paperback, it is still capital reading.

Roncarati, Bruno. *Viva Vino 200 + DOC & DOCG Wines and Wine Roads of Italy*. Wine and Spirit Publications Ltd, Harling House, 47-51 Gt. Suffolk Street, London S.E.1 1986. The latest on DOC & DOCG wines by the London Correspondent for Italian wine trade publications. Foreword by Hugh Johnson.

Veronelli, Luigi. *Il vino giusto*. Milan, Rizzoli Editore 1981.
Veronelli might almost be described as the André L. Simon of Italy. His articles and books on Italian gastronomic matters and Italian wines are rightly respected.

Veronelli, Luigi. *Matrimoni d'Amore: Guida alli accostamenti cibi-vini*. Editore del Sole, Milan 1984.
A guide to the marriage – or love-match as the author has it – of food and wine.

Some Italian Cookery Books

The following books are those I consulted most frequently while first researching for this book in Italy during 1952, and while writing it in England in 1953 and 1954. They are listed by author, in alphabetical order.

Anon. *Il Cucchiaio d'Argento*. Ed. Domus. First published 1950. 3rd ed. 1951.

Artusi, Pellegrino. *La Scienza in Cucina e l'Arte di mangiar bene*. First published 1890. 50th ed. Casa Editrice Marzocco, Firenze 1950.

Boni, Ada. *Il Talismano della Felicità*. First published c. 1932: 13th ed. Ed. della Rivista Preziosa, Roma 1947.
Ada Boni's work is one of the great modern classics of Italian household and regional cookery. American and English translations or rather adaptations of *The Talisman of Happiness* published since the 1950s give little idea of the splendour of the original.

Boni, Ada. *La Cucina Romana*. Ed. della Rivista Preziosa, Roma 1947.
A rare and important small collection of popular, and often now vanished, Roman specialities and recipes.

Denti di Pirajno, Alberto. *Il Gastronomo Educato*. Ed. Neri Pozza, Venezia 1950.
A delightful collection of essays by an Italian nobleman who was also a well-known physician and cookery writer.

Galleani, Giuseppe, *Come si cucina il riso*. Ed. Ulrico Hoepli, Milano 1929.

Ghinelli, Dott. Italo. *Le Conserve di Carne*. Ed. Casanova, Parma 1950.
Deals with the production on a commercial scale of hams, salame, and other pork products.

Marinetti, F.T. *La Cucina Futurista*. Milano 1932. Reprinted by Estate of F.T. Marinetti 1981.

In 1982 a French translation of Marinetti's famous book was published as *La Cuisine Futuriste* by Editions A.M. Metaillie, 5 rue de Savoie, 75006 Paris.

Origoni e Schwarz. *Il Tesoro della Cucina*. Tosi, Roma e Milano 1947.

Rossi, Emanuele. *La Vera Cuciniera Genovese*. Casa Editrice Bietto, Milano 1948.
An interesting compilation of Genoese regional recipes.

Scappi, Bartolomeo. *Opera*.
The most celebrated of all Italian cookery books, first published in Venice in 1570. Scappi was *cuoco secreto*, or personal cook, to Pope Pius V. The book was reprinted many times. Among editions I have seen at auction are those of 1598, 1622, and 1643. Original copies in good condition, with all the plates intact - there should be 27 and a portrait of Scappi as a frontispiece – will probably fetch (1987) upwards of £2,000. Among later editions one of those in which the plates are in the finest state is the 1643 (although the portrait is usually lacking, or possibly was never present). It is from the 1643 that the photographs in this present illustrated edition of *Italian Food* were taken.
A facsimile of the 1570 edition of Scappi's great work was published in 1981 by Arnaldo Forni of Sala Bolognese (Via Gramsci 164).

PERIODICALS

La Cucina Italiana. Monthly publication. Via S. Antonio Zaccaria 3, Milano.
Among contributors to the magazine during the 1950s was Duke Alberto Denti di Pirajno (see above), and there were frequent – and sound – articles on the regional cookery of Italy. Later, in 1967, *La Cucina Italiana* published a fine book of regional recipes by Anna Gosetti della Salda (See below).

ADDITIONAL LIST 1987

The following list includes historical works and essays on Italian gastronomy as well as cookery books and a few works on the duties and functions of stewards employed in princely and other noble households. These latter books were an important feature of Italian gastronomic literature from the third quarter of the sixteenth century down to the very end of the seventeenth. The duties of the carver – a vital functionary in the organisation and service of banquets and ceremonial meals – and instructions in the art of ornamental folding and pleating of napkins or *piegatura* were also given in some of these remarkable books. Menus for dinners, banquets, collations and outdoor receptions at which the authors of the books had played an important part were reproduced, and since the stewards were required to have a sound practising knowledge of cookery, recipes were often given as well.

Alberini, Massimo. *Storia del pranzo all' Italiana*. Rizzoli, Milan 1966.
Outline history of the Italians at table, their eating habits, their cookery books. Well chosen illustrations.

Baldini, Filippo. *De' Sorbetti*. Napoli, Stamperia Raimondiana 1775.
Baldini was a physician whose treatise on ices and frozen sherbets was written from the point of view of a man who believed firmly in the medicinal benefits of those confections. A new edition, enlarged to include a chapter on the properties and virtues of the pineapple, appeared in 1784. There are no recipes. A facsimile reprint of the 1784 edition was published by Arnaldo Forni in 1979.

Bozzi, Ottorina Perna. *Vecchia Brianza in cucina*. Aldo Martelli, Milan (Viale Piave 1) 1969. Regional recipes of Lombardy.

Bugialli, Giovanni. *The Fine Art of Italian Cooking*. New York Times 1977. The author is Florentine by birth. His recipes are for real, down-to-earth food.

Bugialli, Giovanni. *The Taste of Italy*. Stewart Tabori and Chang. New York 1984 and Conran Octopus, London 1985.

Cavalcanti, Ippolito, Duca di Buonvicino. *Cucina Teorico-Pratica*. Naples.
First published 1837. The second edition, 1839, and numerous subsequent editions, contain a section of recipes in Neapolitan dialect. An interesting work giving the composition of household meals in Naples during the nineteenth century. Recipes are detailed, and Cavalcanti gives a list of necessary kitchen implements and utensils. A facsimile reprint of the fifth edition, 1847, was announced by Arnaldo Forni in 1986 but at the time of writing (May 1987) had not yet appeared.

Chapusot, Francesco. *La Cucina sana, economica ed elegante secondo le stagioni*, etc. 4 vols. Torino 1846.
Chapusot, who was chief cook to the English Ambassador to the court of Savoy in Turin, divided his recipes and menus according to the four seasons. Each volume has four elegant plates and the food described is not nearly as grand or Frenchified as might be expected from the author's exalted position. Torinese weights and liquid measures differed substantially from those of Rome, Naples, Venice and other regions. Chapusot supplies necessary explanations.

Ciocca, Giuseppe. *Il Pasticciere e Confettiere Moderno*. First published 1907. Seventh edition, Ulrico Hoepli, Milano 1941.
With 500 recipes and 30 colour plates showing iced cakes for birthdays, christenings and other special occasions, petits fours, ice creams in champagne goblets, patterns for piped meringue, chocolates in paper cases, miniature iced fancies, all in high art deco taste. Classic recipes for such Italian specialities as *panettone, budino di ricotta, grissini*, plus black and white line illustrations of any number of *dolci fantasia*. Good ice cream recipes.

Corrado, Vincenzo. *Il Cuoco Galante*. First published in Naples at the celebrated Raimondiana Press, 1773.
Corrado was a native of Oritano in southern Italy and became a Celestine monk. He wrote numerous works on food and on the cultivation of vegetables, and was particularly interested in the potato, but appears to have believed that it was a native Italian plant which had travelled to the New World and had been brought back again to Italy. *Il Cuoco Galante* went into many editions and in 1778 was enlarged by the addition of a treatise on confectionery, preserves and ices entitled *Il Credenziere*. The publisher of this edition was Michele Migliaccio, and the book was still printed by the Raimondiana Press. From Corrado's *Cuoco Galante* it is evident that by the 1770s the tomato was already well-entrenched in Neapolitan cookery. He gives several recipes for them (although they are not, as is often stated, the first published in Italian – see Latini below), and many of his vegetable dishes have great charm.

David, Elizabeth. *An Omelette and a Glass of Wine*. Dorling Kindersley, London 1984 and Viking, New York 1985. Also Penguin paperback.
A collection of newspaper and magazine articles which includes an essay on the white truffles of Alba, originally published in *The Spectator* in 1963, and another on a little-known Venetian speciality, a marvellous risotto made with wild hop shoots, in Venice called *bruscandoli* or *bruscandolin*.

Durante, Castor. *Herbario Nuovo*. Rome 1585. Durante was a physician who styled himself 'Cittadino Romano', and who is said – although without firm evidence – to have been one of Pope Sixtus V's doctors. His herbal is an important work of its kind and period and ran into several editions, the sixth appearing as late as 1684. Descriptions of plants, which range far from conventional herbs and vegetables to take in the olive tree, the *melongene* or aubergine, and the tomato, are fairly detailed, culinary uses are given, and of course the health strictures usual at the period. There is a ferocious condemnation of the use of ice and snow for cooling wine and water, and fearful warnings to those who persist in that perverse

practice (was 'drinking out of ice' officially disapproved of by the Vatican in Durante's day?) The delightfully original woodcuts in the *Herbario Nuovo* were designed by a lady called Isabella Parasole.

Faccioli, Emilio. (Ed.) *Arte Della Cucina. Libri di Ricette, Testi Sopra Lo Scalco, Il Trinciante e i Vini dal XIV al XIX secolo*. A cura [edited by] Emilio Faccioli. Edizioni il Polifilo, Milano. 2 vol. 1966.
Important work for the historian of Italian cookery, food products, banquetting, viticulture. Faccioli reproduces complete texts of two 14th/15th century cookery manuscripts, one Venetian and one Tuscan, unearthed and edited by late nineteenth-century scholars, originally printed in limited editions and now unfindable outside the great national and university libraries. The first modern Italian printed cookery treatise, actually written by one Maestro Martino, and included in Platina's famous *De Honesta voluptate et Valetudine vulgare* 1487, is also given by Faccioli in its entirety. There are substantial extracts from nearly all the significant works on carving, stewardship, oenology and viticulture published from the sixteenth century to the twentieth. Glossary. Illustrations from some of the works included.

Frugoli, Antonio. *Practica e Scalcheria da servirsi a qualsivoglia mensa di Prencipe*. Rome, 1631, 1638.
Frugoli was a native of the then independent republic of Lucca and proudly announced himself as 'Antonio Frugoli Lucchese' on his title page. From internal evidence it would appear that he was, or had been, steward to Cardinal Capponi, the Papal Legate at Bologna, and evidently travelled with him to Spain on more than one occasion. Dinners served at Madrid as well as in Rome and other places within the Papal States were recorded by Frugoli. He gives dates and the number of guests served.
The 1638 edition has for some time been scheduled for future publication in facsimile by Arnaldo Forni but in May 1987 had still not appeared.

Gosetti della Salda, Anna. *Le ricette regionale Italiana*. Published by the magazine *La Cucina*

Italiana Via S. Antonio Zaccaria 3, Milan, 1967. A volume of well over a thousand pages, giving some two thousand regional recipes arranged according to province. A magnificent collection. Illustrated with informative line drawings.

Hazan, Marcella. *The Classic Italian Cookbook.* Knopf, New York 1979 and Macmillan, London 1980.

Hazan, Marcella. *The Second Classic Italian Cookbook.* Knopf, New York 1981, and Jill Norman and Hobhouse, London 1982.
Marcella Hazan's Italian cookbooks are widely known in the USA, but perhaps less so to British readers. Very clear and detailed line drawings demonstrating the making of various kinds of pasta, and showing many different shapes, are an attractive and useful feature of these books. Mrs Hazan's husband Victor is an authority on Italian wines. (See below.)

Latini, Antonio. *Lo Scalco alla moderna.* (The Modern Steward.) Naples. Vol. 1 1692, vol. 2 1694.
Latini, a native of the Marche and a papal Count, was steward to the Spanish Prime Minister of Naples. His book was the last of the great series of such works which started publication in the second half of the sixteenth century and spanned the whole of the seventeenth. In Latini's very fat first volume appeared the earliest published Italian recipes for tomatoes which I have so far come across,* and in the second, as noted in my brief summary of the story of water ices and ice creams, the first Italian published recipes for *sorbette*, although an anonymous, undated and apparently unrecorded pamphlet on the same subject and published also in Naples at about the same time may possibly have preceded Latini.

In France, recipes for *eaux glacées* and for the occasional *crème glacée* had appeared in two books both published in 1692. One was Massialot's *Le Nouveau Confiturier*, the second

L. Audiger's *La Maison Réglée.* Audiger, according to his own testimony, had spent fourteen months in Rome, from 1659 to the early weeks of 1661, perfecting his skills in the arts of blending and distilling liqueurs and aromatic waters, 'frozen or not frozen', before returning to France to practise his chosen profession.

Extracts from Latini are given in vol. 2 of Faccioli's *Arte della cucina* (listed above), and in 1986 Arnaldo Forni announced a future facsimile reprint of both parts of *Lo Scalco alla moderna* in one volume of 855 pages.

Lotteringhi della Stufa, Maria Luisa Incontri. *Pranzi e Conviti.* Editoriale Olimpia, Firenze 1965.
The story of Tuscan cookery, from the sixteenth century to the 1960s, taking in Medici wedding banquets and popular treats like the *Salsa Verde* once sold in the streets of Florence. Well-documented history, with sources conscientiously cited, although none is forthcoming for 'those pastrycooks who embarked for France with Catherine de Medici (in 1533) and who on the banks of the Seine laid the foundations of that gastronomic refinement which with the passage of time was to gain world-wide renown'. The Catherine de Medici effect on France's gastronomy is a firmly-entrenched tradition based on somewhat tenuous evidence. It is interesting to find that Signora Lotteringhi della Stufa defers to it. Good illustrations.

Mosta, Ranieri da. *Il Veneto in Cucina.* Aldo Martelli, Milan (Viale Piave 1) 1969.
Regional recipes of the province of Veneto, of Venice and the islands of the lagoons.

Root, Waverley, and the Editors of Time-Life Books. *The Cooking of Italy.* Photographed by Fred Lyon. Time-Life Books, New York, 1968. Illuminating and sometimes beautiful photography. Recipes suffer from over-zealous editing.

Scott, Jack Denton. *The Complete Book of Pasta: an Italian Cookery Book.* William Morrow & Co., New York 1968. An ample volume, with excellently informative line drawings of scores of different types of pasta, accompanied by instructions on how to make them and cook them.

Stefani, Bartolomeo. *L'Arte di ben cucinare.* Mantua, 1662.
Stefani was a Bolognese and head cook to the Gonzagas of Mantua. His vegetable cookery and his fruit relishes and sauces are particularly striking. A facsimile reprint was published by Arnaldo Forni in 1983.

REFERENCE BOOKS

Bini, Prof. Giorgio. *Catalogue of names of fishes, molluscs, crustaceans, of commercial importance in the Mediterranean.* Published (by arrangement with the Food and Agriculture Organisation of the United Nations) by Vito Bianco, Rome 1965.
Bini, Prof. Giorgio. *I pesci delle acque interne d'Italia* or *Fish of the inland waters of Italy.* Published by the Federazione Italiana della pesca sportiva, 1962.
The above two works, by a man who was a world authority on his subject, are detailed, illustrated with accurate outline drawings, and are extremely valuable works of reference. Professor Bini's *Catalogue*, etc. is probably now unobtainable, and for the majority of British readers will have been superseded by Alan Davidson's *Mediterranean Seafood* (see below), but so far as I know nothing has replaced Bini's work on the freshwater fish of Italy.

Cavanna, G. *Doni di Nettuno.* G. Carnesecchi e Figli, Firenze 1913.
A fascinating and learned account of Mediterranean fishes, with illustrations, a few unusual recipes, and a table of names in Italian dialects, also Provençal, French, German and English.

Davidson, Alan. *Mediterranean Seafood.* Penguin Books, London 1972.
A scholarly guide to the identification and the cookery of Mediterranean fish, crustacea and molluscs. Accurate line drawings of all fish, names in Latin, English, French, Italian, Spanish, Greek, Turkish, Tunisian and other Mediterranean languages. An anthology of two hundred recipes includes some rare discoveries.

The late Professor Giorgio Bini and his remarkable work, carried out for the F.A.O. in Rome (see above), are fully acknowledged by Mr Davidson, and a recent reprint (1987) in an

---

*One of them is for a tomato sauce *alla spagnuola*, very similar in composition to the modern Spanish gazpacho. Latini's recipe is translated and explained in my article 'Matalda, Giovanna, Giulia', first published in *Petits Propos Culinaires* No. 6, 1980, and reproduced in *An Omelette and a Glass of Wine* pp. 113-19 (see David, Elizabeth above).

enlarged format even includes a section of recipes from the Black Sea. In a book supposedly devoted to Mediterranean seafood that seems a trifle wayward, particularly as Mr Davidson, on his own admission, deliberately omits recipes for salt cod, a Mediterranean favourite if ever there was one, on the grounds that it is an import from Northern seas. Still, in the days of Bartolomeo Scappi, whose famous book, bluntly entitled *Opera* or *Work*, was published in 1570, fish from the Mar Maggiore, as the Black Sea was then called by the Italians, was quite commonly known in Rome. Mainly, the Papal imports from the Black Sea were salted sturgeon and its roe, already processed into caviar. The latter delicacy – probably much saltier that it is today – was a valuable addition when it came to the composition of the frequent meatless meals decreed by the Church in the sixteenth and seventeenth centuries. It is worth noting, by the way, that Pope Pius V, formerly Cardinal Ghisleri, was a man of austere habit who observed his fast days strictly, and who at

all times ate very sparingly. Was it the Pope's ascetism and piety which left his personal cook free to compose his magisterial work? It is odd to think that Pius V was eventually beatified, while Scappi's name has come down to us across four centuries, forever linked with that of Pope Pio Quinto, as the author of the most famous of all Renaissance cookery books. Can there have been a more unsuitably assorted pair in the whole complex history of Italian gastronomy?

Migliari, Maria Luisa, and Azzola, Alida. *Storia della Gastronomia*. Edipem, Novara 1978. Illustrated history of gastronomy from prehistory to the end of the nineteenth century, with emphasis on Italy. Frescoes, mosaics, early manuscript illustrations, still-lifes, paintings, feasting and domestic scenes, popular prints drawn from Etruscan, Egyptian, Roman, Italian, French and Flemish sources.

Westbury, Lord. *Handlist of Italian Cookery Books*. Leo S. Olschki, Firenze 1963.

In the latter part of his life Lord Westbury lived in Rome, where he amassed a magnificent collection of cookery books and works on oenology, viticulture and all subjects related to gastronomy. The bulk of his collection was Italian, but he also owned many rare German and French books and some enviable English cookery manuscripts. Unhappily the author died in 1963, while the book was still going through the press, so he never saw a finished copy of what was to become an indispensable reference book, and one for which all collectors must be grateful. The famous Westbury cookery book collection was auctioned at Sotheby's in February 1965. The prices fetched at the two-day sale made press headlines, and set new records for antiquarian, and even for comparatively modern, cookbooks. For collectors, the days of picking up a seventeenth-century Italian or French gastronomic rarity for a few pounds were gone forever. Copies of the Westbury sale catalogue have themselves become collectors' items.

GUIDES TO FOOD AND WINE IN ITALY

HILE JOURNEYING ROUND ITALY IN 1952 IN SEARCH of regional food and recipes, and later while writing this book, the guide I used more than any other was the *Guida Gastronomica d'Italia*, republished in 1951 from the original edition of 1931, by the Touring Club Italiano, Milano. It is a book to which I still refer frequently.

The editors of the *Guida Gastronomica* did not supply recipes or recommend restaurants, but having amassed a formidable body of information concerning the regional dishes and products of Italy, had collated and classified it province by province. In doing so they were surely making a conscious effort to save their traditional cookery from becoming internationalised in the manner of the Palace Hotel and the chain restaurant. The Italian motor industry, with its beautiful and already world-renowned Bugattis, Lancias, and Isotta Fraschinis, its Alfa Romeos and its Fiats, had evidently understood early that regional gastronomy could be promoted and preserved by tourism rather than destroyed by it, and that the process could be mutually beneficial. Tourism sold cars and petrol, oil and tyres, and if the promotion of those sales also assisted in the rediscovery of Italy's national products and specialities, many of them hitherto unrecorded, so much the better for everyone. In turn hotels and restaurants profited, and their patronage rescued many a minor local industry from oblivion. The 1930s, or at least the earlier years of the decade, were good ones for Italian tourism and the fostering of thriving regional traditions where food and wine were concerned. The promoters of those praiseworthy causes could not know that a second world war and a quarter-century of mass tourism later scores of small industries and local specialities salvaged in the thirties would in the seventies be overwhelmed, buried beneath demolished Adriatic fishing villages and the ruins of minor Mediterranean coastal resorts transformed into immense holiday camps, or deliberately destroyed by bureaucracy in the name of progress.

Among other guides I used at the time I was writing this book, and on later visits, was a particularly valuable one on the food and specialities of Parma and roundabout. This work, by an author hiding under the pseudonym of Ferrutius and entitled *Gastronomia Parmense*, was published by the Scuola Tipografica Benedettina, Parma, in 1952. The fifth edition, enlarged and bound in hard covers, appeared in 1967. The recipes for local dishes are genuine and clearly set out.

The Michelin Guide to Italian hotels and restaurants started publication only in 1957. During my visits from that period on Michelin proved, in many respects, invaluable. But from the first I felt, and still feel, that their star-ratings for cooking should be treated with caution.

In some cases I have found them seriously out of date, in others that showy or Frenchified food and fussy decor have been preferred above the authentically Italian or regional. Sometimes that may be as well. A Michelin star does, unhappily, all too often result in increased prices, lowered standards and disappearance of character in the cooking.

Discursive works on Italian gastronomy were thin on the ground in the early 1950s, but one which I found good reading was Paolo Monelli's *Il Ghiottone Errante (The Wandering Gourmet)*, published in 1935 by Garzanti, Milan. Another book of the same period, Pino Orioli's *Moving Along* (Chatto and Windus, London 1934), is one from which I learned a good deal about wine and food as it had been in southern Italy in the thirties. Orioli was a well-known Florentine bookseller and publisher, and *Moving Along* is the account of a journey in Calabria in company with Norman Douglas, who told me, and repeated in a letter, that he had himself written the book for his friend. It seems to me more than likely that this was true, and the style certainly does smack strongly of Douglas. Whatever the truth of the authorship, the book is a most entertaining one, and I quoted from it several times, most often on the cooking of fish.

Norman Douglas's own *Old Calabria* – no doubts about the authorship in that case – first published in 1915, one of the great travel classics of the twentieth century, and his *Siren Land* (1911), were books I consulted often when I was writing my own. I had known Norman in 1939 and 1940 when he was living in rather impoverished circumstances in Antibes, and in 1951 I had spent some weeks on Capri where he was then living in a friend's villa. I saw him daily, and when I left the island he gave me a copy of his *Late Harvest*, published by Lindsay Drummond in 1948, a collection of writings in which he recollected the circumstances in which he had written many of his books, and also analysed his own feelings about them. Inevitably, there is a good deal about Italy in *Late Harvest*. The book has never been reprinted, but secondhand copies are worth looking for. Norman died on Capri in February 1952, a few days before I was due to leave London for Italy to embark on my researches for the book which became *Italian Food*. He was eighty-two.

When planning my Italian venture, I had for some reason become interested in Sardinia – perhaps D.H. Lawrence's *Sea and Sardinia* was partly responsible – and made up my mind to visit that island, at the time unheard of by the tourist trade. I did in the end manage to get there, and found it fascinating and beautiful. A book I took with me was Charles Edwards' *Sardinia and the Sardes* (1889), a work full of entertaining sidelights on the life of the island. Another was by a French author, the Chevalier Albert de la Marmora, whose *Voyage en Sardaigne 1819-1825* was published in 1826. The Chevalier's admirable description of the Sardinian shepherd's manner of spit-roasting whole animals, sheep, pigs, calves, even mules, is quoted on page 141.

Osbert Sitwell and Tobias Smollett, not exactly a compatible pair, were other authors who accompanied me to Italy in 1952. (In those days I travelled by train. It seemed perfectly normal to take an extra trunk for books.) Osbert Sitwell's *Winters of Content* (Duckworth, 1932), had long been a favourite of mine, and proved a wonderful travelling companion. His evocations of Italian cities and palaces – for example Venice and the Villa Malcontenta – visited in winter, are often quite haunting, and his opinions on Italian wine and Italian cooking, sometimes wayward, are always worth quoting. Of Lambrusco di Sorbàra, the famous sparkling red wine of Emilia, he wrote 'best of all . . . a rare foaming red wine which is quite excellent'. His American contemporary, Frank Shoonmaker, author of *The Complete Wine Book* (Routledge, London 1938), found it on the contrary 'as nearly undrinkable as a well-known wine could be'. Smollett's *Travels through France and Italy*, first published in 1776, is known for the author's tetchy comments. Personally, I find his powers of observation acute and his descriptions of unfamiliar Mediterranean fish such as *datteri di mare* or sea-dates, admirably accurate – and like *Old Calabria* this book was in the old O.U.P. World's Classics series, took up no space, weighed virtually nothing, and could accompany me wherever I chose to go.

To come now to a later book, a real guide, H.V. Morton's *A Traveller in Southern Italy* (Methuen, London 1969), is one I wish had been written earlier. I could have done with it in 1952. Older readers, already long ago beguiled by H. V. Morton, will hardly need to be told how delightful he is as a guide, whether conducting them round some great Norman stronghold or taking them on a stroll through a street market in a modern Adriatic seaport. Here we find him in an Abruzzo hill town, pressed into participation in a sumptuous feast given by the parish priest, and valiantly concealing the fact that he has already eaten a hefty midday snack. Relentlessly, a huge spread of *antipasti* is followed, in succession, by roast chicken, boiled chicken, lamb. Then come puddings, custards, jellies and other sweets. But down in the market place he has already admired 'that medieval presence at every Italian fair, *porchetta*, a roast pig complete with head, stuffed with rosemary and other herbs, and sold in slices between thick wedges of bread'. Morton had of course fallen for a slice of that aromatic roast pork and needed nothing more to satisfy his hunger. In Tuscan towns I have myself often experienced the market-day treat of freshly roasted pork, potently scented with wild fennel and garlic, protected by chewy Tuscan household bread, packed into the picnic bag with olives, some new white cheese, and a bottle of local wine, and borne off, once escape from the crowded market could be effected, to the nearest likely-looking hillside. Those improvised, market-bought picnics are among my happiest memories of golden autumn afternoons in the hills of the Chianti country.

A generation new to H. V. Morton has a lot to look forward to. His instinct for the telling detail, whether of architecture, landscape, costume or historical association, is unerring. An unusual dish, an unfamiliar wine, a colourful display of ice creams in a café, a plantation of magnificent olive trees seen from his bedroom window, are all noted with an enviably sharp and clear eye – and like all good reporters he is on duty twenty-four hours a day. I have not seen his other Italian guides, *A Traveller in Italy* (1964) or *A Traveller in Rome* (1962), but I don't doubt that they are as worthwhile as his excursion into the deep south, where, incidentally, he often remarks on the excellence of the new hotels, contrasting them, thankfully, with those described by earlier travellers, notably Norman Douglas.

Two Italian-language restaurant guides, one now sixty years old and dealing only with Venice, and one comparatively up-to-date, are worth noting. The first, unobtainable outside a reference library when I was in Italy in 1952, is Elio Zorza's *Osterie Veneziane*, first published in 1928 and reprinted in facsimile by Filippi, Venezia 1967. This is a work of historical interest, with contemporary illustrations, anecdotes of the famous who once frequented the taverns, restaurants, and coffee houses of Venice, and evocations of popular festivals and specialities. The second is *Ristoranti di Veronelli*, by Luigi Veronelli, Rizzoli Editore, Milano 1981. Veronelli was recently described in *The Times* as a 'pioneer of connoisseurship' in matters of Italian food and wine. I wouldn't myself have thought that 'connoisseurship' in such matters was as new as that, but the author of the article was evidently writing in all seriousness. For other relevant works by Veronelli see my list of books on Italian wine.

The Ente del Turismo, the Italian tourist organisation, will be found extremely helpful and informative in the matter of local specialities and restaurants or shops where they may be found. There is a local branch of the Ente del Turismo in every town of any size in Italy, and every hotel-keeper knows its whereabouts.

N THE PAST FIVE HUNDRED YEARS NO EUROPEAN country has been more written about than Italy. As the seat of the Vatican, Rome was the great religious centre and place of pilgrimage, and as the ancient capital of the Roman world, the city, with its monuments and its classical ruins, was essential visiting to all who aspired to culture and a polite education. Then there was Venice. From that astonishing civilisation, which had materialised out of the lagoons to become a great marine and mercantile power with a capital which was the wonder of the world, the European trade in expensive spices had been controlled - and it was from Venice that came a little instrument which excrised a vitally civilising influence on European cooking, the table fork. Not that Europe gave it much of a welcome. The English greeted it with ridicule. The French found it decadent and effeminate, and a whole century after its introduction into France by Henri III, third son of Catherine de Medici and Henri II, that great arbiter of seventeenth-century civility, Louis XIV, still preferred to use his fingers at table.

The third Italian city visited by every foreign traveller was of course Florence, capital of the Medici Grand Dukes and centre of the European art world. At the same time it was the city of the fanatical Savonarola, the capital of public festivities, spectacular marriage feasts, theatrical entertainments and firework displays – and the cradle of a game which Europe was to learn to call football.

The Medici rulers of Tuscany prided themselves on fostering science, providing a refuge for Galileo when he was released from the clutches of the Inquisition, employing men such as Bernardo Buontalenti, the great military engineer, to construct canals, design waterworks for their gardens, and supervise the supply of ice and snow for the city.

Fountains and statues to adorn Medici gardens and villas were created by sculptors of the stature of Gianbologna, and in the grounds of Pratolino, the country retreat of the Grand Duke Francesco, who died in 1587, even the grottoes and mechanical water-jokes so much admired by visitors – Montaigne among them – had been the work of the great Buontalenti. When the late Duke's eldest daughter Maria was married by proxy to Henri IV of France in 1600 the festivities in Florence were organised on a scale calculated to make the maximum impression on the French envoys, the assembled ambassadors, the cardinals and the eminent foreign visitors. Who else but Gianbologna should design the models for the sugar-paste statuettes and allegorical centre-pieces or *trionfi* which adorned the banqueting tables? And as for the machinery which turned the marriage feast into a grandiose theatrical spectacle and effected unheard-of transformations under the very eyes of the guests, it was Buontalenti who had designed it all from start to finish.

(There are those who hold that the great architect and innovative military engineer was also responsible for the invention of ice cream, or rather for the discovery of how to freeze it. He certainly *could* have been, but I rather think that the theory was originally based on association and his involvement with the construction and maintenance of Florence's public ice and snow stores).

It was hardly surprising, in view of the reports emanating from Florence, that visitors from all over Europe were anxious to see the palaces and parks and art treasures of these Medici potentates who kept their Florentine subjects entertained with a succession of magnificent public festivities, who on the marriage in 1661 of the Grand Prince Cosimo, the Grand Duke's heir, to the French Princess Marguerite Louise, first cousin of Louis XIV, presented the young couple with a silver four post bed. It was not an auspicious gift. Bride and bridegroom were both unwilling parties to the match, and it heralded the extinction of the Medici line. The stormy, fifteen-year marriage did produce heirs, two sons and a daughter, but all were childless. Both Cosimo, the elder son, and Gian Gastone, his brother, in turn succeeded as Grand Dukes, and with the death in 1737 of the latter, Medici rule in Tuscany came to an end. The last relict of the family, Anna Maria, daughter of Prince Cosimo and Marguerite Louise, who married the Elector Palatine, was widowed and lived on for many years in the Pitti Palace in Florence, her bedchamber furnished with silver tables, chairs, stools and screens, until February 1743. It is the melancholy story of the decay and extinction of the great ruling family of Florence that is the subject of Harold Acton's *The Last Medici*.

As for Naples, a city we know today as a place of decayed palaces and ugly slums where no car, however securely locked, is safe from theft, and where every foreigner is the target of ceaseless and aggressive begging, in the seventeenth century and right up to the end of the eighteenth and the days when Sir William Hamilton married his Emma and young Admiral Nelson appeared on the scene, nearly every visitor who set eyes on the place pronounced it the finest capital of all the Italian states. Not, strictly speaking, that Naples was a state. As travellers were given to pointing out, Naples, Sicily and Sardinia constituted a kingdom, a realm, the only one in the peninsula, and as such in a unique position. That the city and its surrounding territory were for so long under Spanish rule again singled out this southern realm as an area much apart from the rest of Italy. The presence of Spanish soldiers thronging the streets and Spanish warships lying in the Bay of Naples emphasised that apartness. Taxes were heavy. Religious intolerance discouraged English and other protestant visitors, yet for all its disadvantages Naples still seemed to foreigners to be a veritable paradise. The gardens, with their scented roses and groves of lemon, orange, and citron trees surrounding the graceful seaside palaces and reaching right down to the shore, were known throughout Europe. So was the exquisite conserve made from the roses gathered in those gardens – the finest to be found anywhere, declared Scipione Mazzella in his 1586 *Descrittione del Regno di Napoli*.

Neapolitans lived well, importing any delicacies they couldn't produce within their own territories. 'The custom of hearbes spent yearely in Naples amounteth to foure thousand pounds of our money' reported the English traveller George Sandys in his *Relation of a Journey* published in 1611, and according to the French historian Fernand Braudel, in the year 1625 alone Naples imported 1,500 tons of sugar and 500 tons of honey. In modern terms those figures may not sound impressive but in 1625, when consumption of sugar was still barely under way in the rest of Europe, 1,500 tons was a vast amount.

Another import, and one which may have gone some way to account for the high consumption of sugar, was the chocolate so much loved by the Spaniards. Coming relatively early to Naples, and well established there by the last decades of the seventeenth century it was served sometimes hot, sometimes cold, even at the receptions held out of doors on warm evenings in those famous scented seaside gardens. Did the Neapolitans themselves not prefer their own local wines made from the grapes cultivated on the slopes of Vesuvius, and well-cooled with the snow brought down from the highter reaches of that same dangerous, unpredictable mountain? But if their Spanish overlords unaccountably preferred chocolate to wine, at least by the 1690s Neapolitans and Spaniards alike had learned how to enjoy it frozen into a kind of mousse, the first chocolate ices in Italy.

I suppose not every foreigner who visited Rome, Venice, Florence and Naples during the five centuries when Italy was first on the list of places to be seen kept a journal and later published it, but looking along the packed stacks of travel and topographical books devoted in any great library to Italy, or merely studying the subject index, one does get the impression that most of them did. Globe-trotters and sightseers, ambassadors, papal envoys, visiting cardinals, commercial representatives of foreign governments charged with the task of producing confidential reports on the state of trade, art experts sent to buy treasures of every kind on behalf of royal collectors such as Charles I or aristocratic ones like the famous Earl of Arundel, naturalists and botanists seeking plants, medicinal ones in particular, all recorded their impressions of the country and the people, the inns, the roads, the cost of living, the manners, the costume, and very often of the wines they drank, the food they encountered and the way it was cooked and served. From a vast choice of such works I have listed below a small sample, enough to start with, no more.

Acton, Harold. *The Last Medici*. Faber & Faber, London 1932. Revised, illustrated edition Methuen, London 1958. New illustrated edition Macmillan, London 1980.

Acton, Harold. *The Bourbons of Naples 1734-1825*. Methuen, London 1956.

Addison, Joseph. *Remarks on Several Parts of Italy etc in the Yeares 1701, 1702, 1703*. The Third Edition 1726.

Addison found the wine of the Republic of San Marino extraordinarily good and 'much better than any I met with on the cold side of the Appenines'. His journey across those mountains, from Loretto to Rome, took six days. Sometimes he and his companions were shivering on the top of a bleak mountain and a little while later 'Basking in the warm valley, covered with Violets and Almond-trees in Blossom'.

Brydone, Patrick. *A Tour through Sicily and Malta*. 2 vols. London 1776.Written in the form of letters from Brydone to his friend William Beckford of Fonthill. Brydone notes everything unfamiliar in the way of fruit and vegetables that he sees in Sicily. In May 1770 he writes to Beckford about a flowering shrub growing in great plenty around Messina. 'The fruit of this plant is beautiful, round, and of a bright shining yellow. They call it pomo d'oro or golden apple.' Brydone had already spent some months in Naples, and since we know from Antonio Latini writing in 1692, and from Vincenzo Corrado in the 1770s, that the tomato was by that time well entrenched there, it is surprising to find that he had not met with the fruit until he arrived in Sicily. Presumably his stay in Naples had not coincided with the tomato season. Other vegetables new to Brydone, and described in detail, were broccoli, fennel, and *melongene* – one of the commoner names for the aubergine then in use in Italy.

A notable point about Brydone's journeyings about Sicily in the eighteenth century is his reliance on his hot water kettle and tea-making apparatus, and the frequency with which he has recourse to it – an early appearance, I believe, of the English travellers' solace in far-flung places. In Brydone's case it was no doubt the difficulty of obtaining fresh clean water in Sicily which caused him to resort so often to his tea-kettle.

Casola, Pietro. *Canon Pietro Casola's Pilgrimage to Jerusalem in the Year 1494*. M. Margaret Newett BA. University Press, Manchester, 1907.
In Venice, waiting to take ship for the Holy Land, Canon Casola marvelled at the plenty and quality of provisions available there. 'When I saw such abundance and beauty around me I was confused. The bakers' shops which are to be found in one place specially, namely the piazza of St. Mark, and also throughout the city, are countless and of incredible beauty; there is bread the sight of which tempts even a man who is surfeited to eat again. In my judgement Venice has not its equal for this.'

This is Venice in its heyday and Canon Casola is an entrancing as well as an entranced visitor. The famous Rialto vegetable and fruit market has been described by countless sight-seers, but none with more pure joy than Casola. 'There were so many boats full of big beans, peas and cherries – not indeed of every kind as at Milan, but every day in such quantity that it is as if the gardens of the world must be there. The number was so great that I declare that after seeing them, when I turned my back I hardly believed my eyes. . . . I went several times in the morning to watch the unloading of the boats, and the vegetables looked as if just taken from the gardens and very fresh. I know it is difficult for anyone who has not seen these things to believe what I say, because I have fallen into the same error myself – that is, I used not to believe what was told me about them.'

Again, 'so many warehouses full of spices, groceries, and drugs, and so much beautiful white wax! These things stupefy the beholder, and cannot be fully described, to those who have not seen them. . . . I never saw such a quantity of provisions elsewhere'.

David, Elizabeth. 'Savour of Ice and Roses', *Petits Propos Culinaires* No. 8. June 1981. Article describing one of the wedding banquets given by the Medici in Florence on the occasion of the marriage of the French Princess Marguerite-Louise d'Orléans to the Gran Principe Cosimo, heir of the reigning Grand Duke Ferdinand, in August 1661.
'Mad, Bad, Dangerous and Despised', *Petits Propos Culinaires* No. 9. October 1981. Article on the *melongena* or aubergine in Mediterranean cookery from the sixteenth to the twentieth century.
'Vegetables of Mantua'. *Petits Propos Culinaires* No. 12. 1982. Recipes from Bartolomeo Stefani's *L'Arte di ben cucinare*, Mantua 1662, translated and discussed.
'Mafalda, Giovanni, Giulia', *Petits Propos Culinaires* No. 6. 1980. Reproduced in the author's *An Omelette and a Glass of Wine*, Dorling Kindersley, London 1984 and Penguin paperback 1986; Viking, New York 1985. Recipes from three Tuscan women cooks known to the author, 1952 to 1973.

Firpo, Luigi (edited by). *Gastronomia del Rinascimento. A Cura di Luigi Firpo*. Unione Tipografico Editrice Torinese. 1974. This history of Renaissance gastronomy includes a 40-page treatise on salads written by Giovanni del Castelvetro, an Italian who was living in England in the early years of the seventeenth century and was shocked by the contemporary English ignorance of the subject. The work is known in its manuscript form to many cookery historians but is not, to my knowledge, printed elsewhere.

Goethe, Johann Wolfgang. *Italian Journey 1786-1788*. Translated by W. H. Auden and Elizabeth Mayer. Collins, London 1962, Penguin Classics 1970, reprinted 1982. Goethe is a delightful travelling companion.

Goncourt, Edmond et Jules. *L'Italie D'Hier. Notes de Voyages 1855-1856*. Paris 1894. The Goncourt brothers in Florence, Livorno, Naples etc. 'The basic food of the Florentine populace is a cake of chestnut flour larded with pine kernels, the cake is called *Castagnaccio*, a chocolate-coloured cake, displayed for sale in copper cauldrons.' The Goncourts are sometimes surprising: 'In Florence a winter's day is no colder than a summer's night in Paris', they say. Most Florentines would have been amazed to hear such an opinion of their notoriously awful winters. 'The truffles in Florence are the same price as potatoes,' and 'the officers there eat more whipped cream than anywhere else.' The Goncourts' Italian journal was published long after the event, when they had rashly destroyed all their notes. What survived was a skeleton. Even so, the bones still rattle quite effectively.

Labat, Jean-Baptiste (1663-1738). *Voyages du Père Labat de l'ordre des F.F. Prescheurs en Espagne et en Italie*. 8 tomes. Paris 1730.
Père Labat is the finest gourmet and most acute food critic of all foreign visitors to Italy. Whether in Rome inspecting the papal bread ovens, dining in a Roman tavern (discreetly out of sight of the public) or noting every detail of a splendid spread at the table of the Dominican monks in a hospitable Messina monastery, Labat is unsurpassed as a chronicler of the meals eaten by many different classes of Italians during the 1660s.

Lassels, Richard. *An Italian Voyage, or, A Compleat Journey Through Italy. In two parts. The Second Edition with large Additions, by a Modern Hand*. Printed for Richard Wellington, London 1698. (First edition published in Paris 1670.) Lassels, whose book was put together and published posthumously, knew Italy and the Italians well. His last stay there was evidently from 1660 to 1663. He was almost a professional food guide, and critical of Italian cooking, even if table manners were more evolved than in England. 'Every man eats here with his forke and knife,' he warns potential visitors, but on the other hand they over-roast their meat, already 'naturally lean and dry, until they leave in it no juice at all. . . . They scrape Cheese upon all their Dishes, even of Flesh, counting that it gives the meat a good relish.' Before long comes the familar account of how the Italians 'eat all manner of small birds, as Wrens, Titmice etc, and many other great ones, which the English never feed on, as Magpies, Jays, Woodpeckers, Jackdaws etc., and even in Rome 'tis common to see Kites and Hawks lying on Poulterers stalls'. However, 'they have many excellent Fruits, which come to greater perfection than ours. They esteem very much of Chestnuts roasted, and the kernals serv'd up with juice of Lemons and Sugar'. When Lassels gets to Bologna he is impressed by 'the traffick in silks, velvets, olives, leather bottles, gellies, wash balls and little doggs for Ladyes . . . . their *salsiccie* are a *regalo* for a Prince'.

Miller, Lady (Betty). *Letters from Italy*. Two vols. London 1776. Lady Miller's letters are filled with receptions, collations, theatres, and fashionable activities such as taking the steam baths at Pozzuoli outside Naples. At a ball held in the vast royal palace at Caserta Lady Miller meets Queen Maria Carolina who converses with her and reveals that the only food she eats is that prepared for her by her own German cook. (Maria Carolina was Austrian, sister of Marie Antoinette, then Dauphine of France.) In Venice Lady Miller was beguiled by the window displays of the greengrocers' shops, 'dressed in such a manner as discovers a surprising taste in the common people . . . . I observed that ideas drawn from architecture were the favourite fancies of the gardeners who pile up cabbages, lettuces, etc, as columns, and form their capitols, friezes etc, of turnips, carrots, and celery, the flowers and herbs are linked together, and disposed in festoons after the antique'. Socially condescending and not without blue-stocking pretentions, Lady Miller is at the same time a conscientious observer.

Montaigne, Michel de. *The Complete Works of Montaigne, Essays, Travel Journals, Letters*. Translated by Donald M. Frame. Hamish Hamilton, London 1965.

The record of Montaigne's journey from his home in south-west France north to Switzerland, through Germany, into northern Italy and down to Florence was written partly by his secretary, partly by himself. The main motive for his journey was a search for relief from his painful affliction, kidney stones, all too common at the period. Montaigne therefore often went out of his way to visit places where there were natural hot springs and where he could drink the waters or take the baths. For the same reason the food he ate and the wine and water he drank were carefully recorded, as were the effects of the baths on his condition. Montaigne's descriptions of Lombardy and Tuscany, and of, the city of Florence, of conditions in these places, of the inns, the food, the wine, the local people, the acquaintances made on his travels, the meals to which he was invited, even the way a table is set or the bread served, reveal him as an enchanting travelling companion. He notices small pleasures: on February 17th, 1581, 'At this time we had roses in Rome, and artichokes'; and welcomes the gifts of fruit, wine and boxes of quince jelly which he receives along the way.

Moryson, Fynes. *Ten Yeares Travell through the twelve dominions of Germany, Böhmerland, Switzerland, Netherlands, Poland, Italy, Turkey, France, England, Scotland and Ireland.* 1710.
One of the best known of all English travel books. Reading the works of Moryson and his contemporaries and successors one wonders how the English ever came to have the reputation of being inattentive to their food and uncaring about their meals. At any rate when they go on their travels men like Moryson, Lassels and George Sandys (see below) comment at length on the food encountered at inns, often going into some detail about the quality of the bread, the varieties of cheese to be had, and the manner of cooking. Moryson, when he gets to Italy, notes for example the use of olive oil instead of butter, describes a delicate Italian sauce called *savore* made of bread, pounded walnuts and marjoram – one which has survived to this day – and approves of the *gentilezze*, the trifles served as sweetmeats. When it comes to wine he explains the use of the term *brindisi*, meaning to drink a toast to or with someone, records seeing earthen vessels 'full of water wherein little glasses filled with wine swim for coolnesse', and gives a favourable opinion of the muscadine of Montefiaschoni, a wine often singled out by English visitors to Italy at the period.

Piozzi, Hester. *Glimpses of Italian Society in the Eighteenth Century. From the 'Journey' of Mrs. Piozzi.* London 1892.
Mrs. Piozzi was Dr. Johnson's Mrs. Thrale. After the death of Mr. Thrale, a wealthy brewer, his widow married Piozzi, an Italian music teacher. Her friends were hostile to the marriage, considering Piozzi a come-down after Mr. Thrale the brewer. To escape the criticism and unkindness of acquaintances and old friends, the Piozzis left England and made a prolonged stay in Italy. There they were kindly received wherever they went – Genoa, Bologna, Venice, Florence, Naples. Mrs. Piozzi thoroughly enjoyed herself. Her appreciation of her new husband's native country is infectious and the pleasure she took in discovering it comes through everything she wrote about their journey together.

The wonderful fruits of Italy particularly impressed Hester Piozzi. Writing in the summer of 1785, when she was in Florence, she marvelled at the size of the cherries, as large as plums, and in a street market sees somebody's manservant 'weighing two in a scale to see if they came to an ounce'. The figs too were perfection, not by superior size, for they were small and green, but in taste and colour, 'a bright full crimson within', and we eat them with raw ham, I mean ham cured, not boiled or roasted'. Everywhere the bounty of Italian provisions, fruit and vegetables in particular, strikes Mrs. Piozzi. 'Vegetable nature flourishes in full perfection, while every step crushes out perfume from the trodden herbs. ... The scent of truffles attracts, and the odour of melons gratifies one's nerves when driving among the habitations of fertile Lombardy.'

When it comes to Naples Mrs. Piozzi delights in the crammed provision shops, the marvellous abundance of poultry and game, although like almost every other English visitor before and since she remarks less than favourably on the Italian taste 'for small birds, beccafichi, ortolani' etc as the most agreeable dainties'. At Christmas she is entranced by the picturesquely decorated lemonade and coffee stalls of Naples – moveable coffee houses as she calls them – and in Bologna finds 'the best possible food ... rich cream and incomparable dinners every day'. Venice however was marred for her by the importunities of beggars at every turn, on the steps of every church and palazzo, and she was even pestered by them as she stood outside a coffee-house eating an ice – in those days, and for long afterwards respectable women didn't venture inside such establishments. Was it perhaps outside Florian's, opened in St. Mark's Square in 1775 that Hester Piozzi ate her ice that day?

Ray, The Reverend John, FRS. *Travels through the Low-Countries, Germany, Italy and France.* 2 vols. Second Edition, London 1738.
John Ray was in Italy in 1664 and reported in some detail on the provisions to be found in Rome, in Lombardy, in Naples, and in Sicily. Predictably, the dismal list of small song-birds and many others, large and small, to be see in the poulterers' shops was included by the Reverend Ray, with the comment that 'one would think that in a short time they should destroy all the birds of these kinds in the country'.

About Italian truffles Ray makes a curious statement. After a passing mention of those found in Lombardy, he whisks off to Sicily, saying that 'the best of all are gotten there and then sent over into Malta, where they are sold dear', bought, one assumes, for consumption by the knights resident on the island.

In a valiant effort at explaining macaroni and vermicelli to people who have never seen them, John Ray describes these as 'paste made into strings like pack-thread or thongs of white leather. ... Boiled and oiled with a little cheese scraped upon them, they are eaten as we do eat buttered wheat or rice'.

Bread, salads, fruit, carob beans, water melons, cucumbers, love apples (meaning egg-plant or *melongena* rather than tomatoes), Neapolitan and Sicilian cheeses are all described by Ray, but when it comes to what he calls *Caseo de Cavallo* or horse-cheese, he declines to believe, as the locals assert, that they are made from 'buffles milk', because 'we observed not many buffles in those countries where there

is more of this cheese made than of other sorts'. A properly sceptical traveller, the Reverend Ray.

Reresby, Sir John. *The Travels and Memoirs of Sir John Reresby, Bart . . . . Exhibiting a View of the Governments and Society in the Principal States of Europe, During the Time of Cromwell's Usurpation* Etc. Third Edition. Printed for Edward Jeffrey and Son, Pall Mall. London 1831.
Sir John Reresby was a Yorkshire landowner travelling in Europe for the reason given in the title of his account. He was careful to do nothing, such as being seen in Flanders in company with the exiled Charles II, which might put his estates in danger of sequestration by the Commonwealth. In Italy Reresby observes that the government of Tuscany is 'Monarchical', and that 'the Prince lays what taxes he pleases on the people, having always a good competent standing force to keep them in subjection.' In Venice he saw 'most of the canals frozen over, which continued eight days', a sight which reminds him to note the Italian custom of drinking wine cooled with ice or snow. Like so many of his contemporaries Reresby is enthusiastic about the wonderful fertility of the country, the 'abundance of grain, fruits, wines, and much oil, which they generally use instead of butter, except in Lombardy and in the Valley of Pisa'. 'Their wines are the most delicious, especially those of Tuscany, Montefiascone, and a deep red wine which they usually drink at meals, La Lagrima Di Christo, or the tears of Christ, La Vernaza, and the white muscadine, cocubum and Falernum from the kingdom of Naples, with many others are all delicate rich wines; and yet in the Venetian state they drink a great deal of a Grecian sort of wine called Malvoisia.' Reresby is complimentary about the excellent pure wheat-bread, of which they often make a meal, sliced and sopped in wine, less so about the custom which obliges travellers to buy their own victuals and contract with the landlady of the hostelry to dress them. The Italians, says Reresby crushingly, 'are but bad cooks'.

Ross, Janet. *Italian Sketches*. Illustrated by Carlo Orsi. London 1887.
Janet Ross, daughter of Lucie Duff Gordon, author of *Letters from Egypt*, lived in a villa called Poggio Gherardo near Florence, was herself a prolific author, and a prominent member of the English community which in her day flourished in the neighbourhood. Her little book *Leaves from a Tuscan Kitchen*, a collection of recipes supplied by Giuseppe Volpi, her Tuscan cook, is well known to collectors of cookery books. It was recently republished with extra recipes and a preface by Mrs. Ross's great-great nephew Michael Waterfield. *Italian Sketches* is a volume of collected essays previously published in periodicals such as *Fraser's Magazine*, *Macmillan's Magazine* and *Longman's Magazine*. Among the subjects chosen by Janet Ross for inclusion in *Italian Sketches* were the making of olive oil, and vintaging on a Tuscan estate in the summer of 1874, a year in which the yield of grapes had been the greatest since the outbreak of iodium, the disease which twenty-six years previously had devastated the vines. In another essay Mrs. Ross describes the famous Trebbiano grape of Tuscany, 'brilliant yellow, with the sunny side stained a deep brown', and 'the lovely *Occhio di Pernice* or partridge's eye, of a light pink with ruby lines meandering about in every grape, the flavour of which was quite equal to its beauty'.

When lunch for the grape harvesters is brought out from her host's villa, everybody reclines 'round a steaming dish of *risotto con funghi* and a knightly sirloin of roast beef which would have done honour to old England. A big *fiasco* (a large bottle bound round with reeds or straw, and holding three ordinary bottles) of last year's red wine was soon emptied, well-tempered, I should say, with water from the neighbouring well. At a little distance the labourers in the vineyards were enjoying the unwonted luxury of a big wooden bowl full of white beans crowned with *polpette*, little sausages of minced meat and rice.'
An interesting sidelight on the Tuscan vintage as described by Janet Ross was, and presumably still is, at least in part, the putting aside of a certain quantity of white grapes which are laid out on great trays or *stoje* made of canes to be exposed to sun and air for some weeks. These are the grapes used for making the much-loved sweet *Vin Santo* of the Chianti region.

Sandys, George. *A Relation Of A Journey Begun AD1610*. Second edition 1617.
Sandys gives interesting accounts of the Greek islands of Chios and Zante, then under Turkish rule, and of their produce such as currants, mastic and citrus juice in barrels. On Naples and Sicily he is particularly good.

Simetti, Mary Taylor. *On Persephone's Island. A Sicilian Journal*. Alfred Knopf, New York 1986.
Not exactly a visitor's book, since Sicily is in fact Mrs. Simetti's home. She is American, her husband Sicilian, and bringing up a young family she has adapted herself to life on the island, taking a lively interest in its traditions, customs, agriculture, viticulture, cooking, festivals. In one splendid passage Mary Simetti describes a remarkable Christmas cake called *Il Trionfo della Gola*, The Triumph of Greed. A two kilo bunch of grapes made of almond and pistachio paste is set on a base of *Zuccata*, the pumpkin confection so much loved by the Sicilians, and in this case enriched with chopped pistachio nuts and scented with cinnamon. A speciality made by the nuns of a Palermo convent, and a rare survival from the days when sweetmeats and confectionery of all kinds were the special province of the convents.

Vinchant, François. *Voyage de François Vinchant en France & en Italie du 16 Septembre 1609 au 18 Février 1610*. Texte accompagné d'une Introduction par Félix Hachez. Extrait du Bulletin de la Société Royale Belge de Géographie 1896. Société Générale D'Imprimerie Ancienne, Maison Vanderauvera, Bruxelles rue des Sables 16. Brussels 1897.
Vinchant's account of his journey through France and northern Italy deserves to be better known. He is an inquisitive and appreciative traveller. At Vicenza, for example, he finds it a pleasure to see the quantities of white mulberry trees growing both within the town and all round it, and notes that the silk worms which feed on the leaves produce finer silk than that of Rome. At Bolsena the fertility of the soil is aided by manuring. The olives are fine, and the muscadelle grapes growing outside his hostelry hang in clusters so huge that he takes pleasure in cutting one grape at a time, as he would cut into a pear, so

large and firm are the fruit, and at Montefiascone he finds, as other travellers before and since, that the muscadelle wines, both red and white, are the most delicious that could be met with.

After one long ride he arrives at Novarra quite ill from the movement of his horse. But when 'I saw the beautiful yellow peaches that were brought to the table I tasted them, took heart and was cured'. Arrived in Verona, Father Vinchant notes the medicinal plants for which Monte Baldo was famous, and which were much used by the medical faculty of Padua University, and at Pesaro the equally renowned figs, in this case dried ones. As for Florence, they dress with a superfluity of richness, and the same can be said of their banquets. Their best wine is made from the Trebbiano grape which grows around Florence. On his return through France Vinchant unhappily finds the hostelries dirty, from their tables and even to their beds.

INDEX

Where an entry has several page references and one or more of these are of greater importance they are in heavy type.

Abbacchio al forno, 24, **141**
Abruzzi:
    cooking of, 53
    figs, 181
    mozzarella, 207
    pasta alla chitarra, 67
    pears with cheese, 207
    pecorino, 207
    saffron, 27
    wine, 210
Acciughe, 28, 119
    spinaci alle, 166
    See also Alici
Aceto, peperoni all', 200
Acque gelate, 184
Acton, Harold, *The Last Medici*, 219, 220
Addison, Joseph, 220
Adriatic:
    branzino, 121
    brodetto of, 102
    colours of, at Ravenna Marina, 102
    crabs of, 178
    fish of, 109; for soup, 102
    inkfish and scampi on skewers, 115
    octopus, 116
    rospo, 121
    scampi, 114
    sturgeon, 122
Agerola, 207
Agliata, 111

Aglio, 28
Agnello, costolette alla Marinetti, 142
Agnolotti, 29, 73
Agoni, 48
Agrodolce (sweet-sour) sauces, 27, 29, 151, **156**, **158**, **159**, **168**, **170**, **171**, 189, 193
Agropoli, 121, 209
Aguglie, 107, **120**
Alba:
    nougat, 137
    truffles of, 30, 201, 210, 214
Albana wine, 209
Alberini, Massimo, 213
Albicocche:
    gelato di, 185
    in insalata di frutta, 179
    torta di, 176
Ali-bab, *Gastronomie pratique*, 21
Alici, 28, **119**
    al gratin 119
    all'ischiana, 119
    peperoni con, e capperi, 48
    See also Acciughe
Allodole, 151, 157
Alloro, 26
Allumettes, cheese or anchovy, 174
Almond cakes, 177
    pudding, 175-6
Almonds, 26, 29
    in cakes, 177

in pudding, 175-6
in rice salad, 45
Amalfi, wine of, 209-10
Amaretti, 173
Anacapri:
    figs of, 179
    preserved squid, 200
Anchovies, 25, 28, 43, 45, **119**, 129
    in bagna cauda, 28, 192-3
    with crostini di provatura, 96
    au gratin, 119
    ischian, 119
    with pimentos and capers, 48
    in pizza, 97-9
    spinach with, 166
Anchovy allumettes, in Parma, 174
Ancona, 102
    salame Fabriano, 145
Anderson, Burton, 210, 211
Angler fish, 102, 103, 109, **121**
Anguille, 122-5
    arrosto, 124
    in umido, 125
    al vino bianco, 125
Anguilles marinées façon d'Italie, 125
Anita in agrodolce, 156
Anolini, 19, 26, 29, 73, **76**, 141
    pie, 76
Ansonica wine, 211
Antinori, Villa, 211
Antipasti:

insalate, 43-51
agoni, 48
bietole, 161
bresaola, 51
broccoli, 161
buttáriga, 50
caldi (hot), 43
caponata, 169
caponata alla marinara, 50
di carciofi, insalata di, 46
    alla maionese, 46
crostini di mare, 45
culatello di zibello, 50
fagioli toscani col tonno, 46
figiolini col tonno, 46
fave crude, 43, 161
finocchi e cetrioli, insalata di, 48
    e radicchie, 48
frutti di mare, 44
funghi, insalata di, 45, 162
    e frutti di mare, 44
    e scampi, 44
alla genovese, **44**, 145
grancevole, 45
lingua di bue, insalata di, 51
    con salsa verde, 51
misto, 48
olive, 51, ripiene, 51
patate, insalata di, 48, 134
    col tonno, 28, **47**
peperoni, con alici e capperi, 48

gialli, insalata di, 45
alla piemontese, 48
sott'olio, 46
col tonno, 48
polpettone di tonno, 47
pomidoro, insalata di, **48**, 134
col tonno, 47
prosciutto, cotto, 50
di Parma, 50
radicchie, ravanelli, 161
riso, e pollo, 152, **153**,
e scampi, insalata di, 45
salame, 50
salsa per, 44, 195
Sicilian, 169
storione, 43, **122**
tartine al tonno, 47
tartufi, 137
tonno e cipolle, insalata di, 47
uova, sode agli spinaci, 47
tonnate, 47
di tonno, 50
verde insalata, 134, 161
Antonio, cook to Norman Douglas,
74
his ravioli recipe, 74
Anzio macaroni pie, 67
Apicius' cookery book, 144, 193
Apollinaire, Guillaume,
L'Hérésiarque & Cie, 197
Apricot; Apricots:
in fruit salad, 179
ice cream, 185
Italian, 181
tart, 176
Apulia:
fish fried in local oil, 110
mozzarella, 207
olive oil for frying of fish, 110
wine, 210
Aragosta, 112
Aranci caramelizzati, 178-9
Arborio rice, 87
Arigusta, frittelle di, 112
Arista fiorentina, 142
perugina, 142
Army and Navy Stores, 28
Arselle con crostini, 112
Artichokes, 20, 43, 161, **164-5**
boiled, 164
in a fritto misto, 164
hearts of, with fried chicken
breast, etc., 136
in a frittata, 164
with mayonnaise, 46
with peas etc., 43
preparation of, for cooking, 164
in Genoese Easter pie, 164
Jewish, 164-5
Mafalda's, 165
raw for salad, **46**, 164

stewed in oil and garlic, 164
tarragon flavoured, 26
with veal and white wine, 131-2
Venetian, 165
Artusi, Pellegrino, *L'Arte di Mangiar
Bene*, 135, 213
Ascoli, stuffed olives of, 51
Asher, Gerald, 211-12
Asiago cheese, 206
Asparagi, 165
Asparagus (asparagi), 165
of Cavaillon, 165
of Lauris, 165
with Parmesan, 165
of Pescia, 165
wild, 165
Asti, 201
Aubergines, 167, 168
Balkan, Greek, Provençal, Turkish
ways of cooking, 168
in caponata, 169, marinara, 50
in fritto misto of vegetables, 169
pie of, with cheese, 168-9
purée of, 168
sauté of, 168
stuffed, 25, 28, 161, **169**
and veal and mutton pie, 135
Aurora ice, 184
Authenticity of recipes, 21
Auvergne, Cantal cheese of, 206
Aversa, 207
Azzola, Alida, 216

Baccalà, 126
alla livornese, 126
mantecato, 87, **126**
with polenta, 89, 90, 126
polpettine, of, 126
alla vicentina, 126
Bacon, 129
and broad beans, 166
and mushrooms with tonnarelle, 70
and pork with tomatoes and
tagliatelle, 70
French equivalents of, 129
Bagna cauda, la, 28, **192-3**
Baldini, Filippo, 213
Bananas, 181
Barbaresco wine, 210, 211
Barbera wine, 137, 192
Bari figs, 25, 197
Barolo wine, 137, 210, 211
Basil (basilico), **23**, 26, 129, 194
in mayonnaise, 194
in pesto, 193-4
preserved in oil (conservato all'
olio), 200
Bass, 121, 125
grilled, 121
on fennel, 120

roast, 110, 121
Batter for frying, 114
for pancakes, 96
Battipaglia, 207
Battuto, 190
for endives, 169
for fish, 111
for mushroom sauce, 193
Baudroie, 121
Bay trees, as omens of disaster, 26
Bayleaves, **26**
as flavouring for béchamel sauce,
192
Bayonne ham, 35
Beans:
broad, raw as hors d'œuvre, 43, 44,
161
and bacon, 166
dried, 89
French, salad, 130, 161
sformato, 167
and tunny, 28, 43, **46**
haricot, with bollito, 138, 161
with cotechino, 146, 161
in the oven, **89**
and tomato sauce, 66
with zampone, 146, 161
Tuscan, soup of, 28, **56**
with tunny, 28, **46**
Béarnaise sauce, 189
Beccafichi al nido, 157
Béchamel sauce, 26, 65, 189, **192**
Beef:
boiled, 137
consommé, 54
dried, 51
fillet steaks with brandy and
marsala, 138
Florentine steak, 138
Genoese stew, 140
marinading of, 33
réchauffé of, 141
rib, marinaded, 140
roll, 132
Roman stew, 140
saltimbocca, 131
steak, grilled, 129, with tomato and
garlic sauce, 138
with Veronese mushroom sauce,
193
stew, 27, **140-1**
stewed in red wine, 140
stuffed roast, 129, **141**
Tuscan, 129
Beetroot:
leaves, 76, 161
salad, 28
Bel Paese cheese, 29, 86, 93, 96, **206**
cooking properties of, 93
in carrozza, 95
and eggs, 94

Milanese, 95
Mozzarella, as alternative to, 29, 95
Belfrage, Nicholas, 212
Bengodi, 205
Besciamella, 26, 65, 189, **192**
Bibliography, 211-24
Bietole, 161
Bini, Prof. Giorgio, 215
Biondi-santi, Brunello of, 210
Birds, small, with polenta, 89, 157
wholesale slaughter of, 157
Bistecca:
alla fiorentina, 138
alla pizzaiola, 138
alla veronese, 193
Bitto cheese, 207
Blackbirds, 26, 157
Blette, 76
Boar, 151, 159
baked, 159
ham, 151
hunter's, 159
marinading of, 34, 159
roast, 159
Sardinian, 151
with sweet-sour sauce, 159, 193
Boccaccio, 62, 205
Bocconcini, 131
Boccone, squadrista, 125
Boldro, 102, **121**
Boletus, 29, 162
grilled, 162
in vine leaves, 163
Bologna; Bolognese:
bollito, **137-8**, 161
with peperata, 195
Bolognini's restaurant, 131
budino di pollo in brodo, 55
chicken breasts, 30, 151, **152**
cooking, 20, 31, 54
grana cheese, 205
ice creams, 154
lasagne verdi, 64-5
mortadella, 43, 146
supplì, 86
nutmeg used, 26
Pappagallo restaurant, 30, 55, 154
passatelli, 54-5
ragù, 31, 189, **190**
stuffed escalopes, 131
tagliatelle, 64, with ham, 64
tortellini, 77
truffles, white, 30, 77, 130
turkey breasts, 151, **154**
in pastry, 154
veal cutlets, 130
Zia Nerina's restaurant, 30, 190
Bolognini, restaurant and
restaurauteur, 131
Bomba di riso, 85
Bondiola, 144

Boni, Ada, *Il Talismano della Felicità*, 140, 213
Borage (boraggine), 26
Borlotti, 89
Botargue, 50, 211
  with caponata, 169
Bottigleria, 94
Bouillabaisse, 27, 102, 107
Bouillon cubes, 33
Boulestin, Marcel, 40
Bovino, Duke of, 61
Bozzi, Ottorina Perna, 213
Braciolette ripiene, 131
Brain croquettes, 31, 146
Brandade, 126
Branzino, 121
Braudel, Fernand, 220
Bread:
  fried with birds, 157
  rusks, 99
Breadcrumbs, 30-1
Bream, sea, 121
Bresaola, 51
Brieve e Nuovo Modo da forsi ogni sorte di Sorbetti con facilita, 182
Brill, grilled, 111
Broad beans:
  salad, 43, 44, 161
  and bacon, 166
Broccoli, 161, 166
  and polenta, 90
Brodetto alla ravennata, 102
Brodo, 33
  di carne, 33
  di manzo, 54
  pasta in, con fegatini, etc., 55
  di pollo, 33
  ristretto, 54
Brunello di Montalcino wine, 210
Bruscandoli, 214
Bruschetta, 99
Budino:
  di mandorle, 175-6
  di pollo in brodo, 55
  di ricotta, 174
  toscano, 174
Buffalo milk cheeses, 206
Bugialli, Giovanni, 214
Buontalenti, 219
Burrida, 101, **102**, 109
Burrini, 207
Busecca, 137
Buttàriga, 50, 211
Butter:
  in Italian cooking, 81, 130
  with fettuccine, 64
  and Parma ham, 50
  and polenta, 89
  with rice, 85
Buttiri cheese, 207
Byron, Lord, 102

Cabbage, 138, 161
  raw, 192
  sweet-sour, 171
  stuffed leaves of, 171
Cacciagione, la, 26, 27, 29, 151
  recipes, 156-9
Cacciatori, salame, 145-6
Cacciucco livornese, 102-3
Cacio a cavallo, 207
Caciotta, 30, 74, **207**
Caffé:
  gelato di, 185
  granita di, 185
  ricotta al, 174
Cagliari, 26, 28, 151
  market, 50
  fish market, 110
Cake, uncooked chocolate (torrone molle), 174-5
Cake tins, 37
Calabria, 121, 207
Calabria, Old, Norman Douglas, 217
Calamaretti, 43, 102
  e scampi alle stecche, 115
Calamari, 33, **115-16**
  in fritto misto, 117
  e seppie in zimino, 116-17
  in umido, 116
Calamaroni, 102
Calzone, 94, **98**
Campagna, 207
Candied fruit 182, 193, 197, 201-3
Candiero, 184
Candito d'ova, 184
Canelons, 182
Canelloni, 63, **78**
Cannella, 27
Cannelloni, 63, **78**
Canocchia, 102
Cantal cheese, 206
Caparozzolo, 112
Cape sante, 111
  alla griglia, 111
  con sformato di piselli freschi, 167
  in umido, 114
  in zuppa di pesce, 105
Capocollo, 144
Caponata, 169
  alla marinara, 50
Capone, 103
Cappelletti, 19, 73, **74-5**
  in brodo, 74-5
Cappon magro, 109, **125;6**, 189
Caprese, zuppa di pesce, 104
  ravioli, **74**, 96, 97
Capretto:
  al forno, 142
  al vino bianco, 142
Capri:
  caciotta cheese, 207
  fish soup, 104

ravioli, 73, **74**
  wine, 209
Capriolo, montone, uso, 142
Capro roman, risotto in, 82
Caramel oranges, 178-9
Carciofi, 164-5
  frittata di, 164
  alla giudea, 164-5
  insalata di, 46
  alla maionese, 46
  ripieni alla Mafalda, 165
  alla romana, 164
  in torta pasqualina, 164
  alla veneziana, 165
Cardoons, 137, 192
Carne, sugo di, 190
Carni, le, 129-49
Carp (carpione):
  à la Chambord, 122
  in white wine, as for orata, 121
Carrots with marsala, 166
Caruso Brothers, wine, 209-10
Casanova, filletto, 138
Casoeula, 143
Casola, Pietro, 220
Castagne:
  al marsala, 176
  zuppa di, 56
Castellamare, 51
Cavaillon, asparagus of, 165
Cavalcanti, Ippolito, 214
Cavanna, G., *Doni di Nettuno*, 115, 117, 124, 197, 215
Cavoli in agrodolce, 171
Ceci, 30
  con pomidori, 66
  tuoni e lampo, 89
Cefalo, 120
Celery, **25**, 45, 101, 161, 192
  stewed, 140
Centigrade equivalents, 39
Cèpes, 29
  à la génoise, 163
Cephalonian hare, 159
Cerignola, 51
Cerio, Edwin, 74, 89
Cervella, crocchette di, 146
Cervo con salso di ciliegie, 159
Cetrioli, insalata di finocchi e, 48
Chanterelles, 162
Chapon, 102, 103, 126
Chapusot, Francesco, 214
Charcoal grilling, 38
Chard, 76, 161
Cheese, 29-30, 93
  recipes, 95-7
  and basil sauce (pesto), **193-4**
  cream, home-made, 99
  croquettes, 96
  croûtons, 53, 93, **96**
  with eggs and mushrooms, 95

fondue, 30, **95**, 137, 206
  Parmesan, 205
  fried, with eggs, 95
  with fried eggs, 94
  gnocchi, 79
  gruyère, 43, 93
  with ham, 29
  omelette, 94-5
  pancakes, with spinach, 97
  Parmesan, how made, 205
    poor quality of imported, 29, 205
  ready-grated, 93
  and pears, 207
  rice with four varieties of, 86
  St Paulin, 93
  with scrambled eggs, 94
Cheese-grater, 37
Cheese, cream: 20, 36
  gnocchi, 73, 79
  green ravioli or gnocchi, 78-9
  pasta with ricotta, 70
  pasta shells and walnuts with, 70-1
  pudding, 174
  sweet, 174
  in tortelli di erbette, 73, 76
  varieties and makes:
    double, 71
    fetta, 207
    Gervais, 93
    home-made, 99
  See also Mascherpone, Ricotta
Cheeses, Italian:
  in cooking, 29-30
  varieties, 205-7
  Asiago, 206
  Bel Paese, 29, 86, 93, 94, 95, 96, **206**
  Bitto, 207
  Burrini, 207
  caciotta, 30, 74, 207
    cacio a cavallo, 207
  canestrato, 207
  fetta, 207
  fior di latte, 207
  fontina, 30, 91, 95, **206**
  gioddù, 207
  gorgonzola, 206
  grana, 29, **205**
  groviera, 30, **206**
  mascherpone (mascarpone), 31, 70, 174, **206**
  mozzarella, 29-30, 86, 94, 95, 96, 97, 206, 207
  paglierino, 207
  pannerone, 206
  parmigiano, 19, 29, 37, 53, 74, 86, 93, 119, **205**
  pastrorella, 206
  pecorino, 30, 53, 66, 207
  provatura, 96
  provola, 207
    di pecora, 207

provolone, 30, 74, 86, 93, 96, 97, **207**
raviggiolo, 207
ricotta, 29-30, 70, 76, 96, 99, 174, **207**
robiola, 206, goat's milk, 207
robiolina, 206
sardo, 44, 53, 145, 193, 207
scamorza, 207
stracchino, 206
taleggio: taleggino, 206
tomini del talucco, 207
Cherry sauce for venison, 159
Chestnuts:
  with boar, 159
  fried cake of, 157
  with marsala, 176
  'in Mont Blanc', 176
  purée of, 174
  soup of, 56
Chianti, 209, 210-11
Chick peas: cooking of, 21, 30
  and pasta, 89
  and tomato sauce, 66
Chicken, 151
  breasts, 151
    fried, with artichoke hearts, etc., 136
    in butter, 30, **152**
    with ham and cheese, 152
    in pastry, 154
  and egg soup, Pavese, 54
    Roman, 54
  with fruit mustard, 197
  galantine, 30
  grilled, 152
  liver:
    in crespolini, 97
    croûtons, 132, **153**
    sauce, 79, 86, **190**
    sauce with gnocchi, 190
    sauce with rice, 86
    and pea soup with pasta, 55
  in marsala, 158
  in milk, 153
  mousse in broth, 55
  with rice, 83
  salad, 45, 152, **153**
  soup, cream of, 59
  stock, 33
  stuffed, with ham, 153
  with tunny sauce, 153
  with Veronese mushroom sauce, 193
Chiocciole al mascherpone e noce, 70-1
Chiodi di garofano, 27
Chitarra, pasta alla, 67
Chocolate: 220
  ice, 182, 220
  truffles, 176
  in sweet-sour sauce, 193
Chopper, double-handled, 37

Cicala di mare, 87, 102
Cider: in fish dishes, 101
Ciliegie, salsa di, 159
Cima, 129, **135**
Cinghiale, 159
  in agrodolce, 159
  arrosto, 159
  alla cacciatora, 159
  prosciutto di, 151
  sardo, 159
Cinnamon, 26, **27**, 182
Ciocca, Giuseppe, 214
Cipolle:
  insalata di tonno e, 47
  ripiene, 170
  rognoni con, e vino bianco, 148
Cipolline in agrodolce, 170
Cipriani's Locanda, Torcello, 87, 90
Cirio brand tomatoes, 31
Civitavecchia, Stendhal at, 164
Clams, 43, 84, 103
  fisherman's, 112
  with fried bread, 112
  in Genoese fish stew, 102
  soup, 101, **105**
  with tomato sauce and spaghetti, 67
Claviari, 162
Cloves, 26, **27**
Clovisse, 112
Cockles, 67, 84, 101
  in soup with scallops, etc., 106
  as for vongole with pasta, 67
Coconuts:
  how displayed in Venice, 181
Cocuzzata, 197
Cod, 101
  salt, 126
  cream of, 126
  Leghorn, 126
  little rissoles, 126
  preparation of for cooking, 126
  smoked, 126
  Venetian speciality, 126
  Vicenza, 126
Cod's roes, smoked, 50
Cœur à la crème, 31
Coffee:
  cream cheese with, 174
  granita, 185
  ice cream, 185
  and rice sweet, 177
Colquhoun, Archibald, The Betrothed, translation of, 90
Coltibuono wine, 211
Comacchio eel-fishing industry, 122
Como, Lake, 48
Concentrato di pomidoro, 31
Conchiglia dei pellegrini (pesce alla griglia), 111
Confectionery, 201-3
Confettura di fichi, 201

Coniglio al marsala, 157-8
Conserve, 197-203
  di peperoni, 198-9
  di pomidoro, 198
Consommé, 53, 73
Cookery books, list of, 213-16
Copate, 173
Coppa, 29, 35, 66, 144
  various meanings, 43
Coriander seeds (coriandro), 26, **27**, 159
Cornwall, saffron buns of, 27
Corrado, Vincenzo, 214
Cosenza, 119
Costa:
  di maiale alla griglia, 142-3
  di manzo al vino rosso, 140
  d'agnello alla Marinetti, 142
Costolette bolognese, 130
  milanese, 130
Cotechino, 137, 143, **146**, 161
Cotognata, 197
Courgettes, see Marrows; Zucchini
Cozze:
  alla marinara, 111
  pizza con, 98
  al vino bianco, 111-12
  zuppa di, 104
Crabs, 43, 44, 45, 102
  soft-shell, 112
Crawfish, 112, 114
Cream, how used in Italian cooking, 31
Cream cheese, See Cheeses, cream
Crema di mascherpone, 31, 174
Cremona, fruit mustard (mostarda di frutta), 197
  with eels, 124
  with pheasant (fagiano futurista), 157
  nougat, 137
Crespi (pancake), 97
Crespolini, **97**, 209-10
Crespone, salame, 145
Crispelle, 98
Crocchette di cervella, 31, **146**
  di patate, 140, **162**
  di spinaci, 166
Croquettes, 20, 31
  brain, 31, **146**
  cheese, 96
  potato, 140, **162**
  rice supplì, 86
  spinach, 166
Crostini, 53, 56, 131, 148
  arselle con, 112
  di fegatini, 132, **153**
  di mare, 45
  di provatura, 28, **96**
  as hot hors d'œuvre, 43-4
  with soups, 53
  vongole con, 112

Crotone, 119, 121, 151
Croûtons, cheese, 53, 93, **96**
  chicken liver, 132, **153**
  garlic, 101
Cucina Italiana, La periodical, 213
Cucumber and fennel salad, 48
Culatello di zibello, 50, 144
Culpeper, 23
Curnieura, 99
Curry, in fish stew, 101
Curti, rice packers, 87
Custard for ices, 185
Cutlet bat, 37
Cutlets:
  Bolognese, pork, 130
    veal, 130
  lamb, Marinetti's, 142
  Milanese veal, 130
Cuttle fish, 115-16
  and squid in zimino, 116-17

Daily Telegraph, The, 87
Dallas, Philip, 212
Dates, sea, 43, 109, **112**, 218
Dates, stuffed, 142
Datteri di mare, 43, 109, **112**, 218
Daurade, 121
David, Elizabeth, 214, 221
Davidson, Alan, Mediterranean Seafood, 102, 215-16
Deep-freeze, 33
Deep-frying, 38
Demi-sel cheese, 96
Denti di Pirajno, Alberto, 213
Dentice (dentex), 121
Diabolical roses, 177
Diogenes the Cynic, 116
Divorced eggs, 95
Dolce Mafarka, 177
Dolci, I, 173-87, 214
Dons, Les, de Comus, 125
Doughnut, ring, 173
Douglas, Norman, 218
  Moving Along, his letter concerning authorship of, 217
  Old Calabria, 217
  Siren Land, 107, 120, 217
  Venus in the Kitchen, 157
  basil, considers must not be chopped, 23
  fish soups, his opinions of, 107
  pheasant, his recipe for, 157
  ravioli, his cook's recipe for, 74
  sees spotted eagle for sale, 151
Dragoncello, 26
Dublin Bay prawns, 45, 114
  in mussel soup, 104
Duck in sweek-sour sauce, 156
Dumas, Alexandre, in his Grand

Dictionnaire de Cuisine:
his clam soup recipe, 101, 105
inkfish described, 116
pheasant, his recipe for, 157
Durante, Castor, 214

Eagle, spotted, 151
Edwards, Charles, 151, 159, 217
Eels, 102, 111, **122-5**
and fruit mustard, 124, 197
marinaded, 125
roast, 124
stewed, 125
in white wine, 125
Eggplant, *see* Aubergines
Eggs, 93-5
divorced, 95
fried with cheese, 94
with fried cheese, 95
hard boiled, 95
stuffed with spinach, 47
with mushrooms and cheese, 95
omelette, cheese, 94-5
Genoese, 95
poached, on potato purée, 94
with sformato of peas, 167
with prawn sauce, 193
with rice, 95
scrambled with cheese, 94
with truffles, 93
sur le plat, 93
and tomatoes, 94
with tunny mayonnaise, 47
Emilia:
cooking of, 74
cotechino, 146
grana cheese of, 205
pork, 129
zampone of, 146
See also Parma
Emmenthal cheese, 206
Endives, Batavian, in Genoese
ravioli, 77-8
stuffed, 169
Endives, braised, good with
Bolognese veal cutlets, 130
English cooking, 19, 53, 63, 81
E.N.I.T., 86
Ente del Turismo, 218
Episcopio's fish wine, 210
Erbe odorose, 23-6
Escalopes:
Milanese, 130
cold as picnic dish, 130
minced, 132
Perugian, 132
stuffed, 131
Escarole, 169
Euboea, figs of, 181
Evelyn, John, 26

Fabriano salame, 145
Faccioli, Emilio, 214, 215
Fagiano futurista, 157
Fagioli, 89
toscani, col tonno, 28, **46**
zuppa di, 28, **56**
Fagiolini:
insalata di, 161
sformato di, 167
col tonno, 28, 43, **46**
Fahrenheit equivalents, 39
Faina, 30
Famiole: famiglioli, 162
Fasœil al fùrn, 89
Fave, crude, al guanciale, 161, 166
Fedden, Romilly, his minestrone
recipe, 57
and names of Italian wines, 209
Fegatini:
crostini di, 132, **153**
pasta in brodo con, 55
salsa di, 190
with gnocchi, 79, 190
con riso, 86
Fegato:
alla veneziana, 146
di vitello, al marsala, 148
alla milanese, 146
Felino:
salame of, 25, 144, 145
wine of, 145
Fenice, Taverna,
caramel oranges, recipe for, 178
kitchen of, 178
Fennel, 25, 26
bulb or bulbous root stem:
in salad, 43, 45, 161
and cucumber salad, 48
and radish salad, 48
au gratin, 161
as flavouring for pork chops,
grilled, 142
in Perugian roast pork, 142
sformato of, 167
in stuffing for chicken (pollo in
porchetta), 153
seeds, 151
with dried figs, 25
in Florentine salame, 25, 145
with grilled mullet or bass, 120
Ferrara, 205
Ferrutius, *Gastronomia Parmense*, 31,
144, 217
Fesa col prosciutto, 132
Festa, specialities for a, 173
Fetta cheese, 207
Fettuccine, 63, 64
with butter (al burro), 64
with oil, garlic and tomato (alla
marinara), 66
Fichi mandorlati, 197

Fig jam, 201
Figpeckers in their nests, 157
Figs, 26, 179-81
of Abruzzi, 181
with almonds, 197
of Anacapri, 179
dried, of Bari, 25, 197
of Euboea, 181
in fruit salad, 179
and Parma ham, 43, 50, 144, 179
of Sicily, 179
Figuier, Louis, *The Ocean World*, 115,
120-1, 127
Filetto Casanova, 138
Finocchio, 25
au gratin, 161
insalata di, 43, 45, 161
e cetrioli, insalata di, 48
e radicchie, insalata di, 48
semi di, fichi con, 25
Finocchiona salame, 25, 145
Fior di latte, 207
Firpo, Luigi, 221
Fish, 109-27, 215-16
antipasti, 43
boiled, 111
broth, 83
fried: frying of, 110
in garlic sauce, 111
Genoese salad, 125-6
grilled, 110-11
marinaded, 111
Marinetti's recipe for, 125
markets, 109-10
mixed fried, 117
in paper cases, 111
and prawn sauce, 193
roast, 110
soups, Italian, 20, 27, 53, **101-7**
new English recipes for, 105-6
Neapolitan, Norman Douglas
denounces, 107
walnut sauce, 195
See also the names of individual
fish: Minestre; Soups
Fisherman's clams, 111
Flamingoes, 151
Florence; Florentine: 219
beans and tunny, 46
beef steak, 138
Café Procacci, 30
chicken breast, 151, **152**
fennel; fennel sausage, 25
fritto misto, 136
ices, 184
market, 24
mint, 24
risotto, 87
roast pork, 142
and rosemary, 24
rolled pork fillets, 24

rosemary, prevalence of in
Florentine cooking, 24
salame, 25, 145
tripe, 149
truffles, white, in sandwiches, 30
See also Tuscany; Tuscan
Focaccia, 93
Fondue, *see*, Fonduta
Fonduta piedmontese, 30, **95**, 137,
206
alla parmigiana, 205
with rice, 86
Fontina cheese, 30, 91, 206
Formaggi, 29-30, 205-7
Formaggio:
piatti di formaggio, 29-30, 93, 95-7
Forno di campagna, 38
Fortnum's, 28
Fragole:
dei boschi, 181
gelato di, 185
granita di, 185
Fragoline di mare, 44, 109, 116
Franciscan pizza, 98
Frèisa wine, 137
French beans, 130
salad, 161
sformato, 167
and tunny, 28, 43, **46**
French cooking:
influenced Parma, 174
omelettes not to be found in Italy, 93
sauces unlike Italian, 189
use of:
cream, 31
fennel, 25
garlic, 28
rice, 81
saffron, 27
soft cheese, 30
thyme, 24
Frittata, 132
di carciofi, 164
al formaggio, 94-5
Genovese, 95
Frittatine imbottite, 96-7
Frittelle, 20, 44, **96**, 173
di arigusta, 114
Fritto misto, 31, **135-6**, 137, 164
alla fiorentina, 136
di mare, 117
milanese, 136
di verdure, 169
Frogfish, 102, 109, *121*
See also Angler fish
Fromages glacés, 184
Frugoli, Antonio, 214
Fruit (Frutta), 179-81
candied, 182, 193, 197
in Italian sauces, *see* Agrodolce
mustard, 124, 157, 197

salad, 179
See also Preserves
Frying pans, 37
Fumet; fumets, 83, 189
Funghi, 43, varieties, 162
  beccafichi al nido, 157
  fritti, 162, **163**
  à la génoise, 163
  alla graticola, 262
  insalata di, 45, 162, riso e, 45
  minestra di, 56
  ovoli, 162
  polenta pasticciata, 90
  e piselli, tonnellini con, 67-70
  pizza, 93, 98
  porcini, 162
  ripieni, 163
  risotto di, 85
  salsa di, alla veronese, 193
  secchi, 29
  tonnarelle alla paesana, 70
  in umido, 162, **163**
  uova mollette con, e formaggio, 95
Futurist dishes, Marinetti invents, 61

Gaeta, olives of, 51
Galleani, Giuseppe, 213
Gallinaccio, 162
Gallinella, 102
Gamberi:
  imperiali, 115
  salsa di, 193
  zuppa di pesce coi, 104
Gamberoni, 44
Game, 26, 27, 29, 151
  recipes, 156-9
Garbanzos, 30
Garfish, 120
Garlic:
  croûtons, 101
  in Italian cooking, 28
  sauce, 111
Gastronomia Parmense, 217
Gazzoni, Tommaso, 26, 73
Gelati, 184-7
Gelato:
  di albicocche, 185
  di caffè, 185
  di fragole, 185
Genoa; Genoese, 197
  beef stew, 140
  cappon magro, 125-6
  cèpes à la génoise, 163
  clams, 112
  cooking, 213
  Easter Cake, 164
  faina, 30
  fish, market, 109
    salad, 125-6
    soup, 116-17

stew, 101, 102, 109
hors d'œuvre, 44
olive oil in cooking of, 31
minestrone, 57-8
mushroom salad, 45
octopus, 116
omelette, 95
pasta, 67
pecorino cheese, 207
pesto, 20, 23, 28, 53, 67, **193-4**
pizza, 93
ravioli, 26, **77-8**
rice, 83
risotto, 33
salame, 145
sauce, 190
sea dates; sea truffles, 43, **112**
spice trade, 26
stuffed cold veal, 129, **135**
veal, 131-2
zimino, 116
Genova la superba, noisiest city on
  earth, 109
Gente rubia, 151
Gervais cheese, 93
Ghinelli, Prof., *Le Conserve di Carne*,
  23, 144, 213
Gianchetti, 44
Gianduia, 201
Gianduiotti, 137
Giarre, 184
Giglio, 211
Ginepro, 26
Gioddù cheese, 207
Giudea, carciofi alla, 164-5
Giulia, cook to Derek Hill, 79
  her recipe for green ravioli, 78-9
Glaze, 189
Gnocchi, 19, 37, 73, **78-9**
  cream cheese, 79
  with pesto, 194
  di polenta, 89
  potato (di patate), 70, 140, 190
    and chicken liver sauce, 190
  di ricotta, 79
  semolina (di semolino), 19, **79**
  spinach (verdi), 19, 20, 30, **78-9**
Goat's milk cheeses, 206
Goethe, Johann Wolfgang, 221
Goncourt brothers, 221
Gorgonzola, 206
Gosetti della Salda, Anna, 214-15
Grana, 29, 205
Grancevole, 45
Granita, 187
  coffee (al caffè), 185
  lemon (di limone), 185
  strawberry (di fragole), 185
Green peas, 20, 101
  history, 161
  and ham, 166-7

with pigeons, 156
with rice, **84-5**, 86, 166
sformato of, 167
soup, 58
with stewed beef, 140
with tonnellini and mushrooms,
  67-70
with veal stew, 132
Green rice, 86
Green sauce, 195
Gremolata, 132
Greve, 210-11
Grifole, 162
Grill, 38, 110-11, 157
Grissini, 137
Gros sel, 28
Grottaferrata, wine, 209
Groviera, 30, **206**
Gruyère, 30, 43, 74, 86, 93, 96, 206
Guidebooks, 217-18

Haddock in white wine, 121
Ham, 29, 43, 45
  calzone, 94, **98**
  with chicken and cheese, 152
  cooked, 29, 50
  with eggs and macaroni, 66
  with fried eggs and cheese, 94
  with fruit mustard, 197
  green peas and, 166-7
  in Italian cooking, 129
  pizza, 93
  Parma, 35, 43, 179
    how cured, 144
    how eaten, 50
    not smoked, 144
    Roman Apicius's recipe, 144
    raw, 29
  San Daniele, 43, 50, 211
  sauce, 29, **192**
  stuffing for chicken, 153
  tagliatelle and, 64
  and veal and cheese, 131
  and veal and marsala, 131
  veal leg larded with, 132
Hare, 151
  Cephalonian, 159
  marinading of, 34
  with pappardelle, 66, 192
  in sweet-sour sauce, 158, 193
  stewed with pine nuts and
    sultanas, 158-9
Haricot beans, 21
  with bollito, 138, 161
  with cotechino, 146, 161
  in minestrone, 57-8
  in the oven, **89**
  salad of, with tunny, 46
  soup of Tuscan, 56
  and tomato sauce, 66

with zampone, 146, 161
Harrods, 26, 28
Hazan, Victor, *Italian Wine*, 210, 212
Hazan, Marcella, 215
Herbs, 23-6
Herring:
  au gratin, 119
  grilled, 111
  roe and prawn soup, 105
Hill, Derek, his Tuscan cook, 79
Holinshed, 26
Hollandaise sauce, 189
Hors d'œuvres: Salads, 43-51, 221
  anchovies and mushrooms, 45
  artichoke hearts, with
    mayonnaise, 46
    with peas, broad beans etc., 43
  artichokes, raw, 43, **46**
  beef, dried, 51
  beetroot, 28
    leaf, 161
  broad beans, 161
  broccoli, 161
  caponata alla marinara, 50
    Sicilian, 169
  chard, 161
  crab, 43, 44, **45**
  dressing for, 28, 44, **195**
  eggs, stuffed with spinach, 47
    with tunny mayonnaise, 47
  fennel, and cucumber, 48
    and gruyère, 43
    and radish, 48
    raw, 161
  french beans, 161
    with tunny, 28, 43, **46**
  Genoese, 44
  green salad, 134, 161
  ham, cooked, 43, 50
    and figs or melon, 43
    Parma, 43, **50**
  hot variety of, 43-4
  lake sardines, 48
  mixed antipasto, 48
  mullet roe, 50
  mushrooms, raw, **45**, 162
    and scampi, 44
    and shell fish, 44
    in vinegar, 43
  olives, 43, 51
    stuffed, 51
  pimentos, with anchovies and
    capers, 48
    in oil, 43, 46
    Piedmontese, 48
    preserved, for, 200
    with tunny, 48
    yellow, 45
  polpettone of tunny, 47
  pork, rump cured, 50
    salt, and spaghetti, 66

potato, salad, 48
  and tunny salad, 28, **47**
radish leaves, in salads for, 161
rice, salads, 45
  and chicken, salad, 45, 152, **153**
  and scampi, 45
  and shellfish, 45
salame, 50
sheep's milk cheese and broad
  beans, 44
shellfish, on fried bread, 45
  salad, 44
spinach, 161
sturgeon, 122
tomato, 48
  stuffed with tunny, 47
tongue, with green sauce, 51
  salad, 51
truffles, 137
tunny, on bread, 47
  with french beans, 43, **46**
    and onion, 47
  with red pimentos, 43
  with Tuscan beans, 28, **46**
  roe, 50
Horseradish with green sauce, 195
Hungarian salame, 145
Hunter, W. A., *Romance of Fish Life*,
  116

Ice cream: ices, **181-7**, 213, 214, 215
  apricot, 185
  churner, 187
  coffee, 185
  custard for, 185
  digestive properties of, 154
  granite (water ices), 185
  history, 181-4, 219, 220
  made in refrigerator, 187
  strawberry, 185
Imam bayeldi, 168
Importers of Italian products, 34-5
Independent, The, 210
Inkfish, 102, 103, 104
  in burrida, 102
  to clean, 116
  in fritto misto, 117
  preserved, 200
  and scampi, 115
  stewed, 33, **116-17**
Insalata di frutta, 179
Insalate, *see* Antipasti
Ischia, anchovies of, 119
Istrian spinach soup, 56
Italian cooking:
  books on, 213-16
  colour of, 20
  equipment, 37-41
  faults of, 19
  fresh materials in, 19, 21

lavishness, 19
regional nature of, 81, 145, 173-4,
  205-7
  spices used in, 26-8
  typical ingredients, 129
Italian State Tourist Board, 86
Italy, southern:
  garlic, use of, 28
  meat dishes of, 129
  meat quality of, 129, 138
  olive oil, use of, 31
  peperonata, 169-70
  scarole ripiene, typical dish of, 169
  tomatoes of, 31
  tomato sauce, 189

Jarrin G. A., *Italian Confectioner*, 185
Jewish artichokes, 164-5
John Dory, 121
  roast, 110
Johnson, Arthur, 209
Johnson, Viola, 201, 209
Juniper berries, 26
  with mutton, to taste like roebuck,
  142
  with pork chops, 142
  with wood pigeons, 245
Jus, 189

Kettner, *Book of the Table*, 97, 122
Kid:
  roasted, 142
  Roman, 129
  in white wine, 142
Kidneys:
  stewed, 137, **148**
  with white wine and onions, 148
Kitchen equipment, 37
Klephti cooking, 141
Knives, 37

Labat, Jean-Baptiste, 221
Lacrima Christi, 209
Lagrein Rosato, 211
Lake sardines, 48
Lamb:
  with coriander, 27
  cutlets, Marinetti, 142
    with sformato, 167
  in risotto, 2
  roast, 24, **141-2**
  Roman, 129
Lambrusco di Sorbàra wine, 218
  conflicting opinions of, 218
Lampreys, 103, **120-1**
  roast, 110
Langouste, 112
Langoustine, 114

Lard, 31
Larks, 151, **157**
Lasagne:
  baked green (verdi al forno), 20,
  64-5, 190
  making of, 64-5
  col pesto, 67
Lassels, Richard, 221
Latini, Antonio: *La Scalco alla
  Moderna*, 181-2, 215
Latte, 31
  maiale al, 143
  patate al, 162
  pollo al, 153
Lauris, 165
Lauro, 26
Leghorn:
  fish stew, 102
  salt cod, 126
Lemon:
  granita, 185
  juice in salad dressing, 44
Lenticchie:
  e pasta minestra di, 56
  in umido, 91
Lentils:
  with bollito, 161
  brown or German, 91
  with cotechino, 146, 161
  red, unsuitable for Italian dishes, 91
  soup with pasta, 56
  stewed, **91**, 146
  with venison, 159
  with zampone, 146, 161
Lepre:
  in agrodolce, 158
  di Cephalonia, 159
  alla montanura, 158-9
  pappardelle con la, 66
    another recipe, 192
  salsa di, 192
Lesso rifatto, 141
Lievito, 33
Liguria; Ligurian:
  anchovies, 28
  curnieura, 99
  faina, 30
  figpeckers, 157
  green sauces, 189
  olive oil, 31, 32
  pesto, 53
  pizza, 93, 98-9
Limone, granita di, 185
Lina, Tuscan cook, 175
  her uncooked chocolate cake
    (torrone molle), 174-5
Lingua:
  di bue, insalata, 51
  con salsa verde, 51
  di castagne, 162
Liver, calf's, 24

with marsala, 148
Milanese, 146
Venetian, 146
Liver, chicken's:
  croûtons, 132, **153**
  with gnocchi, 190
  with rice, 86
  sauce, 190
  soup with peas, 55
Lobster, 84, 87, 101, 102, 114
  and caponata, 169
  fritters, 114
  of island of Ponza, 112
  of Sardinia, 112
Lodi, grana cheese of, 205
Lombardy and Lombard dishes, 213
  bresaola, 51
  cheeses, 206, 207
  crema di mascherpone, 174
  hams sent to Parma for maturing, 144
  polenta, 89
  rice and risotto, 81, 87
  veal, 129
  See also Milan; Milanese
Lonza, 43
Lotte, 121
Lotteringhi della Stufa, Maria, 215
Loup, or loup de mer, 120, 121
Lucca olive oil, 32
Luganeghe, 146
Lumache, 126-7
  in zimino, 127
Lunetta, 37

Macaroni, *see* Pasta
Macaroons, 29, 173
Maccheroni:
  alla carbonara, 66
  pasticcio di, all'anziana, 67
Mackerel:
  grilled, 111
  in paper, 111
Macrobius, 115
Mafalda's stuffed artichokes, 164
Mafarka, dolce, 177
Magalotti, Count Lorenzo, 184
Maggiorana, **24**
Maggiore, Lake, 122
Maiale:
  costa alla griglia, 142
  al latte, 143
Maionese, 194-5
  tonnato, 153, **195**
  verde, 194
Maldon salt, where to buy, 28
Mandorle, budino di, 175-6
Manzo:
  polpettone di, 134
  costa di, al vino rosso, 140
  ripieno arrosto, 141

stufato, alla genovese, 140
  al vino rosso, 140
Manzoni, *I Promessi Sposi*, 90
Marche, Le:
  brodetto, 102
  caciotto, 207
  Fabriano salame, 145
  pasta ascuitta, 67
Marinading, 33-4
  beef, 140
  eel, 125
  fish, 111
  mullet, 117
Marinetti, F:
  La Cucina Futurista, 62, 213
  his attempts to banish asciutta, 61
  his divorced eggs recipe, 95
  his fish and apple recipe, 125
  his friendship with Mussolini, 62
  his futurist recipes, 61
  his green rice recipe, 86
  his lamb cutlet recipe, 142
  his pheasant recipe, 157
  his rice and coffee recipe, 177
  his roses fried in batter, 177
Marinetti's lamb cutlets, 142
Marinotti estate, 209
Marjoram, **23-4**, 26
Markets, 50, 109-10
Marmora, Chevalier Albert de la,
    Voyage en Sardaigne, 141, 217
Marotta, Giuseppe, on spaghetti, 63
Marrows, baby, or courgettes, 167-8
  fried, 168
  spaghetti with sauce of, 71
  stewed, 168
  stuffed, 25, 28, 137, 161, **168**
  in sweet-sour sauce, 168
  and veal pie, 135
Marsala, 33
  carrots with, 166
  chestnuts with, 176
  in Italian cooking, 129
  liver with, 148
  piccate al, 130
  rabbit with, 157-8
  in risotto, 82
  sole with, 119
  turkey breasts with, 154
  zabaione, 179
Marseilles, 107
Mascherpone, Mascarpone, 31, 70-1,
    174, **206**
Matriciana, spaghetti alla, 66
Mayonnaise, 194
  green, 194
  Italian opinion of mustard as
    flavouring for, 194
  tunny-fish, 47, 153, **195**
Mazzancolle (mazzacuogni), 104, 115
Mazzella, Scipione, *Descrittione del*

Regno di Napoli, 220
Measures, 39-41
  tables, 40-1
Measuring jug, 40
Meat, 129-49
  cold, with fruit mustard, 197
    with green horseradish sauce,
    195
  and peperata, 195
  roll, 134
  sauce, 190
  stock, 33
Medici, Catherine de, 181, 215, 219
Medici, Marie de, 219
Mediterranean, Eastern, 50
Melanzane, 168
  caponata, 169
  caponata alla marinara, 50
  a funghetti, 168
  parmigiana, 168-9
  purè, 169
  ripiene, 25, 28, 161, **169**
  in sformato di vitello, 135
Melon and ham, 43, 50
Menta, **24**, 53
Mentuccia, 34
Merli, 26, **157**
Mezzaluna, 37
Michelin Guide to Italian hotels and
    restaurants, 217
Midolla di pane, 31
Migliaccio, 157
Migliari, Maria Luisa, 216
Milan; Milanese, 61, 197
  calf's liver, 146
  cooking, 57
  panettone, 173
  polenta pasticciata, 89, **90**
  risotto, 27, 33, **81-2**, 87, 132
  salame, 145
  stewed pork (casoeula), 143
  stewed shin of veal (ossi buchi), 132
  veal cutlets, 130
  veal escalopes, 130
  See also Lombardy; Lombard
    dishes
Milk, 31, 182
  chicken in, 153
  pork in, 143
  potatoes in, 162
Miller, Lady, 221
Mincer, 38
Minestre; Zuppe, 30, 33, **53-9**, 73
  asciutta, minestra, 73
  brodetto alla ravennata, 102
  brodo, di manzo, 54
    ristretto, 54
  budino di pollo in brodo, 55
  burrida, 102
  busecca, 137
  cacciucco livornese, 102-3

  con ceci, 30
  di castagne, 56
  di cozze, 104
  crema, di piselli, 58
    di pollo, 59
    di pomidoro, 59
  di fagioli alla toscana, 56
  fredde, 59
  di funghi, 56
  di lenticchie e pasta, 56
  paparot, 56
  passatelli, 54-5
  pasta in brodo, con fegatini e
    piselli, 55
    al pesto, 55
  di patate, 56
  pavese, 54
  di peoci, 104
  di pesce, caprese, 104
    coi gamberi, 104
    alla romana, 103
  di pomidoro, 59
  stracciatella, 54
  di vercolore, **58**, 59
  di vongole, 105
  zimino, 116
    lumache in, 127
    seppie e calamari in, 116-17
  ziminù, 110, 116
Minestrone, 33, 53, 56-7
  genovese, **57-8**, 59
  with pesto, 194
  green (verde), 58
Mint, **24**, 26, 53
Mirto, **26**, 142
Misoltini, 48
Mixed fry, *see* Fritto misto
Modena:
  cotechino, 146
  grana, 205
  passatelli, 54-5
  wine of district, 210
  zampone, 146
Molecche, 112
Mollica di pane, 31
Molyneux, Adam de, 26
Monelli, Paolo, *Il Ghiottone Errante*,
    67, 217
Mont Blanc, 176
Mont Cenis, Lake, 137
Montaigne, Michel de, 210, 219,
    221-2
Montanura, lepre alla, 158-9
Monte Bianco, 176
Montepulciano wine, 209, 210
Montone uso capriolo, 142
Morene, 103, **120-1**
Mortadella, 19, 29, 43, 61, **146**
  supplì, 86
Morton, H. V., *A Traveller in Southern
    Italy*, 218

Morue, 126
Moryson, Fynes, 222
Moscardini, 43, 116, 117
Moscato, 137
  di Siracusa, 157
Mosta, Ranieri da, 215
Mostarda di Cremona, 124, 157, 197
Mouli-légumes, 37
Moussaka, 168
Mousse, chicken, in broth, 55
Mozzarella, 29-30, 86, **207**
  Bel Paese as alternative to, 29, 206
  in carrozza, 19, **95**
  buffalo milk, 207
  in crespolini, 97
  in crostini di provatura, 96
  and eggs, 94
  Milanese, 95
  pizza with, 97, 207
  rarity of genuine, 207
  smoked, 207
  supplì, 86
Muggine, *see* Mullet
Mullet, grey, 120
  grilled, 120
  roast, 110, 120
  roe, 50, 211
Mullet, red: 102
  fried, 31
  in fritto misto, 117
  grilled, 111, **117**
  marinaded, 117
  in paper, 111
  with pesto, 119
  roast, 110
Murry (Morene), 120-1
Mushrooms, 101, 130, **162**
  and bacon with tonnarelle, 70
  cèpes à la génoise, 163
  dried, 29
  with eggs and cheese, 95
  figpeckers in their nest, 157
  fried, 163
  and green peas with tonnellini, 67-70
  grilled, 162
  pizza, in, 93
  raw, salad of, 45, 162
    in salad with shellfish, 44
  and rice, 85, 86
  salad, 45
  sauce, 45, 167, 193
  and scampi salad, 43, 44
  soup, 56
  stewed, 28, **163**
    with mint, 24
  stuffed, 163
  Veronese sauce, 83, **193**
  in vine leaves, 163
  and vinegar, 43
Mussels, 43, 44, 67, 103, 104
  fisherman's, 112

on fried bread, 45
in Genoese fish stew, 102
in pizza, 93, **98**
risotto, 84
soup, 101, 104,
    Venetian, 104
in white wine, 111-12
Mussolini, 62
Mustard, 26
not used in Italian mayonnaise, 194
Cremona fruit, 124, 157, 197
Mutton, 26
Italian opinion of, 129
marinading of, 34
and marrow pie, 135
polpette, 134
roebuck flavour, supposedly with,
    142
risotto, 82
Myrtle, 26
with Sardinian roast sucking pig,
    142
with Sardinian thrushes (tàccula), 26
oil, highly esteemed by
    Sardinians, 26

Naples; Neapolitan, 219-20
aubergine pie, 168-9
beef steak in garlic and tomato
    sauce, 138
calzone, 94, **98**
cheeses of district, 207
cooking, 28, 66, 214
fettuccine alla marinara, 66
fish soups, described by Norman
    Douglas, 107
garlic and tomato sauce
    (pizzaiola), **138**, 189, 192
ices, 181-2, 184
mozzarella highly esteemed in, 207
olive oil in cooking, 31
pasta, 63
pastiera, 173
pizza, 20, 23, 93, **97**
rice (sartù), 85
snails, 127
sorbetti 181-2
spaghetti with clams, 67
salame, 145
sfogliatelle, 174
tomato concentrate, 31
Nasello alla griglia, 111
Nashe, Thomas, 179
Nebbiolo wine, 137
Nepitella, 24
Nerina, Zia and her trattoria, 30, 190
her recipe for ragù, 190
her method of preserving white
    truffles, 30
Neve, 184

Newnham-Davis, Lt-Col., *The
    Gourmet's Guide to Europe*, 32
describes a Piedmontese meal, 137
Nice, 30, 121
Nightingales, 151
Nîmes, 126
Noce moscata, 26-7
Noci, candite 201-3
chiocciole al mascherpone e, 70-1
salsa di, 195
Northcote, Lady Rosalind, *Book of
    Herbs*, 24
Norway lobsters, 114
Nougat, 173, 'soft', 174-5
Novara, 137
Nutmeg, much used in Italian
    cooking, 26-7
grater, 38

Octopus, 102, 103, 104, **115-16**
Olive oil (olio di oliva), 31-2, 44
Apulian, for frying fish, 110
basil preserved in, 200
importance of in Italian cooking, 129
in soup, 53
of Lucca, 32
new with baked bread, 99
prevents rice boiling over, 85
quality of important to Italians, 32
squid preserved in, 200
Olives (olive), 43, 45, 51
with Genoese antipasto, 44
in Ligurian pizza, 98-9
for picnic meals, 207
in Sicilian caponata, 169
in stuffed aubergines, 169
in stuffed Batavian endives, 169
stuffed (ripiene), 51
varieties of Italian, 51
with wood pigeons, 156-7
Ombrina, 121-2
Omelette, 93
artichoke hearts in, 164
cheese, 94-5
Genoese, 95
Italian method of cooking, 93
Onions:
with kidney and white wine, 148
Piedmontese stuffed, 170-1
stuffed, 25, 161, **170**
sweet-sour, 170
and tunny salad, 47
Oranges, 101
caramel, 178-9
Orata, 121
in white wine (al vino bianco), 121
Orfei, Benedetto, 197
Origano, **24**, 53, 129
Origoni e Schwarz, 213
Orioli G., *Moving Along*, 110, 119,

121, 125, 149, 151, 217
Oristano, 211
Oronges, 163
Ortolans, 157
Ossi buchi milanese, 81, 87, **132**
gremolata for, 132
risotto served with, 81, 132
Ostriche, 43, **115**
alla veneziana, 115
Ovarine, 190
Ovoli, funghi, 162
Oysters, 43, **115**
Venetian, 115

Padua struck by pestilence following
    death of bay trees, 26
soppresse salame, 145
Paesana, tagliatelle alla, 70
tonnarelle alla, 70
Paglierino cheese, 207
Palombacci alla perugina, 156-7
Palombo, 102, 107
arrosto, 110
Palourde, 112
Pancakes:
batter for, 96
with spinach and cheese, 97
stuffed, 96-7
Pancetta, 66, 144
Pane grattugiato, 30-1
Panettone, 173
Panforte di Siena, 27, 173
Panna, 31
Pannerone, 206
Paparot, 56
Pappagallo restaurant, Bologna, 30,
    55, 154
Pappardelle with hare sauce, 66
another recipe, 192
Parkinson, *The Earthly Paradise*, 23
Parma:
bomba di riso, 85
cooking, 217
influenced by French, 174
culatello di Zibello, 50; 144
Felino salame, 25, 144, 145
fesa col prosciutto, 132
ham, 35, 43, 179
how cured, 144
how eaten, 50
not smoked, 144
pancetta, 66, 144
pasticcio di anolini, 76
pastries of, 94, 174
pizzette, 94
pork specialities, 145
roll of beef or veal, 134
tomato concentrate, 31
tortelli di erbette, 27, **75-6**
tripe, 149

truffles, white with new
    Parmesan, 205
Parmesan cheese, 19, 29, 37, 53, 74,
    86, 93
how made, 205
sole with, 119
See also Grana
Parmigiana (aubergine pie), 168-9
Parsley, **25-6**, 38
in cheese paste, 194
in mayonnaise, 194
mushroom soup, gives unusual
    flavour to, 56
said to be of Sardinian origin, 25
Partridges:
in broth, 157
roast, 157
Passatelli, 54-5
Pasta asciutta, 20, 23, 37, 43, 53, 54, **61-71**
Anzio macaroni pie, 67
Bolognese tagliatelle, 64, 190
Bovino, Duke of, defends, 61
and chick peas, 30, 89
chiocciole al mascherpone e noci,
    70-1
alla chitarra, 67
controversy about, 61-2
cooking and serving, 63, 215
dish from the Marche, 67
fettuccine, home made, 62, 63, 64
with butter, 64
alla marinara, 66
and Genoese sauce, 190
with green peas, 166
lasagne, 55, 63
green baked (verdi al forno), 64-5
and ragù, 190
macaroni, 62, 63
with ham and eggs, 66
maccheroni alla cabonara, 66
alla marchigiana, 67
pasticcio di, all'anziana, 67
making of, 37, 62
Marinetti's attempts to abolish, 62-3
Marotta, Giuseppe, defines choice
    of, 63
and marrows, 167
origins of, 62
pappardelle with hare sauce (con
    la lepre), 66
with pesto, 194
alla pizzaiola, 192
with ricotta, 70
rigatoni with ham and eggs, 66
with salted sardines (con le sarde),
    67
sfogliatelle, 174
shells with cream cheese and
    walnuts, 70-1
spaghetti, 62, 63
with clams and tomato sauce, 28, **67**

with marrows (con salsa di zucchine), 71
alla matriciana, 66
with oil and garlic, 19, 28, **65**
with oil, garlic and red pepper (all'olio, aglio e saetini), 67
with pork and tomato, 66
with tomato sauce, 190
with tomato and marsala sauce, 192
with tunny sauce (col tonno), **70**, 193
alle vongole, 28, **67**
tagliatelle, 55, 62, 63, **64**
alla bolognese, 64
with ham, 64
with tomatoes, bacon and pork (alla paesana), 70
and walnut sauce, 195
tonnarelle with bacon and mushrooms (alla paesana), 70
tonnellini with mushrooms and green peas (con funghi e piselli), 67-70
trenette with pesto, 67
tuoni e lampo, 89
vermicelli, 63
al pomidoro, 61
with Veronese mushroom sauce, 193
with walnut and parsley sauce, 189
water of Naples district said to produce superior products, 63
water or wine, which drunk with pasta, 62
wheat flour, durum, for pasta products, 63
Pasta in brodo (clear broth), 62
cappelletti in brodo, 74-5
con fegatini e piselli, 55
passatelli, 54-5
al pesto, 55
ravioli in brodo, 74
Pasta frolla (pastry), 173
Pasta sfoglia, 173
turkey in, 154
Pasta in thick soups, minestre and minestrone, 56-8
lentil and, 56
minestra di lenticchie e, 56
Pastella, 114
Pasticciata:
with polenta, 89, **90**
Pasticcio di anoline, 76
Pasticcio di maccheroni all'anziana, 67
Pastiera napoletana, 173
Pastorella cheese, 206
Pastry, 173
board, important of for pasta making, 64, 74
cooks, Italian, fame of, 173

shops of Parma, 174
sweet, for apricot tart, 173
yeast, for pizza, 97-8
Patate, 138, **162**
arroste, 161
crocchetti di, 140, 161, **162**
fritte, 161
gnocchi di, 19, **79**, 140, 190
insalata di, 48
col tonno, 28, **47**
al latte, 162
purè di, 161
con uova, 94
torta di, 162
zuppa di, 56
Pavese, zuppa, 54
Peaches:
preserve of, 197, **200-1**
stuffed, 177-8
in white wine, 178
Pears and pecorino cheese, 207
Peas, chick, cooking of, 21, 30
and pasta, 89
and tomato sauce, 66
Peas, green, 20, 101
in broth, with chicken livers, 55
France, brought to from Genoa, 161
and ham, 166-7
history, 161
with pigeons, 156
with rice, **84-5**, 86, 166
Sévigné, Madame de, writes of, 161
soup, 58
sformato of, 167
with beef stewed in red wine, 140
with tonnellini and mushrooms, 67-70
with veal stew, 132
Pecorino cheese, 30, 53, 66, 207
Penna d'Oca, Milan restaurant, 61
Peoci,
risotto di, 84
zuppa di, 104
Pepe, **28**
Peperata, 195
Peperonata, 169-70
Peperoni:
all'aceto, 137, 200
con alici e capperi, 48
with la bagna cauda, 192
conserva, 46, 137, **198-200**
insalata di, gialli, 45
e riso, 45
alla piemontese, 48
ripieni, 25, 28, 161, **170**
sott'olio, 43, 46
col tonno, 48
Pepper, 26, 28
mill, 28, 38
red, 53, 67, 145
Peppermint, 24

Perch, 122
Pernici:
arrosti, 157
in brodo, 157
Persicata, 197, **200-1**
Perugia; Perugian:
cappelletti in brodo, 74-5
pinoccate, 173
roast pork, 142
veal escalopes, 132
wood pigeons, 156
Pescatrice, 102, 103, **121**
Pesce:
all'agliata, 111
arrosto, 110
in bianco, 111
boccone squadrista, 125
cappon magro, 125-6
in cartoccio, 111
ai ferri, 110
fritto, 110
fritto misto di mare, 117
alla graticola, 110
alla griglia, 110-11
marinato, 111
mercati, 109-10
persico, 122
prete, 102
San Pietro, 121
spada, 121
zuppe di, 101-7
See also Soups; Minestre; and names of individual fishes
Pesche:
ripiene, 177-8
in vino bianco, 178
Pescia, asparagus of, 165
Pestle and mortar, 38
Pesto, 20, 23, 28, 53, 55, 57-8, 67, 79, 119, 189, **193-4**
Petit, A., *La Gastronomie en Russie*, 157
Pheasant:
Futurist, Georgian, Norman Douglas's recipe, etc., 157
and fruit mustard, 197
Phoenician; Phoenicians:
saffron, their addiction to, 27
tripe, 149
Piacenza, 205
Piccate al marsala, 33, **130**
Piccioni coi piselli, 156
Piedmont; Piedmontese:
anchovies, 28
bagna cauda, 28, **192-3**
beans in the oven, **89**
bollito, 137-8
cheese fondue, 95
cheeses, 207
cooking, 31
Il Confetturiere Piedmontese, 202

described by Col. Newnham-Davis, 137
faina, 30
fasceil al fùrn, 89
fonduta, 30, **95**, 137, 206
fontina cheese, 91, 206
mascherpone, mascarpone, 31, 70-1, 174, **206**
mushrooms, 162
olive oil in cooking, 31
paglierino cheese, 207
pimentos, 48
rice, 81, 86, 87
robiola cheese, 206, 207
stuffed onions, 170-1
truffles, white, 30, 130, 137
wines, 210
Piegatura, 213
Pigeon in soup, 54
Pigeons:
bomba di riso, 85
with green peas, 156
Pigeons, wood, Perugian, 156-7
Pignoli, pinoli, *see*, Pine nuts
Pigs of Parma, how fed, 144
Pilchards, stuffed, 119
Pimentos, 20, 28, 43
with anchovies and capers, 48
with bagna cauda, 192
Piedmontese, 48
preserved, 46, 137, **198-200**
as hors d'œuvre, 43
and rice salad, 45
salad of yellow, 45
stuffed, 25, 28, 161, **170**
and tomato stew (peperonata), 169-70
with tunny, 28, 48
in vinegar, 137, 200
Pinado, 207
Pine nuts, 26, **29**, 34, 45, 129
in agrodolce sauce, 189, 193
biscuits of, 173
hare with, 158-9
in mayonnaise, 194
in pesto, 194
in sorbet, 182
Pineapple, 213
Pinoccate, 173
Pinoli, *see* Pine nuts
Piozzi, Hester, 222
Piselli, 20, 161
with manzo stufato, 140
pasta in brodo con fegatine, 55
piccioni coi, 156
al prosciutto, 166-7
risi e bisi, **84-5**, 86
con riso in bianco, 166
sformato di, 167
with spezzatino di vitello, 132
tonnellini con funghi e, 67-70

zuppa crema di, 58
Pissaladière, 93, 98
Pistaches, ragoût de, with Dumas's
    pheasant, 157
Pistachio nuts, 26, 142
    in green mayonnaise, 194
Pitigliano wine, 211
Pizza, 19, 29, **93-4**
    alla casaligna, 97
    con cozze, 93, **98**
    alla francescana, 98
    fried, 98
    Genoese, 93
    ham, 93
    Ligurian, 93, 98-9
    meaning of word, 94
    with mushrooms, 93, 98
    with mussels, 93, 98
    napoletana, 20, 23, 93, **97**,
    pizzette (little pizze), 44, 94, **98**
    Roman, 93
    rustica, 94, **98**
    sardenara, 98-9
    al tegame, 98
    yeast dough for, 33, 97
    yeast pastry for, 97-8
Pizzaiola, **138**, 189, 192
    bistecca alla, 138
Pizzeria, 93, 97
Pizzette, 44, 94, **98**
Plaice, grilled, 111
Platina, 121
Pliny, 126
Plover, golden:
    grilled, 157
    on its nest, 157
Poetto, Sardinia, 28
Pois chiches, 30
Polenta, 62, 87, **89-91**, 157, 159
    with casoeula, 143
    grassa, 91
    Manzoni writes of, 90
    pasticciata, 89, **90**
    with cream of salt cod, 126
    with seppie, 116
    in soup, 56
Polipetto, 116
Polipi, 115-16
Poliporo, 162
Pollame, 151-6
Pollo, 151
    budino di, in brodo, 55
    alla diavola, 152
    insalata di riso e, 152, **153**
    al latte, 153
    al marsala, 158
    in padella, a disappointing dish,
        151
    petti di, alla bolognese, 151, 152
        alla fiorentina, 151, **152**
    in pasta sfoglia, 154

in porchetta, 153
con riso, 83
risotto di, alla sbirraglia, 83
tonnato, 152, **153**
zuppa crema di, 59
Polo, Marco, 62, 181
Polpette, 20, 85, **134**
Polpettine di braccalà, 126
Polpettone, 134
    of tunny (di tonno), 28, **47**
Pomidoro, 31, 62
    concentrato di, 31
    conserva di, 198
    insalata di, 48
    minestra di, 59
    salsa di, 20, 23, 33, 66, 67, 85, 129,
        138, 189, **190-2**
        crudo, 195
        al marsala, 192
    col tonno, 47
    uova al piatto con, 94
    zuppa crema di, 59
Ponza, island, lobsters of, 112
Porceddù, 26, **142**
Porchetta, 24, 218
    pollo in, 153
Porcini, funghi, 29, 162
Pork, fresh:
    Bolognese cutlets, made with,
        130
    cappelletti, stuffed with veal and,
        73, **74-5**
    chops, grilled with fennel and
        juniper berries, 142-3
    with coriander, 27
    Emilian, 129
    fennel with, 142
    Florentine roast, 142
    with fruit mustard, 197
    with juniper berries, 26
    and marrow pie, 135
    Milanese stewed, 143
    in milk, 129, **143**
    Perugian roast, 142
    roll, 134
    Romagna, 129
    rosemary with, 24, 142
    Sardinian roast, 26, **142**
    sucking pig, fennel with, **25**, 142
    rosemary with, 24
    tagliatelle alla paesana, 70
Pork, salt and cured: 213
    coppa, 29, 35, 43, 66, 144
    cured, rump of, 50
    imports, 35
    pancetta, 66, 144
    Parma, ham and other products,
        35, 144
    salt, with maccheroni alla
        carbonara, 66
    with spaghetti and tomato, 66

See also Ham; Prosciutto
Porto Venere, 112
Positano, 71
Potatoes, 138, **162**
    croquettes, 140, 161, **162**
    fried, 161
    gnocchi, 79, 140, 190
    in milk, 162
    Italian methods with, 161
    pie, 162
    purée, 161
        with cotechino, 146, **161**
        with poached eggs, 94, 195
        with zampone, 146, 161
    roast, 161
    salad, 48
    sauté, 130
    soup, 56
    and tunny salad, 28, **47**
Poultry, 151-6
    and peperata, 195
    quality of in England and Italy,
        151
Praire, 112
Prawns, 31, 43, 44, 84
    Dublin Bay, 45, 114
    fish soup with, 104
    in fritto misto, 117
    in Genoese fish stew, 102
    imperial, 115
    sauce, 193
    with sformato of peas, 167
    soup, 101
        with roes, 105
        with scallops and cockles, 106
Preserves, 197-203
    basil, 200
    candied fruit, 182, 193, 197
    Cremona fruit mustard, 124, 197
    fig jam, 201
    peach, 200-1
    pimentos, 46, 137, **198-200**
        in vinegar, 200
    squid, 200
    tomatoes, 198
Prete, pesce, 102
Prezzemolo, **25-6**
Procacci, Cafè, 30
Prosciutto, 29
    cotto, 29, 50
    crudo, 29
    fesa col, 132
    di montagna, 50
    di Parma, 43, 50, **144**, 179
    piselli al, 166-7
    salsa di, 29, **192**
    di San Daniele, 43, 50, 211
    tagliatelle con, 64
Provatura cheese, 96
Provence, 28, 50, 93, 98, 120, 121, 126,
    168

Provola, 207
    di pecora, 207
Provolone, 30, 74, 86, 93, 96, 97, 207
Pudding:
    almond, 175-6
    cream cheese, 174
    an Italian, 175
    Mont Blanc, 176
    Tuscan, 174
Puglie, olives of, 51
Pumpkin, candied, 184

Quaglie, alla grigtra, 157
    risotto con, 82-3
Quagliette:
    di vitello, 135
    or pork or lamb, 135
Quails:
    grilled, 157
    risotto, 82-3
    roast with polenta, 90
Quantities, 38
Quince paste, 197

Rabbit in marsala, 157-8
Radish (radicchie):
    leaves used for salad, 161
    and fennel salad (insalata di
        finocchi e), 48
Rafano, salsa verde al, 195
Ragù bolognese, 31, 189, **190**
Rana or pescatrice, fish, 121
Ratatouille, 168
Ravanelli, in salads, 161
Ravello wine, 209-10
Ravenna Marina, 87, 102
    fish soup of (brodetto), 102
Raviggiolo cheese, 207
Ravioli, 19, 20, 29, 37, 63, **73-8**
    caprese, 73, **74**, 96, 97
    delicacy of ruined by heavy
        sauces, 73
    Genoese, 26, **77-8**
    green, 30, **78-9**
    Italy, how served in 73
    Parma, 27
    verdi, 30, **78-9**
Ray, Cyril, 212
Ray, Rev. John, 222
Réchauffé of boiled meat, 141
Red-currant jelly in sauces, 34, 159,
    193
Redi, Francesco, 184
Reggio di Calabria, 151
Reggio Emilia, 205
Reresby, Sir John, 223
Ricci, 115
Ricciarelli, 173
Rice, 33, 62, **81-7**

with beef scraps, 82
boiled, 37, 85-6
and coffee sweet (dolce Mafarka),
  177
croquettes, 31, 86
with eggs, 95
with fonduta, 86
with four cheeses, 86
Genoese, 83
French cooking of, 81
green, 86
with green peas, 84
Italian cooking of, unique, 81
with lamb, 82
with mushrooms, 85
Piedmontese, 81, 86
pigeons and, 85
and prawn sauce, 193
salads, 45
with chicken, 45, 152, **153**
with scampi, 45
risotto, 81, 86-7
  chicken, 83, 152
  with chicken liver sauce, 86
  with clams or cockles, 84
  with green peas, 84-5
  milanese, 33, **81-2**, 132
    served with ossi buchi, 81, 132
  with mussels, 84
  and prawns, 83-4
  rice for, 87
  with quails, 82-3
  in salto (fried), 84
  with scampi, 83-4
  shellfish, 83, 87
  with tunny fish sauce, 193
  veronese, 83, 193
  white, 82, 83, 84, 156
  of the wine cellar, 86-7
with scampi, 45
sartù, 85
with sugo, 86
and tomato sauce, 66
with tunny, 86
with white truffles, 30, **86**
Richardin, Edmond, *L'Art du Bien
  Manger*, 163, 169
Ricotta, 19, 29-30, **207**
al caffé, 174
alternatives to, 99
in green gnocchi, 78
gnocchi, 79
nutmeg with, 27
with pasta, 70
in puddings and sweet dishes, 173,
  174
Roman, 207
in sfogliatelle, 174
tortini di, 96
Ricottelle, 182
Rigaglie, 85

Rigani, 23
Rigatoni alla carbonara, 66
Rimini, fish soup of, 102
Riso, 62, **81-7**
in bianco, 85-6
  con tartufi bianchi, 86
bomba di, 85
con la fonduta, 86
gamberi, con salsa di, 193
alla genovese, 83
coi piselli, 166
ai quattro formaggi, 86
ricco, 86
risotto, 81, 86-7
  bianco, **82**, 83, 84, 156
  e bisi, 84-5
  in brodo, 33
  in cantina, 86
  in capro roman, 82
  di frutti di mare, 83
  alla genovese, 33
  alla milanese, 27, 33, **81-2**
    served with ossi buchi, 81, 132
  di peoci, 84
  prosciutto in, 29
  con quaglie, 82-3
  in salto, 84
  alla sbirraglia, 83, 152
  di scampi, 83-4
  di secole, 82
  for supplì, 86
  con tartufi, 30
  tonno, con salsa di, 193
  alla veronese, 83, 193
risoverdi, 86
sartù di, 85
supplì di, 86
con tartufi, 30, **86**
uova col, 95
Ritortelli, 73
Robiola; Robiolina, 206, 207
Rock salmon, 101
Roes, soft in soup, 101, 105
Roebuck, mutton to taste like, 142
Rognoni:
  con cipolle e vino bianco, 148
  rifolati, 137, **148**
Rolé di vitello, 132-3
Rolling pin, 37
Romagna, dishes of:
  cappelletti, 74
  cotechino, 146
  pork, 129
  sausages, 146
  truffles, 30
Romana, zuppa di pesce alla, 103
Rome, ancient, cooking, 26, 33, 115,
  120-1, 126
  Apicius's ham, 144
Rome; Roman, 219
  abbacchio, 24, 141-2

artichokes, 164
asparagus, 165
beef stew, 140
broad beans and bacon, 166
cappelletti, 74
cooking, 24, 53, 213
coppa, 43
crostini di provatura, 28, **96**
fish soup, 103, 121
kid, 129
lamb, 129
maccheroni alla carbonara, 66
olive oil in cooking of, 31
olives, 51
peas, 166
pecorino, 66, **207**
pizza, 93
ricotta, 29, 207
spaghetti alla matriciana, 66
  alle vongole, 28, **67**
stracciatella, 54
Roncarati, Bruno, 212
Root, Waverley, 215
Roquefort cheese, 206
Rose diaboliche, 177
Rosemary (rosmarino), **24-5**, 26
  excessive use of, 24
Rospo, 121
Ross, Janet, 223
Rossi, Emanuele, *La Vera Cuciniera
  Genovese*, 77, 213
Rossini, 30
Rosticcerie, 157, 167
  Genoese, 135
  Sardinian, 26

Saffron, 26, **27-8**, 149
  method of using in risotto
    milanese, 81-2
Sage, 24, 26
Saint Paulin cheese, 93
Sala, George A., *The Thorough Good
  Cook*, 57, 122, 175
Salad:
  fruit, 179
  green served with various dishes,
    134, 161
  See also Hors d'œuvres
Salame, 28, 35, 43, 50, **145-6**
  best, unobtainable in England, 50
  cacciatori, 145-6
  cotechino, 137, 143, **146**
  crespone, 145
  Danish, 50
  Fabriano, 145
  Felino, 25, 144, 145
  finocchiona, 25, 145
  Florentine, 25, 145
  Genovese, 145
    with raw broad beans and cheese, 44

Hungarian, 145
Irish, 50
Milano, 145
mortadella, 19, 43, 61, **146**
  in supplì, 86
napoletano, 145
sardo, 145
how served, 50
soppresse, 145
ungherese, 145
zampone, 146, 161
Sale, 28
Salerno, 207, 209
Salmon:
  boiled as for ombrina, 122
  grilled, 111
  in paper, 111
Salse, 189-95
  agliata, 111
  agrodolce, 27, 29, 151, 156, 158, 159,
    168, 170, 171, 189, 193
  la bagna cuada, 28, **192-3**
  besciamella, 26, 65, 189, **192**
  di ciliegie, 159
  di fegatini, 79, 86, **190**
  fonduta, 86, **95**, 137, 206
  di funghi, 167
    alla veronese, 83, **193**
  di gamberi, 193
  genovese, 79, **190**
  per insalata, 44, 195
  di lepre, 66, 192
  maionese, 189, **194**
    tonnata, 153, **195**
    verde, 194
  alla marinara, 189
  di noci, 195
  peperata, 195
  pesto, 20, 23, 28, 53, 55, 57-8, 67, 79,
    119, 189, **193-4**
  di piselli, 166
  pizzaiola, **138**, 189, 192
  di pomidoro, 20, 23, 33, 85, 189,
    190-2
    crudo, 195
    al marsala, 192
  di prosciutto, 29, **192**
  ragù, 189, **190**
  sugo di carne, 189, **190**
  di tartufi, 137
  di tonno, **134-5**, 153, **193**
  verde, 51, 111, 117, 138, 189, **195**
  al rafano, 195
  di zucchine, 71
Salsicce alla romagnola, 146
Salsomaggiore, amaretti of, 173
Salt, 28
Salt beef, dried, 51
Saltimbocca, 131
Salvia, **24**, 26
San Daniele ham, 43, 50, 211

San Gimignano wine, 209, 210, 211
San Pietro, pesce, 121
San Secondo, spalla di, 144
Sandwich:
    fried cheese, 19, 96
    and polenta, 89
    of walnut sauce, 195
Sandys, George, *Relation of a Journey*, 220, 223
Santa Margherita, fish market, 109-10
Sarde:
    pasta con le, 67
    ripiene, 119
Sardenara, 98-9
Sardines:
    lake, 48
    salted with pasta, 67
    stuffed, 119
Sardinia; Sardinian, 151, 217-18, 219
    blackbirds, 26
    boar, 159
        ham, 151
    brigand cooking, 141
    buttàriga, 50, 211
    clams, 112
    faina, 30
    fetta, 207
    fish cooking, 110
        soup (siminù), 110, 116
    flamingoes, 151
    gioddù, 207
    langouste, 112
    larks, 151
    myrtle, 26, 142
        oil used for frying, 26
    olives, 32, 51
    parsley, originated in, 25
    pecorino (sardo), 44, 207
        in pesto, 193-4
    roast sucking pig, 26, **142**
    roasting or baking, 141
    saffron, 27
    salame, 145
    salt, 28
    Sardinia and the Sardes, 151, 159, 217
    sardo (pecorino), 44, 145, 207
        in pesto, 193
    tàccula (thrushes), 26
    tunny, 28
    Voyage en Sardaigne, 141, 217
    wine, 211
    ziminù, 110, 116
Sardo cheese, 44, 145, 207
    in pesto, 53, 193-4
Sartù di riso, 85
Sassari, 26, 32
Saucepans, 37, 38, 85, 90
Sauces, 45, 189-95
    agrodolce, 27, 29, 151, 156, 158, 159, 168, 170, 171, 189, 193

bagna cauda, 28, **192-3**
béchamel, 26, 65, 189, **192**
cherry, 159
chicken liver, 79, 86, **190**
fondue, cheese, 86, **95**, 167, 206
garlic, 111
Genoese, 79, **190**
green, 51, 111, 117, 138, 189, **195**
    with horseradish, 195
green pea, 166
ham, 29, **192**
hare, 66, 192
Italian, basic ingredients of, 189
alla marinara, 189
marrow, 71
mayonnaise, 189, **194**
    green, 194
    tunny, 195
meat, 189, **190**
mushrooms, 167
    Veronese, 193
for mutton to taste like roebuck, 142
olive oil and pimentos, 67
paesana, 70
pesto, 20, 23, 28, 53, 55, 57-8, 67, 79, 119, 189, **193-4**
prawn, 193
ragù, 189, **190**
salad dressing, 28, 44, **195**
tomato, 20, 23, 33, 85, 189, 190-2
    and garlic, **138**, 189, 192
    with marsala, 192
    raw, 195
tunny, 28, **134-5**, 153, **193**
walnut, 195
walnut and cream cheese (for pasta), 70-1
Sausages, Romagna, 146
Savarin, Jeanne, 28
Sbirraglia, risotto alla, 83
Scales, 40
Scallops, 44
    grilled, 111
    prawn and cockle soup, 106
    with sformato of peas, 167
    soup, 105
    stewed, 114
Scaloppe:
    farcite, 131
    milanese, 130
Scaloppine, 33, 167
    al marsala, 130
    alla perugina, 132
    di vitello battuto, 132
Scamorza, 207
Scampi (Dublin Bay prawns or Norway lobsters), 31, 43, 103, 104, **114**
    boiled, 114
    fried (fritti), 114
    frozen, 114

grilled (alla griglia), 115
    and inkfish, 115
    lessati, 114
    and mushrooms, 43, 44
    and rice, 83-4
    and rice salad, 45
    stewed (in umido), 114
Scappi, Bartolomeo, *Cuoco Secreto del Papa Pio Quinto*, 38, 213, 216
Scarole:
    ripiene, 169
Scissors, 38
Sciule piene, 170-1
Scomiglia, 182
Scott, Jack Denton, 215
Scott, Leader, *Tuscan Scenes and Sketches*, 157, 162
Scropetta, Michele, 62
Sea dates, 43, 109, **112**, 218
Sea eels, 120-1
Sea hen, 102, 109
Sea truffles, 43, 109, **112**
Sea urchins, 115
Secole, risotto di, 82
Sedano, 25
Selfridges, 26, 28
Sel gris, gros, 28
Semi di finocchio, 25
Semola, 63
Semolina, 63
    gnocchi, 79
Seppie, 43, 102, **115-16**
    e calamari in zimino, 116-17
    alla veneziana, 116
Serpentaria, 26
Sévigné, Mme de, 161
Sfogliatelle, 174
Sformato, 161, **167**
    french beans (di fagliolini), 167
    green peas (di piselli), 167
    other vegetables, 167
    veal and marrows (di vitello e zucchine), 135
Shakespeare, *Richard II*, 26
Sheep's milk cheeses, 206
Shellfish:
    on croûtons, 45
    with raw mushrooms, 44
    risotto, 83
    salad, 44
    and rice salad, 45
    See also Fish and names of individual fishes
Sherbet, 181-4, 213
Shoonmaker and Marvel, *Complete Wine Book*, 218
Shrimps, 43
    potted, 50
Sicily; Sicilian, 219, 220, 223
    canestrato cheese, 207
    caponata, 169

figs, 179
olives, 51
oranges, 178
pasta con le sarde, 67
stuffed sardines, (Orioli's recipe), 119
swordfish, 121
Siena; Siennese:
    pastry, 173
    panforte, 27, 173
    pecorino, 207
    tarragon, used in cooking, 26
Simetti, Mary Taylor, 223
Siren Land, Norman Douglas, 107
Sitwell, Osbert, *Winters of Content*, 218
Skewers, 37
Smith, Michael, 87
Smollett, Tobias, *Travels through France and Italy*, 112, 121, 159, 218
Smyth, *Sardinia*, 156
Snails, 126-7
    stewed, 127
Snipe with mushrooms, as for beccafichi al nido, 157
Socca, 30
Soffritto, battuto, 117, **190**
Sole (sogliola), 102, 121
    grilled, 111
    al marsala, 119
    with parmesan (alla parmigiana), 119
    and tarragon, 26
    with Venetian sauce (alla veneziana), 119-20
    in Venice, 119-20
Soppresse salame, 145
Sorbàra, Lambrusco di, 218
Sorbet, 181-2, 187
Sorbetières, electrical, 187
Sorbetta d'aurora, 184
Sorrento, 207, 209
    veal of, 129
Soups, 25, 33, **53-9**
    bean, Tuscan, 56
    beef consommé, 54
    brodetto of Adriatic, 102
    broth, cappelletti in, 74-5
        pasta in, with chicken livers and peas, 55
        ravioli in, 74
    burrida, 101, **102**
    cacciucco, 102-3
    Capri fish, 104
    cheese ravioli, 74
    chestnut, 56
    chicken, cream of, 59,
        mousse in broth, 55
    clam, 101, **105**
    cold, 59
    concentrated consommé, 54

consommé, pasta in, with pesto, 55
cuttle fish etc., 116
fish, 20, 33, 53, **101-7**
  Norman Douglas denounces, 107
  English, 105-6
  with prawns, 104
  Genoese, fish stew, 102 (burrida), 110, 116 (zimino)
  minestrone, 57-8
green, **58**, 59
  minestrone, 58
green pea, 58
  ham in, 29
Leghorn fish stew, 102
lentil with pasta, 56
  and tomato, 53
minestrone, 33, 56-7
mushroom, 56
mussel, 101, **104**
passatelli, 54-5
pasta in broth with chicken livers and peas, 55
  in consommé with pesto, 55
Pavese chicken broth and eggs, 54
pesto with, 194
potato, 56
prawn, 101
  and herring roe, 105
Ravenna fish, 102
Roman, chicken broth and eggs, 54
Roman, fish, 103
Sardinian fish, 110, 116
scallop, 105
snails in, 127
spinach, 28, **56**
stracciatella, 54
tomato, 59, cream of, 59
tripe and vegetable, 137
Tuscan bean, 28, **56**
Venetian mussel, 104
zimino, 116
ziminù, 110, 116
zuppa pavese, 54
Spada, pesce, 121
Spaghetti, 62, 63
  all aglio e oilo, 19, 28, **65**
  con funghi e piselli, 67
  alla matriciana, 66
  all'olio, aglio e saetini, 67
  con salsa di zucchini, 71
  col tonno, **70**, 193
  alle vongole, 28, **67**
  See also Pasta
Spalla, 29, di San Secondo, 144
Spanish, possible origin of baccalà mantecato, 126
Spanish olives, 51
Spannocchio, 115
Spectator, 210, 214
Spezie (spices), **26-8**

Spezzatino di vitello, 132
Spices (spezie), **26-8**
Spigola, 102, **121**, 125
Spinach (spinaci):
  with anchovies (all'acciughe), 166
  with bollito, cotechino, etc., 161
  crespolini, 97
  croquettes (crocchette di), 31, **166**
  eggs stuffed with, 47
  Genoese omelette (frittata genovese), 95
  gnocchi, 19, 20, 30, 73
  gnocchi verdi (ravioli), 78-9
  lasagne verdi, 64
  nutmeg, good flavouring for, 27
  in pancakes with cheese, 97
  paparot, 56
  salad, 161
  sformato, 167
  soup, 28, **56**
  with sultanas, 166
  in tortelli di erbette, 73, 76, 97
  uova sode agli, 47
  con uvetta, 166
Sprats au gratin, 119
Squid, 31, 43, 102, **115-16**
  to clean, *see* Inkfish
  stewed, 116
  and cuttlefish in zimino, 116
  in fritto misto, 117
  preserved, 200
Squilla, 87
Stefani, Bartolomeo, 215
Stendhal at Civitavecchia, 164
Stoccafisso, *see* Baccalà; Cod, salt
Stock, 33, 54
Storione, 43, **122**
  roast, 110
Stove, 38
Stracchini gelati, 184
Stracchino cheese, 206
Stracciatella, 54
Stracotto, 27, **140-1**
  in stuffing for anolini, **76**, 141
Strawberries:
  wild, 181
Strawberry:
  granita, 185
  ice cream, 185
Strutto, 31
Stufatino alla romana, 140
Stufato di manzo, alla genovese, 140
  al vino rosso, 140
Sturgeon, 43, **122**
  roast, 110
Sucking pig, 24, 25
  Sardinian roast, 26, **142**
Sugar:
  brought to Europe by Venetian traders, 173

vanilla, 27
Sugo di carne, 189, 190
  and rice, 86
Sultanas, 26
  in brandy and lemon leaves, 197
  with hare and pine nuts, 158-9
  and spinach, 166
  in sweet-sour sauces, 189, 193
Supplì, 86
Sweets, 173-87, 214
Swiss: bouillon cubes, 33
  origin of bresaola, 51
Swordfish, 121

Tacchino:
  arrosto ripieno, 156
  filetti, bolognese, 20, 151, **153-4**
  in pasta sfoglia (Margaret Rose), 154
  al marsala, 154
  stufato al vino bianco, 154-5
Tàccula, 26
Tagliatelle, 63-4
  alla bolognese, 64, 190
  with ham (col prosciutto), 64
  with hare (con la lepre), 66
  with pesto, 67
  with walnut sauce (salsa di noci), 195
  See also Pasta
Tagliolini, 30
Taleggio; Taleggino, cheeses, 206
Tarragon, 26
Tart, apricot, 176
Tartine al tonno, 47
Tartufi bianchi, **30**, 137, 154, 162, 201, 214
  with bagna cauda, 192
  with costolette bolognese, 130
  with filetto di tacchino alla bolognese, 30, 153
  with fonduta, 95, 205
    alla parmigiana, 205
  with petti di pollo alla bolognese, 152
  with polenta pasticciata, 90
  with riso in bianco, 86
  tortellini bolognese, in stuffing for, 77
  uova strapazzate con, 93
Tartufi di cioccolata, 176
Tartufi di mare, 112
Tartufoli, 112
Tegamino, 37
Temperature equivalents, 38-9
Thrushes, 26, 157
Thyme (timo), **24**
Timing, 38
Tomatoes, 31, 214, 220
  and eggs, 94
  concentrate of, 31

preserved, 198
raw for sauce, 195
salad, 48
sauce, 20, 23, 33, 66, 67, 85, 129, 138, 189, **190-2**
  with Marsala, 192
soup, 59
  cream of, 59
stuffed with tunny, 47
varieties of for salad, for sauce, 31
Tomini del Talucco cheese, 207
Tongue:
  with green sauce, 51
  salad, 51
Tonnarelle; Tonnellini, *see* Pasta
Tonnetto, 104
Tonno, 120
  e cipolle, insalata di, 47
  fagioli toscani col, 28, **46**
  insalata di patate col, 47
  alla livornese, 120
  maionese tonnata, 195
  sott'olio, 28
  peperoni col, 48
  pollo tonnato, 153
  polpettone di, 28, **47**
  pomidoro col, 47
  salsa di, 193
  spaghetti col, 70
  tartine al, 47
  uova di, 50
  uova col maionese tonnata, 47
  vitello tonnato, 134-5
Torcello, 87, 90
Tordi, 26, 157
Torrone, 173
  molle, 174-5
Torta:
  di albicocche, 176
  pasqualina, 164
  di patate, 162
Tortelletti, 73
Tortelli, 73
  di erbette, 27, 73, **75-6**, 97
Tortellini, 29, 63
  bolognese, 27, 77
  with cream (alla panna), 31, **77**
Tortiglione, 177
Tortini di ricotta, 96
Totani, 43, 104, **115-16**
  all'anacaprese, 200
Touring Club, Italiano, regional guides, 201, 217
Trastevere, 66
Treccia cheese, 207
Trenette col pesto, 67
Trifle, 174
Triglie:
  in fritto misto, 117
  alla griglia, 117

col pesto, 119
alla veneziana, 117
Tripe, 149
busecca, 137
Florentine, 149
Parma, 149
'Phoenician', 149
Trout (trota), 122, 137
boiled, 122
fried, 122
grilled, **111**, 122
in paper, 111
Truffles:
chocolate, 176
sea, 112
Truffles, white, **30**, 137, 154, 162, 201, 214
with bagna cauda, 192
with Bolognese chicken breasts, 152
with Bolognese cutlets, 130
with Bolognese tortellini, in stuffing for, 77
with Bolognese turkey breasts, 30, 153
with fondue, 95, 205
Parmesan, 205
in polenta pie, 89, **90**
with rice, 86
with scrambled eggs, 93
Truffoli, 73
Trun, 162
Tunny, 43, **120**
and bread, 47
with caponata, 169
with Sicilian caponata, 169
with french beans, 43, 46
fresh, with tomato sauce, 120
mayonnaise, 153, **195**
with eggs, 47
in oil, 28
and onion salad, 47
with peppers, 43, 48
polpettone, 28, **47**
and potato salad, 47
preserved in oil, various ways of using, 28
and rice, 86
roe, 50, 169
Sardinian, 28, 120
sauce, 193
with chicken, 153
and spaghetti, 70
with veal, 134-5
stuffing for tomatoes, 47
in tomato sauce, 120
with Tuscan beans, 28, 46
ventresca of, 28, 120
Tuoni e lampo, 89
Turin, 30, 137
candied walnuts, 201-3
Turkey, 151

breasts, fried with ham and cheese, 20, 151, **153-4**
in flaky pastry, 154
with marsala, 154
and fruit mustard, 197
galantine, 30
Italian, favourite dinner party dish, 151
roast, stuffed, 156
stewed with white wine, 154-5
Turner, *Herbal*, 25
Turtle soup, English, basil traditional flavouring of, 23
Tuscany; Tuscan:
beans, 32
soup, 56
with tunny, 28, **46**
beef, 129, 138
bruschetta, 99
caciotto, 207
cappelletti, 74
chickens, 151
grilled, 152
stuffed with ham, 153
chicken liver croûtons, 153
cooking, 215, 223
frogfish, 121
nougat, soft, 174-5
olive oil in cooking, 31, 32
olive oil in soup, 53
pudding, 174
raviggiolo cheese, 207
ravioli verdi, 78
risotto, 87
stuffed sardines, 119
truffles, 30
wines, 210-11
See also Florence, Florentine
Tusser, *Five Hundred Points of Good Husbandry*, 23

Uccelletti, 157
with polenta, 89, 157
with rice, 157
Udine, 50
Umbria; Umbrian:
bruschetta, 99
caciotto, 207
cooking, 25, 74
chicken liver croûtons, 153
raviggiolo cheese, 207
Uova, 93-5
di bufalo, 207
al burro, 93
divorziate, 95
frittata, al formaggio, 94-5
genovese, 95
mollette con funghi e formaggio, 95

al piatto con pomidoro, 94
con purè di patate, 94
col riso, 95
sode, 95
agli spinaci, 47
stracciate (strapazzate), 93
al formaggio, 94
con tartufi, 93
al tegame al formaggio, 94
tonnate, 47
di tonno, 50
Uva passolina, 197
Uvetta, spinaci con, 166

Valderno, 151
Valéry, Paul, his opinion of Italian cheeses, 207
Valtellina, 51
Vanilla (vaniglia), 27
sugar, 27
in sweet pastry, 176
Veal, 19
cappelletti stuffed with, 73, **74-5**
cutlets, Bolognese, 130
Milanese, 130
escalopes, bread crumbs for, 30-1
with chicken liver croutons, 132
grilled, 130
Milanese, 130
and ham, with cheese, 131
with marsala, 131
leg, larded with ham, 132
Lombardy, 129
with marsala, 130
minced escalopes, 132
piccate, 33
pie with marrows, 135
roll, 132-3
saltimbocca, 131
scaloppine, 33
shin, stewed (ossi buchi), 132
stew, 132
stuffed cold, 135
escalopes, 29, **131**
rolls, 129, 131
with tunny sauce, 28, 129, **134-5**
veal olives, 135
with Veronese mushroom sauce, 193
with white wine and artichokes, 131-2
Vegetables, 161-71
mixed fried, 169
Venice: Veneto; Venetian, 219, 220
Asiago cheese, 206
artichokes, 165
baccalà mantecato, 87, 126
calf's liver, 146
caparozzolo, 112
Cipriani's Locanda, 87

coconuts, how displayed for sale, 181
cooking, 20, 215
coppa, 43
crab, 45, 112
creamed salt cod, 126
Fenice tavern, 178
fish of, 109
food market, 109
forks introduced, 219
John Dory, 121
mullet, red, 117
mussel soup, 104
oranges, caramel, 178-9
Osteriq Veneziane, 218
polenta, 89, 158
rice, use of, 81, 87
risi e bisi, 84-5
risotto, in cantina, 86-7
in capro roman, 82
di peoci, 84
di secole, 82
di scampi, 83-4
rospo, 121
scampi, 109
grilled, 115
sole, 119-20
soppresse salame, 145
spice trade, 26
Trattoria all'Madonna, 87
vegetables and fruit of, 109
wines drunk in, 210
Venegazzu, 211
Venison with cherry sauce, 159, 193
marinading, 34
Ventresca of tunny, 28, 120
Verdure, 161-71
fritto misto di, 169
Vernaccia, 211
Verona; Veronese:
mushroom sauce, 83, **193**
risotto, 83
pasta in brodo con fegatini etc., 55
Veronelli, Luigi, 212
Ristoranti di Veronelli, 218
Verze ripiene, 171
Vesuvio wine, 210, 220
Vialone rice, 87
Vicenza salt cod, 126
Vinchant, François, 223-4
Vine leaves and mushrooms, 163
Vinegar:
pimentos in, 200
in salad dressing, 44
Vino Santo, 197
Visitors' books, 219-24
Vitello, 19
bocconcini, 131
defined, 129
braciolette ripiene, 131
cima, 129, **135**

costolette bolognese, 130
costolette milanese, 130
fesa col prosciutto, 132
alla genovese, 131-2
ossi buchi milanese, 132
piccate al Marsala, 130
polpette, 134
polpettone, 134
quagliette di, 135
rolé, 132-3
scaloppine, alla perugiana, 132
    di vitello battuto, 132
saltimbocca, 131
scaloppe farcite, 131
scaloppe milanese, 130
sformato di, e zucchini, 135
spezzatino di, 132
tonnato, 28, 129, **134-5**
Vitellone defined, 129
Vongole:
    con crostini, 112
    alla marinara, 112
    spaghetti alle, 67
    zuppa di, 105

Walnuts:
    candied, 201-3

in honey, 197
in pesto, 194
sauce of, 195
sauce with cream cheese for pasta,
    70-1
Watercress, 101
Weights, 39-41
    tables, 40-1
Welby, T. Earle, *Away Dull Cookery*,
    157
Westbury, Lord, 216, *With Gusto and
    Relish*, 67
Whiting, grilled, 111
Wine:
    in Italian cooking, 33, 129, *see also*
    Marinading
Wines, 209-12
    Albana, 209
    Ansonica, 211
    Barbaresco, 210, 211
    Barbera, 137, 192
    Barolo, 137, 210, 211
    books on, 211-12
    Brunello di Montalcino, 210
    Capri, 209
    of Caruso Brothers, 209-10
    Chianti, 209, 210-11

Coltibuono, bianco di, 211
Felino, 145
Freisa, 137
Grottaferrata, 209
Lacrima Christi, 209
Lagrein rosato, 211
Lambrusco di Sorbàra, 218
    of Marinotti estate, 209
Marsala, 33
Montepulciano, 209, 210
Moscato di Siracusa, 157
Nebbiolo, 137
Pitigliano, 211
San Gimignano, 209
Santo, 197, 223
Tortoli, 159
Trebbiano, 210
Valpolicella, 211
Venegazzu, 211
Vernaccia, 211
Vesuvio, 210, 220
Villa Antinori Bianco, 211
Woodcock, grilled, 157

Yeast, 33
Yoghourt, Sardinian, 207

Zabaione, **179**, 184
Zafferano, 27-8
Zampone di Modena, 146, 161
Zeppole di San Giuseppe, 173
Zimino, 116
    lumache in, 127
Ziminù, 110, 116
Zorza, Elio, *Osterie Veneziane*, 218
Zucchini, 167-8
    in agrodolce, 168
    fritti, 168, 169
    ripiene, 137, **168**
    spaghetti con salsa di, 71
    in stufato, 168
    sformato di vitello e, 135
Zuppa:
    di cozze, 104
    di gamberi, 104
    inglese, 174
    pavese, 54
    di peoci, 104
    di pesce, 27, 53, **101-7**
        caprese, 104
        alla romana, 103
    di vongole, 105
    zimino, 116, 127
    See also Minestre; Soups

$\mathscr{N}$OTES ON THE $\mathscr{I}$LLUSTRATIONS

The illustrations at the opening of each chapter are taken from decorated shovels in the collection of the Accademia della Crusca in Florence, which was instituted in 1582 for sifting the good from the bad in the Tuscan language, and for the publication of correct words. John Evelyn, in his diary for May 1645, described them thus: 'They shew'd us the famous Accademia de la Crusca which is a Hall hung about with Imprises and divices painted, all of them relating to corne seifted from the brann. The seats are made like bread baskets and other rustic instruments used about wheate, and the Cushions like sacks, of satin.' (From *The Diary of John Evelyn*, University Press, Oxford 1959, page 213.) The photographs are copyright Franco Maria Ricci, taken by Massimo Listri, and appear on pages 7, 19, 23, 37, 43, 53, 61, 73, 81, 89, 93, 101, 109, 129, 151, 161, 173, 189, 197, 205 and 209.

Acknowledgement is also due to the following for permission to reproduce copyright photographs: Bavaria Verlag, Munich, 124; Osvaldo Böhm, Venice, 21, 46, 110, 111t,b, 118, 146; J.-L. Charmet, Paris, 27rh, 50, 83, 168, 195; DACS, 170, 171; Dagli Orti, Paris, 22, 36, 40, 71, 135, 136, 137, 171, 177; Franco Maria Ricci/Massimo Listri, 54, 55, 127, 164, 192; Giraudon, Paris, 24c, 128; Riccardo Gonella, Turin, 158; Haynes, Hanson & Clark, 31; Foto Murgioni Nadia, Rome, 34l,r, 35, 51, 112, 130, 169; Pastificio Lensi SpA, Vinci, 68-9; Pedicini, Naples, 18, 45, 52, 108, 115, 144; Retrograph, London, 66, 67, 78; Ricciarini, Milan, 77, 97, 134; Ricciarini-Simion, Milan, 60, 62, 63, 65, 70; Roncaglia, Modena, 27lh, 140; SCALA, Florence, 20l,r, 33, 38, 41, 42, 47, 48, 49, 57, 58, 59, 72, 74, 75, 76, 82, 84, 88, 90, 91, 92, 96, 98, 99, 100, 102, 104, 106, 113, 114, 116, 117, 119, 120, 122, 131, 133, 139, 141, 143, 145, 148, 149, 150, 153, 155, 156, 163, 165tr, 166, 170, 175, 176, 180, 181t,b, 182l, 183, 185, 187, 188, 191, 193, 194, 196, 198, 199, 200, 202, 204, 206, 207, 208.

PICTURE RESEARCHER: JENNY DE GEX